Using Young Adult Literature in the English Classroom

Second Edition

John H. Bushman

University of Kansas
Lawrence, Kansas

Kay Parks Bushman

Ottawa High School
Kansas

Merrill,
an imprint of Prentice Hall

Upper Saddle River, New Jersey
Columbus, Ohio

Library of Congress Cataloging-in-Publication Data
Bushman, John H.
    Using young adult literature in the English classroom / John H. Bushman, Kay Parks Bushman.—2nd ed.
      p.   cm.
    Includes bibliographical references and index.
    ISBN 0-13-457052-9 (pbk.)
    1. Literature—Study and teaching (Secondary) 2. Young adult literature, American—History and criticism—Theory, etc. 3. Young adult literature, English—History and criticism—Theory, etc. 4. Language arts (Secondary) 5. Reading (Secondary)   I. Bushman, Kay Parks. II. Title.
    LB1631.B798   1997
    428'.0071'2—dc20   96-2108
                                                                                                                              CIP

Cover art/photo: Wassily Kandinsky, Bauhaus Archive/E.T. Archives/London/Superstock
Editor: Bradley J. Potthoff
Production Editor: Patricia S. Kelly
Copyeditor: Robert L. Marcum
Design Coordinator: Jill E. Bonar
Text Designer: Kip Shaw
Cover Designer: Proof Positive/Farrowlyne Assoc., Inc.
Production Manager: Patricia A. Tonneman
Electronic Text Management: Marilyn Wilson Phelps, Matthew Williams, Karen L. Bretz, Tracey Ward

This book was set in ITC Galliard and Swiss 721 by Prentice Hall and was printed and bound by Quebecor Printing/Book Press. The cover was printed by Phoenix Color Corp.

Printed in the United States of America

10 9 8 7 6 5 4 3 2

ISBN: 0-13-457052-9

Prentice-Hall International (UK) Limited, *London*
Prentice-Hall of Australia Pty. Limited, *Sydney*
Prentice-Hall of Canada, Inc., *Toronto*
Prentice-Hall Hispanoamericana, S. A., *Mexico*
Prentice-Hall of India Private Limited, *New Delhi*
Prentice-Hall of Japan, Inc., *Tokyo*
Simon & Schuster Asia Pte. Ltd., *Singapore*
Editora Prentice-Hall do Brasil, Ltda., *Rio de Janeiro*

For Eric

*May he experience the joy and satisfaction of
young adult literature in and out of the classroom.*

Preface

While there have been changes in the traditional English curriculum in middle and high schools, we believe more must be done. We believe that young adult literature—with its conflicts, themes, protagonists, and language—should be present in the curriculum to provide the necessary transition to the adult literature we hope students will eventually discover and learn to enjoy. This genre deserves the attention that is currently given the classics by those who aspire to teach English and by those who are already teaching English. Therein lies the motive for writing this book. *Using Young Adult Literature in the English Classroom*, Second Edition, is written for both prospective and experienced English teachers as they begin and continue the process of selecting the literature curriculum for their students. The book provides guidance both for choosing reading selections and developing teaching ideas.

NEW TO THIS EDITION

We have made changes in the second edition of *Using Young Adult Literature in the English Classroom*, changes we think readers will appreciate. We have updated the references significantly to provide the reader with information about the most current young adult literature. We also have two new chapters, one on reader-response theory and its classroom potential, and one on technology and its use with young adult literature. What we haven't changed is the conversational tone of the first edition. We believe that both students in preservice programs and experienced teachers who want up-to-date information about young adult literature want to read about it in a short, clearly and concisely written, classroom-oriented work.

TEXT ORGANIZATION

The content of the book is very much classroom oriented. In Chapter 1 we discuss the characteristics of young adults and how this literature meets their interests and needs. In Chapter 2 we focus on the literature itself, providing criteria by which teachers may evaluate young adult literature. The research and theory, along with classroom applications, of the reader-response approach to teaching literature is the subject of Chapter 3. In Chapters 4, 5, and 6 we focus on the classroom itself and how teachers can effectively incorporate young adult literature into the curriculum. Chapter 7 encourages teachers to evaluate their use of the classics. Chapter 8 provides literature for a diverse ethnic, cultural, and national population. Chapter 9, one of the new chapters, addresses technology and how teachers may use it effectively in conjunction with young adult literature. Chapter 10 addresses concerns that many educators have about censorship. Chapter 11 briefly reviews the history of young adult literature.

To involve readers in this text, we suggest that they keep a "Learning Log" as they interact with this book. In addition to jotting down ideas as they read, readers can use our suggested ways to respond at the end of each chapter. Readers are thus able to participate in the reading/writing connection process that we suggest is beneficial for students to use.

To make this book as useful and accessible as possible, we have supplied three appendices, one providing general teaching information and two supplementing the young adult literature information given in the text. Appendix A provides readers with a variety of resources (books, journals, and organizations) they may use for support when teaching young adult literature. Appendix B lists the works of literature that we have cited in each chapter. We have also indicated which of these titles are more appropriate for the middle school student.

Appendix C contains a long list of young adult books in various categories that we feel are appropriate for use in middle school and high school classrooms. This information supplements the lists of titles and brief annotations that we provided in Chapter 6 as a representative sample of young adult literature.

ACKNOWLEDGMENTS

Many individuals contributed in some way to the preparation of this book. Our students, both experienced and prospective classroom teachers, have readily given of their ideas and suggestions about unique and interesting teaching strategies. As we discussed these contributions, they became a part of our thinking of new and interesting ways to look at young adult literature.

Other contributors influenced us in more specific ways. They need to be thanked directly for their contributions to different chapters: Donald Lind (Hutchinson, Kansas), Chapter 1; Pamela J. Levitt (Lawrence, Kansas), Chapter 3; Victoria Tate (Robert E. Clark Jr. High, Bonner Springs, Kansas) and Lois Stover (Towson State

University), Chapter 8; and Elise Biggerstaff (Westside Middle School, Shawnee Mission, Kansas), Chapter 9. We also thank Carlena Haney, Todd Goodson, Ted Fabiano, Sarah Raben, Jean Ketter, Sandy Asher, Kristin Wilson, Shawn Secrest, Susan Harper, Sue Pierce, Travis Hansen, Diane Strang, and Paul Clark. We also wish to thank our production editor at Prentice Hall, Patty Kelly, and freelance copy-editor Robert L. Marcum for their valuable contributions to the content and structure of this edition.

In addition, we thank the reviewers for this edition: Ruth Cline, Emerita, University of Colorado; James L. Collins, State University of New York at Buffalo; James E. Davis, Ohio University; Patricia P. Kelly, Virginia Tech; Teri S. Lesesne, Sam Houston State University; and Elizabeth Poe, Radford University.

Finally, we say "thank you" to the creative authors of young adult literature for their devotion to the genre which has allowed teachers to more easily turn their students on to the world of reading.

Brief Contents

Contents

Chapter 3
Using Reader Response to Begin   45
with Pamela J. Levitt, University of Kansas

About the Authors

John H. Bushman is Professor of Curriculum and Instruction (English Education) at the University of Kansas, Lawrence. He is also director of The Writing Conference, Inc., a nonprofit organization established to provide services and materials that support the teaching of writing and literature. Bushman, a frequent contributor to national journals in English education, has written three books in addition to *Using Young Adult Literature in the English Classroom* (with Kay Parks Bushman): *The Teaching of Writing*, *Teaching the English Language*, and *Teaching English Creatively* (also with Kay Parks Bushman). He is a frequent workshop leader and consultant on the teaching of English/language arts. He is active in NCTE and ALAN.

Kay Parks Bushman teaches English and serves as English department chair at Ottawa High School, Kansas. She is former president of the Assembly on Literature for Adolescence, National Council of Teachers of English (ALAN), Associate Chair of the Secondary Section and member of the Executive Committee of NCTE. She is co-author with John H. Bushman of *Teaching English Creatively*, as well as *Using Young Adult Literature in the English Classroom*. In addition, she contributes to national journals in English education and serves as a consultant to publishing companies.

1

Young Adults and the Literature that Meets Their Needs and Interests

Adolescence and preadolescence are difficult, unsettled periods for young people. They are no longer children; they are not yet adults. It is a time of change: a time for physical growth, sexual awareness, emotional upheaval, and cognitive development. Because we are teachers or librarians who work in some way with young adults, it would seem imperative that we know about these developmental stages through which young people pass. The well-known saying seems appropriate here: We don't teach English; we teach students. Teaching young adults requires familiarity with the characteristics of this age group.

If we agree that the research and theory about young adulthood is accurate and that it gives us important information on what happens to young adults during preadolescence and adolescence, then it is also important that teachers know about young adult literature and how it meets the interests and needs of these young people who are confronting a range of experiences in their physical, intellectual, moral, and reading development.

YOUNG ADULT LITERATURE: A DEFINITION

This genre of literature has been called many names over the years: *literature for adolescence, adolescent literature, adolescent fiction, junior teen novels,* and *juvenile fiction.* Due to the pejorative nature of the term *adolescence,* most have moved away from that term and have settled on *young adult literature.* Publishers seem intent on using the term *juvenile fiction,* but most school people don't like the term *juvenile. Young adult literature,* then, seems to be a the common term for that literature written for or about young adults.

Young adult literature has many common characteristics: Conflicts are often consistent with the young adult's experience, themes are of interest to young people, protagonists and most characters are young adults, and the language parallels the language of young people. Most definitions would include all of these components (Auten, 1984; Carlsen, 1980; Fuller, 1980). Donelson and Nilsen (1989) offer this definition: "any book freely chosen for reading by someone in this age group" (preface). This seems very broad, but young readers "freely choose" specific books because they include the characteristics listed.

YOUNG ADULT LITERATURE: THE RIGHT CHOICE

Contemporary adult society is a nonreading society, and some studies suggest that people read less as they grow older (Heather, 1982; O'Connor, 1980; Trelease, 1982). Other research indicates that adults read less than one book a year: Angelotti (1981) concludes that the literature programs in schools have produced less than 5 percent of adults in the United States who read literature. Perhaps Slatoff (1970) states the problem best:

> It is hard to remember that upon graduation most of them stop reading little more than trivia and go on to live their lives, both inner and outer, as though nothing had happened to them. It is hard to remember that almost everything about a classroom,

about the relation of student and teacher, about the structure of the curriculum—in short about the total environment in which we teach literature—helps to produce this unhappy condition and is at best alien and at worst hostile to the fullest comprehension and experiencing of literature. By this I mean mostly that all of this defines a world in which literature is not really relevant except as a subject for study and in which a full literary experience is not likely to take place. (p. 175)

Carlsen and Sherrill (1988) have collected reading autobiographies from teachers and have shared excerpts in *Voices of Readers,* an interesting collection of statements about reading habits. Generally, most respondents stated that their love for reading occurred in spite of what was done in schools. Some developed their appreciation of literature in school, but it usually did not occur until very late in high school or even in college. However, these respondents were English teachers who, we would assume, have a stronger relationship to reading than other adults.

It seems that schools have accomplished just the opposite of what they intend to do: They have turned students off from reading rather than made them lifelong readers. How has this happened? Teachers have failed to choose literature that enables students to become emotionally and cognitively involved in what they read. If students are asked to read literature that is not consistent with their developmental tasks, they will not be able to interact fully with that literature. As a result, students who do not interact with the literature are left with learning only *about* literature. For example, most tenth graders know little about *Macbeth* other than a very cursory view of the plot, but they know a great deal about the Elizabethan Period, Shakespeare, the Globe Theatre, and the rest of the trappings that accompany the study of this classic play.

Sadly, this is an accurate picture of the literature programs in many middle and secondary schools that still have students move chronologically through the literature anthology and choose the traditional classics as their outside reading. Students are simply unable to connect the text with their goals, level of development, and experience. Language development affects cognitive development and vice versa: Students at this age read at a much higher level of ability when they are reading something that matches their developmental interests and goals (Anderson, 1983). The attitude found in this classical literature curriculum seems to be that the schools have a "body of literature"—a *canon*—to be taught to students, whether they can read it or not. Therein lies the problem. Most students cannot read classical literature well (i.e., they cannot have a personal involvement with it). Students think of the literature as something that they cannot understand; therefore, they think they are not intelligent individuals.

This literary elitism forces students to have an unhealthy, negative attitude toward their ability and, as a result, leads to nonreading when they leave school. If schools and teachers want students to understand what they read, to interact with the literature so that they can make connections to their own lives, to make critical judgments that will enhance their intellectual, emotional, and moral development, and, perhaps most importantly, to become lifelong readers, schools and teachers must evaluate the literature curriculum and make the necessary changes so that students can, indeed, achieve success in these areas.

PIAGET AND COGNITIVE DEVELOPMENT

Piaget (Piaget & Inhelder, 1969) believes that cognitive changes from infant to adult are the result of a developmental process. He suggests that this process occurs in four stages: the sensorimotor period (birth to 2 years), the preoperational period (2 to 7 years), the concrete operational period (7 to 12 years), and the formal operational period (12 years to adulthood). Although these stages give the appearance of a start-and-stop process, the theory suggests a gradual movement from any one period to another. In addition, there are transitional periods between these stages.

Since this book deals primarily with literature read by preadolescents and adolescents, the later periods, concrete and formal operations, are emphasized. During the concrete operational stage, young adults become more independent in their thinking. They can think logically, classify, and show relationships. The real world is extremely important to these young people. Their thinking revolves around immediate and concrete objects rather than concepts and abstractions. The research indicates that at this stage the preadolescent is able to think backward as well as forward in time.

As preadolescents move out of the concrete operational level, they take on more of the formal operations. These operations develop at this time and are retained throughout the adult life. During this time, the adolescents are able to apply logical operations to all classes of problems. It is during this final stage that abstract thinking prevails. These adolescents are able to reason about abstract propositions, objects, or concepts that they have not directly experienced. At this time, young people are able to hypothesize and use deductive and inductive reasoning.

Middle School: Appropriate Literature, Appropriate Responses

Middle school students have ample opportunity to relate experiences about themselves as they react and respond to what they read. The responses are personal, usually based on real experiences. *Chernowitz* (Arrick), for example, enables middle schoolers to respond at this appropriate level. The primary emphasis of the novel deals with prejudice. At the concrete level students are able to share their personal experiences with this theme. They relate to each other specific examples of how they have faced ethnic, religious, and other kinds of prejudice and what specifically they have done to overcome these prejudicial actions. Other works—*Daniel's Story* (Matas) and *Sworn Enemies* (Matas)—also with this theme, work well with middle schoolers. While middle school students work with these and other such books at the concrete level, older students may take a different approach, perhaps dealing in a more sophisticated way with the topic of prejudice by exploring its effects on society.

Some students object to the ending of *Whatever Happened to Janie?* (Cooney). At the middle school level, students explore why the novel ends as it does. Now that Janie has decided to call the Johnsons, her birth parents, will she go back to them? Using this novel as their basis, students can also discuss making decisions and living with the consequences. Through a variety of ways—writing, discussions, creative drama—middle school students can extend the ending of the novel, with either Janie staying with the Springs or returning to the Johnsons, and discuss how each of those decisions would affect her future.

Humor plays an important role in *Bel-Air Bambi and the Mall Rats* (Peck). As a response to that novel, students can relate this humor to a concrete experience. For example, mornings around many homes are disastrous. Parents are struggling with each other and with their children. All need to use the bathroom at the same time; all need to eat breakfast and get off to work or school. Items temporarily lost cause further distress. Students may write a humorous response, using an incident that they have experienced while keeping in mind Peck's strategies of writing humorously.

Middle school students frequently read *Beardance* (Hobbs), Will Hobbs's 1993 sequel to *Bearstone* (1989). Many readers can relate to Cloyd, the 15-year-old boy who is so very determined to make sure that the surviving bear cubs go free. Cloyd's determination is very believable. Many young people at this age have strong feelings about social concerns and are willing to carry out their beliefs. While few may be able to travel to the mountain wilderness to save bears from destruction, many can and do take on responsibilities in their own communities. These middle school students can share these real experiences that they have had and can share how they overcame obstacles to succeed with what they were trying to do.

High School: Appropriate Literature, Appropriate Responses

Research (Piaget & Inhelder, 1969) indicates that most high school adolescents are able to reason at the formal operational level. In general, these students have reached intellectual maturity, and most are able to think in a systematic manner, to reason by implication at the abstract level, and to bring together variables through synthesis. Most students in the upper grades are able to make a statement or pose a problem about a work and defend or solve that particular response, showing the level of reasoning appropriate for students who have moved into the formal operational level.

Using the following statement, "Sometimes novels leave you with the feeling that there is more to tell," students can develop an idea or thesis that was begun in the literature but needs to be continued. For example, after reading *Beyond the Chocolate War* (Cormier), students respond to the condition of Trinity School and what it will be like in five years. If students were to suggest a third Chocolate War novel to Cormier, what would they tell him? For example, what would Archie be like as a 30-year old? Students also may wish to respond to the ending of *The Giver* (Lowry):

> Downward, downward, faster and faster. Suddenly he [Jonas] was aware with certainty and joy that below, ahead, they were waiting for him; and that they were waiting, too, for the baby. For the first time, he heard something that he knew to be music. He heard people singing.
>
> Behind him, across vast distances of space and time, from the place he had left, he thought he heard music too. But perhaps it was only an echo. (p. 180)

Certainly, students have the opportunity to explore the possibilities of what happened to Jonas and the baby. Did they escape? Were memories restored to them? To those left behind?

Students who read *Cold Sassy Tree* (Burns) respond to Grandpa's words: "I can forgive a fool, but I ain't inner-rested in coddlin' hypocrites" (p. 99). The response shows how the reader interprets this idea and how Grandpa comes to make the statement. Students can go on to consider how this message may be important to them today.

Fallen Angels (Myers) offers readers many opportunities to respond. A character sketch showing the changes that Richie goes through enables students to understand the important incidents of the war and what effect they have on him. Showing growth of a character from the beginning of the novel to the end asks students to bring together important considerations that effect change. Other students may choose to single out the most difficult aspect of fighting a war, based on this novel, and explain why. Still others may conduct a more personal investigation by interviewing Vietnam War veterans about their feelings toward the war, specific incidents, and their relationships with other soldiers. Students can then compare this information to the novel, making some personal comment about how realistic the novel is.

In his novel *Eva,* Peter Dickinson provides older students with a controversial issue: transplanting the brain of a 13-year-old into the body of a chimpanzee. Readers may dismiss the work as science fiction, but this reality is getting closer and closer. Human-to-human transplants have been in existence for many years and now are quite common. In the late 1980s, the transplanting of a baboon's heart into a human body was quite controversial. Can the reverse, suggested by Dickinson's novel, be far behind? Certainly, the book gives students many issues to investigate, such as the moral and ethical issues of animal and human transplants and the degree to which society will accept the results of medical technology. Higher level thinking about thought-provoking issues can find its way into student responses, both written and oral.

Responses about freedom, human rights, and the use of language to obfuscate will certainly follow the reading of *Forbidden City* (Bell). The story of 17-year-old Alex and his father, a cameraman for the Canadian Broadcasting Corporation, tells of the nonviolent-turned-violent demonstration at Tian An Men Square in the spring of 1989. Issues that may surface include the following: How far will people go to secure freedom and human rights? With the use of doublespeak and euphemism, how do we know if the government is telling the truth? What forms of language abuse occur in the United States government? Who best serves as agents for change, adults or students? High school students probably have attained the intellectual level to undertake these questions with a higher degree of sophisticated thinking and to respond with more complex, in-depth, and abstract reasoning.

THE DEVELOPMENTAL TASKS CONFRONTING ADOLESCENTS

What are the special needs and expectations of adolescents? What are the major developmental tasks that confront teenagers? Erikson (1963) suggests that the major task of adolescence is the formulation, or reformulation, of personal identity. Middle and high school students are primarily engaged in the task of answering the question "Who am I?" Marcia (1980) describes a series of stages or classifications of identity that teens may adopt as they grow into adulthood. These stages represent products of considerable effort at sorting out concepts of self in relation to parents, peers, authorities, and society in general.

Havighurst (1972) outlines lifetime developmental tasks for healthy individuals that include a series of tasks that confront adolescents. In his view, the principal needs of adolescence are emotional and social development, rather than intellectual growth. Since the adolescent developmental tasks presented are comprehensive and useful to classroom teachers who wish to understand the internal struggles of their maturing students, a closer examination of Havighurst's tasks is warranted. As we discuss each of the tasks, we have suggested young adult literature that may reflect the developmental struggle that the young adult is experiencing (Figure 1.1). The literature does not necessarily have the task as its central theme, but the developmental task is part of the character's behavior.

The first task is achieving new and more mature relations with age-mates of both sexes (Havighurst, 1972). Mature relationships are here viewed as adult relationships; girls are looked upon as women and boys as men. As younger children, social grouping tends to be same sex, characterized by secret gangs and clubs. During adolescence teens mature sexually and develop strong interests in themselves in relation to the opposite sex. Young people become deeply occupied with social activities and social experimentation.

School is the primary arena where this socialization takes place. Gaining the approval of peers of both sexes becomes a powerful influence on the behavior of adolescents. What may appear minor issues of choice develop into shattering dilemmas of conformity or expressions of individuality.

Failing or delaying this developmental task results in poor social adjustment and interferes with progress in other developmental tasks. Havighurst suggests that delay, unlike complete failure, probably means an unhappy adolescence but not a permanent inability to achieve mature adulthood.

Although it is not the primary emphasis in Greene's *The Drowning of Stephan Jones,* this developmental struggle is clearly reflected by Carla and Andy as they try to relate to each other, and also as they try to be accepted by their peers. Certainly, this struggle is also experienced by Jerry, Archie, and Obie in *The Chocolate War* (Cormier). The struggle that emerges among the young people who travel the Colorado River in the Grand Canyon in *Downriver* (Hobbs) also shows this concern for peer acceptance, but at what price?

Achieving a proper masculine or feminine social role is the second developmental task. Again, the point is developing an acceptable adult social role. The task of achieving manhood or womanhood is complicated by the contemporary ferment over social roles, the erosion of traditional models, and lack of clarity for replacements. Cormier provides for these emerging social roles in *We All Fall Down.* Buddy struggles with who he is, what he has become, and who he wants to be. Jane, the moral model, falls in love with Buddy, as he does with her. The struggle then begins for both young people.

Achieving new and more mature relations with age-mates

The Chocolate War, Robert Cormier
Deliver Us from Evie, M. E. Kerr
The Drowning of Stephan Jones, Bette Greene
Out of Here, Sandy Asher

Achieving a proper masculine or feminine social role

Out of Control, Norma Fox Mazer
Shepherd, Julian Thompson
We All Fall Down, Robert Cormier

Adapting to physical changes and using the body effectively

The Cat Ate My Gymsuit, Paula Danziger
Freak the Mighty, Rodman Philbrick
Lizard, Dennis Covington
One Fat Summer, Robert Lipsyte

Achieving emotional independence from parents and other adults

Everything Is Not Enough, Sandy Asher
The Car, Gary Paulsen
David and Della, Paul Zindel
Loch, Paul Zindel
Sniper, Theodore Taylor

Preparing for marriage and family

First a Dream, Maureen Daly
Mr. and Mrs. Bo Jo Jones, Ann Head

Preparing for an economic career

Jesse, Gary Soto
Make Lemonade, Virginia Euwer Wolff

Acquiring a personal ideology or value system

Crazy Lady, Jane Conley
Sisters, Gary Paulsen
Skin Deep, Lois Ruby
Staying Fat for Sarah Byrnes, Chris Crutcher
Unfinished Portrait of Jessica, Richard Peck

Achieving social responsibility

Dogwolf, Alden Carter
The Giver, Lois Lowry
Nothing But the Truth, Avi

During the third developmental task, the adolescent adapts to physical changes and using the body effectively. During adolescence young people learn what their adult bodies will be—short, tall, wide, narrow. Not all bodies are shaped or function as their owners desire. The task as defined by Havighurst is pride or tolerance of one's body and the ability to use and protect the body satisfactorily.

There are at least two components to teenage anxiety regarding physical growth. First is the concern about developing into a satisfactory adult body. What if I don't like the way I look, the way I am? Will others accept me as I am? The second and more immediate adolescent crisis regarding physical growth has to do with the timing of physical changes, particularly the development of adult sexual characteristics. Since everyone develops on a different schedule, and girls generally develop more rapidly than boys, adolescents experience keen interest in their own growth in comparison to peers. If development is delayed, considerable teenage anxiety and social confusion can result. Teens also struggle at significant depths about physical flaws, real or imagined, that provoke a genuine concern: Am I normal?

Many young adult novels have characters who struggle with their bodies. Paula Danziger's *The Cat Ate My Gymsuit* and Robert Lipsyte's *One Fat Summer* seem to be representative of the literature. Richard Peck tackles the issue in *Remembering the Good Times*. The struggles that come with disfigurement are handled by Dennis Covington in *Lizard*. *Freak the Mighty* (Philbrick) brings together two unlikely characters: Maxwell, an extremely large boy who has learning disabilities, and Kevin, a very small boy who is a genius.

The fourth developmental task is achieving emotional independence from parents and other adults. Again, the goal is an adult relationship with parents rather than the dependence of childhood, a process that is problematic for all parties. Young adults are ambivalent about leaving the security of childhood for the strange, complicated, threatening world of adulthood. Parents want them to become mature adults, but they also wish to protect their children, innocent and inexperienced as they are, from the ravages of the adult world. The stage is set for miscommunication, rebellion, authoritarian behaviors, and irresponsibility.

Teachers, as authority figures, are frequently targets of adolescents who are working to establish their personal independence. It's important to understand the conflicts, both internal and external, that drive teenage activity in relation to this task so that teachers can avoid being drawn into misplaced hostility and confrontation.

Sniper (Taylor) involves Ben's struggle coming to terms with the relationships among adults at the wild animal refuge and at the same time having to handle problems associated with a sniper trying to kill the animals. All of this occurs while Ben's parents are on an adventure of their own. A lot of growing up takes place in a short period of time. Michael (*Everything Is Not Enough,* Asher) is perhaps the classic example of this developmental task. This 17-year-old has everything a young adult could want: loving parents, summers at the beach, a job waiting for him in his father's business. But Michael wants to make it on his own. He wants to be independent from his parents, but he doesn't want to hurt them.

The preparation for marriage and family is another concern for the emerging adult. Adolescence is a period in which strong attractions develop between the sexes and the possibility of marriage and family is entertained. Obviously this fifth task connects with others, especially those of establishing satisfactory peer relationships with the opposite sex and establishing independence from parents. We believe that early young adult literature reflected this struggle more than the current literature does. Perhaps contemporary young people do not feel that the preparation for marriage and family is as important to them at this age as it was twenty years ago; perhaps the shift in attitude toward varying lifestyles has influenced them not to consider marriage and family as an immediate concern. The literature may, then, reflect an alternative attitude, as displayed in the homosexual relationships found in *The Drowning of Stephan Jones* (Greene) and *Deliver Us from Evie* (Kerr), rather than an attitude that leads to marriage. An earlier work, *Mr. and Mrs. Bo Jo Jones* (Head) does reflect the marriage and family theme, albeit as a necessary arrangement due to an unplanned pregnancy. Maureen Daly seems to continue this theme from an earlier novel (*Seventeenth Summer,* 1942) to her 1990 novel *First a Dream.*

The sixth developmental task is preparing for an economic career. A significant part of moving from childhood to adulthood is involved with achieving economic independence, the ability to make a living, and in choosing a satisfying occupation. During adolescence the young adult progresses in both these objectives with part-time work, summer jobs, chores, and other means of making money. Readers see this with LaVaughn (*Make Lemonade,* Wolff) as she works as a babysitter for a teenage mother to earn money for college. Certainly at a different level, the three young people in Harry Mazer's *When the Phone Rang* find themselves in immediate need of financial assistance. Kevin, Lori, and Billy want to remain together as a family after their parents are killed in a plane crash; but this means sacrifice from each of them. This financial concern is brought about more quickly than usual, but nevertheless, it is there to confront them. Jesse and his brother Abel (*Jesse,* Soto) struggle to make ends meet in junior college as they see that education is their only hope of escaping a world of physical labor in the farm fields of California.

Acquiring a personal ideology or value system to guide the individual in ethical decisions is Havighurst's seventh developmental task. Adolescents tend to be interested in sampling various world views, religions, political stances, and philosophical problems. Much of life, both in adulthood and adolescence, is made up of choices that reflect the values and ideals of the chooser. Young adults begin to critically evaluate their parents' values and ideas, which in childhood were passively accepted as universal truths.

In *Unfinished Portrait of Jessica* (Peck), the title character comes to terms with her father. He could do no wrong; he was her idol. Jessica learns the hard way that what she thought was true was, indeed, quite the contrary. As she grows up, she develops her set of values and begins to exercise them. This struggle to achieve an appropriate value system also occurs in Fred in *The Chemo Kid* (Lipsyte).

The final developmental task Havighurst outlines is satisfactorily achieving social responsibility. Satisfactory interpersonal relationships have already been addressed; this developmental task involves discovering one's role in relation to social groups and to participate as a member of the community and a citizen of the state and nation. Adolescents discover that their personal desires, beliefs, and behaviors affect, or potentially affect, groups beyond their own families.

Readers see this struggle in Philip Malloy (*Nothing But the Truth*, Avi) as he learns quickly how his actions affect many people, some closely connected to him and others who are not. His decision to hum along as the national anthem is played during his school's opening exercises sets in motion a series of charges and counter-charges regarding respect, freedom, and patriotism. Readers struggle with his motives as well as with the motives of the others involved. There is a sense, however slight, that Malloy begins to realize the consequences of his actions as the series of events go further than he intended. However, ultimately, as in most good literature, the reader makes the final decision.

ADOLESCENTS' DEVELOPMENT OF MORAL JUDGMENT

In Havighurst's (1972) model, the personal value systems or moral ideology that characterize the tasks are derived primarily from social interaction. Kohlberg (1976) critiques the social learning model of moral development, suggesting that the model assumes that the development is the internalization of external cultural rules. He criticizes moral development in the social interaction model by arguing that the basic motivation for morality is rooted in the pursuit of social reward and avoidance of social punishment. "Environmental influences on normal moral development are defined by qualitative variations in strength of reward, punishment, prohibitions, and modeling of conforming behavior by parents and other socializing agents" (p. 48).

As an alternative approach to adolescent development and construction of moral judgment, Kohlberg (1968, 1976, 1987) describes a cognitive developmental approach that builds on ideas and concepts originated by Dewey and Piaget. The primary characteristic of the cognitive developmental understanding of adolescence is the concept of *stages*. The stages of adolescent development and establishment of moral ideology are age linked and organized in an orderly sequence.

Dewey (1895/1964) links moral development to cognitive development in a discussion about the objectives of education:

> The aim of education is growth, both intellectual and moral. Only ethical and psychological principles can elevate the school to a vital institution in the greatest of all constructions—the building of a free and powerful character. Only knowledge of the order and connection of the stages in psychological development can insure the maturing of the psychical powers. Education is the work of supplying the conditions which will enable the psychological functions to mature in the freest and fullest manner. (p. 273)

As we have noted, Piaget's work (1932/1965, 1971) suggests that as a person ages, sequential stages of intellectual development are achieved. These stages are not only age linked, but they also feature increasing complexity. During adolescence, for example, the teenager's transition from a concrete operations stage of intellectual ability to formal operations thinking, which is characterized by abstractions and ability to hypothesize and test for possibility, is a significantly higher order of thinking ability.

Kohlberg (1984) develops and refines a hierarchy of moral development stages that parallels the intellectual stages of Piaget's theory of human development. The hierarchy consists of three levels: preconventional, conventional, and postconventional or principled. In turn, each of the three levels consists of two stages, for a total of six stages.

At the preconventional level of moral development that characterizes younger children, the child is self-centered, basically unable to consider the interests and claims of others. Doing right is motivated by the desire to avoid punishment, obey rules, and yield to the superior power of others, usually adults. The conventional level appears in conjunction with the adolescent age period. This level is characterized by moral decision making based on interpersonal activity. Motivation for doing right is based more on caring for others, the Golden Rule, and the desire for others to see the individual as a good person.

The postconventional or principled level is generally attained in adulthood. An individual at this level has distinguished and adopted principles for moral reasoning and action for herself. This person also recognizes that these moral principles occasionally conflict with social rules, posing moral dilemmas that the person resolves with principled ethical judgments. Crucial to Kohlberg's theory on moral development is the idea that higher stages are also better stages of moral reasoning and action—better, not merely different. This concept is important to educators because it implies that students cannot merely change through moral education: They improve or raise their level of moral reasoning and judgments. "Nevertheless, holding development as the central aim of education, we do argue that a higher moral stage is a better stage in solving moral problems as problems of conflicting interests and claims" (Kohlberg, 1984, p. 292).

Kohlberg's theory proposes a close link between age, intellectual development, and moral development. As an individual matures, she grows in mental stages (Piaget, 1971) and through the moral stages of Kohlberg's hierarchy (Kohlberg, 1984), beginning with stage one at the bottom and progressing toward stage six at the top. Kohlberg further states that intellectual development is linked to moral development so that an individual could not achieve a higher moral judgment than could be supported by that individual's intellectual development. "Moral stage theory postulates parallelisms between cognitive stages and moral stages, and that attainment of a given cognitive stage is necessary but not sufficient for the attainment of the parallel moral stage" (Kohlberg, 1984, p. 309).

Thus, at age 7, a child may have achieved the concrete operations ability to use logic. Possession of concrete operations level of intellectual capacity is necessary, but not sufficient, to rise to the second stage of Kohlberg's hierarchy. At the beginning of adolescence, the individual may begin developing capacity for formal operations and more complex mental abilities. Formal operations capacity is necessary, but not sufficient, to rise to the third and fourth stages of moral development.

The key concept here is in the "necessary, but not sufficient" relationship between intellectual development and moral development. Kohlberg asserts that individuals may progress in mental capacity through concrete operations, beginning formal operations, basic formal operations, and consolidated operations without progressing past the second stage of moral development. However, an individual with postconventional moral judgment capability must, of necessity, have developed mental capacity well into formal operations. Adequate intellectual development is necessary, but not sufficient, to cause a rise in moral development.

The following four young adult novels have characters that seem to reflect the developmental theories of Piaget, Havighurst, and Kohlberg. The characters struggle with their identity, with their relationships with adults and other adolescents, and with their choices, which often suggest their concern with moral questions of right and wrong.

Jacob Have I Loved

Sarah Raben (1991), a student at the University of Kansas, offers the following description of how Paterson's *Jacob Have I Loved* (1980) could be used in the classroom. She suggests that the novel fits in well with the developmental tasks that young people are experiencing.

Louise was born and raised on Rass Island, one of the few surviving fishing islands on Chesapeake Bay. The novel, set around the end of World War II, outlines Louise's life in a place where life, which really had not changed for years, is finally changing. Like many young adults, Louise has many problems: young love, family rivalry, relations with her parents and grandmother, experiencing her first job, and discovering a vocation—all developmental tasks listed by Havighurst.

Louise is a twin, and her sister Caroline seems to be the darling of the family. Caroline has an excellent singing voice, and the whole town is proud of her. Louise, however, feels she has nothing special to offer and, therefore, feels alone.

Louise must find herself during the course of the novel. The reader watches her struggles in discovering friendship with Call, one of the boys on the island who also feels somewhat left out because of his obesity. Thus, one of the developmental tasks is illustrated in Louise and Call's relationship: When grade school ends and both find themselves alone, they find each other. They form their own group of friends based on personal affinity; each finds another whose personality meshes with his or her own. They move past the friendship of convenience.

Later in the novel more intimate relationships are explored when Call goes away to war and Louise discovers she has developed stronger feelings for him while waiting for his return. Interestingly, this novel deviates from "boy meets girl." Upon his return, Call turns to Caroline for love and not Louise.

Louise also experiences development in the vocational category. She finds she is drawn to the water as the men on their little fishing island have been since it was settled. For Louise, a woman, the call of the sea is considered improper, yet the family does not turn down the money she earns from crabbing. Though she is considered rough and unladylike, Louise feels a certain pride in her accomplishments because she is able to help support her family.

Louise finally asserts her independence from her parents and discovers that all along they have given her just as much support as her sister was given. Eventually, Louise moves from her first job to choose a vocation: She leaves the sea to work with the people of the Appalachian Mountains as a nurse-midwife.

As these events take place, the reader watches Louise struggle through her jealousy of her sister and her bitterness toward her grandmother. Through Louise's thoughts and actions the reader watches as she forms her own value system and shifts from external to internal locus of control.

Louise also exhibits typical teen problems in terms of her physical self. Because of her work, her skin is roughened and dark, unlike her fair and delicate-skinned sister. Louise tries moisturizer to improve her cracked and dried skin, but with little success.

Jacob Have I Loved traces the entire gamut of developmental tasks. It reads well, and students should be able to have that personal involvement with the text.

Out of Control

Out of Control (1993) by Norma Fox Mazer provides numerous opportunities for young people to react and respond to conflicts and issues that are quite relevant to their lives. Mazer's young adult novel is the story of three "all-American boys," Rollo, Brig, and Candy, nicknamed the "Lethal Threesome," who have been best friends since grade school. Although they seem to have everything going for them, including brains, popularity, sports abilities, and school leadership positions, they are all bothered, or threatened, by beautiful, smart Valerie Michon, whom they love to tease and taunt. Valerie, however, does not succumb to their "innocent" little threats of blocking her way in the hallway, but, instead, stands up to them—a behavior they find inappropriate and threatening to their images. Then one day, convenience leads to an outrageous opportunity as, during a school assembly, Valerie leaves, with the threesome following her into a deserted school hallway where they sexually molest her—an incident that they claim to be "no big deal," until Valerie decides to report the incident to the school administration. However, the boys' attitude is seemingly reinforced by the actions of the principal, who, wanting to brush the incident under the carpet to spare possible negative repercussions to the school's reputation, simply suspends them for a few days.

It is at this point in the novel that several characters must come to terms with what has happened and decide how they will deal with the situation. Will they cover it up and go on as if nothing out of the ordinary has occurred? Or will they address the crime head on, make the incident public, and appropriately deal with the three boys?

Readers will especially identify with the internal conflicts experienced by Rollo Wingate, who, although having participated willingly in the hallway incident, finds himself riddled with guilt. The other two try to convince him that they didn't do anything wrong. When Brig and Candy take off on a ski trip during the suspension time, Rollo is left behind to wallow in his guilt. The fact that Rollo's father has expressed his own shameful feelings toward Rollo's participation in the incident only makes him feel worse. As a result, Rollo must come to grips with how he actually feels about what he did and, then, decide what he will do about it. But when he reaches the conclusion that he must take responsibility for his own action, separate from the pressures of Brig and Candy, he also concludes that he must make amends with Valerie—an act he knows will bring an end to his lifelong friendships with the other two. Many readers will relate to Rollo's needing to take responsibility for mistakes, seeking forgiveness, and dealing with such consequences as changing one's own identity while, in the process, risking the loss of relationships of the past.

Other readers will certainly identify with the inner conflicts experienced by Valerie, who, in some ways, is assertive enough to ignore some widely practiced, age-old behaviors. While others who have viewed for years the ornery, masculine-bonding behaviors of Rollo, Brig, and Candy have accepted them with a nonchalant, boys-will-be-boys attitude, even when having been personally victimized, Valerie refuses to succumb to them. In doing so, she risks being labeled with derogatory names, not only by the boys but also from both male and female observers. But, like Rollo, she too must answer to herself. She must decide the degree to which she is to blame for having invited the incident in the hallway. At the same time, she must decide how important it is to herself to risk further abuse by pushing the issue and going public to press charges against the boys outside the school arena. And then there's Rollo, who does seem sincerely sorry for his part in the matter. Can she forgive him? And if she does, can she let her feelings for him influence what she still knows she must do? Readers will have strong connections to Valerie as she comes to terms with her own responsibilities, makes decisions, deals with the possible consequences, finds it in her heart to forgive, and trailblazes past old stereotypes to protect her own dignity.

Through *Out of Control,* Mazer has courageously opened up for classroom discussion the issue of sexual harassment, a situation that is manifest in our nation's high schools, and, in doing so, may effect change in the daily victimization of many young people.

The Crazy Horse Electric Game

Chris Crutcher writes for young adults and incorporates issues relevant to young people. *Chinese Handcuffs, Stotan!, Running Loose,* and *The Crazy Horse Electric Game* are all worth noting.

Willie, the protagonist in *The Crazy Horse Electric Game* (1987), is a talented baseball player who gets seriously hurt in a water-skiing accident and has to learn how to walk and speak all over again. This accident and the resulting injury place an insurmountable barrier between Willie and his parents. Willie finds it more and more difficult to relate to them and they to him. His parents have already lost a child to SIDS and simply cannot cope with Willie's problem. One night Willie hears his parents arguing over his problem; soon afterward he leaves home and travels to California.

Willie's struggles with his injury as well as with his parents and their lack of understanding are two very honest conflicts that any young adult might have to face. Havighurst (1972) states that the goal is an adult relationship with parents rather than the dependence of childhood, a task that is problematic for all parties in the process. Willie believes that under these conditions he can't have an independent relationship with his parents, so he leaves the family.

Willie travels to Oakland, California, by bus, not knowing where to go or what to do. After Willie arrives, his life at first does not get any better—he is beaten and robbed by a street gang. A pimp befriends Willie and takes him to his house. After his body mends, Willie enrolls in OMLC (One More Last Chance) High School, which provides Willie with physical and mental therapy. He does odd jobs for his benefactor as well as for the school to help pay for the tuition.

Willie works intensely to improve physically. With the help of gifted teachers, he learns how to use his mind and body in harmony to compensate for his injuries, and to once again play sports.

After he recovers, Willie returns home, but the situation there is not as he had hoped. His parents are divorced, his mother has remarried, and his father has become an alcoholic. In addition, his one-time girlfriend resents him for not letting her, as well as his parents, know where he was all this time. Knowing he is not yet ready to cope with all of this, Willie returns to California to start anew.

A number of issues confront the young adult reader: parent–young adult relationships, young adult independence, and differing lifestyles. One of the more challenging moral dilemmas that Willie faces occurs in California when the gang that attacked him comes for him again and burns the school where Willie is working. As the building burns, Kam, the gang leader, attacks Willie, but Willie is able to overcome him. The building burns quickly, and the gang members run away, leaving Kam injured in the building with Willie. Willie realizes that he must get out of the school to survive but knows that Kam, the gang leader, will surely die if not helped. He begins to leave without Kam, knowing that Kam doesn't deserve to be saved, but then stops and returns to rescue him. Young adult readers will certainly have plenty to discuss after reading this Crutcher novel.

Downriver

Downriver (Hobbs, 1991) involves some of the issues raised in *The Crazy Horse Electric Game* and also will involve students in discussions of moral development. *Downriver* is a tale of adventure as seven young people pirate two boats and equipment and travel through the Grand Canyon. The young people are a part of Discovery Unlimited, an outdoor education program for young people at risk. It is the story of the rafting down the Colorado River, but more than that, it is a story of how leaders emerge and what they become; it is the story of how young people challenge authority, work through conflicts within the group, and struggle with their own identities.

The novel is written so that students can make connections with the story and the characters. Some will relate to the adventure of rafting down the Colorado River; others will be more concerned with the concept found in Discovery Unlimited. Some readers will wonder why Heather left before the Canyon trip. Others certainly will identify with Jessie's problems at home: a father that doesn't understand her and a stepmother that infringes on Jessie's time with her father.

Downriver challenges students with other issues: Is it necessary to have rigid rules in groups like Discovery Unlimited? How are leaders of unorganized groups selected? Did Troy take on the leadership role or was it thrust on him? When do young people know that their agenda is not as important as that of the group? How does Troy change throughout the novel? What motivates his actions? Do the students know of other students like Troy? What has become of them?

The characters have very definite characteristics: Freddy becomes close to Jessie and challenges both Troy's relationship with her and his authority with the group. Star sees dark omens in her Tarot cards, and Adam, the practical joker, finds that the group has problems. How does each change throughout the novel, and what do they learn about themselves and each other?

From a moral standpoint, readers can respond to Troy's throwing the map over the falls, Freddy's encounter with the scorpion, and Jessie, Freddy, Adam, Rita, and Star leaving without Troy and Pug. What is the moral consideration, and how would the students have responded if they had been the characters? How have the characters grown morally? Some would argue that most of the characters move from the first stage to the third stage of Kohlberg's model.

In the end, Jessie and Star are back with Jessie's father. She has reconciled with her stepmother; Freddy is in southwestern Colorado, close to Jessie's home, getting rehabilitated; Rita is back in New York; Troy has been caught by the police in L.A.; and Adam is back working with Al, the leader of Discovery Unlimited. Students can discuss their feelings about how each of the characters fared as the novel comes to a close. After what they did, were they treated fairly? Do the students believe that the characters learned from their experiences? Did the students learn from the characters' experiences?

One of the reasons for choosing this novel for classroom reading is to help students respond to the moral issues and dilemmas experienced by Jessie and her friends. Through discussion or writing students try out their ideas, compare and contrast their ideas with those of their peers, and make some moral judgment about the decisions that Jessie and her group made and their consequences. By sharing all of the ideas, moral development is increased.

Young adults experience this moral development of characters as they read other literature as well. They see the growth that takes place with Adam and Miriam in *Miriam's Well* (Ruby), with Jimmy in *Somewhere in the Darkness* (Myers), with Freddie in *The Original Freddie Ackerman* (Irwin) with Bert in *If Rock and Roll Were a Machine* (Davis), with Marie in *I Hadn't Meant to Tell You This* (Woodson) with Robert in *A Day No Pigs Would Die* (Peck), with Ponyboy in *The Outsiders* (Hinton), with Carla in *The Drowning of Stephan Jones* (Greene), with Jess in *Bridge to Terabithia* (Paterson) and with many, many more characters in young adult literature.

Many young adult novels offer the quality of literature suggested in these examples. This literature provides the reader with a variety of conflicts and issues, and the student's response depends on the stage of moral development the reader has attained. Young readers may respond effectively to literature in which there are issues of right and wrong. Older readers have more interest in literature that focuses on social expectations. Sometimes the books themselves will fit into these categories by emphasizing one level of development.

Other novels have a full range of conflicts and issues—all within the same book. This literature offers settings that are realistic to all young people, characters that include the range of social economic status, and realistic conflicts that help young adults make that transition from the somewhat sheltered life of adolescence to the sometimes stark, cruel life of adulthood. Categories in which we frequently find novels with both positive and negative treatment include family relationships, friends and society, racial and ethnic relationships, identity, and sexual relationships, most of which are mentioned in Havighurst's stages of developmental tasks.

READING DEVELOPMENT OF THE YOUNG ADULT

Students not only develop physically, intellectually, and morally in stages, they also develop their reading appreciation in stages. Many sources discuss the stages in the development of reading (Brewbaker, 1989; Donelson & Nilsen, 1989; Early, 1960). Carlsen (1980) makes three generalizations about the reading patterns of young adults that are helpful as classroom teachers make selection decisions for students. First, he suggests that chronological age is more important than mental age in determining what a young adult will enjoy reading. Given 13-year-olds of varying cultural backgrounds, development, and school ability, he believes they will be interested in reading the same kinds of books. For this reason, Carlsen thinks the tendency to push and pull gifted young adults into adult literature and the traditional classics is ill advised and risks creating resistance and barriers that will carry far into the reader's future.

Second, Carlsen suggests that reading preferences are determined culturally as well as by age. For example, there are significant differences between what adolescent boys and girls are willing to read outside classroom experiences. Again, lack of awareness and teacher insensitivity to these differences may result in students developing resistance to reading.

Carlsen's third generalization about adolescent reading habits holds that most young adults make reading selections based on the subject matter of the book rather than literary merit, language difficulty, or complexity of the story. A young person may choose a difficult book if the subject matter is of significant interest; simple books may be rejected if the subject is boring.

Carlsen (1974) also presents five overlapping satisfactions in reading appreciation. In contrast to some stage hierarchies, a young person moving from a lower to a higher level of reading appreciation doesn't leave the lower stage for the higher stage. In this construct the higher stages incorporate and expand on the lower stages, much in the way that larger concentric circles incorporate and expand on small circles.

The first stage of reading appreciation Carlsen labels *unconscious delight*. Here a reader becomes lost in the story, experiencing intensely and personally the events, places, and people. Action and twists of plot are the most attractive parts of the reading experience.

Toward the beginning of adolescence and moving through adolescence, readers are concerned with having vicarious experiences along with seeing oneself in the literature that they read, Carlsen's second and third stages of reading development. At this point readers seek situations that parallel their own life situations and issues. Readers also identify with characters in the story; they can test new roles, new feelings, and new responses to challenges through reading experiences.

The fourth concern, philosophical problems, evolves at the point in adolescence when the initial tasks of self-identity are basically resolved and attention shifts to wider society and the happenings of the world in which the teenager lives. Reading interests move beyond the experiences of the characters in the story to the interpretations and meanings of the writing. Issues of relationships, values, and human responsibility characterize the reading interests of adolescents at this level, obviously requiring more complex material.

The last stage Carlsen describes is an adult reading level, or at least a level generally attained in adulthood. This level is *aesthetic delight,* wherein the literature must be satisfactorily presented and reader concerns focus on the art of the presentation: its style, thematic treatment, structure of the story, and the subtlety and harmony of the writer's craft. Obviously, this stage is the most sophisticated and may well be beyond the comfortable ability of most high school students.

The value of Carlsen's hierarchy of reading appreciation for middle and high school teachers lies in the realization that a representative classroom of adolescents will generally contain young adults scattered across all five stages. Treating the entire class of students as though they were homogeneous results in problems, potential reading resistance, and frustration for both students and teacher. Not all students will find the same books useful, desirable, or even readable. The task for teachers is to know the students, become familiar with stages of adolescent growth, understand the needs of students, and familiarize themselves with the level of reading the students have achieved. Then teachers can satisfactorily guide and match readers to material that entertains, enlightens, and challenges them to greater maturity.

MEETING THE NEEDS OF SPECIAL STUDENTS

This chapter has focused on meeting the developmental, moral, and reading interests and abilities of students in general. Young adult literature speaks directly to young people in middle and secondary schools. Teachers can meet the range of ability and interest among young adults by carefully selecting literature appropriate for the developmental levels found in the classroom. Although "regular students" may be easy to describe, teachers may need to pay some attention to two special groups: those students who are considered "at risk" and those who are considered "gifted."

The At-Risk Student

All students are probably at risk to some degree, but some are more at risk than others. Generally, those "more at risk than others" are students who are in danger of failure and are less likely to complete school successfully. *At risk* is a new term—a term that describes those students who are not specially labeled as "special education" students. At-risk students may have problems with school success and achievement. In fact, they probably will drop out of school before graduation. Some educators have characterized at-risk students as those who never contribute to class, have very little or nothing to say when called on, often daydream, and generally do not respond to classroom activities. These students often see success or failure as beyond their control; they blame others for what happens to them. In the recent past, most at-risk students have been characterized as those with a low socioeconomic status; however, more study has revealed that all socioeconomic levels have young people at risk.

For the purposes of this book, we are interested in those students who are at risk in reading. These are not necessarily remedial reading students, but students who have not had positive experiences in reading for a variety of reasons. For some, reading and schooling go together. They hate to read and they hate school. As they see it, school has not been good to them. Because of what has been given to them to read, they have not developed into good readers. They struggle with almost everything given to them in the classroom to read. Other at-risk students have the ability to read the letters and words on the printed page, but they have no desire to read anything that is not required. Even the required literature makes little sense because it has no meaning to these students. In either case, at-risk students in reading will not be productive in the academic experience of the classroom or in the social/community arena after leaving school.

What can be done? Some of the risk factors mentioned—socioeconomic status, financial resources, past educational success or failure—may be beyond the direct control of teachers. However, decisions about what literature is used in the classroom and what strategies are used to teach that literature lie right at the feet of the classroom teacher.

As we note throughout this book, young adult literature serves the young adult well. It is written from the perspective of the young people, their experiences and levels of reaction. Adult literature (or at least that literature most often found in the middle and high school curricula) is written from different perspectives. Students find it difficult to relate to Brönte's *Wuthering Heights,* Thackeray's *Vanity Fair,* or Austen's *Pride and Prejudice,* but they find delight in reading *Miriam's Well* (Ruby), *Tunes for Bears To Dance To* (Cormier), *Killing Mr. Griffin* (Duncan), and Chris Crutcher's *Stotan!*

Why are these novels more attractive to the young adult reader? An adolescent can better relate to the characters and plot. A youthful protagonist with an adolescent point of view helps at-risk students make connections. The characters are highly independent. They may not seem realistic to adults, but they are very realistic to the young readers. They offer hope to the young reader—hope that things can change, improve, succeed. They give hope to be able to cope with all that seems wrong with being a young adult. They see these novels showing responsibility (e.g., the young adults have to deal with the consequences of their own decisions).

If we want at-risk students to continue reading in the middle and high schools, we must provide them with materials that they will read. In discussing reading difficulty, Langer (1984) states: "While syntax, word length, and vocabulary have been shown to affect text difficulty, more recent views of reading comprehension suggest that ease of comprehension is also a function of the reader's knowledge and experiences . . . the contextual variables that affect and are affected by the purpose for reading and the environment surrounding the reading experience" (p. 122). In other words, students will comprehend more if they have previous knowledge about what they are reading. Young adult literature makes the connections between reading and experience.

Several books meet the direct needs of at-risk students since the protagonists of the novels are at risk. Travis (*Taming the Star Runner,* Hinton), an unmotivated young man, can't seem to get his act together. He is capable but unable to do something with this ability. Travis' father was killed in the Vietnam War. Travis is in trouble with the law—he tried to kill his stepfather because he could no longer endure the man's physical and verbal abuse.

Finally, his mother sends Travis to live on a horse ranch with his uncle Ken, his father's brother. Travis does not do well in school, he has very low self-esteem, his aggressive behavior is self-destructive, and he doesn't trust people. However, as Travis interacts with his new environment, his new living situation, and his new friend Casey, he begins to learn that he does have good qualities and self-worth. He writes a book. At first he doesn't like to talk about it, but he begins to see that it's all right to be a writer. He gains Casey's respect, and he helps Jo, a friend involved in a murder. His relationship with Ken grows stronger, and he begins to trust. He comes to the realization that incidents in his life don't have endings, only pausing places. At the end of the novel, Travis realizes that there is hope and things will improve.

Wart, Son of Toad (Carter) also involves a young adult who would be considered at risk. Wart—his name because his father is called Toad by his students—has many problems that seem to get in the way of success. His mother has died; his father is the hated biology teacher at school; Wart wants to enter Capstone, a vo-tech school, but his father wants him to do well so that he can go to college; his father also constantly hovers over him and urges him to do well in school; and because of his low self-esteem, Wart frequently gets into trouble in school.

The reader experiences the roller-coaster ride Wart takes with his life experiences. He sometimes wants to do well in school to please his father; other times he wants to drop out. There are times when he feels that he can get his act together and do well enough to get into Capstone. Many at-risk students ride this roller coaster every month in school. These students will relate well to *Wart, Son of Toad.*

The Gifted Student

Some teachers and many more parents feel that young people who are labeled *gifted* should read only the best literature, and the best translates into reading the classics. (Reading the classics will be covered in detail in Chapter 7.) If educators accept the developmental processes of the young people, the choice of literature becomes paramount in the success of gifted students. It is folly to believe that a gifted student who excels in reading and writing will be able to interact with literature that has been written for adults in a language and style that is quite different from contemporary literature. Success in reading relates strongly to the life experiences the reader brings to the literature. If the experience is lacking, if there is no understanding of the moral issues presented, and if the general attitude toward the work is negative for whatever reason, gifted students will have difficulty making the kind of personal response that we want them to have. Educators must present literature with which the student can interact, not just analyze.

> Insofar as we divorce the study of literature from the experience of reading and view literary works as objects to be analyzed rather than human expressions to be reacted to; . . . insofar as we favor form over content, objectivity over subjectivity, detachment over involvement, theoretical over real readers; insofar as we worry more about incorrect responses than insufficient ones; insofar as we emphasize the distinction between literature and life rather than their interpretations, we reduce the power of literature and protect ourselves from it. (Slatoff, 1970, p. 168)

Intellectually gifted students can read the words, phrases, and sentences very well. We are not concerned about the students' ability to mechanically read the works. It is their ability to *respond to* the literature that is so important. For this reason we believe that teachers should not remove young adult literature from the gifted student reading program. This literature addresses problems in the realm of the moral, emotional, and experiential levels of young adults. The tragedy is that classroom teachers give classic literature to students whose experience and developmental levels are limited, therefore preventing students the joy and success of reader response at its highest level and, perhaps, encouraging students to function only at the analytical level.

In young adult literature, gifted students can read about themselves, or at least about characters that are gifted in some way. Just as the literature about at-risk students may be helpful for those students, literature with gifted characters may provide emotional and moral growth for the gifted student. The gifted student may indeed feel some of the same concerns of the at-risk students: isolation, emotional instability, social indecisiveness. Young adult literature may, indeed, validate their own experiences, attitudes, and uniqueness. Reading literature with characters who have similar concerns and differences may help these students overcome some of their own problems. Painfully aware of how giftedness may lead to isolation and the fear of socializing, gifted students may find some solace in Ursula LeGuin's *Very Far Away from Anywhere Else*. Students may find it easy to relate to the experiences of Owen Thomas Griffiths, the exceptionally bright senior in that novel. LeGuin's novel also lets readers respond to many important issues: the need to conform, the cost of conformity, the "handicap" of being intelligent, boy-girl relationships, and being true to yourself.

Bonnie and Paul Zindel's novel *A Star for the Latecomer* serves the gifted reader well. Brook Hillary is a senior at a special high school for talented teens who are trying to break into show business. She is a dancer and has been encouraged her entire life by her mother, who is convinced she is star material. When Brook discovers that her mother has cancer, Brook becomes more determined to obtain her first breakthrough before it's too late for her mother to experience it with her. She eventually gets invited to dance on television, which pleases both Brook and her mother. On her mother's death, Brook finally realizes that she now has to live her life for herself and gives up her dancing world to find the real Brook Hillary. Students who face insurmountable parental or peer pressure to succeed may find this young adult novel helpful.

Nonfiction young adult literature meets the needs of the gifted student as well as other students found in the classroom. In her study of reading habits of gifted junior high students, Carter (1982) found that many of these students were reading nonfiction works even though most of the assigned reading in the classroom was fiction. We believe students will find *Into a Strange Land: Unaccompanied Refugee Youth in America* (Ashabranner & Ashabranner, 1987), *New Kids in Town: Oral Histories of Immigrant Teens* (Bode, 1986), *Chapters: My Growth as a Writer* (Duncan, 1982), *The Way Things Work* (Macaulay, 1988), *Rescue: The Story of How Gentiles saved Jews in the Holocaust* (Meltzer, 1988), *Voices from the Civil War* (Meltzer, 1989), *Crews* (Hinojosa, 1995), *Speaking Out: Teenagers Talk on Sex, Race, and Identity* (Kuklin, 1993), and *Straight Talk About Death for Teenagers: How to Cope with Losing Someone You Love* (Grollman, 1993) and other such works most interesting and enjoyable. Duncan's *Chapters* would be most appropriate for those students who write well and wish to make a career in writing.

In addition to the appropriate content and the developmental levels, young adult literature provides quality writing, writing that students should read and discuss to help them in their own writing. After reading *After the First Death, Bridge to Teribithia, Roll of Thunder, Hear My Cry, Miriam's Well, The Giver,* and *The Chocolate War,* for example, readers quickly realize that they have read emotionally powerful, carefully crafted, well-written works of literature. These novels contain all the components of recognized literary masterpieces. Students can do with these novels all that can be done with the classics: make personal responses, undertake literary analysis, and identify universal themes and specific techniques and strategies characteristic of the author's craft. The issues raised confront students with ample subject matter for creative and critical thinking. Analysis of theme, character development, and plot structure are but a few of the additional literary activities in which students can become engaged.

⇗ Learning Log Responses ⇗

Write an entry at least a page long showing your understanding of the periods we call *preadolescence* and *adolescence*.

Explain Havighurst's developmental tasks and develop a position statement (two or three paragraphs) on their importance to middle school and senior high school classroom teachers.

Write a reflective entry in your journal in which you address the issues of moral development and reading interests as they apply to you as a teacher of literature.

REFERENCES

Anderson, P. (1983). Practical applications of language learning theory in the middle school and junior high. In Bergdahl, D. (Ed.), *Research in the teaching of the English language arts* (pp. 1–7). Athens, OH: Southeastern Ohio Council of Teachers of English.

Angelotti, M. (1981). Uses of the young adult literature in the eighties. *English in Texas, 13,* 32–34.

Auten, A. (1984). All about adolescent literature: Pro and con. *Journal of Reading, 28* (1), 76–78.

Brewbaker, J. (1989). I like happy endings. You don't. *English Journal, 78* (6) 66–68.

Carlsen, R. (1974). Literature IS. *English Journal, 63* (2), 23–27.

Carlsen, R. (1980). *Books and the teenage reader.* New York: Harper & Row.

Carlsen, R., & Sherrill, A. (1988). *Voices of readers: How we come to love books.* Urbana, IL: National Council of Teachers of English.

Carter, B. (1982). Leisure reading habits of gifted students in a suburban junior high school. *Top of the News, 38,* 312–317.

Dewey, J. (1895/1964). In R. D. Archambault (Ed.), *On education: Selected writings* (pp. 271–279). New York: Modern Library.

Donelson, K., & Nilsen, A. (1989). *Literature for today's young adults.* Glenview, IL: Scott, Foresman.

Early, M. (1960). Stages of growth in literary appreciation. *English Journal, 49* (3), 161–167.

Erikson, E.H. (Ed.). (1963). *The challenge of youth.* Garden City, NY: Anchor.

Fuller, L.B. (1980) Literature for today's adolescents: A historical perspective. *English Education, 11* (3), 131–141.

Havighurst, R. (1972). *Developmental tasks and education.* New York: David McKay.

Heather, P. (1982). *Young people's reading: A study of the leisure reading of 13–15-year-olds.* Paper presented at the annual meeting of the United Kingdom Reading Association.

Kohlberg, L. (1968). Early education: A cognitive-developmental view. *Child Development, 39* (4), 1013–1062.

Kohlberg, L. (1976). Moral stages and moralization. In T. Lickona (Ed.), *Moral development and behavior* (pp. 47–52). New York: Harper & Row.

Kohlberg, L. (1984). *Essays in moral development. Volume II: The psychology of moral development.* San Francisco: Harper & Row.

Kohlberg, L. (1987). *Child psychology and childhood education.* New York: Longman.

Langer, J. (1984). Literary instruction in American schools: Problems and perspectives. *American Journal of Education, 93,* 107–132.

Marcia, J. (1980). Identity in adolescence. In J. Adelson (Ed.), *Handbook of adolescent psychology* (pp. 98–112). New York: John Wiley & Sons.

O'Connor, M.E. (1980). *A study of the reading preferences of high school students.* Arlington, VA: ERIC Document Reproduction Service. (ED 185524)

Piaget, J. (1932/1965). *The moral judgment of the child* (M. Gabain, Trans.). New York: Free Press.

Piaget, J. (1971). *Science of education and the psychology of the child*. New York: Viking.

Piaget, J., & Inhelder, B. (1969). *The psychology of the child*. New York: Basic Books.

Raben, S. (1991). *Arguments for the increased use of young adult literature in the high school classroom based on recent related research*. Unpublished master's project, University of Kansas, Lawrence, KS.

Slatoff, W. J. (1970). *With respect to readers' dimensions of literary response*. Ithaca, NY: Cornell University Press.

Trelease, J. (1982). *The read aloud handbook*. New York: Penguin.

2

Evaluating Young Adult Literature

The enjoyment of reading must be an integral part of the classroom to foster the positive attitude toward literature that is necessary for lifelong reading. We want our students to enjoy the literature now, but we also want them to continue this enjoyment as they proceed to higher education or become productive members of society.

The role, then, of the classroom teacher is to walk that fine line between having students read for the pleasurable act that it is and read to increase their powers of literary analysis and, thus, become members of an educated, literate society. To this end, teachers will want to make decisions carefully concerning the literature curriculum: its design and how it is delivered to students. In addition, teachers will want to structure lessons that will enable students to independently evaluate the quality of the literature they are reading. To know that we like a work is great; to know why we like it is even better.

CONSIDERING STANDARD LITERARY QUALITIES

Authors (writers) are concerned about a number of literary techniques as they bring a piece of literature to publication. Students (readers) are involved with these same literary strategies as they finish their study of the work. Both writers and readers ask questions during the process of writing and reading. What works for young adult readers? What conflict will draw the readers' attention and sustain it throughout the work? How many characters should there be? How involved can they become in the conflict? Will the setting be an integral part of the conflict or a minor consideration? How these literary elements work in the literature determines the degree to which we as readers suggest that the work has quality.

Plot

In interest surveys, young adults usually comment that they like novels that are realistic; i.e., novels that have conflicts in which young adults can find themselves and can realistically decide the solution to that conflict. Authors usually give the young adult reader just what they want. They hook them at the beginning and, through a carefully crafted story line, keep the reader to the end.

In the opening lines of *Killing Mr. Griffin,* Lois Duncan grabs the reader and never lets go: "It was a wild, windy, Southwestern spring when the idea of killing Mr. Griffin occurred to them" (p. 5). Margaret Mahy uses the "hook" to get to her readers in *Memory:* "Groping his way through darkness, certain he was no longer on the right path, Jonny suddenly saw a square of light appear ahead of him—the window of a house. His long scramble through unrelieved blackness was almost over" (p. 1). The relationship to reality is crucial. This holds true for fantasy and science fiction works as well. The reality in this literature may be defined in a different way by the author, but it is defined and attended to.

This reality is found in four plot types:

1. Protagonist against self: *The Contender* (Lipsyte), *Running Loose* (Crutcher), *The Accident* (Strasser), *Driver's Ed* (Cooney)

2. Protagonist against society: *I Am the Cheese* (Cormier), *The Secret of Gumbo Grove* (Tate), *The Giver* (Lowry), *Miriam's Well* (Ruby)

3. Protagonist against another person: *Jacob Have I Loved* (Paterson), *Deathwatch* (White), *Sworn Enemies* (Matas)

4. Protagonist against nature: *The Voyage of the FROG* (Paulsen), *The Haymeadow* (Paulsen), *Dogwolf* (Carter), *Downriver* (Hobbs)

Nonfiction has similar types. Certainly, Meltzer's works are included in the individual-against-society type, and Bunting's *The Great White Shark* and Reed's *The Dolphins and Me* fall into the protagonist-against-nature group. We have to be careful, too, not to consider one and only one category of plot structure for many of these works since some will easily cross over. For example, *Deathwatch* pits Ben and Madec against each other, but the force of nature—lack of water, the canyon walls, the sharp rocks—also plays an important part in the novel.

How the novel ends also provides criteria for determining quality. Is it predictable from the start how the conflict will be resolved? All young adult novels considered quality novels will keep the readers guessing. Although most will come to some solution, others may not. We are not sure just how Benji will turn out in Childress's *A Hero Ain't Nothin' But a Sandwich*. The ending of Greene's *The Drowning of Stephan Jones* will shock and, perhaps, frustrate readers. Most novels, too, will end "the way we want them to." The romance in most of us wants everything to turn out well. However, Cormier jolts us into realizing that life just isn't like that. Most readers want Archie (*The Chocolate War*) "to get his" and they want Miro (*After the First Death*) to be caught and Kate to remain alive, but that isn't the way life is.

Other novels that give emphasis to plot structure:

Avi, *The Man Who Was Poe,* 1989

Robert Cormier, *I Am the Cheese,* 1977

Robert Cormier, *Fade,* 1988:

Robert Cormier, *We All Fall Down,* 1991

Robert Cormier, *In the Middle of the Night,* 1995

Lois Duncan, *Don't Look Behind You,* 1989

Sherry Garland, *Song of the Buffalo Boy,* 1992

William Sleator, *The Duplicate,* 1989

Paul Zindel, *Loch,* 1994

Characters

Young adult literature traditionally has characters with whom young adults can identify. Sometimes the plot may not be strong, but because of the well-developed characters readers feel that they are experiencing the conflict. How the characters are presented determines to some extent the quality of the work. If all characters are flat (i.e., they are not fully developed and they do not change), then readers will not relate to the novel.

If, however, the characters are dynamic, round characters, readers will know fully about that character and can appreciate the many levels of growth that take place. Given the limitations of the young adult novel, most minor characters may be flat, but readers can expect the protagonist to be fully developed. At times, however, perhaps due to the length of the novel, main characters as well as the minor characters are archetyped; i.e., they play a particular symbolic role. Archie (*The Chocolate War,* Cormier), Stella (*Home Before Dark,* Bridgers), and Polly Prior (*Remembering the Good Times,* Peck) are used this way.

Are characters motivated to do what they do? To answer this question, readers look at the interaction between and among characters. Do characters respond realistically to each other and to the events that confront them? Young adult literature has been criticized because the young adults in the literature do not relate positively to adults. This may have been true of earlier young adult fiction, but more recent literature offers more of a balance. Of course, adults should not be portrayed in a totally positive way because that is not a realistic view. Many young adults are, indeed, struggling with their relationships with their parents and other adults, and to be realistic, their literature should not be presented in any other way. However, positive adult role models can be found: Max the swimming coach (*Stotan!,* Crutcher), Nora Baines (*The Day They Came to Arrest the Book,* Hentoff), Coach Sherman (*Chinese Handcuffs,* Crutcher), Miss Edmunds (*Bridge to Terabithia,* Paterson), and Big Ma, Mamma, and Pa (*Roll of Thunder, Hear My Cry,* Taylor).

Other novels that give emphasis to character development:

Sandy Asher. *Out of Here,* 1993.

Sue Ellen Bridgers, *All Together Now,* 1979

Jane Leslie Conly, *Crazy Lady!* 1993

Dennis Covington, *Lizard,* 1991

Chris Crutcher, *Ironman,* 1995

Peter Dickinson, *Eva,* 1988

Gary Paulsen, *Sisters,* 1993

Richard Peck, *Princess Ashley,* 1987

Ann Rinaldi, *Wolf by the Ears,* 1991

Ann Rinaldi, *Finishing Becca,* 1994

Lois Ruby, *Skin Deep,* 1994

Setting

Most readers would argue that *The Chocolate War* (Cormier), *Beyond the Chocolate War* (Cormier), *Roll of Thunder, Hear My Cry* (Taylor), *Deathwatch* (White), *The Island* (Paulsen), and *Downriver* (Hobbs), to mention a few, would not be successful if it were not for the dull, drab, almost sterile Trinity School, the Mississippi of the early 1930s, the naked desert, an island in northern Wisconsin, and the Colorado River in the Grand Canyon. In each of these novels, the setting is paramount for the success of the literature. Even though the setting in each novel is strong, it is not overpowering. It allows for strong characterization and plot development. It adds to the success; it plays a unique role.

In other works, the setting—time and place—enables the readers to move beyond or back from the present. Most fantasy and science fiction would not be possible without mythical worlds or futuristic settings. In *This Place Has No Atmosphere*, Danziger takes her readers to a new colony on the moon. We move in and out of reality in L'Engle's *A Wrinkle in Time*. Historical fiction draws on the appropriate time and place for its honest depicting of events. *Across Five Aprils* (Hunt), *My Brother Sam Is Dead* (Collier & Collier), *Summer of My German Soldier* (Greene), *The Bloody Country* (Collier & Collier), and *Number the Stars* (Lowry) depend greatly on a particular time period in the past. The novels of Mildred Taylor as well as Robert Newton Peck's *A Day No Pigs Would Die* are in a sense controlled by the 1920s and 1930s of rural Mississippi and rural Vermont, respectively.

Other novels that give emphasis to setting:

Sue Ellen Bridgers, *Permanent Connections*, 1987

Alden Carter, *Up Country*, 1989

Alden Carter, *Dogwolf*, 1994

Jean Craighead George, *Julie*, 1994

Will Hobbs, *Bearstone*, 1989

Will Hobbs, *Downriver*, 1991

Will Hobbs, *Beardance*, 1993

Hadley Irwin, *The Original Freddie Ackerman*, 1992

Gary Paulsen, *Hatchet*, 1987

Gary Paulsen, *The Haymeadow*, 1992

Richard Peck, *Unfinished Portrait of Jessica*, 1991

Ann Rinaldi, *In My Father's House*, 1993

Theme

Does the work have some redeeming value? Does it speak to readers about universal values and human conditions? Young adults ask these questions when they consider the quality of the literature. Taylor clearly demonstrates the importance of family, ownership of land, and the treatment of the human being in her novels. The themes found in S. E. Hinton's books relate well to the young adult because there is the spirit of hope in each one. Although the protagonists are up against all odds, either put there by themselves or by society, hope remains that the human spirit will overcome the odds.

As in the other literary aspects, there is a balance. In Cormier's *The Chocolate War,* the theme that evil is not limited to any given segment of society is strong, but it does not overpower the plot and characters. Most young adults reading *Mote* (Reaver) will get so caught up with character interaction and the solution to the killing of Mr. Holder that only later do the students sense the importance of each human being, despite the social, racial, or economic group to which each belongs.

Other novels that give emphasis to theme:

Avi, *Nothing But the Truth,* 1991

Caroline Cooney, *Driver's Ed,* 1994

Chris Crutcher, *Staying Fat for Sarah Byrnes,* 1993

Chris Crutcher, *Ironman,* 1995

Bette Greene, *The Drowning of Stephan Jones,* 1991

M. E. Kerr, *Deliver Us from Evie,* 1994

Lois Lowry, *The Giver,* 1993

Norma Fox Mazer, *Out of Control,* 1993

Walter Dean Myers, *Somewhere in the Darkness,* 1992

Gary Paulsen, *Nightjohn,* 1993

Richard, Peck, *The Last Safe Place on Earth,* 1995

Jon Ripslinger, *Triangle,* 1994

Lois Ruby, *Miriam's Well,* 1993

Point of View

Authors have choices to make when they begin to write. What point of view will be most effective to tell the story? Certainly, the omniscient point of view is widely used, establishing the author's presence in all of the characters. Readers know the motivations and actions through each character. Robert Cormier chose this point of view in *The Chocolate War.* We get inside the minds of Jerry, Archie, and Goober through the "all-knowing" storyteller.

The first-person point of view is more limiting. The reader knows events and other characters through the eyes, ears, and mind of one character. The limitation is that the reader cannot get into the minds of the other characters. Some authors get around this problem by moving the point of view from character to character, perhaps by chapter. This technique is used by Lois Duncan in *Killing Mr. Griffin* and

Alice Childress in *A Hero Ain't Nothin' But a Sandwich*. However, the first-person narrative point of view tends to connect more personally with the young adult reader. A bonding occurs between the young adult character and the reader.

Other novels that give emphasis to point of view:

James Bennett, *Dakota Dream,* 1994

Caroline Cooney, *What Happened to Janie?,* 1993

Carl Friedman, *Nightfather,* 1991

Gloria Miklowitz, *Good-bye Tomorrow,* 1985

Gary Paulsen, *Nightjohn,* 1993

Suzanne Fisher Staples, *Shabanu: Daughter of the Wind,* 1989

Ann Rinaldi, *Wolf by the Ears,* 1991

Paul Zindel, *The Pigman,* 1968

Paul Zindel, *Loch,* 1994

Style

The storyteller's style affects the decisions the author makes. For example, is the language of the character appropriate? Young adult literature that incorporates profanity is often criticized. On the other hand, the author's style could be criticized if that language was *not* used by the characters in the novel, especially if the characters would normally use that language. The language found in Cormier's novels fits the characters and events that he chooses. It would be ludicrous if Myers did not use profanity in *Fallen Angels* when depicting soldiers in the midst of the Vietnam War. The question raised relates to appropriateness. How far does the author go in depicting the reality of the situation?

Another area related to language is the manner in which characters use language appropriate for their age and educational levels. In telling her story in *Roll of Thunder, Hear My Cry* (Taylor), Cassie does not talk as an adult, and she should not. Young adult slang is found throughout *The Outsiders* (Hinton), *Downriver* (Hobbs), *The Pigman* (Zindel) and many other novels, as it should be, since it helps the young narrator tell the story with some credibility.

Style affects more than word choice for dialog. Most authors will not have their teenage characters involved in events or carrying out actions that most young adults would not normally do. A few authors may come close to crossing over the fine line between actions of teenagers and adults. For example, Paulsen's *Voyage of the FROG* has been criticized because David's thoughts and behavior are very adult-like.

Other novels that give emphasis to style:

Sandy Asher, *Out of Here,* 1993

Avi, *Nothing But the Truth,* 1991

Janine Boissard, *A Matter of Feeling,* 1988

Olive Ann Burns, *Old Sassy Tree,* 1992

Robert Cormier, *The Chocolate War,* 1974

Robert Cormier, *After the First Death,* 1979

Robert Cormier, *In the Middle of the Night,* 1995

Chris Crutcher, *Chinese Handcuffs,* 1989

Chris Crutcher, *Ironman,* 1995

James M. Deem, *3 NBs of Julian Drew,* 1994

Dallin Malmgren, *The Ninth Issue,* 1989

Gary Paulsen, *Sisters,* 1993

Virginia Euwer Wolff, *Make Lemonade,* 1994

Considering Other Literary Elements

In addition to these standard literary qualities, authors use other literary elements and young people should explore their use as they read and study this literature.

Alliteration

Alliteration is certainly not the most important technique in a writer's craft, but it is used frequently and does offer a more poetic tone to the narrative if used carefully. *Secret, Silent Screams* author Joan Lowery Nixon piques readers' interest by using alliteration in her title. We find alliterative phrases in Roth's *The Iceberg Hermit:* "rant and rave" (p. 2), "catch catnaps" (p. 21), and "lazy lumps" (p. 44). In contrast, an excessive use of alliteration occurs in Peck's *Dreamland Lake* as Flip, a main character, reads a passage from a book describing the early days in his town's history: "we point with particular pride to the pioneer perseverance" (p. 14) of the early settlers. Even the main characters acknowledge and are slightly irritated by the overuse of p's. Teachers could contrast the *Dreamland Lake* examples with the more positive use of alliteration to help students understand its effectiveness.

Metaphor and Simile

Authors traditionally use metaphors and similes to help the reader understand an idea or situation by comparing or contrasting it with another. The important point for young writers is that they should make every effort to use new comparisons rather than trite and overused ones.

Betsy Byars, author of *Cracker Jackson,* uses metaphor to describe the uncomfortable pause that develops out of silence. "It was such a long pause that it seemed to

Jackson that it grew, it developed, the way a stream you can step across at one place becomes a creek, a river, a sea" (p. 92). In *Taking Terri Mueller* (Mazer), Terri berates herself because she doesn't say the things she thinks and feels. Her best friend tells her that she "sits on [her] thoughts until they hatch" (p. 157). Nightmare's terror slowly fades in *Night Fall* (Aiken) as the narrator notices that her fear "slowly receded, uncurling its grip on me tendril by tendril, leaving only its aftermath" (p. 34).

In describing Buddy in *Everything Is Not Enough*, Asher uses the metaphor: "He's a human pillow, a 6-foot one-inch, blue eyed pillow with no sharp edges anywhere. Not fat, just fluffed up" (p. 10). Author Alice Childress uses simile to tell the reader about Rainbow's feelings in *Rainbow Jordan*. Rainbow's friend steals a can of sardines for the girls' lunch. When Rainbow finds out, she is so upset she can barely swallow her lunch and thinks it "tasted like sadness, not sardines" (p. 63). After a very unsuccessful date, Tucker in *Dinky Hocker Shoots Smack!* (Kerr) vows never to go on a date again. He states that "the likelihood of his ever going through an evening like that again was about as sure a thing as hot snow falling or cold water boiling" (p. 56).

Flashback

A memory or retelling of a past event that has importance to the immediate story line can be used most effectively. Both *Dreamland Lake* (Peck) and *The Outsiders* (Hinton) are told entirely using flashback. In fact, at the end of Hinton's novel the reader realizes that the story has been Ponyboy's paper for English class. In both novels, the main characters retell events that led to a change in their outlook on life.

Many authors, however, write much smaller sections using flashback. In *Taking Terri Mueller* (Mazer), Terri finds out that her father has kidnapped her and that her mother is alive. She constantly replays her father's confession while sorting through her emotions. By using Terri's memories, the author lets the reader know what happened in the past while making Terri's feelings known. When James runs from the police in *The Contender* (Lipsyte), Alfred races to their secret hiding place of years past, sure that James will be there. When Alfred enters the cave, he reflects on their many adventures in the cave and the close feelings he and James shared.

Robert Cormier had to incorporate some of the story line in *The Chocolate War* into *Beyond the Chocolate War* so that the latter could stand alone as a piece of literature without the reader having to have read the first novel. He uses flashback to do most of that. Ray Bannister (and the reader) learns about the chocolate sale that occurs in *The Chocolate War* through Obie in a series of flashbacks. *Z for Zachariah* (O'Brien) uses flashback extensively. For example, at the beginning of Chapter 3, Ann writes in her journal:

Now it is night. He is in my house. Or possibly not in it, but just outside it, in a small plastic tent he put up. I cannot be sure, because it is too dark to see clearly. I am watching from the cave, but the fire he built—outside the house, in the yard— has burned down. He built it with my wood. He came over the top of Burden Hill this afternoon. (p. 20)

She then proceeds to tell about the arrival of Loomis and what occurred during the time up to nightfall.

Other works that use flashback often are *Sex Education* (Davis), *About David* (Pfeffer), *Remembering the Good Times* (Peck), *After the First Death* (Cormier), *The Crazy Horse Electric Game (Crutcher),* and *Jacob Have I Loved* (Paterson).

Foreshadowing

Foreshadowing is an author's technique for giving clues or hints to the reader about forthcoming action. In *A Wrinkle in Time,* L'Engle uses this device to let the reader know that even though Charles Wallace is only 5 years old, he is a very important character. "How did Charles Wallace always know about her? How could he always tell . . . it was his mother's mind, and Meg's, that he probed with frightening accuracy" (p. 11).

We learn of two important incidents that will occur in the future in *A Day No Pigs Would Die* (Peck) through foreshadowing. The reader is prepared for the slaughter of Pinky through similar acts found in nature: the hawk killing the rabbit and the shooting of the squirrel. Examples of the cycle of life and death foreshadow the death of the father. In Cormier's *Beyond the Chocolate War,* the climax of the novel centers around Obie's use of a guillotine to get back at Archie. Cormier plants the seed through foreshadowing early in the book: "Obie would be watching him [Bannister] closely now, anticipating his every move. And anticipation was fatal to illusion, making it difficult for Ray to use misdirection, a magician's most powerful tool. He wondered if he should tell him about the guillotine" (p. 31).

Effective Beginnings

Frequently young adults have trouble starting their writing. Although we as teachers have an abundance of prewriting strategies to help these young writers get through this period of "blank paper stare," young adult literature may be an effective source to show how published writers begin. We have on occasion suggested to teachers that when their students are at this stage they simply bring to class four or five young adult novels and read the opening lines of each novel. After a brief discussion of the strategies and techniques used, students are better prepared to begin their work. These models, coupled with the prewriting ideas that have been generated, work to make the job of getting started easier. Figure 2.1 gives the opening lines of several well-known young adult novels.

Humor

Making the reader chuckle or even laugh out loud is always a refreshing attribute of literature. Young adult literature is no exception. Whether the author emphasizes humor or simply sprinkles it throughout the work, most readers can find an appreci-

From *Killing Mr. Griffin* (Duncan, 1978). It was a wild, windy, southwestern spring when the idea of killing Mr. Griffin occurred to them. (Hook)

From *The Chocolate War* (Cormier, 1974). They murdered him. (Hook, surprise)

From *The Kolokol Papers* (Bograd, 1981). In the middle of the night, men came and took my father away in a big black car. I heard the knock at the door, heard my father slowly descend the stairs, followed by my mother, heard the door open and the sound of voices, heard the footsteps of several men up the stairs, loud, over the protests of my parents. (Informing detail, an incident)

From *Running Loose* (Crutcher, 1983). The year started out pretty smooth. Probably would have ended up that way, too, if Becky had stayed around or if I hadn't quit the football team and made myself look like the jerk of the Universe, though I still say quitting was the only thing to do, and I wouldn't change that. (Hook, character)

From *Dicey's Song* (Voigt, 1982). And they lived happily ever after. Not the Tillermans. Dicey thought. That wasn't the way things went for the Tillermans, ever. She wasn't about to let that get her down. She couldn't let it get her down — that was what had happened to Momma. (Character)

From *No Dragons To Slay* (Greenburg, 1983). Six months ago, I got sick. It wasn't a simple matter of taking two aspirins and drinking plenty of chicken soup. Instead, my whole life got turned around. I lost my hair, they pumped my body full of drugs, and most of the time I dragged around like some zombie escaped from Transylvania. It wasn't a nervous condition, so don't think I went bananas and ended up in a loony bin. (Character, an incident)

From *Sex Education* (Davis, 1988). This is a story I would rather not tell. It is a stick caught in my throat, gagging me, choking its way up, and now I am stuck with it. I don't want to tell it, but Hirsch says I must and Hirsch is my doctor. He says there is healing in telling, telling even the worst. But what he doesn't understand is that I don't want to get well. So. There. Now I've said it. (Character, an incident)

From *A Wrinkle in Time* (L'Engle, 1968). It was a dark and stormy night. (Setting)

From *The Accident* (Strasser, 1988). "If you go up there, Matt, I'll never talk to you again." "I just want to try it once," Matt Thompson said. "What's the big deal?" (Dialogue)

FIGURE 2.1
Opening lines of selected novels

ation for its use. In *Me, Me, Me, Me, Me: Not a Novel,* Kerr writes of her life using language and highlighting humorous situations. It's a funny, funny book!

Other writers simply play with the language. Danziger, perhaps, is the most notable. Her works are filled with humor, especially puns. In *This Place Has No Atmosphere,* the reader may react negatively to the abundance of puns, as does one of the characters: "'But Sir Hal . . . how can you rescue me from the dragon when none appears on yon horizon?' He continues to hold my hand and rush me along. 'I'm rescuing you from draggin' along and being late for the meeting.' 'Oh, yeck. That pun is perfectly awful'" (p. 108). Danziger also has fun with the characters' names in this novel: Juna, Aurora, Starr, Cosmosa, Rita Retrograde.

Crutcher tells a very funny story about an overweight youngster named Angus Bethune in the short story "A Brief Moment in the Life of Angus Bethune." Crutcher treats some very serious topics—obesity, homosexuality, bulemia—but with a touch of humor. For example, Angus's dance partner tells him that she is bulemic but under treatment for it. He responds:"'Actually,' I say, 'I even tried it once [sticking his finger in his throat to force vomiting], but when I stuck my finger down my throat, I was still hungry and I almost ate my arm'" (p. 23). Other works that emphasize humor include *Those Summer Girls I Never Met* (Peck), *The Pigman* (Zindel), *If This Is Love, I'll Take Spaghetti* (Conford), *Space Station Seventh Grade* (Spinelli), *Alice in Rapture, Sort Of* (Naylor), *The Crazy Horse Electric Game* (Crutcher), *Don't Care High* (Korman), and *Bel-Air Bambi and the Mall Rats* (Peck).

Imagery

Unlike picture books for young children, novels rely on words to create pictures in readers' minds. These word pictures help readers to know what the characters look like—how they dress, what their features are, and so on. Authors use imagery to help readers see what can't be shown them in pictures. These images also help to set the time and place of an event in the literature. Certainly, authors use imagery to set a mood. Early in *The Chocolate War,* Cormier gives the readers a number of pictures to help establish the mood:

> The sun vanished behind floating clouds, Archie brooded, isolating himself again. The wind rose, kicking puffs of dust from the football field. The field needed seeding. The bleachers also needed attention—they sagged, peeling paint like leprosy on the benches. The shadows of the goal posts sprawled on the field like grotesque crosses. Obie shivered. (p. 14)

Will Hobbs describes Cloyd's first sighting of a black bear in *Beardance.*

> The trail led down the mountain into the timber, where the bear had stopped to dig up a squirrel's cache and to overturn a log for the ants and grubs underneath. Cloyd tracked the bear upslope now, far from any trail, and thought he'd lost it when he emerged from the forest at the tree line. The bear wasn't above him on the open, grassy slopes as he'd hoped. But when he crouched and then crawled up to the very top of the Divide, with the wind blowing stiffly in his face, there the black bear was, not thirty feet away, sitting on its haunches and sniffing the wind. (p. 42)

Personification

Authors often quite effectively give human traits to animals or other nonhuman objects. Sue Ellen Bridgers (*All Together Now*) uses personification along with sensory experiences to enrich readers' responses:

The metallic thump of the baseball gave the neighborhood a new pulse, a heavy, lonely, throbbing sound. All through the long afternoon it toned, like a knelling bell, their lethargy, their indifference, their unspeakable failure. (p. 151)

Readers will remember the wonderful effect of Taylor's use of personification in *Roll of Thunder, Hear My Cry* when she describes the school bus as it approaches the trench in the road:

The bus rattled up the road, though not as quickly as we had hoped. It rolled cautiously through a wide puddle some twenty feet ahead; then, seeming to grow bolder as it approached our man-made lake, it speeded up, spraying the water in high sheets of backward waterfalls into the forest . . . the bus emitted a tremendous crack and careened drunkenly into our trap. . . . Then it sputtered a last murmuring protest and died. . . . (p. 40)

Symbolism

Again, *Roll of Thunder, Hear My Cry* serves us well with its use of symbolism. Taylor treats the land as symbols for the family's freedom and independence, and effectively uses thunder to symbolize impending trouble or danger. To some extent, the trees on the Logans' land symbolizes a place to be safe and secure.

As mentioned, Cormier uses symbolism in *The Chocolate War* to help create the mood: "The shadows of the goal posts definitely resembled a network of crosses, empty crucifixes" (p. 17).

In *Blue Heron*, Avi, to some extent, uses the heron as a symbol for timidity of the boy who has grown up in a home isolated by wilderness.

Hyperbole

We use hyperbole or exaggeration a great deal of the time in our daily conversations, as when we say things like, "I was so shocked at what he said, I almost died." Well, of course, the speaker didn't almost die, he simply wanted to exaggerate his feelings. Authors use this technique as well to make points. The title of Cormier's *The Chocolate War* doesn't suggest a literal war. Chris Crutcher uses hyperbole in a more humorous way, but one that is still quite effective. In *Ironman*, Bo is writing to Larry King (this is a major part of the book as Bo thinks Larry King is the only adult who will listen to him) about the choices he has. Due to his obnoxious behavior he can either have home tutoring with Ms. Conroy or join the Nak Pack, Mr. Nak's Anger Management class. Bo says,

Now Larry, I gotta tell you what kind of choices I was being offered here. I took Geography from Conroy as a freshman, and the woman can flat put you to sleep. And the second your forehead splats onto the desk, she calls your parents; has a phone right there in her room. Next thing you know you're wiping the drool off your chin and she's standing over you with the handset saying your dad wants a word with you. My biggest worry about home tutoring is that she'd then know where I live. On the other hand, there's the Nak Pack. That's what they call it, no kidding, Larry, and if you wanted to put a major crimp in Clark Fork's future crime wave, you'd call an air strike down on their next meeting. (p. 19)

Allusion

An *allusion* is a reference to something that is generally known or understood. Often, readers find Biblical and mythological allusions in literature. For example, when someone has a great deal of stress or is working through a tremendous problem, others may say "that's his cross to bear," making reference to the Biblical story of Jesus having to carry his cross to the place of crucifixion. In young adult literature, we find, perhaps, one of the best-known allusions. Robert Cormier's *I Am the Cheese* is an allusion to the old nursery song and game, "The Farmer in the Dell." Cormier connects this allusion even further: the family name is Farmer. Readers may make the connection between the novel and the allusion when they think of the last two lines of the rhyme: "The rat takes the cheese" and "The cheese stands alone!"

Cormier calls on a nursery rhyme again in his novel *We All Fall Down*. The allusion is to the song, "Ring Around the Rosy," which refers to the Black Plague. When people got a rosy rash, they rubbed themselves with herbs and posies, but fell down and died.

Chris Crutcher, a masterful writer, uses allusion in many of his works. Specifically, in *Staying Fat for Sarah Byrnes,* he characterizes one of the orderlies in the hospital as "Schwarzenegger Number One" (p. 121) in reference to the actor/body building guru Arnold Schwarzenegger.

Main Character as Writer

Like Gary Paulsen's *The Island* (discussed in Chapter 4), other young adult novels feature a character as writer. Although there are not many, a few novels emphasize writing in addition to the central theme. One such novel is Hinton's *Taming the Star Runner.* Travis, a troubled teenager from the city, is sent to stay with his uncle on a ranch in the country. Travis may be the macho, cool, city kid, but he is also a writer who has finished his first novel and sent it off to a publisher. The novel's most noteworthy point is Travis's attitude toward his writing, the audience to whom he thought he had written, and his overall concern with changing any part of this "finished" writing.

Hunt's *Up a Road Slowly* emphasizes writing through its 11-year-old narrator. Julie turns to writing for companionship. She also gets advice from Haskell Bishop, her uncle who also writes. He gives her the same advice teachers tell their students today: Write from your own experience. He also wants her to revise her writing. Julie says: "He would make me do a paper over, pointing out a hackneyed phrase, a

FIGURE 2.2
Writing models in young adult
literature

> **The Writing Process At Work**
>
> *The Man Who Was Poe,* Avi (1989)
>
> *The Moon and I,* Betsy Byars (1991)
>
> *Chapters: My Growth as a Writer,* Lois Duncan (1982)
>
> *The Outsiders,* S. E. Hinton (1967)
>
> *Taming the Star Runner,* S. E. Hinton (1988)
>
> *Me, Me, Me, Me, Me: Not a Novel,* M. E. Kerr (1984)
>
> *The Island,* Gary Paulsen (1988)
>
> *Author! Author!,* Susan Terris (1990)
>
> *David and Della,* Paul Zindel (1993)
>
> **Therapy/Reflection**
>
> *Chinese Handcuffs,* Chris Crutcher (1989)
>
> *Ironman,* Chris Crutcher (1995)
>
> *Sex Education,* Jenny Davis (1988)
>
> **Journalism**
>
> *Summer Smith Begins,* Sandy Asher (1980)
>
> *Forbidden City,* William Bell (1990)

contrived situation, a paragraph of strained dialogue" (p. 168). Students will recognize the situation.

Paul Zindel's plot in *The Pigman* includes writing as John and Lorraine state that they are going to write a "memorial epic" to Angelo Pignati. They decide to write because it will help Lorraine's unhappiness over the Pigman's death. They need to write it down before they "mature and repress" (p. 6), and they both believe that writing will lead to understanding.

Three novels take the forms of journals and may help students in the process of writing their own journals. We learn about the troubles and conflicts in *Eva* by Dickinson, *Z for Zachariah* by O'Brien, and *A Gathering of Days: A New England Girl's Journal, 1830–32* by Blos through their own journals. *A Gathering of Days* is particularly interesting because Cassie, the 13-year-old narrator, records everyday activities that are important to her as well as personal feelings about events in her life. Figure 2.2 lists young adult literature that uses writing in some significant way.

Atkins (1988) suggests that the structure of a novel as a whole can be used to teach the structure of a formal essay. She offers *A Day No Pigs Would Die* (Peck) as an example to follow to teach a structured three-part essay. She suggests that the first

Journals/Diaries

Alicia: My Story, Alicia Appleman-Jurman (1988)

Stotan, Chris Crutcher (1986)

Black Swan, Farrukh Dhondy (1993)

Eva, Peter Dickinson (1988)

The Beginning of Unbelief, Robin Jones (1993)

A Haunting in Williamsburg, Lou Kassen (1990)

Robyn's Book: A True Diary, Robyn Miller (1986)

A Family Apart, Joan Lowery Nixon (1987)

Z for Zachariah, Robert O'Brien (1974)

About David, Susan Beth Pfeffer (1980)

The Year Without Michael, Susan Beth Pfeffer (1987)

The Girl in the Box, Ouida Sebestyn (1987)

The Secret Diary of Adrian Mole, Aged 13¾,
Sue Townsend (1982)

Marked by Fire, Joyce Carol Thomas (1982)

The Amazing and Death-Defying Diary of Eugene Dingman,
Paul Zindel (1987)

A Begonia for Miss Applebaum, Paul Zindel (1989)

The Pigman, Paul Zindel (1968)

3 NB's of Julian Drew, James M. Deem (1994)

chapter in which Rob assists the cow in giving birth to twin calves serves as the novel's introduction. The reader sees Rob's emergence as a man—the central theme or thesis. The body of the book deals with Rob's raising of Pinky through the pig's slaughter. Here, Rob understands what it means to be a man. The conclusion describes Rob's father's death and Rob's assumption of manhood. Atkins suggests that "With this model before them, the students should understand the basic organizational structure of a piece of writing—be it novel or essay" (p. 202). Atkins then suggests that students write an essay about manhood using all the component parts of the writing process.

The connection of reading and writing is clear. The research from a variety of sources is strong: Reading leads to writing and, in turn, writing leads to reading. Author Richard Peck has said many times: "Nobody but a reader ever became a writer." Donald Murray (1982) states it this way: "Writers act as their own first readers, scanning and rescanning their own prose to evaluate the content, form, and language of the material they produce" (p. 146). The two processes are combined: When young people read, they create meaning for themselves; when young people write, they create meaning for themselves and others.

Probst (1986) believes that "at the basis of the conceptions emerging today of literature and its teaching is the assumption that knowledge is made and that it must be made by each of us. It is an epistemology that ties together language, literature, and composition. The making of meaning is a linguistic process, the formulation and testing of propositions and assertions; literature is the reservoir of meanings made, the visions others have had; composing, both oral and written, is the act of forging our own visions" (p. 67). In addition, as students make meaning of what they read and what they sense in the world around them, they are more eager to do something with this meaning when they write.

With this attitude in the reading/writing connection, students give more serious attention to both. They feel more comfortable responding and creating. Because of this, they are able to identify and analyze the writer's craft and make some transfer to their own writing.

CONSIDERING YOUNG ADULT AUDIENCE APPEAL

Experience tells us that young adults do get turned on to reading when they read literature that meets their interests and fulfills their needs. Experience also tells us that that literature does not, for the most part, come from the literary canon that is on the curricular menu in most middle and high schools. What is it that gets students excited about reading? Why is it that many young adults will not take the time to plow through a Keats poem but will stay up half the night reading Paul Janeczko's or Mel Glenn's poetry anthologies? Why is it that juniors won't read Hawthorne's *The Scarlet Letter* but will read Speare's *The Witch of Blackbird Pond;* won't read Thoreau's *Walden* but will read Paulsen's *The Island;* won't read much of anything given them from the established curriculum, but will read Chris Crutcher's *Running Loose* and ask, "Has this author written anything else?", and then proceed to read everything that Crutcher has written.

The answer is that there are qualities found in young adult literature that simply are frequently not found in the more traditional literature—qualities that draw young adults to read and enjoy.

One of the most significant qualities that draw young adults to reading is the existence of characters they can relate to in situations they are familiar with. For example, students who have had to suffer the threats of peer pressure would be drawn to the conflicts between the main characters in Michael Cadnum's *Breaking the Fall,* Richard Peck's *Princess Ashley,* William Eliot Hazelgrove's *Ripples,* or Lois Ruby's *Skin Deep.* Along the same line, students who are experiencing the joys and conflicts of dating would be interested in reading about the teen relationships in Maureen Daly's *Acts of Love,* Jon Ripslinger's *Triangle,* or Todd Strasser's *A Very*

Touchy Subject. Students having to deal with family conflicts would relate to the situations in Paula Danziger's *The Divorce Express,* Hadley Irwin's *The Original Freddie Ackerman,* ar Alden Carter's *Dancing on Dark Water.* We also have students in our classes who might be suffering some personal conflicts, dealing with abuse, illness, or death. For outside reading, those students might want to read about the abusive relationship in Chris Crutcher's *Chinese Handcuffs,* the grandfather's illness in Norma Fox Mazer's *After the Rain,* or Becky's death in Chris Crutcher's *Running Loose.* Even given an unfamiliar setting, young adult readers can become interested in the plot because they can relate to the similar feelings, needs, and interests of the teenage characters. As a result, students will find a connection to the apartheid situation in Sheila Gordon's *Waiting for the Rain,* the persecution of the Jews in Carol Matas's *Daniel's Story,* the massacre in Tian An Men Square in William Bell's *Forbidden City,* and the fight for civil rights in Ellen Levine's *Freedom's Children.*

On the other hand, young adults also find themselves interested in unique people and situations—characters, settings, and storylines that are different from themselves but that they can still make some connections to. As a result, students enjoy the aliens in William Sleator's *Interstellar Pig,* the facially deformed Lucius Sims in Dennis Covington's *Lizard,* the futuristic colony on the moon in Paula Danziger's *This Place Has No Atmosphere,* and the adventure of saving the monstrous sea creatures in Paul Zindel's *Loch.*

Concerning style, many young adults are more likely to appreciate a more direct plot compared to that often found in traditional classics, which include a great deal of description before and within the storyline—a storyline that often covers a large period of time. Young adult literature, instead, usually begins effectively and directly with a hook, dialogue, or action and covers a shorter period of time. Robert Cormier's *We All Fall Down* exemplifies directness of plot from the very beginning with the intense action-packed description of the trashing of a suburban house. The novels of Lois Duncan, Will Hobbs, and Gary Paulsen are also good examples of directness of plot in that, although we have a sense of setting in their books, it comes across through the action and dialogue of the characters.

A final area of interest to explore in young adult literature is the nature of the ending. Much to many teachers' disappointment, most young adults like a neatly tied-up ending—one with closure that provides all the answers so the student is burdened with no more thinking. However, the characteristic of most young adult literature is to provide a thought-provoking ending—one which frequently leaves some loose ends for the reader to ponder, question, and extend. For example, at the end of Susan Beth Pfeffer's *The Year Without Michael,* Michael is still missing, leaving the reader to wonder what happened to him and whether he will ever return. With the multiple interpretations of Robert Cormier's *After the First Death,* students must decide for themselves not only the interpretion of the title but also whose death or deaths actually occurred. And in Lois Lowry's *The Giver,* the reader is left to wonder whether Jonus actually reached Elsewhere and what happened to the society he left. Although these open-ended pieces are conducive to creating activities that will extend the students' thinking and interpretations, it is even more rewarding when the students also grow to appreciate this characteristic of the literature.

❧   Learning Log Responses   ❧

How do you determine the quality of a book? Explain what a book has to do or have to be a quality book for use in your classroom.

Choose a specific young adult novel and write a rationale for its use based on the qualities found or not found in the work.

Select a specific young adult novel that has a thought-provoking ending. Explain two different activities you would use to help students extend the storyline on the basis of their own interpretation and thus enhance their understanding of the novel.

REFERENCES

Atkins, J. (1988). *The use of young adult literature to teach writing.* Unpublished doctoral dissertion, The University of Kansas, Lawrence, KS.

Murray, D. (1982). Teaching the other self: The writer's first reader. *College Composition and Communication,* 33, 140–147.

Probst, R. (1986). Three relationships in the teaching of literature. *English Journal,* 75, 60–68.

Using Reader Response
to Begin

School boards, parents, administrators, and teachers have often expressed concern about literary study, but middle and high school curriculum planners seldom alter their teaching perspective in response. Perplexing and unresolved issues about teaching and learning persist, despite scholarly attention to literature instruction. Some scholars do provide insight. According to Langer (1990), problems in literature teaching stem from a lack of research:

> There has been little systematic improvement in literature instruction in the past 25 years in spite of the efforts of many individual teachers across the country to bring systematic improvement to the teaching of literature. . . . There has been virtually no research on the teaching of literature, no change in the "objectives" that guide program development, no changes in materials that guide instruction, and no rethinking of what counts as success in literature classes—either for teachers or for students. (p. 812)

Langer's words are alarming to literature teachers who must confront these curriculum issues and who hope to instill in students a lifelong love of reading. It is distressing that our nation's greatest natural resource, its young people, is graduating and leaving school yearly without a desire to read. Verbal scores on the 1993 national SAT exam dropped one point from the previous year (Rau, 1994). Rau, an English teacher, comments, "It's no surprise reading scores dropped this year on the SAT college admissions test. . . . Our young people aren't reading anymore" (1994, p. 3A).

Literature instruction for decades focused on teaching information, analyzing the text, and in the end, teaching and seeking specific knowledge about the text. Probst (1988a) expresses concern with this information approach to literature study. According to his analysis, teaching literature as information only evolves from an outdated organizational scheme, which directs students to study facts rather than literature:

> Conceived of as a body of information, the literature curriculum tends to become a course in literary history or genre . . . a typical curriculum . . . will focus on American literature in the eleventh grade and British literature in the twelfth . . . the courses are most often arranged chronologically. As a result, the class is likely to concentrate on historical matters, examining the literature in terms of periods, dates, major authors, major works, and so on. (p. 203)

Historically, literature study developed as an academic discipline centered on information, evolving in the late nineteenth century from such closely related disciplines as classical studies. Probst (1988a) points out that nineteenth-century educators viewed literature the same way they viewed the classics, as "a subject to study and know"; therefore, "knowledge about the literature rather than sensitive reading of the literary works" was the important focus (p. 197). Anderson (1986) adds that literary study was closely aligned with the demands of college entrance exams as early as 1874. "The study of literature at that time was informed by the arguments of Matthew Arnold on the function and purpose of literature study, and Arnold maintained that the avowed purpose of literature study was initiation into and maintenance of 'high culture,' representing the best thoughts and words of western civilization" (p. 19).

With the twentieth century, attitudes changed about the role education played in the community. The focus shifted from preparing students for college to a concern of preparing them for practical pursuits. Reform came to the English curriculum soon thereafter, and an important development in that revision was the Bureau of Education *Bulletin Number Two,* assembled by James F. Hosic, a founder of the National Council of Teachers of English (Probst, 1988a, p. 197). As the social times changed, and with the help of the Commission on the Reorganization of Secondary Education, more emphasis was placed on individual needs in English rather than focusing attention on college-bound students. The psychological needs of students came to the forefront, and English as a subject was thought more as "a tool for effective living, so that students would be prepared, not just for the academic life, but for life in whatever role they might have to play" (p. 198). While some positive things came from this philosophy, such as the change in focus from the discipline to the student, other problems emerged. This period produced the idea that literature was only useful as a pastime: "It was 'English for leisure,' nothing more" (p. 198). There never seemed to be a middle ground wherein both the student and academics were treated with equal consideration.

The academic treatment of English as a discipline attempted to reestablish the coursework as a serious and "scholarly" endeavor (Probst, 1988a, p. 200). The late 1960s, however, brought another conference to the fore and again change was in the offing. The Dartmouth seminar of 1966, "attended by about fifty prominent English educators from the United States, Britain, and Canada," was highlighted with the British philosophy of "making the work personally significant to the students" (p. 201). This was truly a major change in how educators were to view English as a discipline. Finally, many years after Louise Rosenblatt's groundbreaking work on reader-response theory, other scholars were reacting to her philosophy. The change from analyzing to responding to literature was beginning to gain interest, but it was only experimentally used in the United States at this time, and that rarely.

Again, there seemed to be a shift from concern with subject matter back to students' needs. From within the "swinging pendulum," between concentrating first on the subject, then on the student, a pervasive influence had emerged—teaching literature as a body of knowledge and focusing on literary heritage. But the main point of this historical influence is that "the vacillation back and forth from student-centered to discipline-centered has not produced a conception of literature adequate to support the curriculum" (Probst, 1988a, pp. 202–203).

In the midst of the pendulum swings, one important perspective has been overlooked—a method that offers hope for revolutionizing an outdated literature curriculum. Rosenblatt's (1991) reader-response theory, first written in 1938, provides a theoretical base for students to personally respond to reading material. Her theory embraces a method of teaching literature that has the capacity to change students' view of reading. The following passage outlines her perspective on the readers' potential relationship with literature:

> Our eyes must always be directed toward that dynamic interaction between the work of art and the personality of the reader. The aim will be to increase the student's abil-

ity to achieve a full, sound reading of the text, and to broaden the personal context of emotions and ideas into which this response will be incorporated. The development of literary appreciation will depend upon a reciprocal process: An enlargement of the student's understanding of human life leads to increased esthetic sensitivity, and increased esthetic sensitivity makes possible more fruitful human insights from literature. (p. 273)

Rosenblatt's perspective on the relationship between the reader and the text opens an opportunity for students to partake in an active process whereby they must accept responsibility for much of their literary experience. Instead of a system in which teachers control and limit anticipated responses with "objective" questions, students now contribute to the knowledge pool by providing personal reactions. Rather than teaching literature as a body of knowledge dispensed by the teacher and digested by the student, Rosenblatt offers a method in which reading literature is merely one segment of a process. Literature is much more than a subject that produces information and knowledge; it is a means that, when fully developed, promotes personal growth and, in the process, aids students in making their own knowledge, knowledge that prepares students to become lifelong readers because they will have gained the confidence to read and discover on their own.

Donelson (1989) both captures the goals most teachers desire their students to reach and provides a sound rationale for changing our traditional curriculum in hopes of developing lifelong readers:

> . . . And that really is what a good literature program is. The authors we read and think about and worry about and doubt become part of us as we become part of them. If literature doesn't become part of our hearts and our guts and the guts and hearts of our students, then what is it good for? And that is our responsibility and our joy, to know so many different books and stories and poems and to present them so that young people will take some of them in and become wiser and nobler people because of the literature—and us. (p. 26)

THEORY AND RESEARCH

We feel strongly that the fundamental purpose of any middle or high school literature curriculum is, through developing the love of reading, to promote lifelong reading, whatever secondary goals a particular curriculum may have. Most scholars applaud this purpose; their research works toward implementing that goal. Rosenblatt (1991) considers it the essential reason for teaching literature: "Few teachers of English today would deny that the individual's ability to read and enjoy literature is the primary aim of literary study" (p. 64). Yet, not only have curriculum designs failed to meet this goal, often literature courses have accomplished the opposite effect. Not only are students leaving high school not enjoying literature classes, they aren't reading much, if anything, after school. Research tells us that contemporary adult society is a nonreading society, and some studies suggest that people read less as they grow older (Heather, 1982; O'Connor, 1980; Trelease, 1982; Binz, 1993);

other research indicates that adults read less than one book a year. Angelotti (1981) concludes that the literature programs in schools have produced fewer than 5 percent of adults in the United States who read literature.

From a research perspective, several variables interact to diminish desire to read for school or for pleasure. Why this is happening needs closer analysis. Purves (1992) agrees that students "do not read for enjoyment, for enlargement of their understanding, or from a desire to appreciate the classics"; rather, they read with a focus "upon issues of format, spelling, grammar and other surface features rather than on content" (p. 22). Probst (1987) attributes poor organization of curricula to the growing disinterest in reading during and after high school: "it is arranged as if knowledge about literature is the crucial matter, thus the predominance of courses emphasizing literary history, genre, and terminology and of tests demanding the memorizing of information about authors, texts, events" (p. 28).

Applebee (in Probst, 1988a) refers to the established curriculum pattern of teaching literature as a means of teaching literary history, authors, genres, and skills such as analysis of plot or character in order to attain knowledge: "In this arrangement, literature is knowledge—information to acquire, to remember, and be tested on" (p. 28). Reemphasizing the detrimental effects of teaching literature as "information to acquire," Rosenblatt (1991) comments on the long-term impact of an information-driven curriculum: "It is not at all surprising that so few of even our college graduates have formed the habit of turning to literature for pleasure and insight. The novel or play or poem has been made for them too much something to know 'about,' something to summarize or analyze or define, something to identify as one might identify the different constellations on a star map" (p. 59).

Developing Lifelong Readers

As a result of research, a shift away from information is beginning to occur, however slightly. With this move a concern for the role of students is evolving in literature instruction. Probst (1988a) argues "that literature is experience, not information, and that the student must be invited to participate in it, not simply observe it from outside. Thus, the student is very important—not simply a recipient of information, but rather a maker of knowledge out of meetings with literary texts" (preface).

Juxtaposed with the problem of teaching literature as knowledge, another misfortune occurs in high school instruction. Often, mistakenly, English teachers think they are teaching literacy when in fact they are teaching and testing students on how well they can determine what the teacher wants. Hynds (1990) explains that often teachers thought they were "measuring 'performance'" (p. 247), when in fact they were actually testing how well students could determine the teachers' expectations and answers. This is not unusual in teaching literature. Because the focus is on the text and on testable knowledge, often a student's real learning is overlooked, and is rarely tested. "In schools, teachers and curriculum builders often assume that training better readers (i.e., raising scores on competency tests) will result in a more literate populace. As a result, teachers constantly remark, 'I don't have time to let the kids read and write what they like. That won't be on the competency exam!'" (Hynds, 1990, p. 249).

As long as no one challenges our existing literature curriculum, teachers and schools will go on teaching under the same precept—if students can perform on tests, then it naturally follows that they must be gaining knowledge from and loving to read literature. Again, Hynds (1990) illustrates that teachers and administrators continually misinterpret classroom behaviors: "Thus, through a complex social construal process, students learn what teachers will and will not accept. Because some readers can so easily masquerade reading skills as reading interests, some of them may graduate from formal schooling and then never pick up a book. In this case, no amount of training in literacy skills can make them literate" (p. 254). She further explains that the social effects of classroom discussion and a student's personal response to the text are the ingredients that produce literacy:

> . . . readers become literate not simply by learning literacy skills but by participating in an elaborate socially construed system. As they develop notions of themselves as readers through participation in reading communities, they develop both intellectual and social competence for bringing what they know about life into the text. The degree to which they 'bring life to literature and literature to life' (Hynds, 1989) is related to the likelihood that they will continue to read beyond their years of formal schooling. (Hynds, 1990, p. 255)

It is essential that teachers and others who help design high school curricula begin reinterpreting student behavior and motivations. Driving home the point that teachers often misinterpret students' motives and learning, Hynds (1990) relates a story about Jay, a student she studied closely for a clearer perception of reading behavior. He performed well on his class assignments and essays but actually didn't like English or reading at all. His teacher, however, was under the impression that Jay was an exemplary student and, therefore, must love reading and English class. According to Hynds's (1990) study, Jay's teacher was wrong: "My studies of adolescents revealed that readers can be competent and can demonstrate that competence in the classroom, yet fail to see themselves as 'readers,' and consequently, seldom read for their own pleasure" (p. 249). In Jay's own words, he doubted that he would read much at all after graduation: "Jay had developed 'literacy skills,' but not 'literate behaviors.' He was capable of comprehending and demonstrating competence to his teacher when a grade was involved. However, he rarely saw reading as an end in itself, and only occasionally put his competence to use in understanding and identifying with literary characters" (p. 249).

Students, especially middle and high school students, are not likely to pursue literature with a scholarly passion; however they *will* read as a form of self-indulgence. When used for the best reasons, self-indulgence can serve as "an attempt to see more clearly who one is and where one stands" (Probst, 1988a, p. 4). This perspective provides students more opportunity to grow with the literature they read, and challenges them to create new knowledge. "Exchange with the text can become for the reader a process of self-creation" (p. 21). Curricula that endorse a reader-response base for teaching literature help promote the possible gain for students. As Rosenblatt (1956) explains, it ensures their love of reading:

> Once an organic relationship has been set up between young readers and books, many kinds of growth are possible, and the teacher can proceed to fulfill his function. Above all, students need to be helped to have personally satisfying and personally meaningful transactions with literature. Then they will develop the habit of turning to literature for the pleasure and insights it offers. (p. 67)

Rejection of a curriculum based on studying literature solely for factual knowledge is the first step in aiding students' growth toward an attitude of lifelong reading. Moreover, students who have experienced a classroom wherein reader response is the basis of instruction will discover the transformational process of learning. As Probst (1987) aptly points out, "Literature's value resides not in information it imparts but in experience it enables us to have. . . . Literature enables each of us to shape knowledge out of our encounter with it" (p. 27).

Students' Evolving Literary Understanding

Focusing on literature as a means of knowledge is merely one change that must transpire in school curricula. Another problem confronting teachers and administrators in teaching literature to a group of young people is dealing effectively with the students' differing intellectual development. Researchers have identified several stages of, and patterns to, young adults' developing literary understanding. Carlsen (1980) suggests three general developmental stages of literary interest. The first, early adolescence, occurs from about ages 11 to 14. Students at this level are characterized as having interests in animal stories, adventures, mysteries, the supernatural, sports, coming of age in different cultures, stories about the home and family life, and fantasy. Middle adolescence, roughly ages 15 to 16, typically is characterized by interests in nonfiction adventure, longer historical novels, mystical romances, and stories of adolescent life. Carlsen's third stage, late adolescence, from approximately ages 17 to 18, is the period of transition to adult reading. Here this age group searches for personal values, social questions, strange experiences and unusual circumstances, and the transition to adult roles.

Where Carlsen's study suggests a definite trend in interest for students, Hynds's (1990) research challenges the idea that comprehension and literary analysis are enough to promote better reading skills. In her studies, she discovered "that readers operate out of a variety of social perspectives that influence their conceptions of how to read, respond to, and demonstrate understanding of literary texts" (p. 245). Hynds distinguishes between the approaches students take in reading. If, for example, they read for pleasure, students are "story-driven," responding to and "motivated most often by an engaging plot or interesting characters"; however, when they read for school assignments, students read for the teacher's tests, and therefore, are "largely 'information-driven'" (pp. 245–246). The implication is that students read with a different intent depending on the assigned purpose. But it further suggests that if students are reading for pleasure (in or out of class), they are searching for a story that will entice them to engage and maintain their interest.

Beach and Wendler's (1987) study moves the issue of reading development a step beyond Carlsen's research. They examined differences in ability to respond to literature based on age levels, comparing eighth graders, eleventh graders, college freshmen, and college seniors in their ability to draw inferences about characters, acts, and perceptions. The results make evident how significant the developmental differences are both in terms of student performance and in the selection of literature "The results suggest that from early adolescence to young adulthood, readers shift from a 'describer orientation'—conceiving of characters in terms of immediate surface feelings or physical behaviors to conceptions of characters in terms of long-range social or psychological beliefs and goals" (p. 286). This important finding reveals that the younger age group does think in terms of analysis beyond the most basic level. Further, they found evidence that the older, more mature college students had increased developmental abilities to "infer social/psychological meanings for characters' acts" (p. 294). In curriculum planning this knowledge is salient because often part of the problem for students is that they are developmentally incapable of achieving their teachers' expectations of analysis or interpretation. The maturity factor in older students makes selection of reading material more critical. More difficult works should be geared toward older rather than younger students. This is an important point of contention in the selection of literature.

Probst (1987) provides a challenge to high schools that want to redesign their literature curriculum. He suggests that rather than "arranging literature courses in terms of genre or history, we might conceive of the curriculum as an opportunity for students to explore the significant issues in their lives and in the culture, issues about which they must develop convictions" (p. 30). Inherent in his alternative route to teaching literature is the reader-response approach to reading. As noted Rosenblatt established this theory as early as 1938, and reinforced the idea with instructional information in subsequent publications, but it was only in the late 1960s and early 1970s that some teachers in a few schools actually incorporated the theory into their actions. Rosenblatt (1991) outlines the significance of the student/reader: "The really important things in the education of youth cannot be taught in the formal didactic manner; they are things which are experienced, absorbed, accepted, incorporated in the personality through emotional and esthetic experiences" (p. 180).

Teaching literature then, should be an ongoing process between reader and the text, as expressed by Probst (1987) as he expands the concept of literature in the classroom: "Literature thus invites us to participate in the ongoing dialogue of the culture. It presents to us what others have experienced and how they have made sense of that experience, and it invites us to take those perceptions, combine them with our own, and build out of the mix the conceptions and visions that will govern our lives. Literature provides us not knowledge ready-made but the opportunity to make knowledge" (p. 28).

Probst further explains that predetermined meanings of words, ideas, and issues are nonexistent; rather it is our interpretation, our response to the words and the writers, and our reflective and critical thoughts that form cultural meaning: "I read Shakespeare, then, and [Richard] Peck, not to submit to them, not to absorb unreflectingly and uncritically their visions and their values but to think with them" (1987, p. 28).

The transaction between reader and text (reader response) is the focus of change in literature curricula. Probst (1988b) identifies this intricate relationship by borrowing a metaphor from Annie Dillard explaining this transaction between reader and text: "'The mind fits the world and shapes it as a river fits and shapes its own banks.'" (quoted on p. 378). He goes on to explain the metaphor: "The relationship between reader and text is much like that between the river and its banks, each working its effects upon the other, each contributing to the shape the literary text ultimately takes in the reader's mind" (p. 378). This denotes an important distinction between the two types of literature curricula discussed, placing the quest for knowledge on one end of the curriculum continuum and literature as a process focusing on the relationship between the reader and the text at the other.

The Response-Centered Curriculum

A response-centered classroom is an important alteration of curriculum, one that meets Hannson's (1992) criteria for a "good" instructional method: "We believe that if students are to see reading as a vehicle for lifelong learning, then, *how* we teach is just as important as *what* we teach. In a good reading or literature program, *how* and *what* we teach are orchestrated so that no one is in doubt as to *why*" (p. 260). Inherent in this change of focus from text to reader, and providing another link to middle and high school level interest, is the demand for an alternative selection of literature.

For the transaction between reader and text to succeed, teachers must alter their methods of literature selection for the classroom. Which literature is taught in what classes has been an issue of great importance. According to Kolb (1990), "The question of what books are to be required in our schools is, with the exception of salaries, the chief topic of concern among teachers, administrators, and school boards" (p. 35). Selection is intrinsically connected to the longstanding use of textbooks. According to Applebee (1989), "the literature anthology was the most frequent source of materials (used 'regularly' by 66% of the teachers)" (p. 29). By and large, then, teachers base their literature selection on which textbook the school uses. Hannson (1992) reiterates concern for the near-total reliance on textbooks:

> What we currently see being taught in classrooms—regardless of grade level—is a standard body of texts, primarily narrative, preselected for use by someone other than the teacher or the students. . . . At the secondary and college levels, publishing houses and editors of anthologies do the selecting. As we travel across the county, we see a disappointing sameness to what students are reading. Students and teachers tend to approach these texts in habitual and uninspired ways. (pp. 259–260)

In arguing both sides of an established literary canon, Kolb (1990) suggests, "Literature can be thought of as the embodiment of the great ideas of human civilization, or as the voice of social protest; as a manifestation of a specific society in a specific time and place, or as the product of an individual artistic consciousness. . . . Literature can be understood as a confirmation of the reader's experience, an explanation of that experience, or an enlargement of experience" (p. 39). The question remains—which material best meets this criteria? Rosenblatt (1991) is more concerned that students be provided with literature that they can relate to. She suggests that if students are to truly participate in literature as a process of learning and developing skills and interest, then the selections must provide connections:

> The reader brings to the work personality traits, memories of past events, present needs and preoccupations, a particular mood of the moment, and a particular physical condition. These and many other elements in a never-to-be duplicated combination determine his response to the peculiar contribution of the text. For the adolescent reader, the experience of the work is further specialized by the fact that he has probably not yet arrived at a consistent view of life or achieved a fully integrated personality. (pp. 30–31)

In other words, no one—not the teacher, the parents, or the critics—can experience literature for us. She explains:

> The reader of the poem must have the experience himself [as] he is intent on the pattern of sensations, emotions, and concepts it evokes. Because the text is organized and self-contained, it concentrates the reader's attention and regulates what will enter into his consciousness. His business for the moment is to apprehend as fully as possible these images and concepts in relation to one another. Out of this arises a sense of an organized structure of perceptions and feelings which constitutes for him the esthetic experience. (pp. 32–33)

It is essential that teachers adopt Rosenblatt's view of the reader's role in literature if they hope to encourage young people to want to read again and again. But perhaps even more important is her understanding of the importance of connecting student to text in dictating the future for lifelong reading: "If the language, the setting, the theme, the central situation, all are too alien, even a 'great work' will fail. . . . Books must be provided that hold out some link with the young reader's past and present preoccupations, anxieties, emotions" (1991, p. 72).

Rosenblatt (1991) explains the inherent reasons that literature must match students' needs, experience, and maturity levels: "It is not enough merely to think of what the student *ought* to read. Choices must reflect a sense of the possible links between these materials and the student's past experience and present level of maturity" (p. 42). In particular, the link between a student's "emotional maturity" and the material selected is crucial in helping students achieve that sense of success that ultimately produces confident readers. Rosenblatt explores how much of the student's whole being is involved in this intricate process of appropriate selection:

> The whole personality tends to become involved in the literary experience. That a literary work may bring into play and be related to profoundly personal needs and pre-

occupations makes it a powerful potential educational force. For it is out of these basic needs and attitudes that behavior springs. Hence, literature can foster the linkage between intellectual perception and emotional drive that is essential to any vital learning process. (p. 182)

Selection is a crucial dimension of altering our national problem of students' lagging interest in literature classes. One basic problem inherent in the selection process is the insistence on teaching "classical" literature. We suggest that this insistence is partially due to historical circumstances, which have encumbered literature curricula with selections that don't meet the needs of today's youth.

Curricula of the 1980s and 1990s continue this tradition of including the literature of the past—the literature most commonly called "the classics." Those who call for school and curriculum reform often make suggestions about the English curriculum, usually demanding literature that will help students understand their literary heritage. (For a more detailed discussion of classroom use of the classics, see Chapter 7)

We state our concerns about the use of the classics here because this study relates directly to the reader-response theory. A teacher's zest to provide students with the great literature of the world so that they may have an understanding of basic cultural issues may have the opposite result—students may very well stop reading all together. Rosenblatt (1991) provides perspective about overwhelming students with the standard "classical" selection: "In our zeal to give our students the proper literary training, we constantly set them tasks a step beyond their powers, or plunge them into reading that practically requires the learning of a new language" (p. 215). She follows this argument with the notion that classic literature has often been introduced to students when their experience is inadequate to connect in any way to the ideas and issues in those works.

Hynds (1990) suggests many of the merits of including literature of interest to students. It is, after all, a link in helping students "view themselves as literate," and this will ultimately lead them to continue a lifetime pattern of reading: "Finally, no matter how sophisticated the curriculum or the classroom library, readers must *want* to read and must see the value in becoming readers before they view themselves as literate" (p. 251). When reading literature, students must be "engaged" in some way with the text or novel they read. If they cannot grasp the plot or make meaning from the work, then they really aren't interacting with the text.

More evidence introduced by Hynds (1989) illustrates the effect of teaching young adult literature. Her study provides evidence that students interact with greater success when reading works they are capable of connecting with: "Readers who brought a greater range of interpersonal constructs to their reading" (p. 31) appeared more internally motivated and not dependent on teachers, parents, and peers. In contrast, readers with little congruence in their peer and character impressions were not consistently motivated to read for its own sake, and as a result, were unable to create connections between literature and life.

Young adult literature adds life to an otherwise boring, traditional curriculum. Probst's (1987) compelling argument defines the parameters of gain from young adult literature and dispels the myth that "traditional literature" is best for students.

He also points out the ease with which students may be able to engage in reader response, which may not be the case with the older literature:

> Adolescent literature must have a significant place in the curriculum, then, because it deals with the issues students are likely to be confronting, and so it directly and openly invites the sort of encounter we have been alluding to. It touches their lives, addressing issues that matter, raising questions that are likely to interest them. The transactions they may have with it are likely to be significant, rather than trivial and superficial. We must not judge the literature solely on criteria of worth that deal only with features of the text. We must instead judge it on the likelihood that the students' transactions with it will be of high quality—that is, committed, interested, reasoned, emotional, personal. It is of little significance that students remember twenty years from now the distinction between metaphor and simile—far more significant that they have felt the shaping effect of metaphoric language, and that they have profited by it. (p. 28)

CREATING A CLIMATE FOR USING READER RESPONSE

Like any successful program, a reader-response approach to teaching literature requires carefully using classroom strategies to achieve the desired results. Along with creating a climate conducive to active learning, the teacher must learn and exhibit behaviors that promote trust and consistency for students. The teacher creates classroom atmosphere, and the first step is arranging the room in a manner that promotes an environment for open discussions. Next, the teacher's behaviors must encourage an environment of cooperation and trust. After all, teachers can only hope to achieve the desired results in the classroom if students first feel a sense of security to pursue openly active learning (Bushman, 1994).

Classroom climate may predict the success or failure of any diligently planned curriculum. Essential to a response-centered method of teaching is developing trust between teacher and students. Preparing the students for a trust relationship begins with room arrangement. The classroom should provide an environment that radiates warmth so that quality communication will result whether in class discussion or in a one-on-one conversation between teacher and student. The classroom arrangement must enable the students to easily see and hear one another. For example, circular seating often accomplishes the communication goals effectively. It is not necessary, however, to keep this arrangement at all times. Change may keep the atmosphere fresh and alive. Mostly, the teacher's concern should be to promote a feeling to students that she cares about their success—"a place where kids feel like working and enter with expectations and a 'what are we going to do today?' feeling" (Kirby & Liner, 1988, p. 23). In other words, the classroom arrangement should convey to students that this is a place for sharing ideas, discussing freely, and specifically, feeling safe in that process.

Once the seating arrangement has created an atmosphere of warmth, then comes the most critical ingredient to a successful response-centered program—the teacher's behavior. A teacher's attitude is the primary tool that can persuade a student that the lesson, the methods used, and, ultimately, the literature itself are critical to learning. Kirby and Liner (1988) suggest that a teacher's role is to develop "the psychological climate" (p. 25) in such a manner as to foster trust. Although their book focuses on writing classrooms, the idea suits any class wherein a teacher subscribes to effective behaviors. Creating this climate is not easy, and an important balance between inviting students to think and respond freely and maintaining authority and control is just one component that teachers must sustain if success is to prevail. Probst (1988a) addresses one key for success, discussions. Offsetting the teacher's authority role with an attitude of trust in students is one way of establishing student confidence:

> If the discussions are to invite the responses and perceptions of the students, it is necessary that these responses and perceptions be welcomed. The teacher must let the students know that their comments are solicited and will be given consideration. . . .
>
> A delicate balance is required. The teacher must establish an atmosphere in which students feel secure enough to respond openly, but must not deceive them into believing that initial responses are sufficient. Nor, on the other hand, should he make students think their responses are invited to provide the teacher and other students with clay pigeons to shoot. If responses are ridiculed, there will soon be few responses left to ridicule. This is not to say that response-based teaching demands the intimacy of a sensitivity session . . . but it does require reasonable freedom from fear of castigation or mockery, and from obsequious submission to the authority of the teacher or the author. The classroom must be cooperative, not combative, with students and teachers building on one another's ideas, using rather than disputing them (p. 25).

Teacher behaviors, providing they are appropriate and sincere, can create the potential for an exciting literature experience; this is an integral part of connecting students to that event. Therefore, using a response-centered curriculum requires a special type of teacher, one who teaches rather than instructs. This distinction is basic to ensuring the success of a response-based classroom. The difference in the terms is partially an attitude toward students and is explained in Eisner's (1985) text, *The Educational Imagination,* in which he distinguishes between *instruction* and *teaching:* "To 'teach' is softer than to 'instruct'" (p. 181). He follows with an integral reason for teaching as opposed to using instructional methods, stating that "this is why the term *instruction* is more likely to be used by those whose orientation to curriculum is technological and who want to maximize effective control over the content and form of what children learn in school. *Instruction* is a term more suited to a manual than is the term *teach.* Instruction is less apt to be associated with the adventitious, with what is flexible and emergent, in short, and what is artistic, than is teaching" (p. 181).

Certainly, teachers are called on to be "artists" in a response-centered classroom. They must be creative in all aspects of classroom management so that students become personally engaged in responding to literature and teachers sustain a fresh approach to students' responses.

One specific behavior that teachers must maintain involves discussing student responses. Classrooms that have focused on literary analysis, or on literature for the sake of knowledge, will have an especially difficult task ahead because students have learned through experience that teachers have a specific answer in mind. Expected responses and preconceived notions, apart from matters of factual recall, do not enhance response-centered class discussion. Rosenblatt (1991) suggests that students will need guidance in evaluating their own reactions to the work, but instead of imposing specific ideas or "patterns, the teacher will help the student develop these understandings in the context of his own emotions and his own curiosity about life and literature" (p. 66). If the teachers display this attitude, they will create an environment wherein students begin to "feel" their responses instead of the anticipated answers that teachers have expected in the past.

The teacher's demeanor will determine the success of a response-centered program. Leadership, exhibited through questioning techniques and by facilitating group discussions that reflect their own insight into what students think about when reading, will be the key as to whether trust will develop. When students recognize that the teacher is not guiding them to a specific response and that they can speak without fear of disapproval, they will sense consistent behavior. One way for teachers to prepare for students' responses is through understanding their own reading responses. Buckley (1992) suggests that teachers first explore their own reading habits before leading students through a reading journey. In the context of an imaginary institute for educators, she sets two objectives—the first to study teachers' reading habits and the second to have them discover how students read:

> The purpose of the first objective is to develop reflective teachers who seriously think about how they themselves read, discerning as best they can the peculiarities of human comprehension. . . .
> [The] second objective calls for a new curriculum for teaching literature to elementary and secondary students. This objective . . . is easier only because it follows and benefits from the understandings gained from the first. Generating ideas on how to teach others naturally follows in the wake of discoveries born from self-teaching. To teach literature with poise and confidence, teachers need to experience and internalize the subject. If the institute aspires for a different teaching of literature, then the new ways of literature must first become part of the teacher, not just part of the curriculum. Change the teacher, the institute hypothesizes, and then students will change accordingly (p. 46).

It is important to remember that teachers cannot be thrust into a response-centered method, they must understand it, believe in it, and ultimately, want it to work for students.

Critical to response-based literature are teachers who are both sensitive to students and sincerely responsive to the unexpected. Teachers must be able to "hear" what students are responding to, which involves much more than merely listening to answers. Once students learn that the teacher is interested in their insights, trust can evolve. Ultimately, as Rosenblatt (1991) counsels, teachers must establish a classroom climate that will induce students into a "spontaneous response" (p. 108). Achieving this level of facilitation will provide the necessary tools to help students love reading; however, to complete the desired results, students must be provided with literature that provokes their interest enough for them to read it.

As we have noted, reading literature that motivates students and stimulates ideas relevant to them is essential as they enlist response-based skills. Probst (1988a) reminds us, "If we are to begin our teaching with students' responses, we need literary works that provoke responses, stimulating students to think, feel, and talk. Without such works, awakening interest in discussion and writing can be very difficult. The teacher is forced to trick students into temporary interest in something that doesn't really appeal to them" (p. 113).

CLASSROOM STRATEGIES FOR TEACHING THE LITERATURE

As we have noted, the young adult literature chosen in middle and secondary schools provides young adults with subject matter that relates to areas that are important to them. How we teach that literature is important, too, since what teachers have students do with the literature enables young adults to make the connections necessary between their reading and their world.

Traditionally, teachers have spent considerable time teaching about literature, and students have, therefore, not been truly involved with the literature itself. "We must keep clearly in mind that the literary experience is fundamentally an unmediated, private exchange between a text and a reader, and that literary history and scholarship are supplemental. Studying them may or may not contribute to understanding of the private exchange, but it cannot be substituted for that immediate experience" (Probst, 1984, p. 7). It would seem, then, that teachers must do everything in their power to foster the relationships that students have with the text; therefore, the classroom becomes the nurturing center for that reading experience. Students feel comfortable sharing the meaning of literature and how it relates to their particular world.

Rosenblatt (1938) and Probst (1984) write of the interconnection of teacher, text, and student. Although the literary experience is between the reader and the text, the growth of that experience most often takes place in the classroom, so the teacher and students play an important role in this reading development. To make some sense of the text, readers draw on their thinking about past events, relevant experiences, and general knowledge. Sharing this process with the teacher and classmates fine tunes their understanding of the text.

Beach and Marshall (1991) suggest that students respond by engaging, describing, conceiving, explaining, connecting, interpreting, and judging. When young adult readers make emotional responses and reactions to the text, this engagement comes in many ways: "I love this book!," "This is great!" "What a dumb story!" Readers can react to the book as a whole, or they may respond to a particular part: "That character was a jerk!" When describing, students reproduce or restate what is in the text. This is a rather low-level response, but the information may be necessary to reach the meaning.

Students move beyond this describing process by making connections between the text and their experience (conceiving). As students explain the text, they are offering reasons why certain actions occur or why characters do what they do. The process increases the perspectives that students have on their reading. At a higher level of response, students make connections to the text with their knowledge of language, literary conventions, and social conventions to make meaning.

When students interpret what they have read, they say, "What does this text say?" We all understand at one level of reading and generalize to another level. Jerry's decision not to sell chocolates in *The Chocolate War* (Cormier) is more than just one student's decision not to enter into a school's money-making project. And lastly, students respond by judging the quality of the work. They evaluate the characters, the plot, and the author's craft.

Teachers have an important role in fostering this reader response. They also share in the responsibility of helping students with their developmental tasks, growing moral judgment, and reading appreciation. The classroom pedagogy that teachers choose can make or break a student's development in these areas. We believe that creative oral and written activities with young adult literature will have a positive effect on young people.

Group Discussions

The interaction that occurs among young people within a large or small group enables students to check their responses to literature against the responses of other students. This interactive process helps students adjust their thinking or reinforce their positions as they hear other responses. Students can ask for clarification if ideas and positions are not presented clearly; they can ask for elaboration if they need more information for a better understanding of the issues under consideration. If students feel that a statement has little supporting evidence, they can ask that the student give justification for making the point.

For example, a student responding to Peck's *Are You in the House Alone?* suggests that the treatment of Allison and Phil at the end of the novel is appropriate. Another student quickly agrees. Hearing no further evidence from either student, others may ask for a justification of that position. In their responses, the students show their understanding of the novel in relation to their perceptions of the world in which they live. There is at this point a heightened moral awareness (Yeazell & Cole, 1986) of the incident in the novel as it relates to the world of these two students. Certainly, the additional discussion that follows would enhance further moral reasoning skills.

There are additional processes that enhance thinking skills. Students may find that by comparing and contrasting incidents and characters in two or more young adult novels, they have a better understanding of the issues under discussion. The group discussion also fosters evaluation. Students make evaluative statements about what they read. When students make statements with the words "good," "great," and "super" in them, they need to offer sound reasoning why and on what basis they feel that the quality of the work should be described with those or similar words.

One way to help students respond to their reading is by using response questions similar to those listed in Figure 3.1. Questions such as these help students to move through their emotional responses to the work at first. There may be many more questions and areas to discuss, but these would get to the meat of any novel discussion. Of course, these questions could be used when the discussion slows down. Perhaps the first and foremost question to ask in the response-based discus-

What is your first reaction after reading this novel?

What feelings or emotions does this novel evoke in you?

What character(s) do you particularly like? Why?

What character(s) do you particularly dislike? Why?

Do any characters in this novel remind you of people you know?

Are you like any character in the novel?

What fears or concerns do you have for the characters?

What decisions do you feel were particularly good/bad?

What memory does the novel help you to recall?

Would you change any part of the novel? The beginning? The ending?

What questions do you have about this novel?

What do you think is the major point of the novel?

Does this novel remind you of any other literary work?

Comment on the author's writing style.

FIGURE 3.1
Response-based questions

sion is, "What do you want to say about what you read?" These questions may be inserted periodically after the discussion has begun.

After students develop a strong sense about their relationship with the literature, they then move to the more analytic questions that cause the reader to think about the genre itself and about the author's craft.

Creative Drama

Role playing and improvisation expand the boundaries of experiences for students so that they develop a more complete understanding of themselves and of the literature they are reading. Through role playing and improvisation, students are able to think as characters would think and act as characters would act. Students take on a persona different from their own and work at making that character come alive as they perceive what that character would be like if he were alive. The process is much like Kohlberg's (1987) role-taking. Although Kohlberg's role-taking may not be solely related to literature study, it certainly seems to be an appropriate model for understanding character motivations and actions. Students get inside the characters and play out their emotions, making choices and decisions based on the readers' understanding of those characters.

Role playing works well as students respond to and interact with *Mote* (Reaver). Chris and Billy confront a number of conflicts throughout the novel: white supremacy, black supremacy, murder, individual rights, and others. One important societal issue, although of secondary importance in the novel, concerns the placement of individuals who are mentally or physically disabled. Should they be placed in institutions or remain in the family home? Students role play Chris and Billy as they discuss this conflict as it relates to Leon, Chris's mentally retarded friend. This issue is also found in Bridgers' *All Together Now.* Students role play Casey and Alva (brother of Dwayne) concerning the placement of Dwayne. Alva wants to place his brother in a hospital; Casey does not think it is necessary. Are there reasons for removing Dwayne or Leon from society? Or are the reasons that people have for doing this self-serving? Are there stronger reasons for letting them remain with their families? Such effective moral issues can be a part of most creative drama activities.

The right of extremist groups to exist also provides an interesting moral question for students to debate. After finishing *Mote,* students may role play representatives of the Black Brigade and the ERWA on the issue of their right to exist.

Most young adult novels provide for interesting role-playing situations. The moral dilemma is most often at the heart of the novel's conflict. Students can use creative drama to explore the concerns of Henry and Zelda (*A Begonia for Miss Applebaum,* Zindel), Tracy and Brad (*The Twisted Window,* Duncan), Annemarie and Ellen (*Number the Stars,* Lowry), Jerry, Archie, and Obie (*The Chocolate War,* Cormier), Eric, Jack, Dill, and Nicki (*Night Kites,* Kerr), Chelsea and Ashley (*Princess Ashley,* Peck), Jerry, Bonnie, and Sheila (*Sheila's Dying,* Carter), Louie and Becky (*Running Loose,* Crutcher), Sam and Ollie (*No Kidding,* Brooks), Alex, Christy, and Shannon (*Good-Bye Tomorrow,* Miklowitz), Wren, Kevin, and Sam (*Notes for Another Life,* Bridgers), Dillon and Jennifer (*Chinese Handcuffs,* Crutcher), and Paul Moreaux (*Fade,* Cormier).

Writing

A number of activities use writing as the principal mode of responding. Responding reports, journals, the narrative, and the personal essay help students make a personal response that draws on their ability to create meaning of what they have read. We include a brief comment on each of these strategies in this chapter; a more detailed account about the use of writing and its relationship to the literature appears in Chapter 4.

RESPONDING REPORTS.   Students can make these reports in place of the traditional book report. Book reports have been the nemesis of students and teachers for years. Responding reports emphasize reading the work and responding to it primarily by writing. They do not emphasize looking up specific information to find "right answers." When the novel has been read as a class novel by all students, teachers can use these reports to assess students' understanding of the work.

Responding reports help students to become personally involved with the literature. They begin by having students make personal responses; i.e., they become engaged with the reading. How is this novel related to the reader? What emotions and feelings are felt by the student? After students have read and written about the novel on a personal level, they are ready to move to a more "intellectual" level. They now think about the author's craft: What strategies and techniques did the author use so that students have the responses that they have?

Responding reports also integrate reading and writing. In doing this, students enjoy the totality of the novel by responding to the ideas presented and by understanding the techniques used by the author. We believe that students feel more at ease when responding to a work in this way since they are in control of how they respond: how they structure their responses, what they include, and what they omit. As a result, they will grow in their understanding of their novel in particular and of literature in general.

For example, in *Chinese Handcuffs,* students could respond to Crutcher's use of detail and description, the major themes of suicide and sexual abuse, and how they view the novel in terms of what it means to a young adult in today's society. There also could be an open response: Choose any passage in the novel that you find meaningful. Quote it and comment on its importance. (See Figure 3.2)

THE JOURNAL.   We view the journal as a source for making deposits and withdrawals, much like a checking and savings account in a bank. To carry the analogy one step further, the bank account grows as interest is added periodically. Growth also takes place in the journal entries because students have thought about those ideas since making them. The journal can be the place where students record their reactions to their reading as they are reading. This response is not formal and is certainly not evaluated by the teacher. Students may wish to list the characters and a one- or two-sentence description of each; it is a place to record facts and important information about plot, setting, and theme that may be useful in later discussions or written responses. They may wish to record quotes that they want to remember, connections to their experiences, and interpretations that they make as they are reading. Journals serve students well for continued use throughout the study of a particular novel.

The journal acts as a testing site for students' thinking. Coming to some understanding of a literary text is a process much like the process of writing: Readers do not come quickly to a complete understanding of the meaning of a piece of literature. It often takes time, and it takes a testing of ideas about meaning. Students can write informal drafts in their journals to get at that meaning. We have learned much about the "writing to learn" movement and how writing helps readers and writers in all content areas to increase critical and creative thinking and, therefore, to arrive at understanding. Many readers say that they really don't know what they mean until they can speak or write about it. Often the meaning changes as they spend time working through their understanding by writing.

We frequently ask our students to write response papers on the young adult novels they read. They often say that their thoughts about a particular issue or question in a novel change as they move through the first draft of that paper. Many suggest that they use the journal in making these initial drafts. The very act of writing triggers other responses they have not used previously. Some ideas are abandoned; others are

Dillon, the main character in *Chinese Handcuffs,* writes unsent letters to his dead brother as a way of coping with problems that seem unsolvable. In the space below, tell how you feel about that process. Could you use the unsent letter to work through problems that you may have from time to time? Tell how you deal with difficult problems. What outlet do you use to achieve release from the tensions that problems cause?

Respond briefly to each of the following:

- What is your first reaction after reading *Chinese Handcuffs?*

- What feelings or emotions does the work evoke in you?

- Do any of the characters remind you of people that you know? Do not name the individuals, but describe how these people whom you know are like the characters in the novel.

- What is the major point of the novel as you understand it?

As has been noted, Dillon uses the unsent letter. Indicate in which situations (about what concerns) did Dillon write the unsent letters and indicate what effect they had on him.

Choose one of Dillon's letters to Preston and take on the point of view of Preston and respond to the letter. Become Preston for a short time and respond to Dillon's concerns.

Chris Crutcher uses similes frequently in his novel. The following are but a few:

. . . I was drawn to her like a masochist to hot tongs (p. 15).

The whistle blew. . .Coach Sherman motioned to Jennifer, who approached like a racehorse following a tough workout, shoulder-length blond hair clinging to her neck like a wet mane, her long sinewy legs glistening with sweat (p. 18).

My emotions churn inside me like a hurricane, and when it's at its worst, I can only lay back and let them take me away (p. 59).

- Look through the novel and find at least five more similes and list them below.

- Now, comment on the effectiveness of using such a device. Why would an author use the simile?

- Create a short piece of writing (two or three paragraphs) in which you use similes.

FIGURE 3.2
A responding report on Crutcher's *Chinese Handcuffs*

expanded. The journal, therefore, is the place to record information that may or may not be used later and to try out ideas without having to "get it right the first time."

THE NARRATIVE AND THE PERSONAL ESSAY.   The journal has its uses, but it is not meant for evaluation. At times, however, teachers want students to write a more formal piece of writing, whether it be developing characters and plot in a story or taking a position about what they have read and supporting that position in an organized way. We support this practice, although we feel that for most students in grades 6 through 10 a less formal piece of writing is more beneficial. According to Wadsworth (1978), many students have trouble writing this formal essay due to the nature of the writing and their lack of formal operational characteristics. Formal writing can come later.

For example, after reading Hinton's *The Outsiders,* students who have had experience with groups could respond in a narrative showing the troubling aspects of school cliques, school gangs, or community gangs. Students may choose the personal essay over a narrative to explore the problems of gangs and their effects on the school or social communities. After reading Avi's *Nothing But the Truth,* middle school students may respond by relating a personal experience in which they told the truth as they knew it but others saw it in a different way; older students may write a more formal essay in which they explore the use of half-truths and obfuscated language to achieve a particular result.

RESPONDING TO *In the Middle of the Night:* An Example

In this section, we describe a sample reader-response classroom exercise, using Robert Cormier's 1995 novel *In the Middle of the Night* as our text. A very important part of the literature selection for any English/language arts classroom is choosing material that is age appropriate. We have given much attention to this topic in this chapter; it seems appropriate to offer a minimal reminder as we select a novel for study as an example of what can be done in a response-centered classroom. If we expect students to have sufficient experience for a response, they must be able to relate in some manner to the assigned literature. Karolides (1992) states the significance of using appropriate literature: "The language of a text, the situation, characters, or the expressed issues can dissuade a reader from comprehension of the text and thus inhibit involvement with it. In effect, if the reader has insufficient linguistic or experimental background to allow participation, the reader cannot relate to the text, and the reading act will be short-circuited" (p. 23).

With the wide-ranging selection of young adult literature available today, it is not difficult to find adequate reading material that meets the needs and interests of all students. *In the Middle of the Night* is a quality young adult novel that excels in its literary merits as well as in its ability to maintain reader interest. Fifteen- to seventeen-year-old students identify and are involved in reading this novel because of its themes, language, tension, and interesting characters. A brief summary of the novel follows:

> The ringing telephone blistered the night, stripping him of sleep, like a bandage torn from flesh. He looked toward the digital clock: 3:18 in vivid scarlet numbers. Instantly alert, he thought: it's beginning again, but too early—much too early this year. (p. 13)

Eight years before Denny Colbert was born, his father was involved in a tragic accident in which twenty-two children died. And now, as a 16-year-old, Denny is feeling the impact of that tragedy. There are telephone calls, usually late at night, they've gone on for twenty-five years. They start around the first of October, the anniversary of the fire that killed the children. Denny's father has moved his family too many times; so now they must just put up with the calls. This year Denny disobeys his father and answers the phone. He finds himself drawn into a provocative and potentially deadly relationship with the mystery caller—a girl named Lulu, who has never recovered from the injuries she received in the fire that "killed" her. She wants revenge on her "murderer" and wants to get it through his son.

Preparing Students to Read

The first stage of successfully preparing students for a reading assignment is to seize their attention, and to focus it often through writing. (You can choose a variety of methods for focusing students' attention, but writing works very well. Discussion about a relevant topic works well, too; however, for this prereading lesson, we have chosen writing.) Purves, Rogers, and Soter (1990) attest to the strengths of writing and learning, stating, "Extended writing draws out of the mind of the reader more information, more reflection, more wrestling than, for example, either group discussion or brief responses to questions will do" (p. 137). Through writing, students are able to explore topics and at the same time connect these topics to their feelings, fears, and other emotions.

In choosing a topic for the prereading writing assignments, you want to provoke students to think about a central issue in the novel, preparing and focusing students toward an issue that is important in what they are about to read. Stirring a student's interest is essential to the process of response because if they are not motivated, the chances are slim that they will respond with much effort. Another purpose for prereading writing is to help students make a connection to the novel. Experience teaches us that our connections to people, ideas, or objects are a driving force. The writing will internalize for students that their ideas are important, further empowering them.

In the Middle of the Night abounds with themes and issues that will evoke student responses. Prereading activities might include, but should certainly not be limited to, having students write about the following:

Revenge: Have students ever felt so put upon, so angry that they wish to seek revenge from someone? What are their feelings toward that person or persons? Are they really clearly thinking about what they are doing?

Disobedience: Denny answered the phone when his father told him not to. He also met with Lulu when he knew it would be against his father's wishes. Have students write about a time when they did something that their parents disapproved of. What were the consequences? Did they feel that it was so important that they just had to do it?

Guilt: Have students think about a time when they caused something to happen, but it was an accident. Although they did not act purposefully, the students feel that others believe that it was their fault. How do they feel? How did they overcome any guilt that they had?

As you begin, discuss the responses that students wrote in the prereading sessions. Generally, this is a time for students to discuss what they wrote and to share with each other their various topics. At this time, you assign students the novel. After your students have read it, engage them in the following activities. Spread this response-centered work over a few days as students develop their understanding of the novel.

Large-Group Discussion

First and foremost, ask students for an open response to the novel. What did they think about it? What are their reactions to the work? Did they like it? Why? At first it seems important to let students take the lead in the response. Your listening skills are important in this initial phase. As students react, you may need to make followup statements, questions, or acknowledgments to help them clarify, justify, or elaborate their ideas. If the discussion drags, use generic questions early in the discussion and more content-specific questions later in the process. Try to keep these at a minimum and emphasize your spontaneous reactions to students' responses since these are so much more meaningful to students, and they help move the discussion on using students' ideas rather than yours. However, there are times when you will need to ask questions such as the following:

What is your first reaction after reading this novel?

What feelings or emotions does this work evoke in you?

What character(s) do you particularly like? Dislike? Why?

Do any of the characters in this novel remind you of people you know?

Are you like any character in the novel?

What memory does the novel help you to recall?

Content-specific questions that you may incorporate in the discussion include the following:

Why do you think Denny's father represses what happened twenty-five years ago? Why won't he talk about it?

Do you think Denny is justified in breaking his father's rule about answering the phone?

What do you think is Denny's motivation for breaking the rule?

Is Lulu justified in doing what she does? Why or why not?

What kind of wife/mother is Mrs. Colbert? How do you see her?

How dangerous is revenge? Lulu takes her revenge to the ultimate resolve. How believable is that?

Does Mr. Colbert feel guilty? Why do you think he does or does not? What is there in the text that would have you believe this way?

Is Denny's relationship with Dawn believable? Why or why not?

Lulu speaks of being "dead" when the balcony falls on her. She also speaks of Mr. Colbert "murdering" her. What do you believe she means?

Small-Group Discussion

Small-group discussions may give students an opportunity to discuss some of their most important responses before sharing them in the large group. The small group may also be used to allow students to explore further the general responses that they shared in the large group. Students often feel less threatened in small groups and are more willing in that setting to explore ideas. As in the large group, smaller groups must have rules of behavior that enable students to function effectively in the interaction. Students must feel secure with their responses; they must respect the responses of others; and they will recognize similarities among all the responses. You should actively participate in each group by circulating and facilitating where and when needed. It is best, however, to allow students to lead the discussion of the novel. This approach teaches students that they can function with self-sufficiency and without teachers influencing their responses. As Rosenblatt (1991) reminds us, "The reader . . . must have the experience himself. . . . The teacher's task is to foster fruitful interactions—or, more precisely, transactions—between individual readers and individual literary works" (pp. 26–27).

Creative Drama

As we noted earlier, creative drama—pantomime, improvisation, role playing—can be most effective in helping students to respond to what they have read. Creative drama helps students to expand on their responses and the meanings that they have discovered or defined in the large or small groups. For example, an improvisation between Denny and his father concerning his father's refusal to talk about the tragedy enables students to explore the father's motivation. A similar improvisation among Denny, his father, and Lulu would also elaborate on issues presented in the novel but not fully resolved. The improvisation would allow students to use their interpretations to further explore these issues. Further character interpretation can occur through creative drama between Denny and Dawn. Dawn could try to have him share with her why he hasn't been more forthcoming or aggressive with her. A family role play, discussing what to do about the media inquiry, would force students to confront all the issues and perhaps allow students to explore the character of Mrs. Colbert even further.

Writing

You also may choose to engage students with all of the questions and statements mentioned so far in this section of the chapter through either free writing, journal writing, or personal essay writing. Again, whether you address these through writing or discussion is at your discretion as you decide what is more effective for your students. When you wish to use longer pieces of writing, the following ideas may be helpful:

> Monologue: Ask students to take on the persona of a character—Denny, Lulu, Mr. Colbert as an adult, John Paul Colbert as the child—and have them write stream of consciousness to show their thinking at any given moment in the novel.

> Dialogue: In a similar way, ask students to write a dialogue between any two characters at any given moment in the novel—Lulu and David before calling Denny; Lulu and Denny on the telephone; Mr. Colbert with his wife, or with Denny before the phone rings in the middle of the night.

> Character sketch: Use the biopoem (discussed in Chapter 4 and shown in Figure 4.1). After collecting ideas about a character—Denny, Lulu, David, John Paul Colbert, Mr. Colbert—have students take that prewriting and use it in a poetic character sketch.

> Personal essay: Have students respond to the statement, "The sin of the father will be visited upon the son." Students can explore that statement in terms of this novel and also in terms of how they find its meaning in people that they know.

> Expository essay: Have students explore the author's craft. How has Robert Cormier crafted this novel to heighten the suspense, tension, and emotional intensity?

In a response-centered classroom, the writing assignments should challenge the students to further develop their thoughts about the novel and to explore a specific area of interest. Your suggestions are precisely that—suggestions. Students should remain free to choose other topics and other kinds of writing that will better suit their needs. Whatever the form of writing, students should be able to focus their writing toward resolving a disturbing issue or a problem that they see in this novel, something that connects with them and makes it a worthwhile experience.

All of these classroom strategies—large- and small-group discussion, creative drama, and writing—enable students to come to some understanding, some meaning, of what the novel is about and how it is related to them. In doing this, students begin to establish criteria that they can use to make generalizations about meaning. The intent is to help students to become more independent in establishing meaning. One of the major pedagogical problems with using the classics is that many students never become independent. They are always dependent on the teacher for the meaning of the literature; therefore, many become nonreaders, since they feel that they cannot make judgments for themselves (Bushman, 1994).

On the other hand, as Rosenblatt (1991) points out, while students' reactions and impressions are valid, sometimes they will make incorrect assumptions about a novel, especially when they begin discussing beyond their personal impressions. At this point, you must begin exploring in a way that will help students recognize a mistake without destroying or confusing their personal responses. This is a problem that needs delicate attention, especially while students are in the early stages of learning the response-centered process. You will need to help broaden their "base of experience" with literature. As students come to recognize that personal responses are only one segment of a response-centered classroom, hopefully, they will grow with that experience and continue developing their skills because, as Rosenblatt again suggests, students need to develop "mental habits that will lead to literary insight, critical judgment, and ethical and social understanding" (1991, p. 75).

CLASSROOM RESPONSE TO *IN THE MIDDLE OF THE NIGHT*: A TRANSCRIPTION

We reproduce here as illustration a classroom reader response by a small group of students to *In the Middle of the Night*. The portion quoted is only the beginning of a two-day response session.

Teacher: Now that you have finished the book, what did you think of it?

Student 1:   I liked it, but I didn't like it as much as *The Chocolate War* and some of his other novels. It didn't seem to have the same things as his other works.

Teacher: Okay.

Student 2:   I liked it too—I really liked it when I finished it. The more I thought about it, the more I thought there were certain things that I didn't like about it. There weren't as many characters as, say, *Fade*. Also, I think it was easier to know what was going to happen. I think that is probably why I didn't like it as well.

Teacher: Then, you think it was more predictable.

Student 1:   Well, it seems like when he gets to the end he's really, really trying to wrap it up. I know in some of his other novels, you're kind of left deciding where he wants to go with the book.

Student 3:   And I think that this was written for a younger audience than, say, *The Chocolate War* and *Beyond the Chocolate War*. It just wasn't as open ended as the other books.

Teacher: Okay.

Student 4:   I liked the book. The part that was hard for me was I really never felt like there was the depth of understanding of the characters . . .

Teacher: mmm.

Student 4: . . . at least not with the son, Denny. I felt like I understood his father better than I understood him. In *The Chocolate War* I felt comfortable. I knew what was motivating that character, but I really was not sure with Denny. I was always left a little unsure . . . like I can't figure out why he is the way he is because I don't think Cormier did as good a job with that.

Student 3: I wonder if he intentionally did that . . . because of the theme of isolation? That no one really knew Denny, no one really knew the father or the mother . . . so many characters . . . that I wonder if he wanted to give us the feeling of not knowing them, or feel isolated from them the way that they were isolated.

Student 5: I kind of thought that it wasn't the same depth as some of his other ones. I don't think the quality was necessarily less, but that he didn't go into things as much. It still has the trademark, you know, psychological profile. You are working inside a character's mind, as Cormier does.

Student 3: Did any of you think that at one point that, maybe, the brother had a split personality?

Student 5: I thought that he was Lulu, actually.

Student 3: You thought what?

Student 5: I thought that he might end up being Lulu. I thought smoky voice, husky voice.

Student 3: Yea, that's what I kept thinking. I thought that maybe she really did die and that he took on a dual personality.

Student 5: Yea, I was wondering that.

Student 3: Was anyone else surprised that Dave was the brother?

Student 4: No.

Student 5: No?

Student 4: No, not with the foreshadowing that Cormier did. He talked about the rug on his head.

Student 3: That's when I knew.

Student 4: When he talked about that, I figured that he was in the fire, too. I didn't at that point know what the relationship was, but that he was a part of it. It was too pat. The hair grew back in funny tufts from chemotherapy, or something. It was too easy.

Student 5: Really?

Student 3: No, he does have cancer.

Student 5: I think he really does have cancer.

Student 3: He really does have cancer.

Student 5: He would be 27 years old.

Student 1: And when they find him, he does have sores.

Student 3: At first he was in remission, but now it has come back.

Student 5: "The big one."

Student 4: I got the feeling that the scarring . . . maybe I misread it. . . . I got the feeling at the end he was scarred.

Student 3: No, I don't think so. I can find it.

Student 6: He was trapped in there when his sister was trapped. I think he was pulled out before she was.

Student 1: You were talking about Cormier's style. I still think there is enough in this. That's what I like about it. The manipulating part, with the phone. There is just enough of the uneasy feeling. That's what I like about Cormier's writing—the manipulation of people. That's what keeps you involved.

Student 3: Page 169. That is where we are told that "the big one" is back.

Student 4: On page 167, it talks about how his skull is inflamed. That's how I got the scarring idea.

Student 2: I took that as chemotherapy.

Student 4: I don't know why. I guess I associated that with the fire and what happened at the theatre.

Teacher: Would that, would that surface in that way if someone had gone through the theatre experience that many years ago? Would that hair physically be that way because of the fire?

Student 4: I don't know that much about scarring.

Student 5: I don't know that that much about cancer.

Student 6: The skull being inflamed because of chemotherapy. I do know that you have a burning sensation when you go through chemotherapy.

Teacher: What techniques or strategies do you find in this work that you also would find in Cormier's other works?

Student 6: His use of descriptive language. The way he opens his novels. This is not at the beginning, but it's on page 13. "The ringing telephone blistered the night, stripping him of sleep, like a bandage torn from flesh."

Teacher: What image do you get from the word "blistered?"

Student 2: The fire.

Student 5: One of my favorite words, I think. It really has a lot of connotative meaning. He used it in such a powerful way. "The phone vomited forth." It was something . . .

Student 1: That's the one that I'm trying to find, too . . . because I thought that was vintage Cormier.

Student 5: Exactly.

Student 4: I like the way he contrasts that with the blandness of Denny's life at home. You know, that his parents are almost emotionless. The mother's pretty in a fading way, turning pastel. There are vivid nighttime activities; the day is like wheat paste.

Teacher: Are there other techniques that you want to talk about?

Student 1: I think the moving back and forth in time is quite interesting. Also he shifts the point of view.

Teacher: What effect does that process have on you, the reader?

Student 6: Well it kept my mind working until I found what was going on. It kept me engaged in the reading.

Student 3: It also gives the perspectives of different characters. Not just one character, but the perspective of all characters.

Student 5: This might be the young adult version of Faulkner. You know, dealing with multiple narratives, not that he tells you, but you have to figure that out along the way.

Student 7: I did go back and reread the first few chapters because I thought I missed so much when I read it the first time. I was trying to figure out what was going on. So when I did go back, I found that I did miss so many things. I was concentrating on the story instead of some of the details.

Student 1: He has a lot of minor characters that serve a purpose. I was trying to think—the kid who was beat up, the girlfriend Dawn. He brings those minor characters in to have an important part even though they are not major.

Student 3: I like the way he weaves the characters together. The action of the father is somewhat similar to Hansen. The father says that his job is to absorb the pain. He offers himself to do that. Similarly, Hansen, instead of fighting back, absorbs the blows. So there is a connection there. "Why didn't you fight back?" You could say that to both Hansen and the father. Hansen's response was really one of the themes of the novel. "Why don't *you* get involved?" Denny doesn't get involved. In all the places he has lived, he doesn't get involved. And when he does get involved, something happens. Like when he got involved in the play, someone stood up in the audience and pointed to him and said, "How could you make him be a part of this?"

Student 1: His parents kind of objected to his having a job. They have a thing about that. He is starting to have a sense of confusion.

Student 3: Even answering the telephone. They won't let him answer the telephone.

Teacher: Why won't they let him answer the phone?

Student 5: A protective thing. They didn't want him to hear all—they probably anticipated that someone like Lulu would pop up.

Teacher: Well, that's—we know that, don't we, because the father has been working through this and is trying to keep it away from his son.

Student 2: He feels like he is to blame for this and he doesn't want his son to take the brunt of someone's violence. I think it is interesting when we talked about getting involved. The one time he does get involved, he almost dies from it. I mean . . .

Student 3: The father?

Student 2: No, the son. Because he doesn't get involved all these times that the phone is ringing, and he finally does get involved and talks to Lulu and almost dies. I think that is really interesting that that was happening.

Student 5: Did anyone else have an uneasy feeling when he was doing that?

Student 3: Yes, yes.

Student 5: Didn't it seem that all of a sudden he jumped to a place where he is really familiar with her?

Student 2: He trusts her!

Student 5: Exactly. And your're thinking: You're siding with the parents. On this—human error. Right.

Student 3: I wanted him to call Dawn. Forget about that phone call.

Student 7: I thought it was interesting that the father seemed, like to me, through the whole thing, was trying to protect his son and make sure he was not exposed to these people with the calling and didn't want to deal with that. But I thought that was the reason for the way he was—didn't want him to have a job, didn't want him to drive. Just protect him, protect him. And so he has experienced little in life. He's missing out on a lot.

Teacher: To what extent is there a relationship between that and the way he treats Dawn?

Student 2: He never calls her. I think that has something to do with the fact that he never gets close to people.

Student 6: He had a girl friend earlier—Cloie. He didn't, I mean, it made him mad when he first met Dawn since she reminded him of her. So he has sort of shut down in establishing relationships.

Student 2: I don't think he has ever been taught because every relationship he has ever built he is torn from because . . .

Student 3: The social immaturity. . . . I think it goes back to the theme of isolation. And with the father, after the fire the father is isolated, the mother says to the father, I mean, the mother says to the son: "Are you sure you should go out for a walk?" And so they are isolated. He grows up and he's still isolated; the parents don't have friends; they are isolated. The son doesn't have friends; he chooses isolation. And, and, the ending of these books—*The Chocolate War, Beyond the Chocolate War, Fade,* they—I don't finish them and have a sense of well-being and fulfillment. So sad, I hate to finish this book. I don't have any hope for Denny. He is still isolated. He chose the "no comment." Like the father had chosen the "no comment." Instead of letting people get into their lives and choosing intimacy, they are still sitting there with the father behind the paper. . . . It's sad for me; it was depressing.

Student 5: I agree with you in a way. I also found myself admiring his decision to back his dad's philosophy but only because his father explained why he did it pretty well. The father at least gave a reasonable justification of his actions. And I respected Denny for following him on that. I think it is more his father's problem than his. He is adversely affected; but I think the father has a deeper guilt.

❧   Learning Log Responses   ❧

What advantages do you see when you have your students use the reader-response approach to literature?

How would you build a classroom climate conducive to using reader response? Why is a positive climate important when using the reader-response method?

Choose a piece of literature and design two different reader-response activities for that work.

REFERENCES

Anderson, P. M. (1986). The past is now: Approaches to the secondary school literature curriculum. *English Journal, 75* (8), 19–22.

Angelotti, M. (1981). Uses of the young adult literature in the eighties. *English in Texas, 13,* 32–34.

Applebee, A. N. (1989). The background for reform. In J. A. Langer (Ed.), *Literature instruction: a focus on student response* (pp. 1–18). Urbana, IL: National Council of Teachers of English.

Beach, R., & Marshall, J. (1991). *Teaching literature in the secondary school.* Orlando, FL: Harcourt Brace Jovanovich.

Beach, R., & Wendler, L. (1987). Developmental differences in response to a story. *Research in the Teaching of English, 21* (3), 286–296.

Binz, W. P. (1993). Resistant readers in secondary education: Some insights and implications. *Journal of Reading, 36,* 604–615.

Buckley, M. H. (1992). Falling into the white between the black lines. In N. J. Karolides (Ed.), *Reader response in the classroom* (pp. 45–58). White Plains, NY: Longman.

Bushman, J. H. (1994). *Creating a positive classroom climate.* Ottawa, KS: The Writing Conference.

Carlsen, G. R. (1980). *Books and the teen-age reader.* New York: Harper & Row.

Donelson, K. (1989). If kids like it, it can't be literature. *English Journal, 78* (5), 23–26.

Eisner, E. W. (1985). *The educational imagination.* Englewood Cliffs, NJ: Merrill/Prentice Hall.

Hannson, G. (1992). Readers responding—and then? *Research in the Teaching of English, 26* (2), 135–147.

Heather, P. (1982). Young people's reading: A study of the leisure reading of 13–15-year-olds. Paper presented at the annual meeting of the United Kingdom Reading Association.

Hynds, S. (1989). Bringing life to literature and literature to life: Social constructs and contexts of four adolescent readers. *Research in the Teaching of English, 23* (1), 30–61.

Hynds, S. (1990). Reading as a social event: Comprehension and response in the text, classroom, and world. In D. Bogdan & S. B. Straw (Eds.), *Beyond communication: Reading comprehension and criticism* (pp. 237–256). Portsmouth, NH: Boynton/Cook.

Karolides, N. J. (1992). The transactional theory of literature. In N. J. Karolides (Ed.), *Reader response in the classroom* (pp. 21–32). White Plains, NY: Longman.

Kirby, D., & Liner, T. (1988). *Inside out: Developmental strategies for teaching writing.* Portsmouth, NH: Boynton/Cook.

Kohlberg, L. (1987). *Child psychology and childhood education.* New York: Longman.

Kolb, H. H., Jr. (1990). Defining the canon. In A. L. Brown Ruoff & J. W. Ward, Jr. (Eds.), *Redefining American literary history* (pp. 35–48). New York: Modern Language Association of America.

Langer, J. A. (1990). Understanding literature. *Language Arts, 67,* 812–816.

O'Connor, M. E. (1980). *A study of the reading preferences of high school students.* Arlington, VA: ERIC Document Reproduction Service (No. ED 185524).

Probst, R. E. (1984). *Adolescent literature: Response and analysis.* Englewood Cliffs, NJ: Merrill/Prentice Hall.

Probst, R. E. (1987). Adolescent literature and the English curriculum. *English Journal, 76* (3), 26–30.

Probst, R. E. (1988a). *Response and analysis: Teaching literature in junior and senior high school.* Portsmouth, NH: Boynton/Cook.

Probst, R. E. (1988b). Transactional theory in the teaching of literature. *Journal of Reading, 31* (4), 378–381.

Purves, A. C. (1992). Testing literature. In J. A. Langer (Ed.), *Literature instruction a focus on student response* (pp. 19–33). Urbana, IL: National Council of Teachers of English.

Purves, A. C., Rogers, T., & Soter, A. O. (1990). *How porcupines make love II.* White Plains, NY: Longman.

Rau, S. (1994). Verbal SAT scores dip. *Lawrence (Kansas) Journal World,* 25 August, p. 3A.

Rosenblatt, L. M. (1938). *Literature as exploration.* New York: Noble & Noble.

Rosenblatt, L. M. (1956). The acid test for literature. *English Journal, 45* (2), 66–76.

Rosenblatt, L. M. (1991). *Literature as exploration* (4th ed.). New York: Modern Language Association of America.

Trelease, J. (1982). *The read aloud handbook.* New York: Penguin.

Wadsworth, B. (1978). *Piaget for the classroom.* New York: Longman.

Yeazell, M., & Cole, R. (1986). The adolescent novel and moral development. *Journal of Reading, 29* (4), 292–298.

4

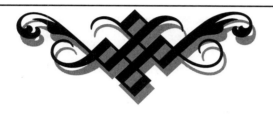

The Reading/Writing Connection

Children learn to read from writing and learn to write from reading. The theory that supports this premise is extremely strong, as discussed in this chapter. However, the practice in schools has been long in coming. Although in the past each discipline was taught in isolation, today the integration of reading and writing is much more accepted. "Any teacher of composition or of literature over the past decade recognizes that we have experienced a radical shift in our approaches to both subjects" (Burkland & Peterson, 1986, p. 190).

Burkland and Peterson go on to say that reading and writing were formerly considered solitary activities, but new studies indicate that readers and writers develop knowledge through shared and discussed information. In addition, teachers do not need to feel that they are short changing either area; rather, they are forging a lasting bond between the student, the literature, and the writing that develops from the literature.

A RATIONALE

Reasons abound for teaching reading and writing in combination. Although writing and literature can be taught within a thematic process, many times they are not. As a result, students feel a lack of personal involvement, especially with isolated writing assignments. Literature, then, along with the theme approach (if it is used), provides the needed context in which to write and learn about writing. Students may find the literature connection helpful as they make connections to ideas and themes expressed in what they read. Writers must find that commitment toward what they are writing. This is difficult to achieve when working through a sterile writing assignment that has not come out of the writer's own desire to write or is a response to something heard in a class discussion or something read in a literature study.

Elbow (1981) suggests that the only valid justification for a writing program is the creation of more capable writers who produce better writing. Practicing writing in isolation may lead to improvement, but at some point student writers need the visual model. For example, they must interact with the published writing of "real" authors. By interacting with that writing, students come to a consensus about what authors do. When students realize that authors deliberately choose certain words and that they begin sentences and paragraphs differently depending on the effect they wish to make, students begin to emulate and experiment, trying to find the best strategies for them and, thus, becoming more capable writers.

It helps students to know that authors first concentrate on the development of ideas and that the emphasis on mechanics comes at the end of the process; that they move through the writing process rejecting the idea that a polished product can be written in one setting; that they understand that the writing process is recursive and not linear (i.e., they write, think, rewrite, etc., frequently throughout the process); and that they may use a list of ideas that they want to include—but a list to which they are not restricted. They know that the act of writing produces more thinking which, in turn, produces more writing.

When making the connection between reading and writing, students do not need the grammar book to learn the language conventions used in writing. Through literature, students will see the use of metaphor, simile, dialogue, imagery, and the many other conventions that authors use effectively. By using literature, students see for themselves the influential effect that these conventions have on readers. Students can carefully examine the choices that the authors have made and transfer them to their own writing.

The study of literature has not gone through the turmoil that the teaching of writing has experienced. Some educators may argue that teaching isolated skills (such as grammar) still benefits young people, and many still believe that answering questions after reading a work is the way to learn the one and only meaning of the piece. However, very few now believe that literature terms and conventions should be taught without experiencing them in the reading process, and most teachers follow, in their own particular way, the reader-response theory.

Most literature and composition anthologies printed prior to 1990 and used in many classrooms today contain chronologically divided American and British literature with composition suggestions for students that result in what Tchudi (1986) calls "pseudo-academic expository essays" (p. 252). Tchudi denounces this practice: "For too long, English teachers and professors have ignored the developmental needs and interests of their students while promoting curricula distant from those students" (p. 254). These texts are primarily concerned with a knowledge-level understanding of what was read. Writing is used to respond to questions that check comprehension, rather than using the reading to inspire original, thought-provoking essays. The traditional use of writing does not encourage response with the literature since the intent of most anthologies seems to be to emphasize the "right" interpretation. As a result, students are asked to interact with questions raised by editors of the books rather than with the authors of particular selections.

Teachers who practice the reader-response theory believe that literature provides young people with universal themes that interact with their own goals, desires, visions, values, and morals. Students are able to experience vicariously the actions and emotions of others and compare and contrast these experiences with their own. Literature, and certainly young adult literature, allows students to see that others face similar decisions and share their problems and concerns. Rather than promoting "distant curricula," writing that ties the literature and the student's world together helps students formulate answers to their personal dilemmas.

THEORY AND RESEARCH

The theory and research shows a strong relationship between reading and writing. This has not always been the case. Even within the last ten years many educators were still arguing that reading was simply a decoding task and that writing was the encoding task—two unrelated processes. A move to reconsider the connection between reading and writing began in earnest in the early to mid 1980s. Educational theory and empirical research now provide evidence for this new thinking about the reading/writing connection.

For many years, most classroom teachers have known that skills were not successfully transferred from one area to another. This transfer did not occur because the skills usually were taught in isolation. For example, most educators, from the elementary classroom to the university level, know that a grammatical knowledge base does not transfer to writing ability, although many classroom teachers continue the practice. No research supports it. This grammar issue most clearly represents how research and practice collide, with research losing out to ineffective practice. This is not true with the reading/writing question. Here, research has led the way.

Noyce and Christie (1989) use schema theory, which explains how the mind assimilates information, to explain the missing link between skills and reading/writing. "Comprehension occurs when text information is assimilated into an already existing schema or when the schema itself is changed so that it can accommodate new information from the text" (p. 7). Therefore, the authors suggest, if comprehension does not occur, it is due to a lack of assimilation into existing schema. Given this information, teachers can include additional instruction to help students revise their schema to lead to better comprehension.

Schema theory not only explains reading comprehension, but it also bridges the connection between reading and writing. Since the two areas are related, activities aimed at increasing reading comprehension will enhance the writer's skills. "The same schemata that are used for reading comprehension are also utilized during the writing process" (Noyce & Christie, 1989, p. 8).

Burkland and Peterson (1986) also found evidence to support schema theory. They examined the work of David Bleich, Louise Rosenblatt, Linda Flower, James Britton, and Lev Vygotsky and learned that these authors believe that our minds make connections between symbols and experience and "out of already developed and developing cognitive schemata" (p. 191). Through experience, readers and writers constantly revise their schemata while they read, write, and interpret.

The transactional approach is also used to describe the reading/writing connection (Sternglass, 1986). In this view, as readers read, they are creating new meaning for themselves, "meanings that did not exist independently before either in the mind of the author or of the reader" (p. 151).

Uttero (1989) connects the use of reading, writing, and cooperative learning. Working together, students find meaning in their reading through their writing. Uttero's research indicates that readers and writers complete several steps during reading and writing. Both processes mobilize prior knowledge, create a model of meaning, and ask readers to monitor their thinking and reading strategies. Through cooperative learning, students express their ideas both orally and in writing and receive feedback on their progress. Peer groups, along with teacher support, enhance students' reading and writing development.

Blanchard (1988) states that the Report of the Commission of Reading in 1985 "strongly emphasizes the need to view all language processes—listening, speaking, reading, and writing—as interrelated and mutually supportive" (p. 60). He indicates that writing activities enhance reading comprehension. Blanchard and the other sources mentioned in this section are convinced that more learning occurs when students write in response to and about literature.

Ronald (1986) discusses expressive writing (writing for oneself and reflecting on that writing). She states that "expressive writing assignments can begin to accomplish that reintegration of reading, writing, speaking, and listening" (p. 238). By constantly rereading their own writing, students become more aware of their meanings and the connections they are attempting to make.

Theory Into Practice: The Classroom Connection

Bromley (1989) states that "both research and theory support the notion that combining instruction in reading and writing in the classroom enhances children's literacy learning" (p. 122). She presents three major reasons for making connections between reading and writing: Both skills develop at the same time; each reinforces the other; and through reading and writing, language is used for communication.

To make these connections, Bromley uses *buddy journals,* a written dialogue between partners about the books that they are reading. Buddy journals provide a real audience for writing, promote cooperation between students, and build interest and confidence in writing. Bromley (1989) states that buddy journals "make the connection between reading and writing obvious for children" (p. 129).

Gilles (1989) advocates the use of literature study groups. While reading the books they have chosen, students write comments, questions, or concerns in literature logs, and then they meet in groups to discuss what they have read. The literature logs serve as a focus for the discussion and as a reminder to students about concerns they wanted to address. Students involved in literature study groups discuss the book seriously by linking it with their own experiences. Each member of the group, including the teacher, is responsible for critiquing and analyzing the book. Gilles believes that when teachers respond as an equal member of the group, they model more sophisticated interpretation strategies. In addition, this process practices the theory that meaning is made as people discuss and interpret what they read.

Harste (1990) discusses the development of literacy and details suggestions for a successful literacy program:

1. Language is learned through use rather than through practice exercises.
2. Children need to be given opportunities to make language their own by making connections with their lives and background information.
3. Children learn best in low-risk environments where exploration is accepted.
4. A well-designed reading/writing program should provide ample opportunities for daily reading and various types of writing.

Harste emphasizes the need for daily, open-ended discussions and activities based on literature and writing. Open-ended activities allow students to become involved based on their own interests because "reading . . . is sharing meaning about texts, [while] writing is not simply a process of recording on paper already-perfected ideas but also a vehicle for organizing thought" (p. 318).

Improvement of reading and writing skills was Raphael and Englert's (1990) goal. To attain their goal, they administered a set of curriculum materials that guide students through planning, organizing, writing, editing, and revising. Their research indicates that both reading comprehension and writing skills improve as students use language, engage in peer-editing and peer-shaping groups, and internalize the strategies they have learned. The authors conclude that learning modes show students that reading and writing are active, ongoing processes.

McMahan and Day (1983) argue against the sole use of essays as springboards for writing in the composition class. Instead, they assert, imaginative literature, short stories, and poems have several advantages over essays. Literature provides an emotional response often not found in essays. "Imaginative literature deals with individual human experience and . . . it can provide an incentive to students to write out of their own experiences" (pp. 111–112). After students read, discuss, and write about the literary work on a personal level, they are ready to analyze the piece itself. The literature provides the writer with specific details and examples for analyzing aspects of the literature, such as character and plot development.

Tierney and Leys (1986) examined studies that show that stories children read influence what they write. For example, a group of first graders who read the traditional first-grade readers full of choppy sentences and little detail wrote in that same style. They conclude that writers are influenced by what they read and mimic the writing style of poorly written as well as well-written works.

Sheley (1983) found that literature could be a model of written language as well as a global view of human experience. "Literature enlarges the student's knowledge and understanding of human behavior for it exhibits thoughts and feelings which are often concealed in real life" (p. 123). When writing from literature, students become aware of the author's intent and discover that writing is not a mysterious event that just happens. As students become more accomplished writers, they begin to see the choices that authors make.

Wilson (1983) found that literature had a positive effect on the writing style of nonstandard English-speaking students. Neither weeks of red correction marks on writing assignments nor extensive grammar exercises had motivated students to analyze their writing habits. However, after providing prolonged exposure to interesting literature, the students' writing skills improved because "students need to read before they write . . . in order to hear mentally and internalize the rhythms and patterns of written standard English" (pp. 116–117).

Wilson also discovered that the quality of writing increased when students first discussed the literary work and then wrote about it. Their compositions showed mature insights often not present in writing without a literature base, and their language patterns improved. Any continuing difficulties in standard English usage or content problems were addressed using student writing during the revision stage.

Fitzgerald (1989) argues that revision in writing and critical reading use similar thought processes since a mutual relationship exists among authors, readers, and texts. For example, authors know that readers expect the text to have continuity and to follow a line of reasoning. Because they keep their readers in mind, writers continually compare the actual with the desired text. "Through the comparisons, writers judge the degree of consonance (match) or dissonance (mismatch) between authors' and readers' goals and what's in the text" (p. 44). When dissonance occurs in writing, the revision process begins. Dissonance develops in critical reading when the reader experiences confusion or skepticism over an author's words.

Fitzgerald suggests group conferences to aid the thinking processes involved in revision of writing and critical reading. Students focus on consonance and dissonance between authors, readers, and texts. The teacher sets a positive tone and models comments and suggestions.

Atwell (1987) believes students should choose what they read and write in the English classroom. A workshop atmosphere permits students of all abilities to think and to learn through literature and writing since the classroom workshop "accommodates adolescents' needs, invites their independence, [and] challenges them to grow" (p. 40). According to Atwell, writers must constantly read and be exposed to a variety of written material, including prose, poetry, fiction, and nonfiction. Children who are given the freedom of choice over their own reading and writing material will show the teacher that reading and writing is important to them.

Romano (1987) asks students to be active learners by challenging them to "use written language to uncover their mental processes of reading, their changes in thinking, their developing awareness, and their emerging understanding" (p. 143). Romano often finds that students' literary insights differ from those given in teacher's manuals. Therefore, rather than use the manual and risk stifling his students' mental maturity, he allows students to find their own meaning in the literature they read. Romano gives his students the independence necessary to interact with and write about literature in their own way. Students "need not listen to a teacher tell them what to think. They think" (p. 145).

These researchers all acknowledge that learning advances occur when writing and literature are treated as interrelated subjects. As noted in the research, the concept is not relegated only to theorists but has practical application in the classroom. By nurturing the reading/writing connection, teachers encourage students to take more responsibility for their own learning while they become more competent and discriminating readers and writers.

TEACHING THE LITERATURE

The rest of this chapter suggests how teachers can benefit from the theory and research just mentioned. In the following pages, we show how we would teach, using selected pieces of young adult literature, the reader-response theory, the writing process, literary elements, and writing and reading skills.

Our approach is holistic: We would teach the reading/writing components frequently found in the English classroom through the study of literature. These skills and processes are not taught in isolation but as a comprehensive study of a piece of literature. We are not suggesting tearing apart a piece of literature bit by bit through a minute analysis of these selected skills; rather, we suggest that readers enjoy the totality of a work by responding to the ideas presented and by understanding the techniques the author uses so that readers learn to make that response. We are concerned that readers do not see themselves as writers and writers do not see themselves as readers. Through the rest of the chapter, we hope that readers of young adult literature will be able to note specific writing strategies that they, in turn, can use when they are writing.

We had to make decisions concerning the arrangement of this material. Do we organize it around the skills and processes or around the selected literature? We chose the literature even though there is a danger of viewing isolated skills listed under particular young adult novels and thinking that these skills should be taught in isolation. However, nothing could be further from our intent. The work is treated as a whole, and the skills are there to be taught as students respond to the work.

Readers will note that we emphasize students' responses to reading and writing. We believe that students need to start with their emotions and feelings and then move forward to more sophisticated responses. Our strategies are to help students make their responses, know why they respond as they do, trust their responses, and respect the responses of others. In earlier writing (Bushman & Bushman, 1994), we have called that process moving from the emotional level to the intellectual level. Others have used such terms as *engaging, describing, conceiving, explaining, connecting, interpreting,* and *judging.*

Throughout this book we emphasize the importance of young adult literature in the classroom. We use young adult novels because they relate well to adolescents. The ideas presented are often consistent with their experiences, the books have young adults as protagonists, the language of the literature parallels the language of adolescents, and the quality of the literature demands its presence in the English classroom. We strongly believe that no longer are the classics the only quality literature and the only works that teachers can use to teach composition and literature skills. Therefore, we strongly support the premise that young adult literature must take its rightful place in schools.

The eight works selected for this study are *The Chocolate War* (Cormier), *Roll of Thunder, Hear My Cry* (Taylor), *Chinese Handcuffs* (Crutcher), *Lasso the Moon* (Covington), *Remembering the Good Times* (Peck), *Killing Mr. Griffin* (Duncan), *The Giver* (Lowry) and *The Island* (Paulsen). We have selected these works because they have the qualities that characterize them as "good literature" and because they are often read by students. Most, if not all, can be used in a classroom study. Of course, we are well aware that any one piece of literature at some time could be held up to the censor; but given that consideration, these pieces are often taught by English teachers in middle or secondary schools.

The Chocolate War

Jerry Renault, a ninth grade student at Trinity High, an all-boys Catholic school, refuses to participate in the school's annual chocolate sale. At first Jerry refuses because of an order given by Archie, an upperclassman who leads the Vigils, a secret organization bent on intimidating non-Vigils and antagonizing the school's administration. The pranks and strong-arm tactics clearly show the power and control that this underground organization has over the student body as well as over the school officials. No one dares to challenge the Vigils.

But Jerry does. After ten days without selling chocolates, Jerry is supposed to join in the effort to sell. He doesn't. The challenge has begun. This act is a definite affront to the Vigils, especially to Archie's control, and to the administration, which has engaged the Vigils to make sure the chocolate sale is successful. For a while, Jerry becomes a hero because he made a decision that no one had ever had the courage to make. But the full powers of Archie and Brother Leon, the chief administrator whose reputation is at stake, and the loss of his closest friends cause Jerry to stand alone in his struggle to fight the establishment. The novel ends with Jerry receiving a savage beating before the mob-like student body while Brother Leon looks on from a distance. Jerry is defeated physically and emotionally. He had "dared to disturb the universe" and realized that he shouldn't have. The novel ends with the depressing feeling that the bad guys had won and there is no hope. But perhaps this novel reflects, at least to some degree, a realistic society.

READING/WRITING ACTIVITIES

You can stimulate interest in reading the novel by involving students in a prereading discussion on fundraising events in their school. Do clubs and organizations or the school as a whole have students sell candy, candles, jewelry, or magazine subscriptions? What do students think of that process? Has there been any comment by parents or the community about this practice? Have students make a journal entry about how they feel about this practice of selling items for school-sponsored programs.

A second area to investigate involves particular students. Has anyone refused to participate in the fundraising? Through discussion or a journal entry, have students explore why they chose not to participate. At this time, introduce the novel and briefly describe the story so that students are aware of the relationship between the practice found in their school and one of the many themes found in the novel.

As a third prereading activity, ask students to place a response on a continuum about the statement "Life Is Fair." At the extreme left is the statement, "Life Is Never Fair"; at the extreme right is the statement, "Life Is Always Fair." Students place their mark somewhere between these two extremes. This activity should be completed before reading to help some students who, after reading, react to the novel as not being realistic. We believe it is important for them to connect to what they and others have said about the fairness of life.

You may choose to assign the novel to be read completely before the discussion over it, or you may choose to assign sections with discussion following each reading. Certain advantages and disadvantages accompany each procedure. We feel that it is beneficial to discuss the novel as a whole and not in parts; however, assigning chapters or sections helps students who may not be motivated to stay on task. Students, however, usually do not have trouble finishing *The Chocolate War.*

As students begin working with the novel, they will want to respond in writing to what they have read. What is their first reaction to the book? What is their gut reaction to what happens to Jerry? Do they know other students who are like Jerry?

Archie? Have they ever had a Brother Leon as a teacher? Specific names are not shared in the class discussion, but students will want to share information about people they know who have these same character traits. Although you may want to return later for further exploration of the ending, have students initially respond in their journals about the ending: The bad guys seem to win, and the innocent character lies there broken, physically and emotionally. Soon after this writing, have students meet in groups to discuss their ideas with each other.

Characters in *The Chocolate War* provide complexities to which high schools students can relate. One way to begin the character study is through the biopoem (Figure 4.1). This structured response helps students understand a variety of character elements. Using the biopoem structure, students choose characters from the novel—Archie, Jerry, Brother Leon, Goober, and others—and write a poem as a tool for understanding. Discuss these biopoems with students. You may want to use these as a prewriting activity for the suggested character sketch or some other writing assignment.

A number of other writing assignments emerge from a study of this novel. Students may explore the theme of the nature of man and respond to Caroni's thoughts after being detained by Brother Leon: "And he did see—that life was rotten, that there were no heroes, really, and that you couldn't trust anybody, not even yourself" (p. 87). Along the same theme, they might write in response to Archie's thoughts on people: "You see, Carter, people are two things: greedy and cruel" (p. 175). Students could very well explore the questions, Do I dare disturb the universe? Why did Jerry have that poster in his locker? Did he indeed disturb the universe? To what extent was he successful? Do you think that Cormier believes that one should, indeed, disturb the universe? What parts of your universe do you think ought to be disturbed?

In addition, students may choose to do an "I Search" paper in which they investigate someone who they believe has dared to disturb the universe and was success-

FIGURE 4.1

Biopoem

From *Roots in the Sawdust* (p. 222) by A. Gere (Ed.), 1985, Urbana, IL: National Council of Teachers of English. Adapted by permission.

Line 1: First name

Line 2: Four traits that describe character

Line 3: Relative (brother, sister, friend, etc.) of _____.

Line 4: Lover of _____ (list three things or people)

Line 5: Who feels _____ (three items)

Line 6: Who needs_____ (three items)

Line 7: Who fears_____ (three items)

Line 8: Who gives_____ (three items)

Line 9: Who would like to see_____ (three items)

Line 10: Resident of _____

Line 11: Last name _____

ful. More serious students may study the original source for the "dare to disturb the universe" theme by reading T.S. Eliot's "The Love Song of J. Alfred Prufrock." Through discussion or writing, you also will want to explore other areas: peer acceptance, human motivation, evil manipulation, hypocrisy, and isolation.

You must allow time to analyze the writer's craft. Cormier makes choices that have a direct influence on the reader. We react and respond to the literature due to his decisions about word choice, setting, use of symbols, and other literary techniques. For example, students explore how the mood of the novel is established right from the beginning. Cormier uses three words to begin: "They murdered him" (p. 7). Immediately we wonder who? How? As the book continues, the reader might think that the struggle on the football field answers our questions about the hyperbole. But as we read on, we realize that there is more to it than just trying out for football. Cormier ties the idea of murder together in the next-to-last chapter when Jerry says: "Just remember what I told you. It's important. Otherwise, they murder you" (p. 187).

The setting and its description helps to establish the feeling that we carry throughout the novel. "The wind rose, kicking puffs of dust from the football field. The field needed seeding. The bleachers also needed attention—they sagged, peeling paint like leprosy on the benches. The shadows of the goal posts sprawled on the field like grotesque crosses" (p. 14). Cormier continues the description with additional symbolism: "The shadows of the goal posts definitely resembled a network of crosses, empty crucifixes" (p. 17). The plot would not be as disturbing without the contrast with this religious setting.

The description of the Vigils' meeting place reinforces the dark, drab picture: "The small room behind the gym was windowless with only one door leading to the gymnasium itself: a perfect spot for Vigil meetings—private, the solitary entrance easily guarded, and dim, lit by a single bulb dangling from the ceiling, a 40-watt bulb that bestowed only a feeble light on the proceedings" (p. 29). *Imagery*—the pictures that the writer paints with words—jumps out from the printed page. Imagery is used again and again to help establish tone:

> Scarlet splotches glistened on his cheeks as if he had been made up for some grotesque stage show. (p. 58)
>
> Leon looked up, smiling, a smile like the kind an undertaker fixes on the face of a corpse. (p. 67)
>
> Sweat moved like small bugs on his forehead. (p. 10)
>
> The moist eyes that reminded Coroni of boiled onions (p. 83)
>
> a toy boat caught in a whirlpool (p. 7)
>
> through crazy cornflake leaves (p. 9)
>
> the two pieces of broken chalk abandoned on the desk, like white bones, dead men's bones (p. 84)
>
> He tossed in his bed, the sheet twisted around him like a shroud, suffocatingly. (p. 90)
>
> October leaves which fluttered to the ground like doomed and crippled birds (p. 91)

In addition to studying the imagery, you will want to help students see the use of metaphor and simile as they help achieve this picture painting. Cormier also uses flashback, alliteration, allusion, personification, and foreshadowing, but not to the same degree.

You may also want to involve students in a study of names so they can see the degree to which Cormier chose names to strengthen the mood. It was not an accident that the gang was called the Vigils. The name is a shortened form of *vigilante*. Students can investigate the meaning of the term and show why Cormier would make that choice. Students can also investigate the meanings of *Archie*. Why might Cormier choose that name over some other one? What about *Goober*? *Obie*?

Roll of Thunder, Hear My Cry

This novel, winner of the 1977 Newbery Medal, is one of Taylor's many books that focuses on the Logan family (others include *Song of the Trees; Let the Circle Be Unbroken; The Road to Memphis*). In this novel the reader experiences the physical survival of the Logans as well as the survival of the human spirit. This tightly constructed novel with strong characterization and universal themes of prejudice, self-respect, and family love tells of the struggle between races in Mississippi during the Depression. In addition, the central theme of owning one's own land runs through this powerful conflict.

Cassie, a 9-year-old black girl, learns how owning land and having a place of their own puts the Logans in a position that their sharecropper neighbors will never achieve. This importance is acknowledged in Papa's comments to Cassie: "If you remember nothing else in your whole life, Cassie girl, remember this: We ain't never gonna lose this land. You believe that?" (p. 115). Papa also explains this to Stacey: "You were born blessed, boy, with land of your own. If you hadn't been, you'd cry out for it while you try to survive" (p. 155).

Over a period of a year (1933), we share with Cassie the deterioration of racial innocence. We struggle to understand as Cassie struggles to understand why she and her brothers must attend a black school, which is below standard; why they must use hand-me-down books; why they must walk to school while the whites ride buses; and why the blacks had to put up with the night riders, the burnings, and other discriminating acts of the whites with seemingly no recourse. Cassie learns through these and many more difficult experiences what it means to be black.

READING/WRITING ACTIVITIES

To motivate students to read this novel, you may wish to have students write what it was like when they were younger and were ready to start a new year of school. When they were 9 or 10, did they ride a bus to school, did their parents take them, or did they walk? Students then discuss their writing in groups. At this point, lead a whole class discussion on the point of choice in the decisions about how students were to travel to school. How would they feel if they were forced to travel in a certain way due to the color of their skin? Once you have discussed this, have students read aloud the first chapter of the novel.

A number of incidents in this first chapter can lead to many writing experiences. One of particular interest is the comparison of the two schools that the children of the area attend—blacks go to Great Faith Elementary and Secondary School and the whites go to Jefferson Davis County School. Taylor describes these two schools well. We learn who goes to each school, how the students travel to the schools, the names of the schools, the conditions of the books and the schools themselves, and many other details that are necessary for the reader to distinguish between the two schools. A writing assignment that could easily follow this reading involves the use of comparison and contrast. Through their reading, students will gather details (prewriting), make some order out of what details they have generated and begin the writing process (drafting), and then share their writing with partners and groups for final revision (revising).

Students can study and perhaps use the various techniques that authors use to strengthen their writing. They may use a lot of detail to strengthen characterization, for example. It would seem that Taylor has chosen to use symbols to strengthen the elements of the theme—danger, prejudice, and destruction. To a lesser extent, Taylor uses the school bus as a symbol for oppression and prejudice. The two schools also may be considered symbols representing the conditions under which each race is educated.

To a greater degree, however, Taylor uses thunder as a symbol for impending danger. She uses this strategy throughout the novel to increase the sense of danger, suspense, and power. Early in the novel when Mr. Morrison comes home with Papa, the reader learns that he has been fired from his job because he got into a fight. As this is revealed, Taylor describes him as having a "deep, quiet voice like the roll of low thunder" (p. 27). Again, while Mr. Avery is telling about the night riders, there is "a clap of deafening thunder" (p. 46). Thunder is heard again just before Papa, Morrison, and Stacey were to return from Vicksburg with a wagon load of supplies (p. 158). We learn that they were ambushed by night riders. As they are telling what happened on the road, the reader again is told that they didn't hear the truck carrying the bullies because "of the rain and the thunder and all" (p. 162).

Thunder strengthens the theme in Chapters 11 and 12. It is used to introduce Chapter 11 and then again as the children return T.J. to his home. We hear it often throughout this section of the novel, and it becomes stronger as the plot moves to its end. When Papa and Morrison go to save T.J. from the lynch mob and Papa sets the cotton on fire to distract attention from the lynching, Taylor builds the suspense: "Then we sat, very quiet, as the heat crept sticky and wet through our clothing and the thunder banged menacingly overhead" (p. 198).

After taking students through this discovery of thunder as a unifying element in the novel, you may wish to have students create an essay in which they examine another object that Taylor has used repeatedly throughout the novel. For example, a particular pattern is developed with trees. In the essay, students trace the unifying element and identify its effect on the theme. Certainly, during this activity much discussion occurs about each of them that occurs in the novel and how the theme holds the work together and helps to make the work whole. Therefore, in this writing activity you can help students to pull together the details that support their thesis just as the author did with the theme in *Roll of Thunder, Hear My Cry*.

At the end of the novel, T.J. is taken to jail. We leave him there as the novel closes. This provides an excellent opportunity for students to write what they believe will happen to T.J. This writing can take many forms. A simple essay can provide a summary of what has happened and what has led to the arrest. It can also include the position of the writer on what should take place. Since a trial does take place in the sequel—*Let the Circle Be Unbroken*—students can divide into groups and write a trial sequence in which the various characters provide the content for judgment. Students will have to predict what will, in fact, occur in the future. The activity would certainly encourage reading the next Taylor novel since most students would want to know if what they predicted is, in fact, what Taylor has happen in the sequel.

Chinese Handcuffs

Dillon Hemingway has had to deal with his older brother Preston's bout with drugs as well as Preston's crippling injury resulting from a motorcycle joy ride. However, when forced to witness Preston's suicide, Dillon is left with guilt, wondering if he could have prevented the tragedy. He fights in his brother's memory by seeking revenge on Preston's gang, whom Dillon blames for driving Preston over the edge. Then, Dillon struggles to renew a relationship with Preston's girlfriend—to whom Dillon has always been attracted himself—only to learn that she is the mother of Preston's child—a gift left behind. To cope with his brother's death, Dillon writes Preston unsent letters to try to communicate his unspoken emotions. Dillon also seeks refuge in training for the grueling triathlon, which is frowned on by the school coaches who wish Dillon would concentrate on using his athletic abilities to better their own high school teams.

When he pursues a relationship with Jennifer Lawless, Dillon learns that her seemingly perfect role as star basketball player is also an escape from her difficult life at home. As their relationship develops and Dillon earns her trust, Jennifer reveals her history of sexual abuse by her stepfather. As much as Dillon wants to help Jennifer, she convinces him that there's no way for her to win because her stepfather is a prominent lawyer who knows how to play the system to his advantage. However, when Jennifer learns that her mother is pregnant, thus creating another child to suffer in a world of sexual abuse, Jennifer's escape through sports is no longer enough. It is Dillon who not only saves her from a desperate suicide attempt but also secretly sets a trap to finally put an end to her misery.

READING/WRITING ACTIVITIES

As a prereading activity, students can respond in writing about how they cope with difficult problems. Everyone has an outlet that they use to release tension. Some students go for long walks; others get belligerent and take it out on family and friends. We know one student who was a fairly good piano player, and he would simply stay at the piano until he had worked through his problem or at least had some temporary solutions worked out. Dillon, the main character in this novel, writes unsent letters to his dead brother. How do we cope? One activity asks students to write about something that they have had to deal with that they wouldn't wish on anyone else. How did they deal with it? What strategies did they use? Students may wish not to share their particular problems, but they probably will share the techniques that they used to cope with these problems. Following the writing and discussion, introduce *Chinese Handcuffs*.

Once again, it is important for students to make their personal responses to this book. To help them do this, you may wish to have students respond to some of the following questions:

- What is your first reaction to the novel?
- What feelings and/or emotions does the work evoke in you?
- What character(s) do you particularly like? Dislike?
- Do any of the characters remind you of people that you know?
- What memory does the novel help you recall? Have you been in a similar situation?

Of course, at some point in the activity, you will want to move students to perception, interpretation, and evaluation of what they have read:

- Would you change the ending of the novel? If so, how?
- What do you consider to be the most important word, phrase, or quote in the novel?
- What reaction or explanation of the title do you have?
- What fears and/or concerns do you have for the characters?
- What is the major point of the novel?
- Does this novel remind you of any other literary work?
- What is your final reaction to the work?

Certainly, these are but a few of the questions and areas that you and your students should explore. In most cases, when students begin responding to literature such as *Chinese Handcuffs,* no list of questions is necessary, but it is good to have a few questions in reserve if there is a lull in the discussion.

Dillon Hemingway uses writing in an interesting way. On many occasions, he writes unsent letters to his dead brother Preston. Early in the novel, Dillon witnesses Preston's suicide, the last resort for Preston after losing the battle with drugs. Dillon is devastated by this act and throughout the novel takes his various concerns to Preston via the unsent letter technique. He writes about his feelings about the suicide; the daily taunting of his principal at school; his experiences in triathlon training and in being the trainer for the girls state champion-bound basketball team; his interest in Stacy Ryder, Preston's old girlfriend; his interest in Jennifer Lawless, the star basketball player; and the concern he has for Jennifer's past history of sexual child abuse with her stepfather. Discuss with students how these unsent letters were helpful to Dillon. What effect did they have? How was Dillon able to use them? Dillon uses them to sort through his feelings and concerns. Although the letters are not sent and there really is no audience to respond, Dillon feels that by doing this, he will be able to work things out.

After this discussion, you may choose to have students write an unsent letter. Students may wish to consider questions or responses to the characters' actions, or they may wish to write about a problem that concerns the author. In a more private way, students may wish to write an unsent letter in which they each share private thoughts concerning a problem with which they have had to cope. At the conclusion of this activity, you may want to suggest to students that the unsent letter technique may be helpful as they sort through their problems throughout their adolescent and adult lives.

After reading the novel, students know a great deal about Dillon, but not as much about his brother Preston. There is enough information, however, for students to take on the point of view of Preston and respond in writing to one or more of the unsent letters that Dillon writes. If Preston could respond, how would he answer Dillon's concerns?

Crutcher uses many techniques well. He uses hyperbole to make a point, the metaphor and simile for comparisons, and allusions to Shakespeare. He uses flashback very effectively, and students could learn from its use. The reader learns a lot about Dillon and Preston in Dillon's unsent letters, in which he uses the flashback technique. We also learn of Jennifer's trauma, her feelings, and her agony through her flashbacks to her sexual abuse. After a thorough discussion of this literary technique, students can practice using this element in their writing. In a narrative, students can relate particular information about characters or the plot through flashback.

Lasso the Moon

Sixteen-year-old April Hunter lives in an island community off the coast of Georgia where she moved with her father Jack, a well-known and successful cardiologist whose alcoholism caused him to lose both his license and his marriage to April's mother. However, since Jack is currently in recovery, he has obtained a provisional license, allowing him to oversee some of the poor residents of the island. One of his patients is Fernando, a kind yet strangely enigmatic illegal alien from El Salvador who suffers from heart disease.

Working at an elite riding stable, April becomes acquainted with Fernando and learns about the terrible conditions in El Salvador that he narrowly escaped. Eventually they fall in love. But, when the immigration service starts looking for Fernando, rumors spread that he was involved in some situations in El Salvador that caused some Americans to lose their lives. As a result, he goes into hiding until he can find a way to return to El Salvador and to his own family, including his own daughter, and leaves April behind, sad yet respectful of the man she still loves.

READING/WRITING ACTIVITIES

An important first step for readers to analyze any piece of literature is for them to ask themselves how they feel about the work. When using *Lasso the Moon,* you might have students begin by reflecting on the title. What do they think it means? Why would Covington choose to title the novel in this way? You might ask students to respond to April as a believable character. Did they like her? What were their reactions to Jack and Fernando? Did their opinions of April, Jack, and Fernando change while reading the book? If so, when and how? Did the plot make sense? Was the style of the book effective? Did the author choose an effective point of view to relay the story? After the students have finished reading *Lasso the Moon,* they should individually respond in writing to several of the aforementioned questions. Encourage students to be honest and thorough in their responses.

After reading each student's opinions of *Lasso the Moon,* make copies of all of the responses for each of the students. Have them read through all of the response sheets, taking note of general impressions of the book by the class, as well as where each writer tends to agree and disagree with other class members. You may feel it appropriate to discuss various responses to seek clarity and further support for the opinions stated. Following this discussion, assign students to write a critical book review using the responses collected from the entire class, treating their classmates respectfully, as valid critics. Rather than address each response, however, students might choose only the few that they feel strongest about. Encourage students to tie their arguments directly to the novel by citing specific passages, actions, and dialogue, as well as citing their classmates by name as their responses are used for support.

At the end of *Lasso the Moon,* April receives a note from Fernando explaining why he had to return to El Salvador. At the same time he shares his strong belief that a father needs to be with his daughter—a belief that April also understands. This message not only affects how April feels about Fernando but also how she feels toward Jack. To help students further understand the relationships depicted in this novel, ask them to consider April's point of view by thinking through her experiences, emotions, desires, and fears. Considering Fernando's actions and the reasons for them as expressed in his note, have students adopt April's point of view and write a letter to Jack, in which they interpret her feelings about her relationship with him. They might include how the relationship has changed since they have come to the island, as well as what April foresees for the future.

Next, have students exchange these letters. Students now assume the identity of Jack, taking into consideration his experiences, emotions, desires, and fears. How will Jack respond to April's letter? Have students write Jack's return letter to April, including Jack's view of their relationship. Although the tone of the letter should be understanding, students also want to clearly explain any differences of opinion they feel Jack would have. These two writing opportunities allow students to share their own interpretations of April's and Jack's characters and to compare their interpretations with those of their classmates.

As an extension, students could then choose one of their own relatives to write about. How would they evaluate the type of relationship with that person? How has it changed throughout the years? What are some unspoken feelings that they would like to communicate to that person? What effect has that person had on them? How do they foresee their relationship changing in the future? Have students write a letter to that relative communicating these ideas.

Remembering the Good Times

The unlikely threesome of Buck, Trav, and Kate have known each other since eighth grade. Buck lives with his father in a trailer next to a gas station, and Kate lives with her mother and great-grandmother Polly on a rundown farm. In contrast, Trav lives in the ritzy suburbs, son of a prominent lawyer. Ironically, it is Trav—with his high-class life that includes tropical vacations and designer clothes—who has problems. It is obvious to Buck and Kate that Trav is overly troubled by a number of things: the fact he is not being adequately prepared for college by his mediocre teachers, indecision on what electives to take, Kate's seeking revenge on the school bully, and having to grow up in a crisis-filled world.

Their closeness to Trav blinds Kate and Buck to his danger signs of suicide, even when Trav gives them several of his personal belongings as presents the day before the tragedy occurs. When the administration organizes a grieving session for Trav in the hopes of preventing a suicide epidemic, old Polly shares her words of wisdom and insight into the incident, thus enabling Buck and Kate to come to grips with their own feelings and continue with their everyday lives.

READING/WRITING ACTIVITIES

As a prereading activity, students can discuss the topic of friendship. A topic to explore concerns the likelihood of three students of differing socioeconomics status becoming close friends. Students should discuss the ingredients that go into making a close friendship. How do students respond to these differences? Is the problem, if there is one, more with adults than with students? Students should culminate this discussion with a position paper on what contributes and does not contribute to a lasting friendship.

After students read and study this novel, you may wish to use the following writing idea for a culminating activity. Students should respond to Kate's and Buck's conversation:

> "Why didn't we say something? I'm talking to you, Buck. People don't pay any attention to kids, but why didn't we make them hear?"
> "We didn't know," I said with my head down.
> "We should have. Think back and you'll see."
> "They added up," Kate said, "and they weren't little. The poem, the pear trees poem. Even that. Remember that? They weren't little things. Why didn't we have someplace—somebody to go to to tell us what they meant?" (p. 166)
> "No, he wasn't," Kate said. "He gave us those presents because he wouldn't need them anymore. Buck, he was saying good-bye. And we were deaf people. We were blind." (p. 167)

Students should go back through the novel and pick up the signs that Trav left. They can group these signs in various categories, similar to those found in the novel.

All of this will lead to a writing assignment: a brochure indicating the signs that may lead to suicide. Before students prepare the brochure, discuss the idea of their audience. To whom is the brochure written? You may wish half of the class to write one for other students; the other half may write the brochure for adults (the administration?). Talk with students about audience: What will be the differences between the two brochures?

A second writing activity involves Kate's comments on page 167: "'I'll tell you one thing,' she said in a low voice, cold. 'I'll grow up, but I'll never trust anything again. I'll never believe in anything or anybody. You can count on that.'" Students should respond to her feelings. Is she justified to feel as she does? Will she change her position as she grows older? Students should decide on a position that they wish to take and move through the writing process to a final paper.

Killing Mr. Griffin

Although senior year is a time when students can traditionally see the "light at the end of the graduation tunnel," there's still one major obstacle left for the seniors at Del Norte High School—perfectionist Mr. Griffin, the hated senior English teacher whose one and only trait is being critical of all of his less-than-good-enough students as he "dumps out F's wholesale" (p. 15). Finally pushed to the limit, Mark Kinney, who already has a history of crime, convinces Jeff Garrett, his girlfriend Betsy Cline, and senior class president Dave Ruggles that it is time that Mr. Griffin is taught a lesson. They plot to kidnap him—not to hurt him, but to scare him enough to tone down. However, to carry off the stunt, they must lure sweet, unsuspecting Susan McConnell into the scheme to draw Mr. Griffin to the kidnapping scene.

Everything works as planned as they take Mr. Griffin up into the hills, tie him up, and leave him blindfolded. When they return after a few hours, however, he is dead—a consequence they had never considered. The group not only has to try to cover up their crime, but they also have to keep Susan from reporting everything to the police. The novel presents a lesson in peer pressure as well as dealing with the surprising consequences of poor decisions.

READING/WRITING ACTIVITIES

Many prereading activities present themselves as you prepare to teach *Killing Mr. Griffin*. In one activity, students share a time when they had planned a sequence of events in the utmost detail, but something went wrong. Ask students to use a jottings list to note the activity and generate the list of steps that they had planned to make this activity take place. Students will need ample time to generate this list. Students then write the one step or action that went wrong to make the complete idea a failure. They then discuss how they explained what they had planned, especially if the activity was less than aboveboard. Discuss this prereading activity in class, then introduce the novel as having a similar plot. The prereading becomes prewriting for an activity that students can do after reading and discussing the novel.

As students read the novel, they will become aware that they learn about the main characters through the characters themselves because Duncan tells the story from different points of view. As we begin the novel, we meet Susan McConnell and learn her views about Mr. Griffin and his class and about some of the other characters. The plot continues in Chapter 2 as the reader learns more from Jeff Garrett, especially how he sees Mark Kinney. The reader meets Dave Ruggles in Chapter 3 and learns about his family. In addition, Dave is confronted by Mark concerning the plot to kidnap Mr. Griffin. The novel continues, using this technique of varying points of view. The reader even sees Mr. Griffin through the eyes of his wife Kathy in Chapter 5.

One advantage of using this literary technique is that students are able to see the events and the people from more than one perspective. In evaluating this technique in literature, students can see the benefits as they transfer this skill to their writing. There are at least three different perspectives of Mr. Griffin in the novel: Kathy's, Mr. Griffin's, and his students'. Thus, readers experience a variety of viewpoints about this man. There are as many perspectives of Mark as well.

For this reading/writing activity, students should create a person whom they can write about from at least three points of view. After creating the individual, students will need to decide on the different people from whose points of view they will present the character. Students will decide how these perspectives will be different: What will be emphasized? How will they indicate that difference? After establishing these viewpoints, students will share in groups and revise their writing. Bring the activity to a close by having students incorporate these characters into a short narrative.

A final activity involves the prewriting the students did in the prereading activity about a plan that went astray. Students create a narrative in which they tell of an incident similar to the one in this novel. In addition, students should describe the events that followed. What happened when things went wrong? How were they able to cope? What did they do? Students can write of a real experience that they had or they can use their keenest imagination.

The Giver

In this futuristic "utopian" society, families are created by selected couples, who may request one son and one daughter. At the age of 1, children are named and given to their chosen families; at 9 they receive bicycles; and at age 12 a ceremony is performed to announce lifetime assignments after the children have been carefully observed for their abilities and interests. They may be assigned to be birthmothers, fish hatchery workers, directors of recreation, laborers, caretakers of the old, nurturers of the newborns, or to other tasks.

As 12-year-old Jonas anxiously awaits the announcement of his assignment, however, he is surprisingly skipped in the traditional alphabetical sequence. Only after all of the other assignments have been made is he shocked and confused to be named the new Receiver of Memories, the most respected assignment of all. His training must begin immediately by the current aging Receiver—now to become

The Giver—to ensure a smooth transition. Jonas works with The Giver to receive all the memories that the society had decided generations ago to do away with to make their lives less complicated and more consistent—memories of war, pain, conflict, divorce, as well as color, music, snow, hills, and love. Eliminating these feelings and experiences has produced a society of "Sameness."

As Jonas first receives, he is delighted with new sensations of sledding down a snowy hillside; but as his training continues, he is overcome with grief and depression, not only for the new sensations of sunburn and warlike tragedy, but also for the realization that others no longer experience many beautiful characteristics.

Jonas is also devastated as he learns the truth behind some of the horrendous acts in his community that, until now, he had been sheltered from. For example, he was aware that as a Nurturer, his father sometimes had to "release" a baby who was not "thriving," allowing the baby to be sent to Elsewhere—an unknown place that everyone associates with positive connotations. When Jonas learns, however, that to "release" babies is to inject them with a lethal solution to end their lives, Jonas is moved to persuade The Giver that it may be time to return the memories to the society. The risk for both is great at this point because they both know that to stop the transition of memories may not allow enough time for a new Receiver to be named and trained and, as a result, the memories would automatically return to the citizens.

In an ending subject to many interpretations, Jonas attempts to carry out his plan by kidnapping Gabe, a baby soon to be "released," and rides off in search of Elsewhere to save himself, the baby, and the rest of his society.

READING/WRITING ACTIVITIES

As a prereading activity, students could describe what they would consider to be a perfect world. Encourage them to consider as many aspects of society as possible, including but not limited to education, experiences, family life, career opportunity, and relationships. They also could include in their description a list of rules or laws they would like to live by. After students share their writings aloud, make a record of the reactions of the other class members for future comparison to the world in *The Giver.*

On pages 80–81 students can experience Lowry's use of vivid word choice and imagery to fully describe Jonas's first experience transferred from The Giver, sledding down a snowy hill. As students read, they will surely want to comment on such vivid words and phrases as "pinpricks," featherlike," "peppered," "whirling torrent of crystals," "propelled," and "glee." Students then choose another experience that Jonas might experience for the first time. Writing from Jonas's point of view and using vivid words and phrases, have them fully describe the situation.

As a good exercise to promote keen critical thinking skills, select quotations from the novel for students to write reactions to. Students can write the degree to which they believe them to be true, how they relate to the world they live in today, or how they relate to another piece of literature they have read. We suggest the following quotations as possibilities:

> "Honor," [The Giver] said firmly. "I have great honor. So will you. But you will find that that is not the same as power." (p. 84)

"The worst part of holding the memories is not the pain. It's the loneliness of it. Memories need to be shared." (p. 154)

"It's the choosing that's important, isn't it?" The Giver asked him.

Jonas nodded. . . . "But now that I can see colors, at least sometimes, I was just thinking: what if we could hold up things that were bright red, or bright yellow, and [Gabe] could *choose*. Instead of the Sameness."

"He might make wrong choices."

"Oh." Jonas was silent for a minute. "Oh, I see what you mean. It wouldn't matter for a *new* child's toy. But later it *does* matter, doesn't it? We don't dare to let people make choices of their own."

"Not safe?" The Giver suggested.

"Definitely not safe," Jonas said with certainty. (p. 98)

Throughout their reading of the novel, students should remind themselves of the perfect world they created and described earlier. Having considered the consequences in *The Giver*, students may then reconsider how they would define and describe a perfect world, perhaps discussing and reconsidering as a class. Then, have the class brainstorm the elements of the society in the novel that they would question. Ideas might include the condition of Sameness; the age-level ceremonies, requirements, and behaviors; or the individual elements removed from memory. Suggest that students put themselves into the world of *The Giver* to choose a situation in the society and write a persuasive "letter to the editor" explaining specifically why this change should occur.

Finally, explore the ambiguous ending of the novel. When Jonas leaves on the bicycle with Gabe, he does so to save Gabe's life as well as to return the memories to the citizens. Readers are left with many questions, however: What really happens to Jonas and Gabe? Do they reach Elsewhere? Do they survive at all? And what about the people left behind? Are the memories transferred to them? If so, what are the consequences? How is Jonas's family affected by his departure? What do they and the other citizens now think about Jonas? What is the tone left to the reader—hope or despair? Rather than simply discuss these questions, have students write an imagined next chapter to the novel in which they consider these questions and provide their own interpretation.

The Island

The Neuton family moves yet again. This time the move takes Wil, a 15-year-old, and his mother and dad from Madison, Wisconsin, to a community farther north in the state. Wil soon finds his special place: the island, a place where he can go to be alone and learn to know nature—and himself. It is also a place for Wil to put aside the outside world—the tension between his mother and father and the local bully that he will have to confront sooner or later. On the island, Wil studies the loons and the fish in the lake. He wants to know all there is to know.

To help him make some sense of the nature that he experiences as well as his own feelings and emotions, Wil writes and paints. He feels the need to create to express himself, and the desire to become a writer or artist is born within him. The people of the community—Wil's father and mother, Ray Brunner, the television crew, the counselor—really don't understand what Wil is doing. A few are moved by his efforts—his new friend Susan, her parents, and a local newspaper reporter. Their support reinforces Wil's sense of purpose, and strengthens his resolution to continue his activities. There seems to be some resolution at the end of the novel when Wil and his father, who has been observing his son from the distant shore, decide to spend time together on the island. Wil realizes that he really doesn't know his father and that he needs to be with him, perhaps on this island, in order to write about "my father."

READING/WRITING ACTIVITIES

This novel, perhaps better than any other, models the writing concepts that are taught in schools: writing to learn and the writing process. Wil says it best as he reflects upon his writing and painting activity on the island: "To paint. To write. To know. To be" (p. 99). You can use this book to help students understand the impact that writing has on thinking and understanding. The power of writing is used as discovery: What do I know and what do I need to find out? In addition, you may show the process that Wil goes through as he collects ideas, reflects them, writes them down, and then returns to the writing later for additional work.

The novel is truly a remarkable piece of literature, not only as it shows a young man in his struggle with growing up, but also as it reflects what we as writing teachers believe to be important in the process of composing. For example, soon after Wil arrives on the island, he sees loons on the water. The reader soon realizes

> There was more here that he did not understand, but he wanted to know. He wanted to know—he wanted to know the loons. Right now he wanted to know the loons and to know all that he could find out about the loons; he wanted to sit and watch them and learn what they were and know them. And if perfection came from that, if harmony came from that, if knowledge came from that, from his being on the island, that was fine. But he wanted to know the loons. This day, his first day on the island, his first full, real day, he would try to learn the loons, learn what made them part of the island as he wanted to be part of the island. (p. 34)

So, Wil spends the rest of that day and the following day watching and studying the loons, and he reflects what he learns. Wil then "kneeled carefully in the grass and willows and took the notebook and pencil out of his pack. At the top of the first page he wrote HERON all in capital letters" (p. 48) and began to write. Throughout the day, "Wil saw many other things, sometimes one thing would lead to two others, and he made side notes about them and would come back to them; but the whole morning he worked on the heron, wrote about the heron . . . " (p. 48). Readers find Wil's finished project in the novel on page 51.

Wil writes about his experiences and his search for understanding of his world and how he relates to it. He writes of his encounter with Ray Brunner at the cafe; he writes about his grandmother. "'So strange,' he whispered. 'So strange to find her here . . . ' 'So strange'" (p. 82). "Then he turned and went to the boat to get his notebook and write about his grandmother while it was still fresh" (p. 82). There is a strong sense that Wil spends a great deal of time writing and rewriting. "He worked all the rest of the day on the piece about his grandmother, and when he had said some of the things he wanted to say and it seemed to be right, he put the notebook aside and ate a cold can of beef stew" (pp. 92–93). We learn about honesty in writing, too.

> The images that came to him were so clear, but when he tried to describe them—no, explain them . . . and there it was, there was the trouble with it. He wasn't writing about his grandmother. He was explaining her. And that, he thought, was not a way to learn about her, about what she had been to him. He took up the notebook again and started to write, and this time he didn't explain or describe; he simply wrote what she meant to him, what she was as he saw her, and it thundered out of him. (p. 108)

It is so important to write about his experiences. Even when he is fighting with Ray Brunner, he thinks about writing about the fight and learning from it. Later Wil writes of his relationship with Ray and how that relationship seems similar to the relationship he sees between a turtle and the lake's fish. So, he writes a piece entitled "The Turtle."

There is so much that this book has to offer students and teachers. In addition to the process model of Wil, the writer, the book also offers examples of free writing at the start of each chapter. Students could use those pieces to make a response. In addition, students could write about how Wil leaves the island, or they could write a newspaper article reporting on his experiences. Certainly they could emulate Wil by trying his observation activities and meditation techniques and write about observations and meditations.

❧   Learning Log Responses   ❧

Choose a young adult novel not discussed in this chapter and describe how you would use it to teach reading and writing skills.

Discuss the relationship between the reading and writing processes. What benefits do you see for your students?

REFERENCES

Atwell, N. (1987). *In the middle. Writing, reading, and learning with adolescents*. Portsmouth, NH: Boynton/ Cook.

Blanchard, J. (1988). Plausible stories: A creative writing and story prediction activity. *Reading Research and Instruction, 28,* 60–65.

Bromley, K. D. (1989). Buddy journals make the reading-writing connection. *The Reading Teacher, 43,* 122–129.

Burkland, J. N., & Peterson, B. T. (1986). An integrative approach to research: Theory and practice. In B. T. Peterson (Ed.), *Convergences: Transactions in reading and writing* (pp. 189–203). Urbana, IL: National Council of Teachers of English.

Bushman, J. H., & Bushman, K. P. (1994). *Teaching English creatively (2nd ed.)*. Springfield, IL: Charles C. Thomas.

Elbow, P. (1981). *Writing with power.* New York: Oxford University Press.

Fitzgerald, J. (1989). Enhancing two related thought processes: Revision in writing and critical reading. *The Reading Teacher, 43,* 42–48.

Gilles, C. (1989). Reading, writing, and talking: Using literature study groups. *English Journal, 78,* 38–41.

Harste, J. (1990). Jerry Harste speaks on reading and writing. *The Reading Teacher, 43,* 388–400.

McMahan, E., & Day, S. (1983). Integrating literature into the composition classroom. *The Writing Instructor, 2,* 115–121.

Noyce, R. M., & Cristie, J. (1989). *Integrating reading and writing instruction in grades K–8.* Boston: Allyn & Bacon.

Raphael, T. E., & Englert, S. E. (1990). Writing and reading: Partners in constructing meaning. *The Reading Teacher, 43,* 388–400.

Romano, T. (1987). *Clearing the way: Working with teenage writers.* Portsmouth, NH: Heinemann.

Ronald, K. (1986). The self and the other in the process of composing: Implications for integrating the acts of reading. In B. T. Peterson (Ed.), *Convergences: Transactions in reading and writing* (pp. 231–245). Urbana, IL: National Council of Teachers of English.

Sheley, C. (1983). Active learning: Writing from literature. *The Writing Instructor, 2,* 123–128.

Sternglass, M. S. (1986). Writing based on reading. In B. T. Peterson (Ed.), *Convergences: Transactions in reading and writing* (pp. 151–162). Urbana, IL: National Council of Teachers of English.

Tchudi, S. (1986). Reading and writing as liberal arts. In B. T. Peterson (Ed.), *Convergences: Transactions in reading and writing* (pp. 246–259). Urbana, IL: National Council of Teachers of English.

Tierney, R. J., & Leys, M. (1986). What is the value of connecting reading and writing? In B. T. Peterson (Ed.), *Convergences: Transactions in reading and writing* (pp. 15–29). Urbana, IL: National Council of Teachers of English.

Uttero, D. (1989). Reading, writing, and cooperation: A dynamic interaction. *New England Reading Association, 25,* 2–7.

Wilson, A. (1983). The study of literature and the development of standard English proficiency. *The Writing Instructor, 2,* 115–121.

5

The Language Connection

The previous chapter noted the extreme importance of the reading/writing connection. We maintain that the language connection is important as well. As teachers strive for an integrated curriculum, using young adult literature to note and study the particular language choices made by young adult authors moves this educational theory closer to an educational reality. Often, little is done with the study of the English language, partly because teachers do not have confidence in the subject matter, and also because of a traditional view that English language teaching means the teaching of formal English grammar. As a result, students often do not enjoy the excitement that can come from a study of various linguistic topics. The beauty of connecting this linguistic study to young adult literature is that students experience how their language works, not through dull, boring worksheets, but through the excitement that can only be found in reading.

It is important that this connection does not turn into a practice that is similar to dull worksheets that kill both the enthusiasm that can come from language study and the excitement about the literature that the students are finally able to enjoy. As suggested in Chapter 3, teachers must have students work with the material they read with all of the strategies and techniques that we have come to use when asking readers to respond to a piece of literature. It is *after* the response—after the joy and excitement of reading and reacting to what is read—that teachers and students take note of the writer's craft. Just as students investigated the use of the simile, metaphor, or the strategy used in the beginning of a piece when looking at particular tools of writing, they will do the same with language study.

The topics are quite broad. We would hope that students and teachers will explore the nature of the English language itself. How have young adult authors used words effectively? To what extent do they use slang? Colloquial expressions? Is there a variety of sentence patterns? Students and teachers should also explore the effective use of dialects. How have authors creatively and honestly used the social and geographical dialects to help achieve their effect in writing a particular work?

An investigation into the use of language manipulation would interest students. An exploration of how characters relate to each other—how they converse with each other to manipulate each other's thoughts and actions—might offer the right source for study before investigating how this process occurs in their own world.

Young adult literature also provides a source for a historical perspective. How is English used in novels with characters from different cultures? To what extent has English borrowed terms and expressions from other languages?

The last area for consideration is nonverbal communication. How do the characters communicate without using words? What effects can be achieved through nonverbal communication? A study of these areas provides students with realistic settings in which to observe others using language devices or strategies. Because language is observed in this way, it becomes alive and has much more meaning for students than the traditional approaches to language study. If done appropriately, it takes nothing away from the enjoyment of reading young adult literature, but, in fact, adds to the pleasure by placing some importance on the author's craft.

THE NATURE OF ENGLISH

Authors use colorful language to make their writing interesting. They use just the right word to convey just the right image. Like painters, they color and shade their writing so that the reader can imagine the scene. For example, in *The Devil's Arithmetic,* Yolen writes the following:

> She and Shifre were set to work with Rivka in the kitchen hauling water in large buckets from the pump, spooning out the meager meals, washing the giant cauldrons in which the soup cooked, scrubbing the walls and floors. It was hard work, harder than Hannah could ever remember doing. Her hands and knees held no memory of such work. It was endless. And repetitive. But it was not without its rewards. Occasionally they were able to scrape out an extra bit of food for themselves and the little ones while cleaning the pots, burned pieces of potatoes that had stuck to the bottom. Even burned pieces tasted wonderful, better even than beef. She thought she remembered beef. (p. 125)

Changing Times (Kennemore), a British work, tells a unique story about the growth of a 15-year-old girl named Victoria Hadley. Kennemore plays a bit with time travel. Victoria is able to move throughout time by setting the hands of her clock. It offers, in both dialogue and narration, a descriptive and vibrant use of language. In describing Mr. Priestly, Victoria states: "He's a revolting disgusting decomposing tail end of a toad's turd. He stinks" (p. 11). Kennemore uses the same vivid language when narrating the story:

> The sound of the alarm was like a pneumatic drill boring into Victoria's brain. She shouted three words at it, all of them obscene in varying degrees, and tried, as usual, to go back to sleep. But there was a noise, an insistent repetitive noise that just shouldn't have been there; try though she might, she couldn't ignore it. Reluctantly she unburied herself, and hazily, through lingering layers of sleep, the truth clicked into place. Her clock was ticking. (p. 24)

In *Chinese Handcuffs,* Crutcher uses language most effectively. He describes Mrs. Crummet's cat as "a three-legged alley Tom with a face like a dried-up creek bed and the temperament of a freeway sniper. Mean cats call Charlie mean. He chewed that other leg off extracting himself from a muskrat trap, and he's utterly willing to let anyone, man or beast, know that experience left him feelin' right poorly toward the world and every living thing in it" (p. 9). Instead of Dillon saying "this may be long" in reference to a letter he is writing, he says "This may be a P.S. worthy of perusal by Guinness, and it's late" (p. 17). And instead of saying "spending money," Dillon says, "He knew he'd probably drop a couple of Abe Lincolns or maybe even an Andrew Jackson on bets" (p. 52).

Crutcher shows his flair for language when he describes Dillon's removal from school: "The Nobel Prize for that little theory was a three-day vacation, do not pass Go, do not collect your lunch ticket" (p. 75). The word choice also is interesting in the following passage: "shoving a plastic bowl under running water in a semivaliant attempt to wash out the SuperBond-like remains of yesterday's granola. He chiseled small bits loose with the handle of a spoon, semiseriously rinsed the bowl again, and filled it to the edges . . . carrying it carefully to the table so as not to break the scientific seal restraining the milk from overflow" (p. 140).

In *Remembering the Good Times*, Peck, too, uses vivid language.

> Across the country road from the horse farm was a big orchard behind us that had definitely seen better days. It was pear trees because of the clay soil, and really jungly. You needed to chop your way through some of it with a machete. (p. 2)

> I heard her—somebody way off, but the trees were leafed out. (p. 2)

> A long time later he [the colt] decided to try standing up. His legs were wild and wobbly and like stilts for him. He couldn't get them sorted out. Then suddenly it worked. He was up, this little knife-narrow body on these spindly knob-kneed legs. (pp. 4–5)

> We fished out a couple of colas and hunkered down on the hot curb in front of the station. (p. 7)

> She noticed shirtless Skeeter Calhoun in his bib overalls making toothpicks out of the taxpayers' investment. (p. 20)

It is interesting to note that Peck uses the phrase *hunkered down* in a slightly different way when he describes the calfing in the opening scenes of *A Day No Pigs Would Die:* "I kicked her. And stoned her. I kicked her again one last time, so hard in the udder that I thought I heard her grunt. Both her hind quarters sort of hunkered down in the brush" (p. 10).

In *Taming the Star Runner*, Hinton uses repetition: "Christopher was the roundest person Travis had ever seen. His chubby face was round. His big eyes were round. His blond haircut was round. His chunky little legs and arms were round" (p. 52). Hinton also incorporates a few slang terms or phrases, as well. Travis says, "What'd Casey do?" Jennifer answers, "Came out and gave me a leg up" (pp. 42–43). Also, when Ken is talking to Travis, he says, "Your mom was a real sweet girl. Pretty, too. She thought Tim hung the moon" (p. 57). And again, when referring to drinking: "Well, yeah, but I can usually hold it pretty good. I can usually put everybody under the table" (p. 99).

Hinton also creates new words, or at least uses words in a slightly different way. Travis's friends are "all those hoody friends" (p. 13). Hinton characterizes sound: "After a while, Travis went to spit in the bug zapper to hear it zit" (p. 39), and "He [Travis] watched the gray horse thunder down the pasture road, clear the gate, and disappear over the ridge" (p. 64). Travis describes his perceptions of what the girls that he was drinking with thought of him since he had to go to the bathroom often: "They probably thought he was tooting up or had the world's weakest bladder" (p. 75). When Travis takes a break from the revisions he has been working on, he looks out the window and observes, "There was the Realtor, in her navy suit and plasticized hair, showing someone around the property" (p. 179).

Teachers may want to use *Park's Quest* (Paterson) to investigate the use of powerful action words used in the narrative.

> The cold salt air stung his nostrils, and his sneakers sank into the damp sand so that he had to struggle to keep up as she jerked him along, not looking at him, just looking at the angry white foam roaring into the land. There was a small boat bouncing about on the waves. (p. 23)

> She loved Park. He knew that. When he was little, she had read to him. He would crawl up on her bed and sit as close to her as he could, smelling her fresh, perfumed soap smell, touching when he could her pale arm, the hairs so blonde they were nearly invisible. He loved to blow on them and make her giggle in protest. (p. 25)

After discussing the use of these words, teachers can have students write a short piece using active, specific verbs rather than overused verbs.

Readers note the use of word choice in a passage from Korman's *A Semester in the Life of a Garbage Bag.* After reading the following from the novel, students can discuss what intent the author had in using such words. What effect was he trying to achieve? "'No way,' said Raymond grimly. 'May Jardine be condemned to the eternal fish fumes of Secaucus if he ever lifts a finger for the greater glory of Danny Eckerman'" (p. 201).

Throughout *Dicey's Song,* Voigt creates beautiful imagery. Dicey's classroom is very hot, and she looks out the window to see "their leaves drooped down, dispirited by the heat. Like dogs' tongues, Dicey thought, and pictured the tree panting with many tiny tongues, maybe even dripping saliva the way a dog's would" (p. 21). Dicey "unrolled the adventures of the summer out, like ribbons. The ribbons unrolled back until Dicey saw her momma's face" (p. 16). Voigt uses language to describe the land, water, and all of nature—particularly the sky and the sun: "The growing darkness turned the sky to the color of blueberries, and long clouds floated gray. Just a band of burning orange was left from the sunset, but the water caught that and transformed it, lying before Dicey like a field of gold. Like cloth of gold" (p. 16).

Questions often arise in class discussions about characters found in literature and how they are portrayed by the authors. What techniques do the authors use to convey just how they want those characters to be seen? The language that they speak often is the telling element, and the reader uses this language to help form some type of mental image of each character. Paterson's *The Great Gilly Hopkins* provides students with interesting use of language. Questions about Trotter often surface due to the language that she uses. Most realize that, although Trotter speaks less-than-perfect English, she is a truly admirable human being.

A study of Trotter's language patterns could be productive. For example, such a study should determine whether Trotter's English actually enhances her powerful use of the language and her image. In addition, students could explore the effects of Mr. Randolph's old-fashioned, flowery, highly literate style of speaking. What effect does this language style have on the reader's image of Randolph? Students could also explore why they think Paterson chose to present him in that way.

THE DIALECT QUESTION

In a society like the United States, language patterns are varied. A variety of dialects are spoken and written daily. Geographical dialects form when the people of a certain region of the country speak and write in a particular way. In general, the United States has three dialect regions: Northern, Southern, and Midland. Within each of these general regions, there are many dialect pockets (Bushman, 1988).

In addition to the geographical dialects, many people speak a social dialect. Taylor (1985) cites eight American social, nonstandard dialects: Appalachian English, Athabascan English (Alaska), black English vernacular, general American nonstandard English, Keaukaha English (Hawaii), New York City nonstandard English, Southern American nonstandard English, and Spanish-influenced English. We believe that students and teachers should be informed about dialects, whether they are regional dialects or social, nonstandard dialects. For example, knowing about black English and the various regional dialects will give both teachers and students a better understanding and appreciation of the English language.

One effective way to carry out that objective is through the literature that young people read. Authors often use vocabulary, idioms, syntax, and a general style in their writing to reflect the culture and society about which they are writing.

The following excerpt is from *To Kill a Mockingbird* (Lee), a novel widely read in secondary schools, although not frequently classified as young adult. Teachers can use this section to show the black dialect in general and also an attitude toward language in particular—an attitude that should be discussed in every classroom.

> "That's why you don't talk like the rest of 'em," said Jem.
>
> "The rest of who?"
>
> "Rest of the colored folks. Cal, but you talked like they did in church."
>
> That Calpurnia led a modest double life never dawned on me. The idea that she had a separate existence outside our household was a novel one, to say nothing of her having command of two languages.
>
> "Cal," I asked, "why do you talk nigger-talk to the—to your folks when you know it's not right?"
>
> "Well, in the first place I'm black—"
>
> "That doesn't mean you hafta talk that way when you know better," said Jem.
>
> Calpurnia tilted her hat and scratched her head, then pressed her hat down carefully over her ears. "It's right hard to say," she said. "Supposed you and Scout talked colored-folks' talk at home—it'd be out of place, wouldn't it? Now what if I talked white-folks' talk at church, and with my neighbors? They'd think I was puttin' on airs to beat Moses."
>
> "But Cal, you know better," I said.
>
> "It's not necessary to tell all you know. It's not lady-like—in the second place, folks don't like to have somebody around knowin' more than they do. It aggravates 'em. You're not gonna change any of them by talkin' right, they've got to want to learn themselves, and when they don't want to learn there's nothing you can do but keep your mouth shut or talk their language." (p. 128)

Another sequence of dialogue, between Huck and Jim in *Adventures of Huckleberry Finn* (Twain) centers on a similar discussion about language and its use. Parts of the novel are not consistent with what we call a young adult novel, but it is read by many young adults and is certainly taught in the English classroom. This passage, along with the one from *Mockingbird,* can lead to a very interesting class discussion.

"Why, Huck, doan' de French people talk de same way we does?"

"No, Jim, you couldn't understand a word they said—not a single word."

"Well, now, I be ding-busted! How do dat come?"

"I don't know, but it's so. I got some of their jabber out of a book. S'pose a man was to come to you and say Polly-voo-franzy—what would you think?"

"I wouldn't think nuffin, I'd take en bust him over de head. I wouldn't 'low nobody to call me dat."

"Shucks, it ain't calling you anything. It's only saying, do you know how to talk French?"

"Well, den, why couldn't he say it?"

"Why, he is a-saying it. That's a Frenchman's way of saying it."

"Well, it's a blame 'ridicklous way, en I doan' want to hear no mo' 'bout it. Dey ain' no sense in it."

"Looky here, Jim, does a cat talk like we do?"

"No, a cat don't."

"Well, does a cow?"

"No, a cow don't nuther."

"Does a cat talk like a cow, or a cow talk like a cat?"

"No, dey don't."

"It's natural and right for 'em to talk different from each other, ain't it?"

"Course."

"And ain't it natural and right for a cat and a cow to talk different from us?"

"Why, mo' sholy it is."

"Well, then, why ain't it natural and right for a Frenchman to talk different from us? You answer me that."

"Is a cat a man, Huck?"

"No."

"Well, den, dey ain't no sense in a cat talkin' like a man. Is a cow a man?—er is a cow a cat?"

"No, she ain't either of them."

"Well, den she ain't got no business to talk like either one er yuther of 'em. Is a Frenchman a man?"

"Yes."

"Well, den! Dad blame it, why doan' he talk like a man. You answer me dat!" (pp. 84–85)

Another piece of literature that is appropriate to use to study language and dialects is a short story, "Who Said We All Have to Talk Alike" (McDaniel). Even though it was not specifically written for young adults, it will contribute much to the study of tolerance and understanding of someone's dialect and idiolect.

Neffie Pike, the main character, is 51 and a widow. She has spent her entire life in the Ozark Mountains. She decides to take a job in California as a nanny, but she soon returns and tells her story about the discrimination based upon her dialect. She added an *r* to many words that did not contain that letter, and she has a rather colorful vocabulary. Her word for toilet was *torelet,* and *worman* for women. The family for whom she worked could not accept Neffie because of her language. A discussion of Neffie, her language and background, and the family's attitude toward her would help students in their understanding of society and its attitude toward diversity in language and people.

The Black Dialect

The black dialect is a broad topic for discussion in the school classroom. A description of the dialect, its characteristics, its history, and its use in America is a must to meet the needs and interests of our diverse society. After some study of the dialect, teachers and students can investigate how authors have used the dialect in their writing. When it is used, it is often found in the dialogue of the characters. Students will find it interesting that authors are not consistent in their use of dialect. Teachers will want to have students investigate this dialect use in the novels they read.

Teachers may want to secure more background and develop a knowledge base that will help students as they investigate this dialect. Briefly, the black dialect, like all dialects, has regular rule-governed obligatory features. Recent linguistic research in this area indicates five systematic differences between the black nonstandard dialect and standard English: optional copula deletion, negative concord, invariant *be,* dummy it, and negative inversion (DeStefano, 1973). The first three are most prevalent in the literature.

Several young adult books include the use of the optional copula deletion: In their dialog, characters omit the *be* form of the verb. For example, in *The Secret of Gumbo Grove* (Tate), Raisin talks with Bunny Walterboro. Bunny says, "She say she tired of your mouth! I told her she better quit talking about my friend 'cause you don't take no mess. That's when she said she was gonna beat—" (p. 27). Later, when Bunny is trying to get Raisin to go to the disco, she says, "Girl, we missin' everything. They jammin' at the school yard. Can't you hear that music?" (p. 28). Again, at the dance, Cracker's voice rolls out over the speaker: "You messin' up my dance, Big Boy. Leave them little sisters alone" (p. 30).

In *Scorpions,* Myers also uses the copula deletion. In a dialogue between Jamal and Mama, Jamal makes reference to a pigeon that has just landed on the window ledge: "He don't even know we here" (p. 11). A moment later, Mama asks Jamal, "So what you going to do?" (p. 12). This structure is found throughout the novel. "Then why Randy want Mack to tell you who to look out for?" (p. 12). "Jamal Hicks, you lying" (p. 12). "'He my ace,' Randy used to say" (p. 13). "'You going to eat the corn flakes?' Jamal said" (p. 118). "'He lyin'.' 'You in the Scorpions?' Darness asked. 'Who you, the F.B.I.?' 'No, man, I'm Harlem Vice, I'm Harlem Vice, and we so bad we got to say it twice!'" (p. 119).

In *Won't Know Till I Get There* (Myers), Earl says, "'You a vandal'" (p. 19). In *Rainbow Jordan* (Childress), Rainbow says, "'Truth is, what else is it but *abandon* when she walk out with a boyfriend, promise to come home soon, then don't show?'" (p. 7). *I Be Somebody* (Irwin) is full of the copula deletion:

> "The thing is, Nimrod," Spicy said, "you talking cigars before tobacco's planted."
> "I talking sense, Spicy," he insisted. "We got to move. We can't stay here. It never going to get better." (p. 1)

The negative concord, or double negative, is found throughout most literature that uses black nonstandard dialect. In Taylor's *Let the Circle Be Unbroken,* a short dialogue between Papa and Uncle Hammer illustrates:

> "Mary still upset with me 'bout Bud?" asked Uncle Hammer, adjusting his mirror.
> Papa slid the straight razor down the right side of his face, stripping away the soap lather. "She got a right to be, don't you think?" Uncle Hammer shrugged and began to lather. "Didn't say nothin' but the truth."
> "Thought you wasn't gonna say nothin' at all.'" (p. 156)

Myers uses the structure in *Scorpions:*

> "I know it ain't real."
> "The Scorpions don't have no fake guns," Jamal said.
> "You ain't no Scorpions." (p. 106)

This feature is also found in the novel *I Be Somebody.*

The invariant *be* is a third feature commonly found in the black nonstandard dialect. Without the "be," the speaker/writer is expressing a momentary condition. With the "be," the speaker/writer is expressing a recurrent action or state. In *Scorpions,* Mama indicates that Jamal will survive over a period of time when she says, "'Mr. Gonzalez don't need nobody [negative concord] every day,' Mama said. 'Jamal be doing okay if he just help us out some'" (p. 123). And again,

> "That's a dollar seventy," Jamal said.
> "I got to tell Indian you working here," Blood said, putting two dollars on the counter. "He been looking for you."
> "What he looking for me for?"
> "You find out when he find your narrow butt." (p. 127)

Rainbow Jordan and *I Be Somebody* also include the invariant be construction. The latter novel even includes this structure in its title.

Other characteristics of the black dialect include lack of the possessive marker, lack of the plural suffix, endings of words lost, the *–ed* suffix added to strong verbs, and the third person singular inflection of the verb form deleted (Baratz & Baratz, 1969). Many examples of these characteristics may be found in all of the pieces of literature mentioned in this section as well as *Do Lord, Remember Me* (Lester), *A Gath-*

ering of Old Men (Gaines), *Mote* (Reaver), and *A Hero Ain't Nothin' But a Sandwich* (Childress). Interestingly, in *Mote,* the black dialect is discussed quite openly between Billy and the detective, Stienert.

In addition to discussing the dialect that they find in their reading, students should also discuss why they think that authors would choose not to use the dialect. For example, there seems to be very little, if any, black dialect used in *Teacup Full of Roses* (Mathis), *Durango Street* (Bonham), *Words by Heart* (Sebestyen), *Hoops* (Myers), *A Little Love* (Hamilton), and *M.C. Higgins, The Great* (Hamilton) although the characters are black and there seems to be no indication that the characters have adopted the standard American dialect.

Geographical Dialects

Regionalisms may be a little more difficult to find in literature. Generally, dialects are more obvious in the oral tradition; however, we do find some examples through vocabulary and syntax. Sometimes authors show the readers what the words or word combinations would sound like through clipping of words and variant spellings. On rare occasions, the main character will tell the reader just how the language is used in the setting of the novel. A case in point is when Wil tells how people use English in Cold Sassy (*Cold Sassy Tree,* Burns):

> "You need to understand that in Cold Sassy when the word *aunt* is followed by a name, it's pronounced *aint,* as in Aint Loma or Aint Carrie. We also say *dubya* for the letter *w, sump'm* for *something,* *idn'* for *isn't,* *dudn'* for *doesn't,* *raig'n* for *reckon, chim'ly* for *chimney,* *wrench* for *rinse, sut* for *soot,* as in train or chim'ly sut, and *like* for *lack,* as in 'Do you like much of bein' th'ew?' Well, I know that how we speak is part of what we are. I sure don't want Cold Sassy folks to sound like a bunch of Yankees. But I don't want us to sound ignorant, either, and pronunciations like *sump'n* and *id'n* sound ignorant. So I'm trying to remember not to use such—except right now to tell how Loma became Aint Loma." (p. 104)

A study of S. E. Bridgers's young adult literature helps readers to come to some generalizations concerning Southern literature. Carroll (1990), who thoroughly studied Bridgers's novels, believes "language becomes an important means by which Southern distinctions are illuminated" (p. 11). Carroll goes on to state that "particularly effective in *Sara Will* (1985) is Bridgers's use of three elements of Southern language: (1) names and phrases that ring true to the Southern ear, (2) the tradition of story telling, and (3) reliance on concrete details drawn from the natural world" (p. 11).

Permanent Connections (Bridgers) is ripe with Southern dialect, which is quite evident in the speech of Fairlee, Coralee, and Grandpa. Fairlee reminisces about his sister when he explains to Rob: "'She's always had a hankering for rings and bracelets and earbobs and the like'" (p. 86). Carroll goes on to show how Grandpa fits into the oratorical tradition, moral absolutes, and the Southern Appalachian dialect, all characteristic of the Southern literature.

A strong dialect flavor is found in Major's *Hold Fast,* written in the dialect of a small coastal town in Newfoundland. *Hold Fast* is the story of Michael, an adolescent whose world is holding strong—everything seems to be working out for him. Then, tragedy comes. His parents are killed and Michael's world changes. Students will enjoy reading the book and discovering the dialect that Michael speaks. Words like the following are found throughout *Hold Fast: baywop* (derogatory term for someone from the coastal community), *caplin* (small fish that comes to shore in Newfoundland), *firking around* (looking through something hurriedly), *flick* (quick), and *shaggin around* (fooling around).

Robert Cormier's books take place around the north central section of Massachusetts, specifically the town of Leominster, Cormier's birthplace. Cormier captures the flavor of the small community in Monument, the setting for *The Chocolate War* and *Beyond the Chocolate War*: "It's a thinly disguised Leominster, I suppose—the spirit of the city rather than the actual place. I've changed the name and everything and I've moved the streets around but it's the same. Yes, I'm lucky that I've got that place—that I can take a ride down to Frenchtown anytime and there it is" (Sutton, 1991, p. 31).

Both Monument and Frenchtown are important settings in *Fade* (1988) and *Other Bells for Us to Ring* (1990). Cormier writes in *Fade,* "The family had settled down in Frenchtown on the east side of Monument in Massachusetts along with hundreds of other French Canadians, living in the three-decker tenements and two-story houses" (p. 4). On each of those three-decker tenements is a *piazza*—a term for porch used in this region of the country. The term *piazza* is used throughout the novel.

This New England flavor is also felt in the rural areas of Vermont in the superbly rich and moving novel *A Day No Pigs Would Die* (Peck). The novel portrays the adventures of Peck's childhood. The setting is rural Vermont, and the language reflects that setting:

> Whatever old Apron decided that I was doing to her back yonder, she didn't take kindly to it. So she started off again with me in the rear, hanging on to wait Christmas, and my own bare butt and privates catching a thorn with every step. (p. 9)
>
> Somebody told me once that a cow won't bite. That somebody is as wrong as sin on Sunday. (p. 11)
>
> "We're beholding to you, Benjamin Tanner," said Papa, "for fetching him home. Whatever he done, I'll make it right." (p. 14)
>
> "Best I be going," I said. "Thank you for the ginger snaps and the buttermilk." "You're more than welcome, Rob," said Mrs. Bascom. "Anytime you come this way, be sure to stop for a how do." (p. 82)

Regional dialects play an important part in the author's craft. Certainly, if the reader could hear the words spoken, the dialect would be even more profound. As it is, the author relies on word choice and expression to convey that added dimension to the work. Students, as they read young adult literature, can note the dialect that authors use.

LANGUAGE MANIPULATION

The use of language to move people to action or to think in a particular way pervades the American culture and is targeted quite often to young people. Adolescents are asked almost daily to buy this product, to act in this particular way, or to accept this point of view. Certainly, activities in the curriculum will share the dangers of blindly accepting these manipulative devices. Teachers may also find ways of presenting the use of manipulative language—euphemisms, doublespeak—through young adult literature. What language devices do characters use on each other to get others to act and think in a particular way? Young people can study this use of language as they read.

Certainly, Cormier's works come to mind as one thinks of this study. In *The Chocolate War,* how does Archie control his Vigils? What language techniques does he use to make them believe in particular ways? The strategies of Brother Leon alone would fill a classroom discussion. Other Cormier novels provoke similar discussions: *After the First Death, I Am the Cheese, The Bumblebee Flies Anyway, Fade.*

Rescue: The Story of How Gentiles Saved Jews in the Holocaust (Meltzer), a nonfiction account of the many self-sacrificing people who risked their lives to hide the Jews from the Nazi forces in Europe, effectively shows how powerful, emotional language can be used for propaganda. Students can discuss the following statements that illustrate this emotional, propagandized language:

> Good Jews? Bad Jews? What difference does it make? All Jews are considered the same. Even the baptized and assimilated Jew is worthless to the anti-Semite. It is no longer a question of religion. The Jews' race, their blood condemns them. (p. 5)
>
> A Gentile Polish teenaged girl is quoted as saying, "Oh, I hate them! The Jews are horrible! They are dirty thieves. They cheat everybody. Jews are a real menace. For Passover they catch Christian children, murder them, and use their blood for matzo." (p. 34)

Meltzer's nonfiction book is a source of euphemistic language. Students can find examples similar to those cited below (emphasis added). They can also explain the real meaning of those words.

> Oskar's subcamp would be closed, too, and the prisoners would go back to Plaszow, to await *relocation.* (p. 63)
>
> The Germans declared martial law and took direct control of the government. Hitler's *experts* on the *final solution* arrived to plan the deportation to the death camps. (p. 90)
>
> No letters of safe conduct or foreign passports for Hungarian Jews from whatever source would permit Jews to escape the *solution to the Jewish problem.* (p. 110)

Tiger Eyes (Blume), certainly a less traumatic novel, is a ripe source for manipulative language. Students should talk about the language Blume uses. There is clear evidence that the characters manipulate each other, persuading each other to do something they may not want to do, by using certain words or phrases or by saying words in certain ways. It is clear that Walter and, to a lesser extent, Bitsy, both want Davey and her family to behave the way Walter and Bitsy think is best. They try to control the family with their language and with their actions.

> "Oh, around," I say. "I like to explore."
> "Just be careful. And don't take any chances."
> "Me . . . take chances?" I picture myself climbing down into the canyon.
> "Don't worry. I don't take chances."
> "Good," Bitsy says. "I'm glad to hear it. This family has had enough trouble."
> (p. 80)
> After dinner Walter wants to see my course schedule. He hits the roof when he finds out that I am not taking a science course.
> "How could they let you register without insisting on a science course?"
> "I wanted to take typing instead," I explain. "I can always take chemistry next year."
> "Typing," Walter says, angrily. "Ridiculous. And next year you should be taking Physics I. You're going to fall behind."
> I feel like telling him that I have no intention of taking Physics I, not next year, and not ever.
> "You have to think of your future," Walter tells me. "You want to get into a good college, don't you?"
> "I don't know," I say.
> "Of course you know."
> "No, I don't! I don't even know if I want to go to college."
> Walter pours himself a glass of brandy, sloshes it around in his glass, then takes a hearty drink. "What do you want to do with your life, Davey?" he asks. (pp. 95–96)

Most of the young adult novels that students are reading lend themselves to the study of euphemisms and manipulative language. Barry is constantly trying to make Harry feel insignificant in *Singularity* (Sleator). If Harry doesn't want to do something, Barry calls him chicken and shames Harry into doing what Barry wants. Other examples can be found in Janeczko's *Bridges to Cross,* Murphy's *Death Run,* and Naughton's *My Brother Stealing Second.*

A HISTORICAL PERSPECTIVE

American English has often been called the "cosmopolitan language" because it has borrowed so much from so many languages that it includes a little of almost every language. Certainly, as students read, they may be aware of words that have been borrowed from other languages. This will be easier if they have studied the history of the English language, even in its most elementary form. This investigation may just happen as students who have some knowledge of language history read the words on the printed page. In fact, students may want to read novels with characters that use English that is influenced by another language.

Park's Quest (Paterson) offers students language study in at least two different ways: the English spoken by a nonnative speaker and the English spoken by native speakers long ago. Thanh, a Vietnamese, uses what we have come to call "broken English." She leaves parts of the discourse out, which is consistent with her native language but not with English speaking. Thanh says to Park: "'Come out where I see you,' she ordered, stepping aside, confident that he would obey. He did, blinking in the bright sunshine. 'I never see you,' she said. 'What you name?'" (p. 57).

Students can discuss this phenomenon and perhaps can name other novels with similar language patterns: *The Prince and the Wild Geese* (Brophy), *Shabanu, Daughter of the Wind* (Staples), and *When Heaven and Earth Changed Places* (Hayslip).

Also in *Park's Quest,* Paterson alludes to the Arthurian legend. Park is on a quest in search of knowledge about his father, as King Arthur and his knights went on quests. As Park dreams of these long-ago quests, he slips into the language of the day." 'Faugh! You are no knight!' the lady cried in disgust. 'You are naught but a kitchen scullion, smelling of garlic and grease. How dare you to presume to be my champion? Dismount fool, and stand aside, lest the Black Knight skewer you on his spear and roast you in the everlasting flames!'" (p. 5).

Students can easily find words with which they are not familiar. They could also discuss the structure of the discourse, giving particular attention to the flair apparent in the language. Some students may want to pursue the investigation further by identifying other characteristics of Middle English.

Kennemore's *Changing Times* also can be used to study language since it has a very British flavor. A comment such as "The day you faint'll be the day I win Crufts" (p. 47) may not be entirely understood by the American reader, but with a little investigation, one can assume that Crufts is some kind of race. Readers may want to study English vocabulary further to find out exactly what Crufts is. The slang used in *Changing Times* is also very British in its origin, frequently using the words *blimey* and *bloody.*

As we think about how language changes over years, we are aware of how words come into the language and how they sometimes disappear. The slang of today may become the standard language of tomorrow. It is interesting to note that words used in earlier times by various groups of people may not now be in use. This can be evidenced in the novel *The Sign of the Beaver* by Speare. This is a story of Matt, a 13-year-old boy, and his relationship with Attean, an Indian boy. As students read this novel, they will invariably find words that are no longer in use: *puncheon tale* (p. 3), *oiled paper* for windows (p. 3), *blunderbuss* (p. 4), *matchlock* (p. 4), *hemlock boughs* for a bed (p. 10), and *boardcloth* (p. 125). Students may then want to ask their parents, grandparents, and much older friends to give examples of common words and phrases that they used when they were young that are not used today.

Teachers could also use *When the Legends Die* (Borland) to teach students about borrowing words from other languages. Many words now a part of the English language were borrowed from Native Americans. Examples include *moccasin, tomahawk, chipmunk,* and *squaw.* In addition to the Native American influence in the novel, the Spanish language is well represented. Words of Spanish origin include *canyon, cinch, rodeo, corral,* and *bronco.*

Julie in *Julie of the Wolves* (George) expresses her feeling and values by first accepting, then rejecting the English language, and then accepting it again at the end of the novel. Students can pinpoint these transitions and speculate about the values Julie believes to be "American" and the values she identifies as "Eskimo." Students with bilingual backgrounds could share how they feel about their first language and their adopted language.

The wolves in the novel have their own language. The wolves' language allows them to express affection, give and take orders, and recognize the leader as well as obtain food and protect themselves. The pups express playfulness in ways that Miyax recognizes as "human." A study of the idea that language is a purely human phenomenon would be appropriate as students read this novel.

NONVERBAL COMMUNICATION

Since language is, phylogenetically, one of man's most distinctive characteristics, we sometimes slip into the error of thinking that all communication must be verbal communication . . . but the language of words is only a fragment of the language we use in communicating with each other. We talk with eyes and hands, with gestures, with our posture, with various motions of our body. (Halpin, 1970, p. 107)

Students are aware of how they communicate nonverbally with each other. They know the meaning of the smirk on the face or the raised eyebrow. They recognize the negative meaning that comes through tone of voice even though the message may be positive. What better way to extend that understanding than to investigate how authors have their characters communicate nonverbally? Readers can note the subtle communication that occurs between and among characters without saying a word.

Here again, young adult literature serves us well. In Lowry's *Number the Stars,* we can see how nonverbal language is used effectively. A few examples are in order: "Kristi clapped her hands in delight" (p. 34); "Ellen stood on tiptoe again, and made an imperious gesture with her arm" (p. 39); and "He made one hand into a fist, and he kept pounding it into the other hand. I remember the noise of it: slam, slam, slam" (p. 41). Students can use these passages and many others to talk about the feelings expressed. Students can explore the novel further to note the facial expressions on the soldiers, how the soldiers move, how they stand, and what messages are sent by these nonverbal communicators.

Everything Is Not Enough (Asher) emphasizes nonverbal communication. Both Linda and Traci effectively communicate to Michael and Buddy to stay away from them without saying a word. Pete communicates one message to Traci verbally ("I love you, I need you") while communicating another to her when he physically beats her.

A discussion of the greater impact of nonverbal communication over spoken words is bound to occur. The issue of adaptations a writer must make to convey a meaning on paper instead of using oral or spoken delivery with gestures and facial expressions should point up the importance of descriptive language that Asher has used. Again, all of this language study must occur after students have made their personal response to what they have read. After this initial emotional response, students are more at ease with the in-depth investigation of these language topics.

❧   Learning Log Responses   ❧

Why is it important for you to connect language study with literature in your classes?

Comment on the interaction between Jem and Calpurnia found on page 107. What generalizations about the language concept discussed can you make, and what application do you see to your teaching?

REFERENCES

Baratz, S., & Baratz, J. C. (1969). Negro ghetto children and urban education: A cultural solution. *The Florida FL Reporter, 7* (1), 1–16.

Bushman, J. H. (1988). *Teaching the English Language.* Springfield, IL: Charles C. Thomas.

Carroll, P. S. (1990). Southern literature for young adults: The novels of Sue Ellen Bridgers. *The Alan Review, 18* (1), 10–13.

DeStefano, J. (1973). *Language, society and education: A profile of black English.* Worthington, OH: Charles A. Jones.

Halpin, A. W. (1970). Theory and research in administration. In J. W. Ketner (Ed.), *Interpersonal speech-communication.* Belmont, CA: Wadsworth.

Sutton, R. (1991). "Kind of a funny dichotomy": A conversation with Robert Cormier. *School Library Journal, 37* (6), 28–33.

Taylor, O. (1985). Standard English as a second dialect? *English Today* (ET2), 9–12.

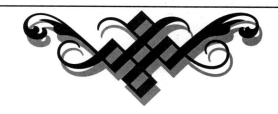

Organizing The Literature

How to use young adult literature effectively confronts teachers as they plan their school year. For middle school teachers, one book for an entire class may be most effective; high school teachers, however, may find that they can place their students in groups of four or five, with each group working with a different book. Some will use a combination of these approaches (Figure 6.1) For reading outside of the class, students normally choose a book from an approved list of books. Discussion of each of these arrangements follows.

ONE BOOK, ONE CLASS

Traditionally, all students read the same work in class. Certainly, on the surface there seem to be many advantages to this arrangement. It is easier for teachers to plan for classroom activities since all students are supposed to start and stop at the same time. Teachers and students can discuss the issues presented in the pages read for the day's lesson. All students, then, are involved with the same issues and can learn from each other the differing points of views held.

In addition, after students finish their personal responses, they can more easily move to the analysis of the qualities of the literature. The entire class can examine plots, analyze characters, and evaluate other literary aspects of the work. When teachers feel that the class has thoroughly examined the novel, they have students complete the process with a project, a piece of writing, or a test that evaluates the students' understanding of the book.

Approach	Instructional Purpose	Classroom Management
One Book, One Class	Attention given to issues presented in one work	Emphasis on large group
Novels Arranged Thematically	Attention given to issues from a variety of works Able to meet a variety of interests and ability levels	Emphasis on small groups with some large-group work
Thematic Units	Attention given to a variety of literary genres and skills	Emphasis on small and large groups
One Book, One Student	Attention given to the reading interest and ability of the individual student	Emphasis on the individual

FIGURE 6.1
Organizational approaches for using young adult literature in the classroom

Some argue that this arrangement does not meet the needs of every student in the class. Experience tells us that not all students in any given class have the same reading interests and abilities. In fact, we've heard it said that the only similarity about a class of eighth graders is that they are called eighth graders. Some may be reading at the fifth grade level; others may be at the 11th grade reading level. All students are moving through the developmental stages—physical, emotional, moral, cognitive—at different speeds.

Knowing this, teachers usually teach to the middle: They choose pieces of literature that will satisfy the majority, if not all, of the students. Often, however, the top of the class becomes bored, and the bottom can't keep up. This can be overcome somewhat by using groups within the class even though each group will still be working with the same novel. The activities can be changed to meet the needs of the specific groups. Teachers are having some success with this approach.

The books listed in Figure 6.2 are books that can be effective if read by all students in the class. We have annotated a few of the books here and have included a longer, more comprehensive list in Appendix C. We hesitate to say that all these books will work for all students in every class. However, all books listed are quality literature and may be used for some classes.

ARRANGING BOOKS THEMATICALLY

For those teachers who believe that their class should not read one book, an alternative arrangement using themes can be very effective. If we believe in the diversity that comes with most classes, more than one book may be needed to meet the interests and abilities of the students. For example, some middle school teachers may want their students to read Paterson's *Jacob Have I Loved* but feel that some students would not respond well to that book. These teachers could also choose Pfeffer's *The Year Without Michael* for the middle range of students and Carter's *Dancing On Dark Water* for those in the lower range. All books center around the families-in-conflict theme. Groups of eight or so students can read one of the three books, and then, because they are bound together with this central theme, students can discuss each book separately and in relationship to each other. Each group may spend time working separately with its book and then join the other groups for a general discussion. Each group may also do projects around its book and then present them to the entire class.

The important concern here is the attempt to meet the needs and abilities of all students and still keep an organization that the entire class can follow. One very important benefit from such an approach is that all students read one book and hear about two others. Students may then choose to read these on their own at a later time. Figure 6.3 presents books that can be grouped around themes. We have also suggested the range of difficulty for each book: higher range, middle range, and lower range.

Thematic Units

This thematic arrangement of literature may be expanded into an effective curriculum design called *thematic units*. This design is more than just arranging three or four novels that are thematically related. The unit involves teaching all the language arts: literature, oral and written English, and language. The emphasis is on integration of the skills and subject matter that are taught in the English classroom. It is much like the whole language approach that is found in many elementary classrooms. The theme—linguistic or social—is the "glue" that holds the unit together. The literature, the written and oral processes, and the language activities are centered in some way around the theme. Most thematic units are 6- to 18-week segments of the curriculum. It is important to note that the theme is the means and not the end. It is a vehicle for teaching the language arts.

The thematic unit is designed to emphasize the process of discovery, much like the reader-response approach in literature and the writing process. Students are able to spend their time more wisely, discovering what is important to them as they explore the investigatory topics that comprise the thematic units. With this approach, students are studying in a curriculum that is based on experience, involvement, and response, all of which are related in some way to the study of young adult literature.

The literature for each thematic unit is not limited to novels. Although the novels may provide the backbone for the unit, other literature, such as short stories, poems, and nonfiction, is included. Whatever literature is chosen, the emphasis is on the response that the student makes; that is, the literature itself and its relationship to the reader. So often in other curriculum designs—chronology and genre—the emphasis is on historical and formal literary characteristics. With thematic units, students' primary goal is not to find out how a particular work fits into an overall historical survey, nor do they spend the majority of their time trying to delineate the formal characteristics of the work (is it a novel, short story, or poem?). It is important to note these characteristics in literature study, but they do not command primary attention. The attention is given to the work itself—what authors have to say and how they say it. In the thematic unit, the chronology may be there in the upper grades in high school, but the genre is there at all levels. By reading these various works, students can consider not only differing viewpoints, but they also see how each author uses different genres to express thoughts on similar topics.

The writing that occurs in the thematic unit is much like the writing that occurs in any other curriculum design. Students use the process to arrive at some understanding of the chosen topic. The unit approach offers, perhaps, one additional component: ideas about which to write. If the theme is relevant to the students' interests, it will provide many opportunities for students to engage in the writing experience. Students may respond in writing to the literature; they can also simply respond to the theme as well.

Since the thematic unit is designed to include all the language arts, the language component is easily incorporated into the total unit. It matters little whether the theme is socially or linguistically oriented—a wealth of material exists for study in

After the Rain, Norma Fox Mazer
> When Rachel learns of her grumpy grandfather's new illness, she accepts the responsibility of visiting him daily, beginning a deeper relationship that continues until his death.

Beardance, Will Hobbs
> A sequel to *Bearstone.* While accompanying Walter, an elderly rancher, on a trip into the San Juan Mountains, Cloyd tries to help two orphaned grizzly bear cubs survive the winter.

Bearstone, Will Hobbs
> Cloyd, a troubled Indian boy, goes to live with Walter, an elderly rancher whose caring ways help the boy.

Beyond the Chocolate War, Robert Cormier
> Conflicts at Trinity High continue as Obie and others question Archie's abusive power.

The Chocolate War, Robert Cormier
> The struggle among Jerry, a Trinity High student who wants to take a stand; Archie, the leader of the Vigils, who wants to control; and Brother Leon, the headmaster of Trinity High, who wants his school to succeed at any cost causes conflict among the student body.

Cold Sassy Tree, Olive Burns
> The small town of Cold Sassy, Georgia, comes alive when Grandpa Blakeslee, a widower of three weeks, elopes with Miss Love Simpson, a woman half his age.

The Contender, Robert Lipsyte
> Alfred Brooks wants to make it straight but his environment in Harlem pulls him in other directions.

Dogwolf, Alden Carter
> Fifteen-year-old Pete, who is part Chippewa, spends a difficult summer fighting forest fires that threaten the northern Wisconsin forest, while also hunting an equally threatening creature believed to be part dog and part wolf.

Don't Look Behind You, Lois Duncan
> April, along with her family, is forced to enter the Federal Witness Protection Program and must leave her friends and successful school life behind.

Driver's Ed, Caroline Cooney
> Three teenagers' lives are changed forever when they thoughtlessly steal a stop sign from a dangerous intersection and a young mother is killed in a automobile accident there.

Flash Fire, Caroline Cooney
> As fire sweeps through a canyon near Los Angeles, young adults whose parents are not around must work together to save themselves.

FIGURE 6.2

Representative literature for one book, one class reading

The Giver, Lois Lowry
  Given his lifetime assignment at the Ceremony of Twelve, Jonas becomes the receiver of memories shared by only one other in his community and discovers the truth about the society in which he lives.

I Am The Cheese, Robert Cormier
  Adam discovers that his family was placed in the Federal Witness Protection Program years ago and now is a victim of his father's enemies.

In the Middle of the Night, Robert Cormier
  Sixteen-year-old Denny lives in the shadow of a deadly accident that involved his father when he was Denny's age, a disaster for which some of the survivors still blame his father.

Loch, Paul Zindel
  Fifteen-year-old Loch and his younger sister join their father on a scientific expedition searching for enormous prehistoric creatures sighted in a Vermont lake, but it soon becomes obvious that the expedition's leaders are not interested in preserving the creatures.

Miriam's Well, Lois Ruby
  Miriam is a teenager who develops cancer. A battle between religious freedom and the courts ensues.

Out of Control, Norma Fox Mazer
  Three teenage boys join together in a spontaneous sexual attack on a girl at their school. The story examines the personal and social values they and those around them hold.

Out of Here, Sandy Asher
  The lives of Stacey Lawrence and other seniors at Oakview High School are interconnected as they move from the first day of school to graduation day.

Skin Deep, Lois Ruby
  Dan finally gets the attention that he has wanted, but he has to become a neo-Nazi skinhead to get it. The novel is ripe with First Amendment conflicts.

Steal Away Home, Lois Ruby
  In two parallel stories, a Quaker family from Kansas in the late 1850s operates a station on the Underground Railroad, while almost 150 years later, 12-year-old Dana moves into the same house and finds the skeleton of a black woman who helped the Quakers.

Stotan, Chris Crutcher
  A high school swimming team learns the importance of friendship and support as each member struggles to deal with his own tragedy.

Middle School

Higher Range	Middle Range	Lower Range
Teen Pressure		
Shadow of the Dragon (Garland)	*Driver's Ed* (Cooney)	*Killing Mr. Griffin* (Duncan)
Friendships		
Waiting for the Rain (Gordon)	*The Moves Make the Man* (Brooks)	*Crazy Lady* (Conley)
Prejudice		
Under the Blood-Red Sun (Salsbury)	*Chernowitz* (Arrick)	*Daniel's Story* (Matas)
Strange and Eerie		
Whispers From the Dead (Nixon)	*A Haunting in Williamsburg* (Kassem)	*Voices After Midnight* (Peck)
Survival		
Deathwatch (White)	*Downriver* (Hobbs)	*Sworn Enemies* (Matas)
War		
Voices from the Civil War (Meltzer)	*Blitzcat* (Westall)	*My Brother Sam Is Dead* (Collier and Collier)

High School

Higher Range	Middle Range	Lower Range
School		
The Day They Came to Arrest the Book (Hentoff)	*Out of Here* (Asher)	*The Crazy Horse Electric Game* (Crutcher)
Victims		
Chinese Handcuffs (Crutcher)	*The Chocolate War* (Cormier)	*Good-bye Tomorrow* (Miklowitz)
Coping with Death		
Sheila's Dying (Carter)	*Phoenix Rising* (Hesse)	*Running Loose* (Crutcher)
Love and Sexuality		
Deliver Us from Evie (Kerr)	*Out of Control* (Mazer)	*Bad Boy* (Wieler)
Echoes from the Past		
Alicia: My Story (Appleman-Jurman)	*Forbidden City* (Bell)	*Just Like Martin* (Davis)
Government Control		
After the First Death (Cormier)	*The Giver* (Lowry)	*Don't Look Behind You* (Duncan)
Unusual Circumstances		
Fade (Cormier)	*Eva* (Dickinson)	*Albion's Dream* (Norman)

FIGURE 6.3

Literature arranged thematically for middle and high school

middle and high schools. Authors' use of dialect, particular word choice, sentence construction, use of euphemisms and doublespeak, and manipulative language provide students with ample material for study.

Oral communication is also an integral part of thematic unit planning. Teachers have long recognized the necessity for and value of classroom discussion, but its quality has slipped until it is often nothing more than a dull recital of names, dates, and other facts. Even well-intentioned teachers may find that the open discussion session they have envisioned becomes instead the familiar "tug of war" as they try to pull answers out of unresponsive students. In most cases, these experiences lead to "teacher-talk," which requires students to function as sponges—soaking up information, which is then wrung out at exam time.

It doesn't have to be this way. The thematic unit approach uses speech and creative drama activities to show students the relationships between all the language arts. Group discussions, impromptu speeches, and interviewing are rewarding activities when linked to particular social or linguistic themes. Speech activities should evolve in response to reading, writing, and viewing. Creative drama helps to expand the boundaries of experience so that students may develop a more complete understanding of themselves, their work, and their relationships to other people. Drama is as effective with composition and language as it is with literature. It adds a more exciting dimension to learning, and it helps to bring about the effective communication that we described earlier.

Improvisation and role playing complement thematic units. Students can interpret themes and conflicts in literature by improvising parallel circumstances, or they can take characters from the work and place them in other situations through role playing. Oral communication is a natural thread that runs not only through thematic units in teaching English but also through the entire educational experience. To teach speech and drama in a way that implies separation from other educational experiences is unfair and certainly unrealistic.

Figures 6.4 and 6.5 present two skeleton thematic units: one for middle school and one for high school. They include objectives, materials, and a few representative activities.

POETRY, SHORT STORIES, DRAMA, AND NONFICTION YOUNG ADULT LITERATURE

Most of the young adult literature mentioned in this book has been of the most common genre: the young adult novel. The reason seems obvious: When one thinks of young adult literature, the novel comes to mind. It has been the mainstay of young adults' reading for more than thirty years. However, the thematic unit examples include poetry, short stories, drama, and nonfiction.

Writing poetry specifically for the young adult audience is relatively new. Very few collections existed a few years ago. Now, more poetry is written by and for young adults, and writers and editors are creating collections for young people. The

Thematic Objectives

The student will:

- Define the concept of hero and heroism.
- Generate a list of criteria for heroes and heroines.
- Investigate the influence of the hero figure in society.

Language Arts Objectives

The student will:

- Develop confidence in his or her written and oral composition.
- Experiment with alternate ways to express ideas in writing and select the one closest to his or her intent.
- Revise, edit, and proofread his or her own writing to make it clear and effective for the reader.
- Examine qualities of writing in others' writing as well as his or her own.
- Identify language items or elements from selected literature that will demonstrate language change and variety.
- Participate in discussion leading toward a goal or solution.
- Describe the power of language found in various forms of communication.
- Identify major traits of important fictional and nonfictional characters and analyze their influence on each other.
- Identify figures of speech in literature and use those elements in their own writing.
- Come to a general understanding of meaning of something read.

Materials

Novels

The Outsiders, S. E. Hinton (all students will read)
Roll of Thunder, Hear My Cry, Mildred Taylor (selected students)
A Hero Ain't Nothin' But a Sandwich, Alice Childress (selected students)

Nonfiction

Eric, Doris Lund (selected students)
People Who Make a Difference, Brent Ashabranner (selected students)
Harriet Tubman, Guide to Freedom, Ann Petry (selected students)

Short Stories

"Great Moves," Sandy Asher
"Playing God," Ouida Sebestyen
"The Fuller Brush Man," Gloria Miklowitz
"On the Bridge," Todd Strasser
"A Hundred Bucks of Happy," Susan Beth Pfeffer

FIGURE 6.4

Thematic unit on heroes and heroines for middle school students

Poems

Selected poems from *Class Dismissed II: More High School Poems,* Mel Glenn
   "Stacey Fowler"
   "Veronica Castell"
   "Dana Moran"
   "Mary Gilardi"
   "Louise Coyle"
   "Clint Reynolds"

Drama
   "Riding Out the Storm," Cin Forshay-Lunsford

Film
   Snowbound
   Blaze Glory
   The Legend of the Lone Ranger

Activities (a representative selection; teachers will want to create others)

1. Have the whole class brainstorm on the word *heroism.* Suggest that students record responses in their journals for later use. Responses may include the students' perceptions of heroes/heroines, specific characteristics that they feel are important to be a hero or heroine, qualities that they see in "real-life" heroes/heroines, and acts that they consider heroic. This list may change as students read and discuss in this unit.

2. After reading Hinton's *The Outsiders,* have students create a biopoem (for example, see Figure 4.1) on one of the characters. Have them follow this with a character sketch. Students should take this sketch through the writing process getting feedback from peer groups and finally finishing the writing into a polished product.

3. To study effective use of language, have students bring in samples of heroism reported in newspapers. Have students examine the language used to describe the hero/heroine. Compare and contrast this use of language to that found in the literature.

4. After students have read the literature assigned to the five groups (Taylor, Lund, Childress, Ashabranner, Petry), have them discuss why the characters do or do not fit the criteria for heroes/heroines that were created at the beginning of the unit.

5. Have students choose one quality that is characteristic of a hero/heroine from the short stories read and write a story in which they emphasize that quality. The writing may be fictional or an incident from their childhood. The writing should then be shared in small groups and polished into a final product.

6. Have students read the poems suggested and compare and contrast the poems' treatment of the theme of heroism.

7. After viewing the films, have students develop a list of qualities of heroism as depicted by the film. How are these qualities similar to those qualities found in the literature? Has time changed how we look at heroism? How can the western hero be characterized? Have the forces of evil changed? To what extent does the Lone Ranger have more personal qualities than the other heroes/heroines discussed in class? Compare and contrast the film as a medium to convey heroic qualities to other forms — the short story, novel, poem, or nonfiction.

Thematic Objectives

The student will:

- Demonstrate an understanding of the thematic concept.
- Investigate attitudes toward death found in selections read and compare and contrast these attitudes with personal attitudes.
- Be able to describe the physical, religious, psychological, economic, and legal aspects of death and be able to demonstrate how these aspects are changing with human tradition.

Language Arts Objectives

The student will:

- Participate in the composing process demonstrating an increased proficiency in oral and written composition while focusing on a specific form of structured written expression.
- Demonstrate an understanding of literature that is varied in form but related in content, and an understanding of the different effects each has on the reader.
- Be able to describe the power of language found in various forms of communication, specifically the language that shapes behavior.
- Participate freely and honestly in small and large group discussions.
- Demonstrate the process of interviewing and then execute that process by interviewing selected people in the community.
- Demonstrate appropriate behavior when presenting an informational report.
- Identify figures of speech in literature, specifically examining simile, metaphor, irony, point of view, foreshadowing, and flashback.

Materials

Novels

So Long at the Fair, Hadley Irwin
Running Loose, Chris Crutcher
The Accident, Todd Strasser (selected students)
Memory, Margaret Mahy (selected students)
Winning, Robin Brancato (selected students)
Good-bye Tomorrow, Gloria Miklowitz (selected students)

Nonfiction

Never to Forget: The Jews of the Holocaust, Milton Meltzer (selected students)

Short Stories

"The Sweet Perfume of Good-Bye," M. E. Kerr
"Jeremiah's Song," Walter Dean Myers
"The Moustache," Robert Cormier
"The Lottery," Shirley Jackson
"The Scarlet Ibis," James Hurst

FIGURE 6.5
Thematic unit on death for high school students

Poems

    "Ian Sinclair," Mel Glenn
    "The Portrait," Stanley Kunitz
    "Incident in a Rose Garden," Donald Justice
    "The Funeral," Gordon Parks
    "Uphill," Christina Rossetti
    "Solace," Dorothy Parker
    "A Dream Deferred," Langston Hughes
    "There Will Come Soft Rains," Sara Teasdale
    Just Give Me a Cool Drink of Water 'fore I Die (collection), Maya Angelou

Drama

    Large Fears, Little Demons, Dallin Malmgren
    A Woman Called Truth, Sandy Asher

Essay

    "The Death of a Tree," Edwin Way Teale

Activities (a representative selection; teachers will want to create others)

1. To help students synthesize their feelings and ideas about death, have them list statements indicating what death means to them. Use the abstraction format: Death is _____. When students have finished, discuss the ideas generated. Have students put their list in their journal, as they will be adding to it as they read the various works in the unit.

2. Have students read some or all of the poems suggested. These poems have a variety of views on death. After students have made their personal responses to the poems, have students compare and contrast these various attitudes among the poets and with the students' attitudes. In addition to the attitude toward death, have students look at the poet's craft: what strategies and devices does the poet use?

3. Investigate the physical, religious, psychological, economic, and legal aspects of death through various resource people in the community. Have students interview a medical doctor; a minister, priest, or rabbi; a psychologist or psychiatrist; a funeral director or insurance agent; and a lawyer. After gathering appropriate information, have students present oral reports to the class; then, each student will present a more formal written report to the class; then, each student will present a more formal written report on the interview in which she or he relates the information to the attitudes expressed in the literature.

4. As a followup activity, have students share characteristics of the language that was used by each person interviewed. How did each talk about death? What particular euphemisms were used? Was the language used consistent with the tone of the interviewee?

5. Have students choose one of the following quotes and develop a well-structured piece of writing. Students should develop their positions on the thesis they choose and support them with ideas offered by authors read in the unit.

"Death is sometimes a punishment, often a gift; to many it has been a favor."—Seneca

"Death: kind nature's signal of retreat."—Samuel Johnson

"Death, however, is a spongy wall, is a sticky river, is nothing at all."—Edna St. Vincent Millay

Teachers are encouraged to discuss these quotes with students and to help students get started through prewriting sessions in class. As students write, they should participate fully in all aspects of the writing process.

6. Through role playing and improvisation, have students present a situation involving death or dying. Students assume the roles of selected characters from literature in the unit and resolve a problem/concern by improvising in the manner of and from the point of view of those characters.

7. This activity could be used as the final project. Students should select a group that will read one of the fiction and nonfiction works listed in the Materials section. After each group has read its work, students will make a presentation about the work to the class. The project should include, but not be limited to, the following:

- A brief personal response to the work: how they felt about it, what it made them think about, whether or not they liked it and why, and other information normally found in a personal response.
- A brief overview of the plot, setting, description of characters, etc.
- How specifically this work fits into the theme of this unit.
- How this work parallels themes found in the other literature read in this unit.
- Characters' attitude toward death.
- Specific devices used by authors to help convey their message.

After the groups have presented their projects, teachers may have students give individual oral and written presentations as well.

FIGURE 6.5, *continued*

same can be said for short stories and drama. Nonfiction has been available longer, but it is now just beginning to become popular in the schools. Young people have been reading it for some time, but it has taken a long time for nonfiction to find its way into the classroom.

Poetry

One of the earliest collections of poetry used for casual reading as well as for the classroom was *Reflections on a Gift of Watermelon Pickle and Other Modern Verse*, edited by Steve Dunning, Edward Lueders, and Hugh L. Smith (1966). An often-read collection by children, young adults, and adults, *Reflections* was comprised of poetry from hundreds of poetry magazines that got favorable responses from young adults. Two other collections followed: *Some Haystacks Don't Even Have Any Needles and Other Complete Modern Poems* (Dunning, Lueders, & Smith) and *Zero Makes Me Hungry: A Collection of Poems for Today* (Lueders & St. John).

Mel Glenn and Paul Janeczko are two contemporary poets that have a primary audience of young adults. Glenn's publications, *Class Dismissed! High School Poems* and *Class Dismissed II: More High School Poems,* became very popular with young adults, probably because the poems have the same characteristics as many young adult novels: The topics of the poems relate well to adolescents; the language is direct, spoken as a young adult would speak; and the protagonists are from a variety of racial and socioeconomic backgrounds. The collections are packaged attractively, with each poem carrying the name of an individual with an accompanying photo, which gives the impression that the poem is written by the young adult pictured. It isn't; all are written by Glenn.

Janeczko, a high school teacher, has achieved success with many collections of poems for young adults. His first was *Postcard Poems: A Collection of Poetry for Sharing,* a collection of poems short enough to send to someone on a postcard. Other Janeczko collections have followed: *Don't Forget to Fly; Strings: A Gathering of Family Poems; Pocket Poems: Selected for a Journey; Going Over to Your Place: Poems for Each Other; The Place My Words Are Looking For;* and *Preposterous: Poems of Youth.* One additional collection—*Poetspeak: In Their Work, About Their Work*—will eventually find itself in most classrooms since it not only contains the poems of many authors, but also because it contains notes from the authors telling how they came to write the particular poems. Figure 6.6 presents a selection of poetry collections suitable for classroom study.

Short Stories

Like poetry, the short story is not new to the secondary school classroom. In most anthologies, the short story is the predominant genre. Most, however, are not written for the young adult. The themes are adult in nature, a few to the point that students do relate positively to them.

Today, the reading in this genre for young adults has broadened greatly. Now young adult authors such as Robert Cormier, Joan Aiken, Robert Lipsyte, Susan Beth Pfeffer, Richard Peck, and Jerry Spinelli, to mention only a few, are included in collections of short stories designed specifically for young adults. Three collections should be noted: *Sixteen, Visions,* and *Connections.* Don Gallo, editor of the three collections, indicates in the introduction the importance of *Sixteen,* the first book: "This book you now hold is unique—in two ways. First, there has never before been a collection of short stories written specifically for teenagers by authors who specialize in writing books for young people. Second, none of these stories has appeared in print before" (p. ix).

Although there is much variety in these collections, there is also some similarity. Many of the stories fit into general themes: cultures, death and dying, and coming of age, to mention only a few. The advantage is that these short stories can be used very effectively in thematic units. Seeing how differing authors treat a particular theme or

Poetry collections that would be of interest to young adults include the following:

Always Begin Where You Are, Walter Lamb
And Still I Rise, Maya Angelou
Back to Class, Mel Glenn
Collected Poems, Robert Hayden
The Dog Ate My Homework, Sara Holbrook
142 Ways to Make a Poem, James Swanson
A Fire in My Hands, Gary Soto
Feelings Make Me Real, Sara Holbrook
Good Night Willie Lee, I'll See You in the Morning, Alice Walker
If Only I Could Tell You: Poems for Young Lovers and Dreamers, Eve Merriam
I Never Said I Wasn't Difficult, Sara Holbrook
In the Trail of the Wind: American Indian Poems and Ritual Orations, John Beirhorst
Johnny's Song: Poetry of a Vietnam Veteran, Steve Mason
Just Give Me a Cool Drink of Water 'fore I Die, Maya Angelou
Lifelines, Leonard S. Moore
Looking for Your Name, Paul Janeczko, ed.
Love and Kisses, Lee Bennett Hopkins
Mindscapes: Poems for the Real World, Richard Peck
My Friend's Got This Problem, Mr. Candler, Mel Glenn
Nothing's the End of the World, Sara Holbrook
Now Sheba Sings the Song, Maya Angelou
Oh, Pray My Wings Are Gonna Fit Me Well, Maya Angelou
Poetry from A to Z, Paul Janeczko, ed.
Rainbow Writing, Eve Merriam
Reflections on a Gift of Watermelon Pickle, 2nd Ed., Stephan Dunning, et al.
Selected Poems, Gwendolyn Brooks
Selected Poems, Langston Hughes
Some Families, Sara Holbrook
Sounds & Silences: Poetry for Now, Richard Peck
Sports Pages, Arnold Adoff
Stardust Hotel, Paul Janeczko
Under All Silences: Shades of Love, Ruth Gordon
Walking on the Boundaries of Change, Sara Holbrook
When Elephants Last in the Dooryard Bloomed, Ray Bradbury
Where Did You Get That Red?, Kenneth Koch
Wishes, Lies, and Dreams, Kenneth Koch

FIGURE 6.6
Poetry collections for young adults

topic can be very beneficial to students. For example, in *Connections,* stories are grouped in four general themes: Encounters, Clashes, Surprises, and Insights. However, each story has a more specific theme such as boy–girl relationships, self-image, and parental and peer relations. It is interesting to note that in *Visions,* more than half of the stories have death or dying as the predominant theme.

Young adult writers have published collections of their own short stories. Robert Cormier, a prolific writer of short stories, has published *8 Plus 1,* an anthology of his stories that were judged exceptional by readers of his novels. Norma Fox Mazer also published collections of her short stories: *Dear Bill, Remember Me? & Other Stories* and *Summer Girls, Love Boys.* Chris Crutcher, whose short stories are found in other collections, has published a collection of his own titled *Athletic Shorts.* Other appropriate collections are listed in Figure 6.7.

Drama

Perhaps *Center Stage: One-Act Plays for Teenage Readers and Actors* (Gallo) will break the drought that students have faced in trying to find dramas written specifically for them. As in his short story collections, Don Gallo has called upon young adult writers to create plays solely for and about teenagers. *Center Stage* is a collection of 10 one-act plays by Alden Carter, Susan Beth Pfeffer, Lensey Namioka, Cin Forshay-Lunsford, Dallin Malmgren, Jean Davies Okimoto, Ouida Sebestyen, Sandy Asher, Walter Dean Myers, and Robin Brancato. As the book jacket blurb indicates, "Some of the plays are comic, some serious; all offer special insights into the concerns and triumphs of teenagers."

Before *Center Stage,* the field was very limited. Students found Aiken's *Street,* Zindel's *The Effect of Gamma Rays on Man-in-the-Moon Marigolds* and *Let Me Hear You Whisper,* and Rose's three-act television play *Twelve Angry Men* to their liking. In 1989, Sandy Asher published a powerful one-act play titled *A Woman Called Truth.* The play tells of the life of Sojourner Truth from the day she is sold away from her family, through her struggle to free herself and her son, to her emergence as a respected advocate of abolition and women's rights. The play is appropriate for young adults as well as adults.

Most of the plays found in anthologies and used in the classroom are the classics and have limited relevance to the young adult. A cross-section of the best dramas now available, some written for young adults and others for adults, appears in Figure 6.8. We hope *Center Stage* creates enough of a stir that other editors and publishers will publish new and creative plays for young adult readers.

Nonfiction

Young adult literature means young adult novels to most people, and some will realize that poetry and short stories are also making inroads. Few will think of nonfiction, although they should because many young adults—and adults—choose nonfiction.

Short story collections that may be appropriate for young adults include the following:

All Problems Are Simple, R. Benard
Am I Blue? Coming Out from the Silence, Marion Dane Bauer, ed.
America Street: A Multicultural Anthology of Stories, Ann Mazer, ed.
American Dragons: Twenty-five Asian American Voices, Laurence Yep
Badger on the Barge and Other Stories, Janni Howker
Bad Behavior, Mary Higgins Clark
Baseball in April and Other Stories, Gary Soto
Blue Skin of the Sea, Graham Salisbury
A Couple of Kooks and Other Stories about Love, Cynthia Rylant
*Do You Like It Here? And Other Stories—Twenty-one Views of the High School
    Years,* R. Benard
Early Sorrow: Ten Stories of Youth, Charlotte Zolotow
Face to Face, Thomas Pettepiece and Anatoly Aleksin
Front Porch Stories at the One-Room School, Eleanora Tate
Funny You Should Ask, David Gale, ed.
A Gathering of Flowers: Stories About Being Young in America, Joyce Thomas
Going Where I'm Coming From, Ann Mazer
Gorilla, My Love, Toni Cade Bambara
If This Is Love, I'll Take Spaghetti, Ellen Conford
I Love You, I Hate You, Get Lost, Ellen Conford
Into the Widening World: International Coming-of-Age Stories, John Loughery, ed.
Join In: Multiethnic Short Stories by Outstanding Writers for Young Adults,
    Don Gallo, ed.

FIGURE 6.7
Short story collections

Nonfiction for Young Adults from Delight to Wisdom (Carter & Abrahamson, 1991) starts with a detailed description of how literature is cataloged in libraries and, thus, gives the reader a sense of how the label *nonfiction* was born. Authors Carter and Abrahamson then offer the following definition of nonfiction: "Simply put, it's any book that's not a novel or a short story" (p. xii). They go on to group nonfiction as "factual books about topics such as the solar system, automobiles, curiosities and wonders, and cooking" as well as "informational works characterized by beautifully written prose, definable themes, unifying structure, and stimulating topics" (p. xii).

If only it were this easy to distinguish between the two forms. Novelists often gather many facts about the topic before any writing is done, and many informational writers make their literature exciting and stimulating for the reader. Perhaps, at best, all of it is just literature, whether it's a fictitious story based on data or a factual account with fictitious embellishments.

Local News, Gary Soto
More Scary Stories to Tell in the Dark, Alvin Schwartz
One Way or Another, Peter Cameron
Out of Time, Aidan Chambers
The People Could Fly, Virginia Hamilton
Point of Departure: 19 Stories of Youth and Discovery, Robert Gold
Rio Grande Stories, Carolyn Meyer
Scary Stories to Tell in the Dark, Alvin Schwartz
Shades of Dark, Aidan Chambers
Short Circuits: Thirteen Shocking Stories by Outstanding Writers for Young Adults, Don Gallo, ed.
Short Takes, Elizabeth Segel
Stepping Stones: 17 Powerful Stories of Growing Up, Robert Gold
The Stone Canoe and Other Stories, John Peyton
Things That Go Bump in the Night: A Collection of Original Stories, Jane Yolen and Martin Greenberg
Thirteen Tales of Horror, T. Pines
To Break the Silence: Thirteen Short Stories for Young Readers, P. Barrett
2041, Jane Yolen
A Very Brief Season, Barbara Girion
Warlock at the Wheel, Diana Jones
Within Reach: Ten Stories, Don Gallo, ed.
A Whisper in the Night, Joan Aiken
Young Monsters, Isaac Asimov

Young people like to read nonfiction. Interest and circulating surveys strongly indicate that children and young adults are avid readers of nonfiction. Interestingly, this interest in nonfiction spans ability levels. Surveys of reading habits indicate that low-ability students are as interested in nonfiction as gifted students are. Most of the surveys indicate that nonfiction is read as casual reading; little is done in the class-room. Because nonfiction has made its mark on young adults' reading habits, it should be a part of the curriculum.

As we noted earlier in this chapter, nonfiction can be easily incorporated into the curriculum as parts of thematic units, as choices when groups read literature, or as choices on students' individual reading lists. Whether the nonfiction is a book on career or college choices, a self-help or how-to book, or one that details the atrocities of the Holocaust, students can and will benefit from the author's craft and the book's content. Carter and Abrahamson, leading advocates of nonfiction, offer a list of non-fiction titles in the January issue of *English Journal* 1990—an article worth reading. Our nonfiction suggestions are listed in Figure 6.9.

Drama selections, some young adult and some not, that may be appropriate and of interest to young people include the following:

The Bad Seed, Maxwell Anderson
Children of a Lesser God, Mark Medoff
The Code Breaker, P. Conley
The Crucible, Arthur Miller
Dags, Debra Oswald
Dancing With Strangers, Sandra Fenichel Asher
Diary of a Young Girl, Anne Frank
Go Ask Alice, adapted by Frank Shiras
Hey There—Hello!, Gennadi Mamlin
Inherit the Wind, Jerome Lawrence and Robert Lee
Langston, Ossie Davis
Little Old Ladies in Tennis Shoes, Sandra Fenichel Asher
Mass Appeal, Ossie Davis
Meeting the Winter Bike Rider and Other Prize Winning Plays, Wendy Lamb
The Miracle Worker, William Gibson
The Night Thoreau Spent in Jail, Jerome Lawrence and Robert Lee
Our Town, Thornton Wilder
The Outsiders, adapted by Christopher Sergel
Pygmalion, George Bernard Shaw
A Separate Peace, adapted by Nancy Pahl Gilsenan
Seven Ages of Anne, Jennifer Fell Hayes
Sunday, Sunday, Sandra Fenichel Asher
Theatre for Youth: Twelve Plays with Mature Themes, Coleman A. Jennings and
    Gretta Berghammer, eds.
The Wise Men of Chelm, Sandra Fenichel Asher
Who Cares?, Gillian M. Wadds

Markets for plays for young people:

Plays, Inc., 120 Boylston St., Boston, MA 02116
Anchorage Press, Box 8067, New Orleans, LA 70182
Dramatic Publishing Co., 311 Washington St., Woodstock, IL 60098
New Plays, Inc., Box 5074, Charlottesville, VA 22905

FIGURE 6.8
Drama for young people

ONE BOOK, ONE STUDENT

This organizational structure perhaps best considers the needs and interests of students. Reading interests and difficulty, developmental stages that young people face, and intellectual ability are all considered before suggesting a book to a particular student. Traditionally, this arrangement has been used for the book report. In most classrooms, teachers have book reports due every 6 or 9 weeks; students usually have optimum choice of reading for this assignment. This organization can also be used from time to time with regular classroom reading.

Leighton (1991) describes a similar program of reading that she calls "saturation reading." When students read their own books, the classroom becomes a reading laboratory. Although teachers usually use one book for the entire class or three or four books with groups, they should not be limited to those arrangements. These three organizations make up a continuum that moves students from the most restrictive to the least restrictive, from dependence to independence in their reading. Therefore, teachers may wish to include all arrangements in the classroom, using the first at the beginning of the year and the third toward the end of the year. In this way, students will have more responsibility for their reading/literature program.

What books should students read? This question frequently gives teachers pause, as there are so many from which to choose. Teachers wonder if they should provide a list from which students choose their reading for a particular assignment. Others question this approach because they see a list as being too restrictive—and all books cannot be listed! The list cannot be all inclusive, but many teachers need lists for suggestions and, therefore, perhaps students need a source from which to select "just the right book."

We have not provided a list of books in this section; we have placed it in Appendix C. Students could readily use many of the books in their individualized reading programs. Teachers will find a wide variety represented. The list includes works by Robert Cormier, Sue Ellen Bridgers, Chris Crutcher, Lois Duncan, S. E. Hinton, Judy Blume, Betty Greene, Paula Danziger, M. E. Kerr, and others—all authors of quality literature for young people.

After students have read their individual books, other students should benefit from this reading. Part of the beauty of reading a wonderful piece of literature is sharing it with others, much like moviegoers share after viewing a film. To have students read good literature but not have them in some way share their reactions to that reading seems unfair and certainly unwise. This sharing can take many forms: formal book talks to the class, sharing in small groups, displays of projects related to the books read, and a variety of writing activities that can be read by other students. We are *not* suggesting that students take a test where no one knows about the responses to the work but the teacher.

The following activities are a few ideas that students can use to share what they have read with their peers. Some are to be written, some are to be oral, some can be either; all, we think, are creative.

1. Two students who have read the same book develop a "meet the author" spot for a talk show. One student assumes the identity of the host/inter-

While it is impossible to list here all nonfiction titles that are appropriate for young adults, we have selected a representative few that will be useful to the classroom teacher.

The Abortion Controversy, Carol Emmens
Ain't Gonna Study War No More, Milton Meltzer
All Creatures Great and Small, James Herriot (and others in the series)
American Dreams Lost and Found, Studs Terkel
Anguished English, Richard Lederer
Balm in Gilead, Sara Lawrence Lightfoot
Black Dance in America, James Haskins
Born to the Land, Brent Ashabranner
Chapters: My Growth as a Writer, Lois Duncan
Cheap Raw Material, Milton Meltzer
Children of the Wild West, Russell Freedman
Columbus and the World Around Him, Milton Meltzer
The Cookcamp, Gary Paulsen
Crews, Maria Hinojosa
Dark Harvest, Brent Ashabranner
Dear America: Letters Home from Vietnam, B. Edelman
Don't be S.A.D.: A Teenage Guide to Handling Stress, Anxiety & Depression, Susan Newman
Dove, Robin Graham
Draw 50 books, L. Ames (series)
The Elephant Man, Frederick Drimmer
Ethics, Susan Neiburg Terkel
Fighting Back: What Some People Are Doing About AIDS, S. Kuklin
The Foxfire Books, Eliot Wigginton
Go Tell It on the Mountain, James Baldwin
The Guinness Book of Amazing Achievements
The Guinness Book of World Records
Heartbreak and Roses: Real Life Stories of Troubled Love, Janet Body and Stan Mack
Homecoming: When the Soldiers Returned from Vietnam, Robert Greene
How to Get into College, Clifford Caine
The Kids Book About Death and Dying: By and for Kids, Eric Rofes
Kids (Still) Having Kids, Janet Bode
Kids At Work, Russell Freedman
I Know Why the Caged Bird Sings, Maya Angelou
Kon-Tiki, Thor Heyerdahl
Lincoln: A Photobiography, Russell Freedman
Maggie's American Dream, James Comer
Me, Me, Me, Me, Me: Not a Novel, M. E. Kerr
Never Cry Wolf, Farley Mowat
The New Read-Aloud Handbook, J. Trelease

FIGURE 6.9
Representative nonfiction books for young adults

Night, Elie Wiesel
Now Is Your Time!, Walter Dean Myers
100 Questions & Answers About AIDS: What You Need to Know Now, Michael Thomas Ford
One More River to Cross, Jim Haskins
People Who Make a Difference, Brent Ashabranner
Presenting Cynthia Voight, Suzanne E. Reid
Presenting Judy Blume, Maryann Weidt
Presenting Madeleine L'Engle, Donald R. Hettings
Presenting M. E. Kerr, Alleen Nilsen
Presenting Norma Fox Mazer, Sally Holtze
Presenting Norma Klein, Allene Phy
Presenting Paul Zindel, Jack Forman
Presenting Ouida Sebestyen, Virginia Monseau
Presenting Richard Peck, Donald Gallo
Presenting Robert Cormier, Patricia Campbell
Presenting Rosa Guy, Jerrie Norris
Presenting S. E. Hinton, Jay Daly
Presenting Sue Ellen Bridgers, Ted Hipple
Presenting Walter Dean Myers, Rudine Bishop
Presenting William Sleator, James Davis and Hazel Davis
Presenting Zibby Oneal, Susan Bloom and Cathryn Mercier
Speaking Out: Teenagers Talk on Sex, Race, and Identity, Susan Kuklin
Straight Talk About Death for Teenagers: How to Cope with Losing Someone You Love,
    Earl A. Grollman
Teenage Fathers, Karen Gravelle and Leslie Peterson
Teens with AIDS Speak Out, Mary Kittredge
Teen Age Perspectives Series, Ruth K. J. Cline, series editor
    Focus on Families, Ruth K. J. Cline
    Focus on Physical Impairments, Nicholas Karolides
    Focus on School, Beverly Haley
    Focus on Sexuality, Elizabeth Poe
    Focus on Teens in Trouble, Daryl Sander
Tell Them We Remember, Susan Bachrach
To Be a Slave, Julius Lester
The Truth About the Ku Klux Klan, Melton Meltzer
Unbuilding, David Macaulay
Voices from the Civil War, Milton Meltzer
The Voices of Rape, Janet Bode
The Way Things Work, David Macaulay
What Makes You Special? Eda LeShan
Woodsong, Gary Paulsen
Zen and the Art of Motorcycle Maintenance: An Inquiry into Values, Robert Pirsig

viewer and the other that of the author. Students can also try another version of the same activity, replacing the author with the main character.

2. Students can give an effective booktalk, giving other students information about their books. These booktalks can be videotaped and placed in the library for others to see.

3. Students who are musical can select background music to enhance an oral reading of specific passages of their book. Students will need to provide background information so the passages will be fully understood.

4. Students who have read the same book can put a character in the book on trial for a crime he or she committed. The students then present the prosecuting case and the defense case.

5. After picking a national or school issue, students compose a speech on that topic to be given by one of the major characters in the book. The speech should reflect the character's personality and beliefs. In groups of five to seven, students share their books with each other. The sharing should include a general overview of the plot, setting, and theme, plus a personal response that should include, but is not limited to, why they liked or disliked the book.

6. Students complete a responding report (see Chapter 3) and then make these reports available in various parts of the room so that other students can read about books that have been read.

7. Students can write one of the following letters about books they have read. The letters are then displayed so other students can read them.

   a. A letter to a friend explaining why the student thinks the book will make enjoyable reading.
   b. A letter from one of the book's characters to another, and a responding letter from the second character.
   c. A letter of advice to a character on how to handle his or her problem.
   d. A letter to the school librarian giving reasons why he should or should not recommend this book to other students.

8. Students take an interesting character, other than the main character, and write an original short story with this secondary character as the main character.

9. Students write book reviews of their books and publish them in a class collection. Teachers may exchange these collections with other classes and other teachers.

10. Teachers organize a book fair in which book projects and book responses are displayed around the room. Students work with other students who have read the same book or books with similar themes to create an original display that represents their books. This display may include, but is not limited to, written responses, collages showing the thematic thread that runs through the books, pictures of well-known actors and actresses who could

play the book characters in a film of the book and why they made those choices, or journals that were kept by students as they read their books.

11. Students present to the class a rationale on why their books should be considered "quality" books. They could include: character development, plot structure, universal themes, and specific examples of the writer's craft.

The importance of these or similar activities is that students are sharing what they have read, which will encourage others to read.

ἓ‍ **Learning Log Responses** ἓ‍

How do you determine the quality of a book? In your learning log, explain what a book has to do or have to be a quality book for you.

What arrangement for teaching literature best suits you? Do you prefer having one book read by everyone, a few books related by theme read by groups of students, or each student read his book? Explain what approach you will use and why.

Choose and read a collection of poetry, short stories, and drama. Write a brief entry about the content of each collection, its appropriateness for young adults, and the way you would use the collection in your classroom.

REFERENCES

Carter, B., & Abrahamson, R. (1990). Nonfiction: The missing piece in the middle. *English Journal, 80* (1), 52–58.

Carter, B., & Abrahamson, R. (1991). *Nonfiction for young adults from delight to wisdom.* Phoenix: Oryx.

Leighton, Dolly. (1991). Saturating students with reading: A classroom lab approach. *English Journal, 80* (6), 81–85.

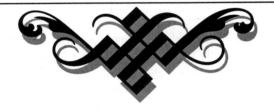

CHAPTER

7

Young Adult Literature and the Classics

Classics: Books people praise but don't read.

Mark Twain

Teachers are torn between teaching the literature that they feel will be most useful to their students and the literature that everyone else thinks that they ought to teach. The struggle is not just with high school English teachers, but with middle and upper elementary language arts teachers as well.

As we visit classrooms and talk to teachers, we find more and more emphasis being placed on what many have come to call "good" literature, the euphemistic term given to the body of literature called "the classics." In fact, a survey that asked 322 public schools to list those books most frequently required in those schools (Applebee, 1989) showed the following ten most frequently cited titles: (1) *Romeo and Juliet*, (2) *Macbeth*, (3) *Huckleberry Finn*, (4) *To Kill a Mockingbird*, (5) *Julius Caesar*, (6) *The Pearl*, (7) *The Scarlet Letter*, (8) *Of Mice and Men*, (9) *Lord of the Flies*, and (10) *Anne Frank: The Diary of a Young Girl*. Interestingly, when compared to a similar study done in 1963, little change has occurred in the nearly thirty years of teaching literature in high schools.

Our concern (in addition to the lack of women and minority writers) is that in the twenty-seven most frequently mentioned titles in the Applebee study, the emphasis is still on literature that has very little relationship to the adolescent. However, at least in the top ten mentioned, *To Kill a Mockingbird, Lord of the Flies, Romeo and Juliet, Anne Frank*, and *Huckleberry Finn* do have some connection to the young adult. When we talk further with teachers about the literature in the classroom, we find that students do not enjoy what they are reading; in fact, many are not reading at all but simply hearing about what they were supposed to read—in essence, hearing a translation of the literature.

Why do teachers feel that they have to teach the classics? What does the research say about the relationship between young adults and the literature they read? What are the alternatives to having a curriculum comprised of just the classics? We explore these questions and others in the following pages.

WHAT DO THE STUDENTS SAY?

In a time of school restructuring, school reorganization, and curriculum evaluation, many "experts" surface to tell school officials what to do and how to go about doing it. Most of these experts, however, are outside of education. Those who work within the schools every day don't have much credibility. Boards of education commission experts to analyze the various components of schooling and to offer assistance in the effort to make changes. Often the two groups—teachers and students—are not asked for input regarding the changes that ought to be made. Therefore, a study such as Sullivan's (1991), who asked her students for information about their reading interests and habits, is refreshing. The results of her survey were not surprising.

> There were a few exceptions. Very few. The trend was clear, undeniable. I can't say that this took me completely by surprise. I have suspected the dark truth for a long time, had been working to develop strategies for counteracting the forces that work in school to separate students from the pleasure and the transforming power of read-

ing. But I had never had to stare the fact in the face like this before. What I saw was painful. It raised difficult questions. It was, ultimately, instructive.

In some cases, school had caused these bright students to abandon reading completely. More often—thank goodness!—enthusiastic readers remained enthusiastic about their own outside-of-school reading and hated (or, at best, remained indifferent to) only what they had to do for school. They clung to the pleasure of reading in spite of us. Sometimes we made them suffer for the choice. (p. 40)

This summary of the students' attitudes toward school literature reminded us of a statement made by a ninth grader we know. He said, "I love to read, but I hate literature." When prompted to continue this thought, he suggested that what he was reading in school had nothing, or at least very little, to do with him. He told us that his book report (one due every 9 weeks) offered some relief since he could, most of the time, choose something that he knew he would like, but what he read in the classroom was, as he called it, "dumb."

Sullivan (1991) asked students to share their thoughts about the literature taught in schools and their relationship to that literature. The details these students offer supports the previous summary. Most have had a very exciting experience with literature during their elementary schooling, but the break in this happy experience comes as they entered junior high/middle school. Their loss of interest in reading generally comes in the seventh or eighth grade and, most of the time, continues through high school. Some students are creative and work things out for themselves. Louis is a case in point:

"Finally in tenth grade I just started reading all the time. At first it was because I actually had spare time, but then I really began reading because I started using 'Mr. Cliff' and then I had tons of time for my own reading." (Sullivan, 1991, p. 41)

Amy makes an interesting point:

"In high school came the assigned movies and textbook reading. They were OK, but I would have liked to go through them a bit faster so that we could have read some more modern things. I hate that we only read 'old' things. In English I read one of the modern short stories that we skipped in class. It was the best story in the book." (Sullivan, 1991, p. 42)

And Melissa:

"In my tenth grade English class, we had to choose something to read off a list. There were all sorts of wonderful things I wanted to read like *Lord of the Flies* and *I Never Promised You a Rose Garden,* but I chose mine too late because I couldn't make a choice. All the best had been taken and I found my self stuck with *The Death of a Salesman*. I hated it with a purple passion! After that assignment was over I went back to the library and found *I Never Promised You a Rose Garden*." (Sullivan, 1991, p. 42)

Although there were a number of relevant choices from which Melissa could choose something that she liked, the tragedy is that there were not enough of them on the list, so Melissa could not read something of her choice, but something that she hated.

There is obviously a wide chasm between what the school offers for students to read and what the students want to read in the literature program. It is also obvious to us that many students will get along some way within this dichotomy, but the question arises, Why should they have to? It is also obvious that many students are not successful—they simply stop reading. Vogel and Zancanella (1991) make an interesting point:

> Some of us spend a great deal of energy trying to draw a clear line between the seri-ous study of "literature" and the undisciplined consumption of "entertainment." Others try to erase such lines so that Stephen King can slide up against Shakespeare. What such maneuvering often fails to take into account, however, are the realities of ongoing literary experiences of adolescents in and out of school. For all the recent quarrels about the canon, about what seventeen-year-olds should know, about who's culturally literate and who ain't, little attention has been paid to the kinds of "literary lives" teenagers lead and to how those lives connect or fail to connect with the learn-ing of literature in English class. (p. 54)

Vogel and Zancanella go on to share the literary lives of four adolescents, and their findings are not unlike Sullivan's. These four adolescents have very little interest in the literature found in the classroom, but do have interest in what they read outside of the school. And that interest outside the classroom is varied. One student has a fondness for romances; another thinks mysteries are great reading. "For Donnovan, school remains a problem. Literature in school means absorbing the viewpoint of the teacher. From his viewpoint his interpretation will always be unaccountably different from those of his teachers" (p. 57). However, Donnovan's love for music, art, and movies shows a different set of interests.

Small (1972) shares Donnovan's concern. He points out that the generally accepted goal of a high school literature program seems to place the student at a great disadvantage while the teacher is placed as the source for the meaning of the literature read. Students have had fewer experiences—and for some, no experience at all—in such areas as marriage and divorce, ambition, greed, and hate, so it is more difficult for them to make honest responses about what meaning is there for them. In contrast, when the content of the book has a teenager as the protagonist and other young adult characters, the balance of knowledge and the authority that is brought to that reading is changed. Young adults are more easily able to evaluate the characters, their problems, and the resolution of these problems.

What Vogel and Zancanella are saying is very similar to the results of Langer's (1984) study, "Literacy Instruction in American High Schools: Problems and Per-spectives." In this study, Langer suggests that literacy instruction is differentially determined by who the students are and what world views and interests they bring to the classroom.

> While syntax, word length, and vocabulary have been shown to affect text difficulty, more recent views of reading comprehension suggest that ease of comprehension is also a function of the reader's knowledge and experiences . . . the contextual variables that affect and are affected by the purpose for reading and the environment sur-rounding the reading experience. (p. 122)

In *Voices of Readers* (1988), Carlsen and Sherrill present excerpts from reading/literature autobiographies of their students. It is interesting to note the authors' summary regarding attitudes toward the classics:

> It seems fairly clear that most of these people's taste had to reach a certain level of maturity before the classics were appreciated. Some mention their senior high school English classes as being responsible for their interest in the classics, but more often, it was not until their college English courses that they began to understand the reasons for labeling a literary work as "classic." Even then, some respondents had been so traumatized by their earlier exposure to a particular title that they could never overcome their distaste for it. (p. 135)

Students seem to be saying that what they are asked to read in school is far removed from their experiences out of school and far removed from what is of interest to them. When students have something to read that reflects their interests, most will read. When this is not the case, students either do enough to get by or simply give up and stop reading.

DEVELOPING LIFETIME READERS

As we have noted, one of the most important goals for any public school at any level is to foster reading so that students develop into lifelong readers. We would argue that schools are not succeeding. Lesesne (1991) surveyed middle school students and found that "almost seventy-five percent of the middle school students reported reading less than one hour daily on a regular basis; twenty percent had read only one book for their own enjoyment in the last six months" (p. 61).

O'Connor (1980) believes it isn't that students in schools can't read, it is that they don't want to read because of the lack of connection between the reader and what is read. Angelotti (1981) concludes that the literature curriculum has contributed to the lack of reading by adults. He suggests that school curricula have produced less than 5 percent of adults who read serious literature. A study of more than 200,000 sixth graders in California revealed that 70 percent rarely read for pleasure (Trelease, 1982).

Results of a study titled, "A Profile of the American Eighth Grader" (1990) completed by the U.S. Department of Education show that eighth-grade students in public, private independent, and Catholic schools have something in common: They don't read much for fun. Regardless of where these students went to school, they spent two hours or less each week reading on their own. Schools have made some attempt to increase the amount of reading that occurs after formal schooling. Programs such as sustained silent reading, directed individualized reading, elective courses that allow students a choice of what they read, and modeling by teachers to show the importance of reading have made some impact, but not much. We still have a society that is made up of many nonreaders.

The research indicates what makes lifelong readers (Lesesne, 1991), and from what students offer about their reading habits in and out of school, an additional change must occur in the English classroom. These add-ons to the English curriculum may provide some help, but the curriculum itself should be modified to include literature that allows students to make some connection between themselves and the text that they read, to find relationships between them and the developmental tasks that they must accomplish, and to read at a level at which comprehension can come with little difficulty. Reading literature in the classroom must be closely related to the independent reading of literature outside of the classroom. Atwell (1987) suggests:

> If we want our adolescent students to grow to appreciate literature, another first step is allowing them to exert ownership and choose the literature they will read. Preliminary to that, we might take a giant step as readers ourselves and acknowledge that the term "literature" embraces more than the risk-free, prescribed junior high canon or second-rate Dickens (*A Tale of Two Cities*), second-rate Steinbeck (*The Red Pony*), and second-rate Hemingway (*Old Man and the Sea*). The last twenty years have witnessed an explosion in the numbers of novels and short stories written expressly for young adults, adolescent literature of such breadth and depth that no teacher need ever apologize for building a curriculum around kids' responses to their own books. (p. 161)

Certainly, out-of-classroom reading does not have to be identical to the in-classroom reading since the classroom should foster growth in literary experiences. But as Probst (1984) indicates:

> If students read with no other purpose in mind than to find and recall information, we may legitimately wonder if they have had a more significant literary experience than that of the student who reads only a summary. (p. 9) . . . If a work touches upon matters in which students have a vital interest, and if the students can read it with enough ease to be able to grasp the fundamental issues, then they may respond strongly enough to the text. (p. 40)

Therefore, the decisions that must be made by teachers and curriculum directors seem obvious: Literature that relates in meaningful ways to adolescents in middle and high schools should be a very strong part of the English curriculum if we want to increase the numbers of lifelong readers. Carlsen and Sherrill (1988) conclude that to produce readers, students at almost every level should be exposed to a variety of reading fare, participate in reader-centered discussions of literature, generate nontraditional book reports, and be allowed freedom of choice in reading fare.

WHY EMPHASIZE THE CLASSICS?

The Back-to-Basics Movements

Throughout modern schooling, there has always been some concern about the quality of education. This emphasis surfaces periodically with new concerns, frequently about different issues. Not long ago, the concern centered on our students being able to compete with students in other countries; in the 1950s, during the Sputnik era, the concern was with the quality of science and math instruction. The nation's school and society went through a much more liberal time during the 1960s and early 1970s.

Following this emphasis on experimentation and self-discovery, educators, some reluctantly, accepted the back-to-basics movement in which teachers and administrators removed most electives comprised of thematic units that emphasized more contemporary literature and replaced this more creative curriculum design with one that emphasized the use of the anthology. This usually provided the student with a chronological presentation of American literature for juniors and English literature for seniors. The anthologies for lower high school and middle school contained literature often thematically related but very little literature that could be identified as specifically for the young adult.

Curricula of the 1980s and 1990s continue this tradition of including the literature of the past—the literature most commonly called "the classics." The emphasis of publications calling for school and curricula reform often includes suggestions about the English curriculum, usually calling for literature that will help students understand their literary heritage. What often is called for is a standardized list—sometimes a list of literary works that all students should have read by the time they leave high school and sometimes a list of educational areas, topics, or concepts that all should know about.

One of the current lists is from E. D. Hirsch, Jr. In *Cultural Literacy: What Every American Needs to Know* (1987), Hirsch sets forth a plan for making cultural literacy an educational priority. He defines core knowledge, wants textbook writers to put more of this information in the textbooks, and wants to develop tests of core learning that can be used by students to measure their progress. His list includes titles, areas, and issues. *A Nation at Risk* (1984) also calls for more emphasis on the study of literature that will increase students' cultural literacy.

Two dangers seem apparent with lists (Mullican, 1991): (1) Whose culture and whose literacy is represented by the lists? It seems that the diverse population is not considered. (2) Lists will probably mean that the "culturally literate need know only titles, not entire literary works" (p. 244). *Educational Leadership* (December 1991– January 1992) discusses this concern for diversity and concern for a cultural literacy.

Our concern is that many students are not cognitively or emotionally ready to read and understand many of the works that appear on these lists. Since American education tries to educate the total population of students with varying ability levels from kindergarten through grade 12, many of these students cannot handle some of the specific works that are recommended. Many are just too difficult. As we read these lists and the tables of contents in anthologies, it is clear that adult literature is being recommended. For example, Charles Dickens wrote for adults: His primary goal was to share with adults the social problems of nineteenth-century England as he saw them, and it was delivered to these adults by periodicals in installments. That information should give teachers pause as they think of selecting literature for twentieth- and twenty-first–century young people. Most of the teachers that we talk to acknowledge that many of their students are not ready for this adult literature.

The Importance of the Anthology

Another very important reason for the continued emphasis on classic literature is the prominent place the anthology has in the English classroom. There is a mystique about placing literature in a hardback collection. Accompanying this collection are strategies on how to use the material, including questions that can be asked prior to, during, and following the reading of any piece of literature. Also, this total package often includes a testing program. By purchasing the anthology package, teachers receive more than just the literature.

Certainly the anthology makes it easier for school districts to buy materials for groups of students spread over a number of grades. But therein lies one of the difficulties. When teachers use a particular anthology, they are assuming that all students in a particular class can and will read the literature found in the book. Evidence indicates the contrary. All eighth graders or eleventh graders are not alike, not even close. The reading level, the emotional level, and the developmental level of adolescents vary significantly in each grade level. We find it difficult to recommend the use of anthologies when teaching a diverse set of students.

Sullivan (1991) mentioned Amy's concern about having to read so many "old" pieces of literature. Amy and many teachers do not realize that including old pieces keeps the cost of the anthology down. Authors of literature that is in public domain do not receive royalty payments when that literature is used in an anthology. Even with this consideration, the anthology is quite expensive, which leaves little money for supplemental reading material. Therefore, the emphasis is given to the literature in the collection.

The Chicken-or-Egg Theory of Classics

The major factor used to determine classics is time. Charles Dickens's literature is considered classic primarily because it has stood the test of time. Of course, classic literature addresses the human condition and has a particular quality that we have come to equate with "great" literature. Time, however, is the deciding factor, since contemporary literature that also addresses the human condition rarely is considered a classic.

A number of questions arise concerning this time element. Have the classics withstood the test of time because they are great literature? Or have they withstood the test of time because they are required reading in college English classes, and because they are included in anthologies that are "read" by thousands and thousands of public school students and read again when some of them go on to college? We pose this question only to suggest further discussion about a very important issue that makes a major impact on the reading program of young adults.

The University Wants Them Taught

The influence on high school literature programs of postsecondary institutions is perceived rather than direct. Colleges and universities do not tell high schools or their teachers what to teach, although this was not always so. During the early and mid 1900s, colleges and universities distributed lists of books that students who graduate from high school ought to have read, and it was expected that students would read the books.

While this is no longer *formally* done, the lists still exist, and teachers who want their students to do well in college often get them so that they can include these books in their high school English classes. They apparently operate on the philosophy that if it is good for college students, it is good for high school students.

It is important to note, however, the type of literature that is often taught in freshman and sophomore courses at colleges and universities. If our analysis is correct, most programs emphasize writing at the freshman level, with some literature in the form of essays and other short pieces. Sophomore English is often a variety of contemporary literature with, again, an emphasis on writing. It is not until the junior year that the British and American canons are taught; and, of course, students who take these courses are English majors or at least, majors who have a close connection to the English field. It would seem to us that the colleges and universities have, through their reading lists and course offerings, forced the teaching of the classics to the high school level. We believe that this practice is inappropriate. In keeping with what we know about the classics, they are by far more appropriate for college-level students.

English professors that we have talked to prefer incoming students that have competent writing, literary analysis, and discussion skills (all of which can be accomplished with quality young adult literature) instead of having a knowledge base of literature that they may or may not have understood in high school.

We should also point out that most college and university teacher education programs for English teachers include a major in English, which usually includes approximately twenty hours in British, American, and world literature with almost all of those coming from the traditional, classic literature. Many colleges and universities will require some study of adolescent literature, but may not have a separate course that connects the adolescent literature with the methods course. English teachers have little to use as models: Their high school literature and their college literature programs are classics oriented.

Guilt

We suppose that some teachers have a sense of guilt if they do not stick with the canon. Certainly, no one can attack teachers for believing that educated people ought to know something of their literary heritage. Generally, the middle and high schools have become the place where that occurs, whether or not it is appropriate for these students. Teachers feel, and rightly so, that they are members of a team and want to be a team player, so if the department chair or the curriculum guide says to teach *Silas Marner*, teachers are hard pressed not to do it even if they feel it's a waste of time. However, there are a few teachers who don't go along with the crowd just because everybody is doing it. We take our hats off to them for the stands that they are taking.

THE CLASSICS AND WHY YOUNG ADULTS HAVE PROBLEMS READING THEM

In addition to the other problems facing young adults and teachers as they read and teach classics, there are two built-in problems that are difficult to overcome: The classics were written for adults, and they were written for an audience that doesn't exist today.

The classics were really not intended to be read by young people at all. Even though this literature may indeed speak to the universal human condition, young people have trouble relating because they have not experienced many of those human conditions. In addition, the classics are written in a style, syntax, and vocabulary that are often quite foreign to young adult readers. Along with the survival of time, the classics are lovingly guarded by some for their stylistic prestige. It is this stylistic prominence that elevates the classic to the high level. Yet it is this elevation that makes appreciation and understanding unattainable for the young adult.

O'Donnell (1983) chronicles attitudes concerning the use of classic literature in the classroom. In this report, she shares the opinion of Robert Carlsen: "It is true that classic literature is one of the most difficult, most subtle and most mature expressions of human beings, so it is no surprise that an understanding and enjoyment of the classics comes, if at all, fairly late in a reader's growth" (O'Donnell, 1983, p. 48). Holbrook (1982) agrees: "Unfortunately, students are often introduced to these often difficult and irrelevant works just when their lives hold so much to distract them from reading . . . it takes a special kind of story to maintain their interest in reading" (p. 378).

Since this understanding and enjoyment of the classics rarely occurs in many students at the middle and high school levels, teachers resort to picking apart and dissecting the literature so that the students can get something out of the classroom presentation. Shaw's (1935) comment, written long ago, may still be appropriate today: "Well meaning English teachers once dissected them [the classics] for us, poked around for the intangible in them, tried to unscrew the inscrutable for us and fixed us for the most part so we shall never open these books again" (p. 110). Robert Frost makes a similar point:

> "I don't want to analyze authors. I want to enjoy them. I want the boys in class to enjoy their books because of what's in them. . . . Youth, I believe, should not analyze its enjoyments. It should live. Criticism is the province of age, not youth. They'll get to that soon enough. Let them build up a friendship with the written word first." (Newdick, 1936, p. 632)

Carlsen and Sherrill (1988) summarize why some adults are not interested in reading:

> The most tragic of all the records, however, are those describing the traumatic experiences that children had with teachers and other adults. They were told they were poor readers, which made them feel inadequate as human beings and thereby fueled their determination to stay as far away as possible from this demeaning activity. Others became embarrassed in front of their classmates because of their teachers' comments about their poor oral reading skills. And still others were forced to read books that they found distasteful because these books were beyond either their comprehension or their interests. (p. 143)

The argument is not that students cannot make literary analyses in what they read or that they should never read a classic. The argument centers around what we know about the young adult, what we know about that body of literature we have come to call "the classics," and how all of this can lead teachers to do what is appropriate for their students. If teachers want their students to hone their thinking skills and they want to use literature to aid in the process, then teachers should select literature that students can understand and respond to. When this happens, students have a common core of knowledge that is suitable for them to use in these thinking processes.

Of course, quality young adult literature can also be explored. It is folly to think that students can respond only to universal themes, literary techniques, and the craft of specific authors by reading and studying only the classics. Literary analysis can and does occur when using most young adult literature recommended for middle and high school. In addition, some students may have progressed to the point where they are emotionally, experientially, cognitively, and developmentally ready to read this traditional adult literature. If this occurs, teachers should encourage students to explore what interests them with the classics, but until then, teachers may find more success if they have students read the literature that is best suited for them. If students can have success with young adult literature, they may very well continue the reading process as they move from the school setting. Daigon (1969) sums up this point of view in his response to a critic of young adult literature:

> Yes, you say, but what of the wisdom of ages, the great ideas and passions of the most sensitive and the most skilled, the great canon of the literary tradition, the great books, the noble concepts, the jewels of our intellectual and aesthetic heritage?
>
> Do we have the courage to confront the cruel reality that the literary heritage barely lives and does so in the minds of a handful of critics, intellectuals, and teachers? And it is losing ground fast as the media revolution and general antagonism to traditions and establishments gain momentum.
>
> If we feel that literature does offer modes of experience and pleasures not otherwise available, and if we feel that these experiences and pleasures are worth passing on to new generations, the principles of relevance, variety, involvement, and developmental appropriateness will surely have to play major roles in literature instruction in the secondary school. If we feel that we cannot or should not do these things, let us honestly put literature away in a museum display case with other relics to be viewed, to be revered, and to be eulogized in hushed tones reserved for the dead. (p. 39)

YOUNG ADULT LITERATURE AS A BRIDGE TO THE CLASSICS

We hesitate to discuss the use of young adult literature as bridges to reading and studying the classics because we are generally opposed to using the classics in the middle and high schools. We firmly believe that 12- to 17-year-olds need to read literature that helps them grow in making literary responses and analyses and that relates to each individual in meaningful ways. To those few juniors and seniors in high school who have grown significantly in meeting their interests and their developmental needs so that they can respond effectively to what they read, we certainly recommend selected classics for the curriculum. However, we do know that many students have not arrived at this level, but the classics are what they will read in their English classrooms.

Our suggestion asks teachers to precede the classics with selected young adult literature that is similar in theme or focus to the classics. In this way, students can succeed at discovering meaning and understanding the literary craft in literature at their developmental level before undertaking the analysis of literature at a higher level. Small (1977) argues: "If you were, for example, trying to teach a child how a jet or automobile engine works, it surely would be better not to use the engines of a 747 or the most advanced racing cars" (p. 56). Experience with making personal responses, analyzing literary techniques, and evaluating the writer's craft with the young adult novel may provide readers with the needed tools in literature study that may help when they are faced with reading adult literature. We'll start by discussing the connecting elements of a few pairings. Additional pairings follow. For a more in-depth study of pairings of young adult literature with the classics, see Kaywell's (1993–1995) two-volume, *Adolescent Literature as a Complement to the Classics*.

The Pairings: A Few in Detail

THE SCARLET LETTER. *The Scarlet Letter* by Nathaniel Hawthorne is found in most high school curricula and is often read by juniors. The novel's complex sentence structure and vocabulary present many problems for high school students. The contemporary student has additional difficulty with Puritanism as well as with some of the complex emotions that Hawthorne includes: despair, anger, grief, guilt, vengeance, and purification by suffering. Hawthorne's use of symbolism and his use of the setting as an emotional companion contribute to the difficulty in understanding the novel.

Samuels and Lowery-Moore (1987) suggest using a young adult novel that offers much the same Puritan atmosphere. *The Witch of Blackbird Pond* (Speare) tells the story of a young girl from Barbados who moves to Connecticut. She finds a very repressive atmosphere.

They also suggest *Sharelle* (Neufeld) because it also offers many similarities to the Hawthorne novel. Sharelle is a young adult who becomes pregnant at a time in her life when she is in need of love and affection. In addition, the reader knows very early in the novel the identity of the child's father; however, Sharelle (like Hester) does not reveal his identity. Throughout the novel, readers see the personal growth that takes place with Sharelle.

Although the Neufeld novel is not of the same quality as the Hawthorne work, it does offer a similar theme for young adults to address before attempting the older work. There are a few questions that may be used to discuss both novels: Did Hester (Sharelle) have justification for having the affair? Why does Hester (Sharelle) keep the identity of the father secret? Does she ever regret her decision? Does Hester (Sharelle) take responsibility for her actions? Is she a good mother? Does Hester (Sharelle) benefit from her circumstances?

Another young adult novel with this theme of unplanned pregnancy is Eyerly's *Someone to Love Me*. Again, the novel is similar in theme to the Hawthorne novel. Students can respond to this work before moving on.

Guilt, a strong force in *The Scarlet Letter*, is also found in Zindel's *The Pigman*. The theme and plot of the two novels are not similar, but the guilt theme is and could be explored by students in the Zindel novel before they read the older work. Shortly after John and Lorraine discuss guilt with Mr. Pignati, he has a heart attack while roller skating with the two young people. Discussing the guilt in the young adult novel may make the discussion in the classic more relevant to the readers. A discussion of the guilt that Louie feels after Becky's death in *Running Loose* (Crutcher) may also help. Students can also discuss the effects of guilt in *The One-Eyed Cat* (Fox).

One other area that may be explored in young adult literature first is the concept of emotionalized landscaping and the symbolism that goes with it. Setting is an integral part of the plot in Hawthorne's novel. Prior to reading *The Scarlet Letter*, students may benefit from reading *Z for Zachariah* (O'Brien), *Roll of Thunder, Hear My Cry* (Taylor), or *Deathwatch* (White). The emphasis on the setting in these young adult novels can help students understand this concept before moving on to *The Scarlet Letter*.

ROMEO AND JULIET.   The book and musical *West Side Story* (Laurents) is an updated, contemporary *Romeo and Juliet* that students can read, understand, and enjoy. The theme is basically the same; the major differences lie in the contemporary language and depth of quality found in the Shakespearian drama. Reading the script of *West Side Story* first may help students come to some understanding of the motivation of the two young people in love, of the interaction of the street gangs, and of the roles that parents play in the lives of young people and in their desire to be together.

A similar theme is found in Mazer's *When We First Met*. Jenny and Rob can't be happier. They both believe their love will last forever. Jenny then finds out that Rob's mother is the drunken driver who killed Jenny's sister. She struggles with loyalty to her family but doesn't want to lose Rob. If this understanding comes through the more easily read literature, more time can be spent on the difficulties found in the Shakespearian drama. Certainly, the fact that students can compare and contrast the two will help in their understanding.

One of the most important themes in *Romeo and Juliet* is the suicide. Young people often find this act very difficult to understand. Even though they may have friends who have committed suicide, they still struggle with it. Reading Peck's *Remembering the Good Times* and Pfeffer's *About David* may help in that understanding. Both young adult authors treat the subject honestly, sincerely, and with great emotional care. Young people may then be able to understand Romeo's and Juliet's attempts when they realize their love cannot be.

If students read Hinton's *The Outsiders*, they can get a sense of what societal gangs are all about and their effects on individuals. How alike are the Montagues and Capulets to the Greasers and Socs? The understanding that comes from reading Hinton's work may transfer when reading about similar actions in *Romeo and Juliet*.

To what extent will young people give themselves to a commitment they have made? Some students reading *Romeo and Juliet* struggle with their decision that if they cannot be together, they will not live. Many novels have protagonists that make a commitment and have the strength to carry it out even when they are faced with great danger. One such novel is *Summer of My German Soldier* (Greene). Patty, a Jewish teenager, puts her life in danger by hiding Anton, her German soldier, after he escapes from a train taking him to a detention camp in Arkansas.

WALDEN.   Two Paulsen novels, *The Island* and *Hatchet,* work well to prepare readers for the more difficult *Walden* (Thoreau). The concept of learning from nature as well as learning through self-discovery runs through both of Paulsen's novels. In *The Island,* Wil finds his island and communes with nature, probing his understanding of what life is about and his relationship to the land and the water and to the life that is found there. In addition, both Wil and Thoreau turn to writing to help make their discoveries meaningful. Readers will relate well to Wil, a teenage boy, as he struggles with the world about him. Readers will also have a better chance of understanding limited isolation and self-study when it is done by one of their own. They can then take this concept to their reading of Thoreau's work.

Similarly, Brian Robeson, the protagonist in *Hatchet,* finds himself alone in the Canadian wilderness with nothing to draw upon but a hatchet, the clothes that he wears, and his will to survive. Although landing the plane in the wilderness was not his choice, Brian learns about himself as he fights to stay alive in the rugged environment. In *The Island,* the interaction with nature is by choice; in *Hatchet,* it is not; but in both, the results are the same: Two young boys learn about themselves, their relationships to the world around them, and the meaning of life as they live it.

In the pairings in Figure 7.1, we have provided one or more young adult novels as companions to the older, traditional adult literature. In these listings, our organizing premise is to find a work with a similar theme—a theme that can more easily be rendered in the young adult novel than in the older work. Having the security of understanding and enjoying the young adult novel may make the job of reading and understanding the classic easier.

Other Pairings

There are other ways of making connections between the classics and young adult literature. For example, if the point of comparison is the general attitude of the region of the country, then it would be helpful to read *Johnny Tremain* (Forbes), *A Day No Pigs Would Die* (Peck), and *Homecoming* (Voigt) to get some understanding of the New England value system before reading *The Scarlet Letter* (Hawthorne). If the connecting theme is what it means to be "Southern," then students might read *Shuttered Windows* (Means), *Roll of Thunder, Hear My Cry* (Taylor), *M. C. Higgins, the Great* (Hamilton), *Home Before Dark* (Bridgers), and *Sounder* (Armstrong) before reading the literature of Eudora Welty, Carson McCullers, William Faulkner, Tennessee Williams, and Flannery O'Connor.

The Life and Strange Surprising Adventures of Robinson Crusoe, Daniel Defoe
The Island, Gary Paulsen
The Goats, Brock Cole
The Island Keeper, Harry Mazer
One Fat Summer, Robert Lipsyte

The Grapes of Wrath, John Steinbeck
A Small Civil War, John Neufeld
Home Before Dark, Sue Ellen Bridgers
Homecoming, Cynthia Voigt
Words by Heart, Ouida Sebestyen
To Kill A Mockingbird, Harper Lee
Roll of Thunder, Hear My Cry, Mildred Taylor
Words by Heart, Ouida Sebestyen
I Know Why the Caged Bird Sings, Maya Angelou
1984, George Orwell
The Chocolate War, Robert Cormier
Beyond the Chocolate War, Robert Cormier
The Kolokol Papers, Larry Bograd

Animal Farm, George Orwell
Bless the Beasts and the Children, Glenda Swartout
The Wild Children, Felice Holman
Great Expectations, Charles Dickens
Is That You, Miss Blue?, M. E. Kerr
Jacob Have I Loved, Katherine Paterson
The Sound of Coaches, Leon Garfield
Harry and Hortense at Hormone High, Paul Zindel
Heart of Darkness, Joseph Conrad
Lord of the Flies, William Golding
Downriver, Will Hobbs
Red Badge of Courage, Stephen Crane
The Last Mission, Harry Mazer
Fallen Angels, Walter Dean Myers
April Morning, Howard Fast
My Brother Sam Is Dead, James Collier and Christopher Collier
The Machine Gunners, Robert Westall
The Odyssey, Homer
Dove, Robin Graham

Anne Frank: The Diary of a Young Girl, Anne Frank
Number the Stars, Lois Lowry
Summer of My German Soldier, Bette Greene
Death of a Salesman, Arthur Miller
Ordinary People, Judith Guest
Remembering the Good Times, Richard Peck
Of Mice and Men, John Steinbeck
All Together Now, Sue Ellen Bridgers
Lizard, Dennis Covington
Lord of the Flies, William Golding
The Chocolate War, Robert Cormier
The Goats, Brock Cole
Moby Dick, Herman Melville
The Slave Dancer, Paula Fox
Old Man and the Sea, Ernest Hemingway
The Voyage of the FROG, Gary Paulsen
The Adventures of Huckleberry Finn, Mark Twain
The Day They Came to Arrest the Book, Nat Hentoff

FIGURE 7.1
Pairings: A listing

The theme of social relationships and social status runs through *The Great Gatsby* (Fitzgerald). Perhaps students should read *Everything Is Not Enough* (Asher), *Permanent Connections* (Bridgers), or *Ordinary People* (Guest) before tackling the Fitzgerald novel.

The law, or at least a trial, plays an important part in *To Kill a Mockingbird* (Lee), *The Stranger* (Camus), and *Billy Budd* (Melville). It may be helpful if students first read *Permanent Connections* (Bridgers) or *Summer of My German Soldier* (Greene). Discussion could center on the connections between the law of the time and how that law was integrated into the trials.

The "decision" theme may be used to make connections among young adult novels and the classics. Although there are many elements to explore in *The Crucible* (Miller), *Kidnapped* (Stevenson), *Of Mice and Men* (Steinbeck), *The Old Man and the Sea* (Hemingway), and *The Pearl* (Steinbeck), the "decisions" element may best be served by reading *Across Five Aprils* (Hunt), *The Catcher in the Rye* (Salinger), *Edgar Allan* (Neufeld), *A Separate Peace* (Knowles), *The Duplicate* (Sleator), or *The Accident* (Strasser).

Our premise is that if teachers are going to teach classics, then they must do everything possible to help their students have success when reading this adult literature. One way, perhaps the most meaningful way, offers students a bridge—something that connects their understanding of the world around them through their literature with the literature of the past, which may have little or no relevance to their world. In this way, young adult literature serves the teacher well.

🙠 Learning Log Responses 🙠

Based on what you have read in this chapter about teaching the classics, present your views on why you will or will not teach them.

Identify a classic not discussed in this chapter. What young adult novel would you use to help your students connect to your chosen classic? Explain the connection. How will you promote in your classroom the concept of developing lifelong readers?

REFERENCES

Angelotti, M. (1981). Uses of the young adult literature in the eighties. *English in Texas 13,* 32–34.

Applebee, A. (1989). *The study of book-length works taught in high school English courses.* Albany, NY: Center for the Study of Teaching and Learning of Literature.

Atwell, N. (1987). *In the middle.* Portsmouth, NH: Boynton/Cook.

Carlsen, G. R., & Sherrill, A. (1988). *Voices of readers: How we come to love books.* Urbana, IL: National Council of Teachers of English.

Daigon, A. (1969). Literature and the schools. *English Journal, 58* (1), 30–39.

Educational Leadership, 49 (4) (whole issue).

Hirsch, E. D., Jr. (1987). *Cultural literacy: What every American needs to know.* Boston: Houghton Mifflin.

Holbrook, H. T. (1982). Adolescent literature: More than meets the eye. *Journal of Reading, 25,* 378–381.

Kaywell, Joan (Ed.). (1993–1995). *Adolescent literature as a complement to the classics* (Vols. 1 & 2). Norwood, MA: Christopher-Gordon.

Langer, J. (1984). Literacy instruction in American high schools: Problems and perspectives. *American Journal of Education, 93* (11), 107–132.

Lesesne, T. (1991). Developing lifetime readers: Suggestions from fifty years of research. *English Journal, 80* (6), 61–64.

Mullican, J. (1991). Cultural literacy: Whose culture? Whose literacy? *English Education, 23* (4), 244–250.

A nation at risk: The full account. (1984). Washington, DC: Commission on Excellence in Education.

Newdick, R. (1936). Robert Frost as teacher of literature and composition. *English Journal, 25* (6), 632.

O'Connor, M. E. (1980). A study of the reading preferences of high school students. Arlington, VA: ERIC Document Reproduction Service. (No. ED 185524)

O'Donnell, H. (1983). Death to the classics. *English Journal, 72* (3), 48–50.

Probst, R. (1984). *Adolescent literature: Response and analysis.* Englewood Cliffs, NJ: Merrill/Prentice Hall.

A profile of the American eighth grader. (1990). Washington, DC: U.S. Department of Education.

Samuels, B., & Lowery-Moore, H. (1987, Winter). Bridging the basics: The young adult novel in a back-to-basics society. *The ALAN Review, 14,* 38, 42–44.

Shaw, L. (1935). Touching the intangible. *Wilson Library Bulletin, 10,* 110–112.

Small, R. (1972). Teaching the junior novel. *English Journal, 61* (2), 222–229.

Small, R. (1977). The junior novel and the art of literature. *English Journal, 66* (6), 55–59.

Sullivan, A. M. (1991). The natural reading life: A high school anomaly. *English Journal, 80* (6), 40–46.

Trelease, J. (1982). *The read aloud handbook.* New York: Penguin.

Vogel, M., & Zancanella, D. (1991). The story world of adolescents in and out of the classroom. *English Journal, 80* (6), 54–60.

8

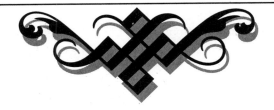

Diversity in Young Adult Literature: Ethnic, Cultural, and National

Picture Stepanov, a handsome 17-year-old who has recently emigrated to the United States from the Moscow area of what used to be the U.S.S.R. He and his family have joined the growing community of Soviet Jews in an East coast urban center. Because of language difficulties and the tremendous culture shock the family faced, his parents did not register him or his sister for public school during their first year in the United States.

Now it is October, and Stepanov is sitting in an American Literature class for eleventh graders at a typical comprehensive high school serving a diverse student body. The teacher is lecturing on Edwards' sermon, "Sinners in the Hands of an Angry God." Stepanov's head is on his desk; his eyes are closed. It's only two months into the school year, and already Stepanov and his teacher have given up. He anticipates failure in this course because he lacks language facility, historical knowledge about the colonization of the United States, and a common cultural background in the Christian faith evident in Edwards' text—all of which contribute to a lack of understanding and, hence, motivation.

The teacher lets him sleep, seeing his lack of attention as reinforcement of her belief that "he doesn't want to learn, to belong." The teacher's lack of response reinforces Stepanov's perception that she does not care, that he is not wanted, that he cannot belong. The literature curriculum has, in this case, not met Stepanov on terms that will allow him to succeed. Instead of drawing him into a common cultural heritage, it has turned him away.

Now picture Natalia. She, too, is a recent immigrant, but her story is different from Stepanov's. She attends a middle school that offers English as a Second Language classes, and her language teacher has managed to find English translations of books from her native land that reflect the adolescent experience. Thus, she practices her developing English competency without having to struggle to make sense of the content of the literature. Her teacher has also shared some of these titles, such as Pogodin's short story collection, *Of Jolly People and Fine Weather,* with regular English language arts teachers. One of them has received permission to use this text in place of a text mandated by the curriculum, a substitution that works well for a unit thematically organized around the concept of "Free to Be Me."

Natalia is invited to the regular English class as a special guest speaker, one with experience and expertise on the cultural information in the text that the other eighth graders find difficult to understand. After her appearance as guest speaker, Natalia leaves the classroom excited, enthusiastic, and eager to continue to learn; the students who talked with her are also excited and enthusiastic, and they are eager to eat lunch with her, to share their experiences, and to learn more about her and her homeland.

When Natalia joins the regular English class later in the year, the teacher uses *A Boat to Nowhere* by Wartski as the first text. This book does not reflect Natalia's exact experiences, but it echoes her own sense of being a stranger in a strange land; the other students connect to the concept of feeling like a "stranger" in the world of adulthood toward which they are moving. Again, everyone learns from everyone else. The classroom has become a place of acculturation because the teacher's attitude and the choice of texts allow everyone to share and respond out of their own experience.

Meeting Curricula Goals

Stepanov and Natalia are real students; there are many Stepanovs and Natalias in our classrooms. They are representative of a growing body of students from many other countries and widely diverse cultural backgrounds. Our classrooms are populated with students from African nations, Asian lands, and Latin American countries, and our classrooms reflect the diversity of the backgrounds of the early settlers of the United States—including those brought to this country in bondage. These students need a literature curriculum that will allow them to feel a sense of belonging.

In fact, all students need a literature curriculum that stretches their perceptions and allows them to appreciate the richness of a contemporary culture woven from the threads of diverse heritages. Without the opportunities to explore a sense of self and to begin to explore the world from different perspectives, it becomes easy for students like Stepanov who experience failure to blame the dominant culture for their failure, as evidenced through the literature. Consider some statistics:

1. In its report, "U.S. Children and Their Families," cited in *Report on Education Research* (1991), the House Select Committee on Children, Youth, and Families indicated that the demographics of the United States are changing. "In 1986, nonwhite and Hispanic women had an average of 2.28 children vs. an average of 1.74 for white, non-Hispanic women" (p. 1). The traditional "majority" is dwindling.

2. Waggoner (1988) notes that the United States is a "multilingual, multicultural country where one person in seven speaks a non-English language at home or lives with family members who do" (p. 69).

3. A report by the Carnegie Forum on Education and the Economy (1986) points out how few members of minority cultures currently choose teaching as a profession. As the diversity of the school population expands (projections for "minority" enrollments by the year 2000 range from 35% to 50%), the diversity of the teaching force is dwindling.

4. After doing a study of major literature anthologies available to secondary school teachers, Romero and Zancanella (1990) note that less than 1 percent of the 1,399 pages in the 1989 Prentice Hall American literature text are devoted to the Hispanic experience in the United States. Other cultures do not fare much better.

Thus, we have a school population of great diversity that interacts with a teaching force composed primarily of those from a white, Anglo-Saxon heritage. This fact "tells [students] something about authority and power in contemporary America. These messages influence children's attitudes toward school, their academic accomplishments, and their views of their own and others' intrinsic worth" (Carnegie, 1986, p. 79). The literature curriculum fails to allow "readers to make powerful connections to works that draw on what they already know and to validate the importance of that knowledge" (Romero & Zancanella, 1990, p. 27).

As Frankson (1990) states, "To develop a positive image of their roles as valuable members of society, minority youth need to see themselves represented in good literature, both in their classrooms and on the library shelves" (p. 30). Using young adult literature by and about minorities—by and about recent immigrants to the United States and by authors from other countries who write for an audience of adolescents in those countries—is one powerful way to help achieve at least four specific curricular goals common to many English language arts curricula: making the connection to all readers through literature, tolerating and appreciating diverse values, articulating relationships between art and culture, and developing habits of reading diverse literature.

Making the Connection to All Readers Through Literature

When students cannot connect to literature, they act, either literally or metaphorically, like Stepanov: They go to sleep. When students do not have any way to feel that their experience is reflected in texts and as a result come to feel that their cultural heritage is either nonexistent or not important, motivation is low. However, when students have an opportunity to explore their own heritage through what Wigginton (1992), editor of the *Foxfire* books, calls *sustained exposure* to it, they become excited about learning in general, and they enter "into a new, unshakably proud relationship with their heritage" (p. 60). He continues:

> Ignorance of our culture leads us to be blind to some of the forces that control our attitudes and behaviors. If we are not led to examine our culture and background, we are denied the potential such study has to influence the acquisition of certain academic skills and content, to evaluate our beliefs in comparison with those of others, to select the best against certain unassailable principles, and to change society. (p. 64)

Writing about the history of young adult literature dealing with diverse cultural experiences, Moir (1989) notes of the period from 1960 to 1980:

> As our social structures and institutions were shaken during the 60's, books for children and young adults changed forever. Real problems of real kids told in real language were fair game for a nation of readers who watched much of the Viet Nam War and the Civil Rights Movement on their television screens. Such topics as racial conflict, divorce, substance abuse, sex and sexuality, death, and child abuse were and are discussed with greater candor and realism. Minority authors, so long silenced by a cynical publishing industry and uncaring society, found new audiences among white and minority readers demanding that books be "relevant." (p. 8)

Moir also points out that, unfortunately, there has been "a paucity of new books by minority writers or themes, especially those by Hispanic, Asian American, and native American writers" (p. 9). Recently, however, the number of young adult books first published in other countries and available here in translation has increased. Heinemann (Boynton/Cook) has made available series of texts under such umbrella titles as "The Caribbean Writers Series" and the "African Writers Series." In addition, many publishers are now distributing booklists of titles reflective of cultural diversity, such as Putnam and Grosset's "Celebrating Our Ethnic Diversity" or Scholastic's "Multi-Cultural Titles," and Kane/Miller, a relatively new company, only publishes children's titles in translation.

Donelson and Nilsen (1980) state that through reading good literature, individuals can explore their unique human qualities while comparing and contrasting them with similarities of human experience that cross cultural boundaries. They also note that good literature written for and about young adults is an especially valuable tool in helping our students relate to the larger world of human experience because young adult readers can immediately connect with the age-level concerns of the adolescent characters in the books. Using young adult literature reflective of diverse cultural experiences helps students who represent minority cultures within the United States validate their own experience and increase a sense of self-worth that comes from knowing "that authors and artists of substance and value come from their culture" (Romero & Zancanella, 1990, p. 29). Also, using such literature with all students helps to move them into an understanding of the pluralistic nature of the U.S. culture, a culture created by the interplay of many different groups.

Thus, teachers and librarians need to be aware of materials that describe life in the United States as experienced by young people from many different backgrounds, such as Tatum's *Mexican American Literature* anthology, Ashabranner's works, such as *To Live in Two Worlds: American Indian Youth Today,* or Yee's *Tales from the Golden Mountain: Stories of Chinese in the New World.* They should provide access for all students to authors whose work reflects the richness of cultures in the United States as shared by recent immigrants. Maureen Crane Wartski, for instance, writes vividly about the Vietnamese refugee experience in such books as *A Long Way from Home,* and Yoshiko Uchida writes about being a Japanese immigrant in *The Samurai of Gold Hill* and *A Jar of Dreams.* Alida Young's *Land of the Iron Dragon* portrays immigrants from China, as does Yep's *Child of the Owl.* Nicholassa Mohr's characters, such as those in *Nilda,* are Puerto Ricans living in the United States, often in New York City, and Gunilla Norris writes about Scandinavians living in the United States in *A Feast of Light.*

Many good young adult books show segments of the American population that are culturally diverse, but about which many students have little knowledge. Rudolfo Anaya, in *Bless Me, Ultima,* and Sandra Cisneros, in *The House on Mango Street,* depict adolescents growing up as Mexican Americans, as do the short stories in *Baseball in April and Other Stories* by Gary Soto. Novels such as Eleanora Tate's *The Secret of Gumbo Grove,* Rosa Guy's *The Friends,* or Sharon Mathis's *Teacup Full of Roses* describe engaging African American characters dealing with the everyday pressures felt by most young adults.

The young protagonists of Jamake Highwater's works, such as *Ceremony of Innocence,* or of N. Scott Momaday's novels, such as *House Made of Dawn* and *The Way to Rainy Mountain,* must wrestle with the question of "Who am I?" while caught between their tribal traditions and the values of the mainstream culture. Reading such novels would allow Native American youth to relate to the text, and all students could compare these struggles to those expressed by Margaret in Judy Blume's *Are*

You There God? It's Me, Margaret. Jane Yolen (*The Devil's Arithmetic*), Chaim Potok (*The Chosen, My Name Is Asher Lev*), Barbara Cohen (*King of the Seventh Grade, Tell Us Your Secret*), Hila Colman (*Rachael's Legacy*), Joan Gerber (*Handsome as Anything*), Gloria Goldreich (*Lori*), and Fran Arrick (*Chernowitz*) have written novels about growing up in the Jewish faith.

Jean C. George, in *Julie of the Wolves,* has created a character struggling to come to terms with her Eskimo heritage. Writers such as Robert Newton Peck (in *Arly*), Barbara Hall (in *Dixie Storms*), or the Cleavers (in *Where the Lilies Bloom*) show what it is like to grow into adolescence while living in rural poverty. George Ella Lyon contrasts this lifestyle to that of the life in the city of Memphis in *Borrowed Children,* and Kathryn Lasky shows the results of the Amish custom of shunning in *Beyond the Divide.*

Tolerating and Appreciating Diverse Values

The New York City Police Department reports that "70% of all bias incidents are now committed by people under 19" (p. 20), a statistic indicating a nationwide trend, according to the Center for Democratic Renewal as cited by Johnson (1989). Berk (1990) notes that when people are forced to interact with individuals they consider "suspect" because of racial and cultural difference, many times they rely on stereotypes, making "estimates of central tendencies associated with particular social categories" (p. 339). The Asian and Pacific Islander Advisory Committee (1988) argues:

> Within many of our schools, racial and ethnic prejudice are an integral part of the social fabric. Instead of being places that provide safe and supportive environments . . . schools have become the sites where children are exposed to racial hostility and intolerance. They must learn to cope with incidents that include name calling, being pushed or spat on, deliberately tricked, teased or laughed at, or being subjected to unprovoked physical harassment and victimization, all of which contribute to feelings of rejection, isolation, and fear. (p. 51)

The traditional literature program offered to secondary students does little to help break down negative stereotypes. To the extent that traditional pedagogy follows from a new critical approach to text, students have little help even in confronting their own values as explored in the literature they read. To be comfortable in an increasingly culturally diverse society, students from the traditional, prevailing culture need to examine their own heritage and related values. They also need to better understand their own culture and to broaden their perspectives by exploring cultures and the ways in which their adolescent experience is alike and different from the adolescent experience reflected in literature about young adults from diverse backgrounds.

A failure to broaden the literature canon would, as Smith (1983) notes, "obviate the possible acknowledgement of divergent systems of values" and tell students there is only one literature—one culture—of value (p. 7). At the very least, using novels by authors such as Laurence Yep (*Dragonwings*), Max Martinez (*Schoolland: A Novel*), or Mildred Taylor (*Let the Circle Be Unbroken*) might serve to make us and our students face the facts about the presence of racism and ethnocentricity in our lives as well as the prejudice and stereotyping that results from our fear of those we perceive to be "suspect" because of their differences.

Ehle (1982), reviewing the research about the influence of literature on readers, states that through reading and vicariously experiencing life from a different point of view, young adults can begin to develop increased tolerance and appreciation for the ways of those who are "different." Stover and Karr (1990) share the responses of students from rural Maryland as they read *Shadows Across the Sun* (Likhanov), a young adult novel from the U.S.S.R. The novel has poetic passages describing the setting of Fedya and Lena's growth toward maturity as they, both age 12, learn something about accepting themselves and caring for another. An eighth-grade girl wrote,

> "This was pretty interesting. I learned things about Russia, about their culture. It was a little hard to relate because I don't have a friend or a relative in a wheelchair. I also don't know any alcoholics. But, I did like the characteristics the author gave to the characters because they were my age and the characters had believable personalities. I like Fedya's perspective on life. He worked to make things o.k." (Stover & Karr, 1990, p. 51)

This young woman enjoyed the book because she appreciated Fedya as a person, found him someone she would like to know. A classmate of hers commented,

> "At first I thought Russia was a stony, cold, ugly place. After reading the novel, I know I was wrong. The novel gave me a better understanding. I like the fact that Moscow is a lot like Baltimore. They have skyscrapers, apartments, people roaming the streets with briefcases and armfuls of shopping bags." (p. 52)

Reading the book made the setting, her vision, of the U.S.S.R. more comprehensible. Perhaps another student, Sam, summarized most eloquently what happened to his initial perceptions of the Soviet Union and life in such a distant place among very different people. Before reading the book, Sam had written in a journal entry that he would "probably die" if he had to live in Moscow. When asked to reflect on his initial journal entries and to comment on what he would change having read the text, Sam wrote,

> "I would change the part about 'I'd probably die' because reading the book I see that it's not that hard to adjust to the Russian way of life, especially with friends like Fedya and Lena." (p. 47)

In fact, Sam and his classmates probably would have a difficult time in Moscow, given the economic turmoil in the newly created states that once made up the Soviet Union and the diversity of cultures within those states. *Playing the Game* by Strelkova portrays this cultural diversity as several young men from various states within the former nation must come to terms with their diverse experiences and values. However, Sam's response indicates a willingness to move beyond stereotypes and to look for, even to celebrate, similarities of experience.

Young adults from diverse cultural backgrounds have concerns in common, and the literature for adolescents reflects these similarities in various cultures. One shared area of interest of young adults from many cultures is related to the individual's school career and future in the work force. Several researchers have documented that concerns about future schooling and career rank very high among adolescents from the United States (Abel & Gingles, 1968), Australia (Nicholson & Antill, 1981) and Canada (Bibby & Posterski, 1985). Novels for adolescents from non-English–speaking countries reveal a similar level of concern about these issues among young adults.

In *The Silver Crest: My Russian Boyhood,* Chukovsky details the importance of a good education for success in Russian society and the problems an underprivileged individual faces in creating a future for himself. Conton's *The African* tells the story of Kisimi, who moves upward in society as a result of his scholastic endeavors, which win him a scholarship. As he pursues his studies, he must make important decisions about how to use his gifts, and he decides he can make a contribution to his country as a politician. Kuroyanagi's *Totto-Chan: The Little Girl in the Window* provides insight into the significance of schooling in the Japanese society. Totto-Chan is a divergent thinker and, as such, has a great deal of difficulty finding a place in traditional Japanese classrooms. She is "saved" when her mother finds an alternative environment, but the tension mounts as they must determine what to do when that school is no longer available to Totto-Chan.

The River Sumida by Kafu captures the confusion of Chokichi as he tries to decide what the future holds for him. Will he follow the path to the university outlined for him by his mother, or will he follow his heart and become an actor? Once he makes a decision, what will the consequences be for his well-being, both emotionally and physically? Christopher is almost a German twin of the Japanese Chokichi, except that the tensions involved in making such decisions about the future are so intense that Christopher decides life is not worth living in *Who Killed Christopher?* (Korschunow). On the other hand, the young male diary keeper of *A Handful of Stars* (Schami) who comes of age in Syria faces the future head on, and his reflections show him taking responsibility for going against the wishes of his family—and for going against the political establishment as well.

Chinua Achebe's somewhat older protagonists in *Things Fall Apart* and *No Longer at Ease* both deal with issues of crafting a future out of a balance between traditional values and the values of the system in which they have been educated. Almazov's book for younger readers, *The Most Beautiful Horse,* presents, with more humor, the similar struggle of a Soviet youth who is attempting to figure out what his skills are and how he can use them to advantage in the world of work.

In all of these works, the young adult wrestles with issues of identity and separating the self from societal and parental expectations as he engages in a quest for a meaningful educational future or career. A second concern for young adults from diverse cultural backgrounds is anxiety about their health and physical development while dealing with puberty and its attendant chaos. Concerns about general health, including height and weight, trouble adolescents a great deal (Bibby & Posterski, 1985; Nicholson & Antill, 1981). Also, young adults are anxious about their physical development (Collins & Harper, 1974), and they wrestle with the issues of smoking and drug and alcohol use, from the standpoint of health as well as of "fitting in" (Eme, Maisiak, & Goodale, 1979).

Evidence of cross-cultural concerns was found through a comparative survey on smoking behavior among youth from China and the United States (Chen & Winder, 1986), but young adult literature from other countries is more dramatic than statistics in giving our young people an appreciation for the similarities they share with peers from other lands and other cultural backgrounds. Any middle school student who has identified with Margaret as she tries to figure out what her 12-year-old body is doing in Blume's *Are You There God? It's Me, Margaret* would also appreciate the Russian book *Shadows Across the Sun* (Likhanov). Fedya, the main character, is at that age when his body is growing and maturing, leaving him feeling gangly and awkward inside it. Also, he feels the first stirrings of sexuality as he becomes friends with Lena. Lena, too, is coping with the awkwardness inherent in puberty, but her situation is complicated by the fact that she is wheelchair bound, a result of polio. Likhanov's book is a tender and gently humorous account of this developing friendship, much of which centers about the efforts of these two characters to feel good about themselves physically.

The Nigerian Aku-nnu, created by Emecheta in *The Bride Price,* loses her father when she is 13. Her selfish uncle adopts her, viewing her as an object to be sold for enough money to allow him to become Ibo chief. Aku-nnu's mother gradually becomes a part of the uncle's household, leaving Aku-nnu feeling lost and lonely. Starved for affection and lacking all concept of self-worth, Aku-nnu falls in love with the descendent of a slave, and at age 15 she elopes with Chike. Young people around the world will be able to identify with the longing, insecurity as a physical and emotional being, and isolation expressed in *The Bride Price*.

Shell, in Anthony's *Green Days by the River,* is also 15 when he must contend with changes in his family situation, compounded by his developing feelings of sexuality, which confuse and trouble him. His confusion in the face of awakening physical desire can be compared to those of Pennington, the working-class British hero in *Pennington's Seventeenth Summer* (Peyton), or to the Russian Dima, whose dedication to the clarinet suddenly must take a back seat to his interest in a young woman in *My Brother Plays the Clarinet* (Aleskin). The French novel, *A Matter of Feeling,* beautifully captures the same feelings from the female point of view as Boissard describes Pauline's experiences with first love. In *Arly,* Peck describes young men growing up in rural Florida who face similar sexual responses; Butler's *Kindred* shows a female slave exploring sexual feelings while confronting the advances of her master. In *Children of the River,* Crew presents a female Cambodian refugee struggling to negotiate between allegiance to her past life and culture and allegiance to the young Oregon boy who loves her.

Although the issue of adapting to a changing body and the resulting passions and stirrings of longing brought about by puberty is not the central theme in any of these works, it is a major factor that contributes to the main characters' confusion. As they try to come to terms with their adult bodies, they find themselves making moral and ethical decisions about who they are in a larger sense. Because adolescents in this country are so concerned with physical appearance, they will easily relate to the characters in these books who are dealing with similar feelings of awkwardness—and with the related issues of how to act out masculine and feminine roles.

A third concern evident in young adult characters from many backgrounds are their efforts to formulate a personal sense of self. Erikson (1959) identifies the major task of adolescence as developing a clear sense of self-definition and integrity, which he terms "identity." Other theorists have noted that adolescents express concern about identity in two ways. The first involves developing a private self through the struggle to answer questions such as, "Who am I?" or, "What is the meaning of life?" The second aspect of the search for identity involves the definition of the self in the public sphere through the struggle to determine how the self should relate to friends, co-workers, teammates, or members of the opposite sex (Violato & Holden, 1988). Mohr's Felita of *Going Home,* who feels like an outsider when she first visits relatives in Puerto Rico and who then has to come to terms with a heritage she has always taken for granted, is a good example of this struggle. Judging from the literature for young adults from other countries, the "Who am I?" question is one of great importance to all adolescents.

Young adult literature offers both lighthearted and serious approaches to the identity issue. Both of the novellas in Aleskin's *My Brother Plays the Clarinet* show young protagonists trying to determine a personal identity separate from that of their parents—or from their parents' expectations for them. In many ways the characters in these novellas compare to Carl Davis III in Guy's *The Ups and Downs of Carl Davis III* or to many of the characters in the slice-of-life stories created by Soto in *Baseball in April and Other Stories.* The tone of these works, however, is light and affectionate; the reader's emotions are treated gently, as are those of the characters, yet the message is clear to all: At some point in one's life, as happens to Zhenya, as well as to Sergei in *My Brother Plays the Clarinet,* there is no one to whom to turn to solve a problem, and facing that problem alone takes the individual a long way toward growing up.

Another example of a gentle treatment of the search for identity is the love story set in Scotland that unfolds in *Emma in Love* (Arundel). Emma, living alone for the first time and struggling to maintain her academic standards, is somewhat distracted by her deepening relationship with her boyfriend. When she goes home with him one weekend to visit his parents, however, she begins to question whether she can remain true to herself and still be involved with him. His expectations mirror those of his father: Both assume that the mother will wait on them, that the men will determine all activities, and that the women will accept without argument their decisions. Most young women can relate to the dilemma facing Emma. Should she give in to her boyfriend's vision and thus give up her professional goals and her growing sense of individual identity for the sake of the security of the relationship? Or should she take the risk of continuing to pursue her studies and hope to find someone who will encourage her to reach her potential? The theme remains a timely one, but the story is told humorously.

In *Balloon Top* (Albery), the same theme is treated much more seriously, and Kana's quest to determine who she is becomes complicated by conflicts between her traditional Japanese family values and her sense of the world as seen through the political uprisings of the 1960s, as well as by conflicts between her desire for others to tell her who to be and her frustration at not being allowed to determine this by herself. The novel opens when Kana is a little girl and describes her view of her mother as all powerful and all knowing. The family faces severe hardship during World War II, which results in Kana's sense of insecurity about the future. This insecurity pushes her to excel, never to take chances, and do what she is told.

As Kana matures, these feelings lead her to become the best student in whatever school she attends and never question the wisdom of her parents' choices. At the same time, she is always painfully aware that, as the first-born child, she somehow failed the family by not being a boy, by not being the heir for which every father prays. Thus, she has no clear sense of what her future should hold. She, as female, certainly cannot expect to take over her father's business. The traditional life for her would be to marry a young man selected by her family who also would inherit the family firm. However, growing up in a changing political climate, she is bright enough to feel uncomfortable with this prescribed view.

Kana thus works to win herself a position at the most prestigious of schools, Tokyo University, and when she is accepted, she leaves her family for 3 years of constant strain as she seeks to balance the conflicting expectations and pressures. Throughout the novel, Kana has trouble thinking an issue through to its logical conclusion and has difficulty acting upon her ideals. As one of her friends tells her, "You may cry your heart out and may even compose an ode after reading *Les Miserables,* . . . but if I ask you to come with me on Sundays to visit old people's homes and orphanages, you tell me you are going to the Takarazuka Girl's Revue" (p. 93). She experiments with political activism, the theatre, and various kinds of relationships with young men, and she even tries to find out what it means to be a liberated female through a sexual encounter.

The book is not easy to read; it is not easy to summarize. The characters and the setting in which they are growing and changing are complex, and the novel does not end with any definite solutions for Kana. But the end is hopeful. Kana promises her father "never to attempt to be someone other than yourself, a great pitfall of the impressionistic young" (p. 111). Because of the realism and the complexities of the issues with which it deals, *Balloon Top* is an outstanding portrait of the confusion and search for answers experienced by young adults.

Similarly, Hamilton's *A White Romance* is an uncomfortable text for many readers because of the realism of her portrayal of the complexities of interracial relationships and of the stereotypes and negative perceptions characters both black and white hold of each other. *The Runner* (Voigt) and *The Moves Make the Man* (Brooks) also show the confusions inherent in an interracial friendship, which nevertheless is a significant factor in helping the main characters determine at least partial responses to the constant adolescent query of "Who am I?" In Porte's *I Only Made Up the Roses* and in the lighter *It's an Aardvark-Eat-Turtle World* (Danziger), adolescent females of mixed heritage wrestle with the identity issue confounded by that mix. In the Australian text *Three Weeks with the Queen* (Gleitzman), a young man learns about his own values as he compares and contrasts them with those of the aunt, uncle, and cousin he is forced to visit in England and with those of a new friend who happens to be a homosexual.

For able young adult readers, Kana from *Balloon Top* and Aku-nnu from *The Bride Price* would be interesting to compare to Shabanu in *Shabanu: Daughter of the Wind* (Staples), the narrator of *Nectar in a Sieve* (Markandaya), Sumitra in *Sumitra's Story* (Smith), or to the two sisters of *The Color Purple* (Walker). These young women from diverse backgrounds all struggle with what it means to be female within the confines of a particular culture. Some, like Sumitra, break with the culture of their birth; others, like Kana, eventually adapt to it; and others find their own solutions. But young female readers from many backgrounds will easily identify with the tensions faced by women around the world who are torn because of the different possibilities they see—or do not see—for their role in society.

Bykov's *Pack of Wolves* provides further proof that the quest for identity is common to young people of both genders from many nationalities. Levchuk, the main character, is a young man, no longer an adolescent, when the novel opens. He is fighting with the Russian army during World War II, and it quickly becomes clear that he has little real conviction about the struggle in which he finds himself. He is basically a self-serving, selfish young man—until he is left the sole survivor of a major skirmish, in charge of the infant born to a female collaborator who disappears during the fight. As he struggles to find shelter and then permanent safety for the infant, Victor, he questions for the first time the meaning of his life, and he takes a long, hard look at himself and his motivations as he cares for the child. The novel ends after he searches for and finds Victor, now grown to adulthood, and he reflects on his own purpose in life as someone who took responsibility for the life of another. Except for the fact that the characters drink vodka, are located in Russia, and eat more potatoes than most U.S. readers would do, this book could easily be about a young American man forced to question the reason for his being.

In each of the stories in *Badger on the Barge and Other Stories* (Howker), the main character is a young person living in Britain whose sense of self and identity is deepened or enlightened as a result of an encounter with an older person. For instance, in the title story, Helen is the younger daughter of a couple that has pinned its hopes for moving up the social scale on the success of her brother Peter, and she has lived in Peter's shadow for years. Then suddenly Peter dies in an accident. Helen's parents seem not to realize she exists, and their attitude affects her own view of herself. When Helen meets Miss Brady, she learns about the need to develop convictions and to go against authority if necessary to stand by those convictions. She then can accept her parents more readily as they are. Helen realizes she will be the one to leave the safety of her known world and to "make it" in a social world about which her parents have only dreamed. As she discovers and uncovers her ambitions and potential, she becomes free to be herself with her parents and even helps them to begin to heal after Peter's death. These well-written stories are filled with poetic language and intriguing, unusual older people and with young adults who are not afraid to grow and learn about themselves as they try to answer the question, "Who am I?"

Finally, young adult novels about characters from many cultures reflect a concern for the adolescent's development of a social self. Issues related to discovering a sense of self in the social meaning of the word focus on characteristics and relationships that are more observable than those related to the personal self (Violato & Holden,

1988). Factors such as personal appearance, relationships with friends, social and athletic activities, and jobs and the stress and relationships associated with them figure into young adults' efforts to answer the question, "Who am I—as I interact with the world? How am I perceived by others?"

Obviously, this category intertwines and overlaps with the others; for example, as adolescents seek to determine their values, they often act on these values in a social context, receive feedback from their peers and adults, and then reflect on their values based on that response. The main character in *The River Sumida* (Kafu) attempts to decide what his career path should be, so he seeks advice from those important to him socially. Most of the books discussed so far in this section of the chapter can provide insight into the significance of social concerns to adolescents.

However, by examining novels from different cultures, it becomes apparent that the kinds of concerns related to the development of the social self cross cultural boundaries, and so do strategies for dealing with those concerns. In *Balloon Top,* Kana depends on others to tell her how to dress, how to speak, and how to act; it is when the advice of her mother or aunt conflicts with that received from her peers or when her parents' conception of her future contradicts that of her friends that she begins wrestling with the inner, and larger, question of "Who am I?"

Similar patterns emerge in Highwater's books, as characters deal with developing a sense of self while juggling the demands of a traditional Native American culture with those of the dominant white culture. Raisen Stackhouse of Tate's *The Secret of Gumbo Grove* must also deal with prejudice and fear as she, a young black would-be historian, must decide how much history could and should be told. Her strategies include comparing the points of view of many adults and contrasting what they say with how they act. *Water Girl* (Thomas) illustrates the strategies, drawn from a more ancient tradition than those practiced by her family, that Amber Westbrook uses to reformulate her sense of identity after a fragment of an old letter shatters it.

Similarly, in *My Mate Shofiq,* Needle tells the story of Bernard, who only starts to think about his prejudices and value system when he reluctantly—almost accidentally—befriends a Pakistani boy. His defense of Shofiq is not acceptable to his British friends, so at first he tries to ignore the Pakistani. However, he enjoys playing with Shofiq, admires Shofiq's skill in physical games, and struggles throughout the book to reconcile these contradictory feelings. This text would make an interesting pairing with *The Moves Make the Man* (Brooks) because of the relationships and themes in both.

In *The Games Were Coming* (Anthony), the reader sees how identity and values are pursued through athletics. As Leon becomes obsessed with training for a great bicycle race, he must confront how this obsession affects his relationship with Sylvia—and she must think about how much cycling defines Leon and whether she should accept that definition or move into another relationship. *Pennington's Seventeenth Summer* (Peyton) and *Who Killed Christopher?* (Korschunow) also illustrate how a young man's choice of leisure-time activity, whether music, fighting, playing pranks, or just "hanging out" with friends, helps him define himself—and, ultimately, gives him the information he needs to begin developing a set of personal values.

The powerful set of texts in *Frankie's Story,* Sefton's trilogy about a young woman growing up within the chaos created by religious and political strife in

Belfast, shows the turmoil of that troubled land—and that sometimes the only option for a young person struggling to find an independent sense of self is to leave a familiar society behind. *Sumitra's Story* also describes the struggles involved in making such a choice—a choice between a sense of identity prescribed by the culture of one's birth and the identity forged by the individual. Sumitra/Sue finally, too, must leave her family to forge both her individual and social selves.

Perhaps the British novel *Witchweek* (Jones) most clearly illustrates the significance of the social context to a young person struggling to develop a clear sense of self. This fantasy involves parallel worlds. In one world, witches with supernatural talents but ordinary appearances exist, despite laws against their existence and laws against helping them to maintain their existence. Prejudice runs high, with extreme consequences for witches who are uncovered. Thus, when a teacher receives an anonymous note stating, "There's a witch in this class," action must be taken.

As the young witches (there are more than one) discover who they are and the extent of the feeling against them, they seek shelter, and they and the reader are forced to confront the issue of fitting in. Just how different is it possible to be, in looks and behavior, before being perceived as dangerous rather than merely eccentric? How far can and should society go in telling its members how to look, feel, and act? Although this book is written in a hopeful key and is a fantasy, the issues it raises are serious and significant to young adults in many cultures.

These same issues are confronted, in part, by Cassie and her family in the very realistic *Roll of Thunder, Hear My Cry* (Taylor) and by the narrator/diary keeper of Schami's *A Handful of Stars*. Students confront these questions when they read about and discuss characters who face social injustices and who must also decide, as Cassie does, whether bowing to the level of her tormenters is a viable strategy for dealing with those who seek to keep her "in her place." Cassie could easily be compared with the young woman in Naidoo's *Chain of Fire,* who must deal with the effects of the unjust apartheid system on her life.

What other similarities and differences in daily life within different cultures might be fruitful discussion topics? Stover and Karr's (1990) students who read *Shadows Across the Sun* developed the following list of similarities between life for adolescents in the U.S.S.R. and the United States: families (divorce, arguments), school and homework, sibling fights, problems with parents, importance of music, respect expected for leaders and teachers, similarities of feelings (falling in love), importance of sports, pets a part of life, and class clowns exist. At the same time, the students acknowledged differences in the cultures, such as those manifested in different food options, different vegetation, different roles of the government in the life of the individual, the place of the disabled in society, different senses of humor and of historical events, differences in the kind and amount of material possessions, and differences in the amount of choice individuals have in creating their futures. By examining individual characters living their own lives as influenced by a particular time and place and then comparing and contrasting these lives to those of other characters and to those of the individuals who comprise a given class, students and teachers can move between the particular and the universal, coming to understand how the individual both does and does not represent a whole community—and how the whole is shaped by the individual.

Reading fiction and nonfiction texts for young adults by authors whose works reflect the cultural richness of the population of the United States and discussing the kinds of topics generated by students interested in exploring issues of identity, both individual and cultural, would be a useful way to help begin to break through the "shadows across the sun" generated by prejudice and stereotyping. Appropriate authors include Jean Fritz (*Homesick: My Own Story; China Homecoming; China's Long March*), Brent Ashabranner (*Born to the Land; Into a Strange Land; Morning Star, Black Sun; The New Americans*), Virginia Hamilton (*A Little Love; Junius Over Far; Cousins; Sweet Whispers, Brother Rush*), Alice Childress (*Rainbow Jordan; Those Other People; A Hero Ain't Nothin' But a Sandwich*), or Walter Dean Myers (*Fast Sam, Cool Clyde and Stuff; Crystal; Fallen Angels; The Outside Shot*).

Articulating Relationships between Art and Culture

As students and their teachers examine the previous topics, they automatically begin to explore the relationship between art and culture. When the literature curriculum focuses only on one culture, traditionally in this country the culture of western Europe, students do not have enough experience to appreciate that an art form both reflects and in some way creates the culture that forms its content.

Through reading, however, we can examine various cultures' treatments of such topics as the conception of family, the role of women and children, the view of technology and the environment, religious practices and beliefs, and other issues related to ethical, moral, and philosophical beliefs. We then begin to understand how the characters within a given text are somewhat limited to choices we may not appreciate, but they also may have options we do not have. For instance, it is difficult to find a young adult novel from an African country that would not raise a few parents' eyebrows because sexual exploration is an accepted—and even implicitly mandated—aspect of young male adulthood. In the Japanese picture book *Hiroshima No Pika* by Maruki, the illustrations that accompany the text vividly indicate a different sense of "afterlife" than that held by many readers in the United States.

Through reading texts from many cultures, students can also explore the nature of language and ways in which language reflects (and sometimes limits) perceptions of reality. For example, young adult novels by Native Americans provide readers with beliefs about our relationship to the environment, which might contribute to the reader's ability to evaluate his or her own attitude. For example, Jamake Highwater, an anthropologist who writes young adult books that reflect the Cherokee/Blackfoot heritage, is quoted by Wilson and Hughes (1981) as feeling

"alienated by the ways ideas find their way into English words. For instance, when an English word is descriptive—like the word 'wilderness'—I am often appalled by what is implied in that description. After all, the forest is not 'wild' in the sense that it is something that needs to be tamed. For Blackfeet Indians, the forest is the natural state of the world; it is the cities that are wild and need taming. . . . Indians do not believe in a 'uni-verse,' but in a 'multi-verse.' Indians don't believe there is only one truth, but think there are many truths." (p. 223)

On a lighter note, young adult readers could compare and contrast the language and style of British novels such as *Handles* by Mark, which provides a handy glossary, or *An Ash-Blond Witch* by Lillington. Young adult readers could explore ways in which texts reflect a different use of language. For instance, in this country, "classical" music refers to music of a particular tradition, music which has its roots in madrigals, Bach's fugues, Chopin's etudes, and so forth. What does "classical" mean in Japan? In Nigeria? How is the term used in a similar fashion in these cultures, and how does it reflect cultural differences? How do texts reflect different understandings of our relationship to the world, a different sense of "truth"?

However, students will be able to understand how a text unfolds as a cultural artifact only if they have experience with texts reflective of multiple cultures. They will be able to appreciate what makes our pluralistic American culture unique only by contrasting it with other cultures, and they will understand the complexity of the American heritage only if they read texts that reflect that complexity. As Ravitch (1990) states:

> At its most basic, our common culture is a civic culture, shaped by our Constitution, our commitment to democratic values, and our historical experience as a nation. In addition, our very heterogeneity sets us apart from other nations and creates styles of expression that the rest of the world perceives as distinctively American. The pluralistic seek due recognition for the ways in which the nation's many racial, ethnic, and cultural groups have transformed the national culture. They say, in effect, "American culture belongs to all of us, and we remake it in every generation." (p. A44)

Developing Habits of Reading Diverse Literature

One of the cries of frustration often heard from English language arts teachers is "How do I get my students to stop reading Sweet Valley High books?" (or other series books, or books representing only one genre). Presenting young adult readers with good texts that lend themselves to discussion in the classroom, that pull readers into the world of the story because they are good narratives, and that have the added appeal of presenting alternative perspectives may (obviously, there are no guarantees!) help broaden our students' reading interests.

There are many, many young adult novels in print today that present both good stories and diverse perspectives—and that satisfy criteria for being termed *literary works of art*. Authors who grew up in the United States as members of minority cultures write about those experiences. Other authors for young adults describe the experience of stepping off a boat or a plane and, in so doing, of being transported from the world of the familiar into a strange new world. Such works document the immigrant experience as lived by contemporary adolescents; others, such as Uchida's *The Samurai of Gold Hill,* describe the immigrant experience from a historical perspective. Students could compare and contrast a freely chosen immigrant experience with the experience of those who were forced to come to this country.

Students also could compare and contrast the experiences of young adult immigrants in the United States with the experiences of immigrants to other countries as portrayed in novels such as *Sumitra's Story* (Smith) or *My Mate Shofiq* (Needle), or in the collections of stories by Dhondy, *Come to Mecca* and *East End at Your Feet,* all about Asian children trying to adjust to life in the United Kingdom. Other books for young adults about the adolescent experience in other countries are now available in translation, such as *Beka Lamb* by Edgell and *Annie John* by Kincaid, both from Caribbean countries; *The Dingo: A Story of First Love* by Freierman, another young adult novel from the former U.S.S.R.; or *A Day in the Life* by Argheta, from El Salvador.

Students might broaden their consumption of science fiction/fantasy works by exploring titles by Westall, such as *Urn Burial,* or by Dianna Wynne Jones, such as *Witchweek,* or by reading a collection such as Ginsburg's *The Air of Mars and Other Stories* from the former Soviet Union. New Zealand, Australia, and Great Britain are a rich source of texts that show just how different life can be in another country, even countries that share a cultural and linguistic heritage. Writers such as Jill Peyton Walsh, Gillian Cross, Catherine Sefton, and Ann Fine are all worth knowing and using.

Resources for teachers such as articles (i.e., Blair, 1991; Stover & Karr, 1990) and books (i.e., *Multicultural Teaching: A Handbook of Activities, Information, and Resources* [Tiedt & Tiedt, 1986] or Banks [1980]) are valuable to the teacher specifically seeking help in using young adult books that reflect cultural diversity. Autobiographical resources such as Rodriguez's *Hunger of Memory: The Education of Richard Rodriguez* or Kingston's *Women Warriors* will help the teacher seeking to empathize with the experience of forging an identity while feeling torn between two cultures. References such as Delpit's "The Silenced Dialogue: Power and Pedagogy in Educating Other People's Children" (1988) or Steele's "On Being Black and Feeling Blue" (1989) also address the question of cultural identity.

Before we try to help students face their feelings of prejudice and ethnocentricity, we need to confront our own attitudes and values. Do we truly think it is valuable to appreciate the likenesses and differences inherent in individual members of the human family? Do we truly want to use literature and the act of reading it as a vehicle for liberating thinking and being for all our students as described by Freire (1990)? What should the goals of the literature program be, and how can we reach all students when more than 100 languages are spoken in some school districts?

Before we revise the entire literature curriculum, we need to think about issues related to the selection of text. We need to avoid tokenism. We need to understand that such terms as *Asian American* or *Hispanic* are umbrella terms encompassing peoples from very diverse backgrounds, and we need to examine those differences, such as those between a middle-class Cuban immigrant to the United States who fled Castro and an illegal alien migrant worker from Mexico. We need to find books that are worth teaching and reading because they are "just plain good," as one future English teacher said when first introduced to Taylor's *The Road to Memphis,* books worth studying because their imagery, symbolism, and style make them works of art.

We also need to recognize that forcing students to read texts they do not like, do not trust, or do not value just for the sake of introducing them to diverse cultural heritages may have the adverse effect of reinforcing their already negative attitudes toward members of those cultures. Thus, we need to read texts recommended in bibliographies such as those in the NCTE publications *Your Reading: A Booklist for*

Junior High and Middle School Students (Samuels & Beers, 1995/1996) and *Books for You: A Booklist for Senior High Students* (Christenbury, 1995). Texts are also recommended in the following: "Chicano Literature for Young Adults: An Annotated Bibliography" (Frankson, 1990), "Black Adolescent Novels in the Curriculum" (Mitchell, 1988), *An Hispanic Heritage: A Guide to Juvenile Books About Hispanic Peoples and Cultures, Series III* (Schone, 1988), and "Booktalking: Going Global" (Rochman, 1989). We need to recognize, too, as Wigginton (1992) points out,

> Inevitably, as teachers and students examine traditions, they will uncover some that are not worth celebrating—some, in fact, that cannot be tolerated in this world. For example, would anyone want to return to the traditional role of the Appalachian woman? . . . To a traditional, fatalistic acceptance of all misfortune? . . . To blood-feuds? . . . We can gradually construct, with our students, a yardstick of ethical behavior against which we can measure those aspects of culture we are studying— treasuring, showcasing, celebrating, amplifying those that pass the test and discarding the rest. There is always much to honor and be proud of, as the more than 6,000 pages of printed material in the various Foxfire books confirm. And as we examine the outdated, and/or dishonorable, dysfunctional, and self-limiting, most of us will silently, simultaneously say to ourselves, "This practice or belief is one I will not carry forward with me into my life or condone in others. We can do better than this." (pp. 62–63)

As teachers, if we use in our classrooms literature reflective of the young adult experience from diverse cultural perspectives, we can demonstrate to our students that we care about them as individuals and that we want them to care about each other. In doing so, however, we must face the realities of anger and discomfort that can arise as topics not frequently addressed are made explicit. Thus, we must create classrooms in which students are both free to express themselves and also free from fear of intimidation when they do, as Aristotle might argue. We can, as Bullard (1992) eloquently writes,

> show them that hatred hurts. Show them how to think critically. Open up new worlds for them to discover. Offer them the tools for change. Create a small caring community in the classroom. Multicultural education is not a substitute for individual attention. But multicultural education, by some definition, is essential. We must help our students find a place in our pluralistic world. In doing so, we must avoid stereotyping, resegregation, indoctrination, assigning blame. We must confront the problems of prejudice and inequality in our classrooms as well as in our society. And, we must remember that as individuals we are not merely expressions of culture; we are also capable of transcending our cultures. In that way, we are all alike. (p. 7)

The resources listed at the end of this chapter should provide a starting point for exploring ourselves as expressions of our cultures, for exploring cultures as created by individuals, and for celebrating diversity and similarity between ourselves and the others with whom we share our world.

❧   Learning Log Responses   ❧

Choose and read one young adult novel mentioned in this chapter and write how you would use it to achieve the goal of having students tolerate and appreciate diverse values.

How will you encourage and help your students to develop lifelong reading habits that will include reading ethnically, culturally, and nationally diverse literature?

REFERENCES

Abel, H., & Gingles, R. (1968). Identifying problems of adolescent girls. *Journal of Educational Research, 58,* 389–391.

Asian and Pacific Islander Advisory Committee. (1988). *Final Report.* Sacramento, CA: Office of the Attorney General, California Department of Justice.

Banks, J. (Ed.). (1980). *Education in the 80's: Multicultural education.* Washington, DC: National Education Association.

Berk, R. (1990). Thinking about hate motivated crimes. *Journal of Interpersonal Violence, 5,* (3), 334–340.

Bibby, R.W., & Posterski, D.C. (1985). *The emerging generation.* Toronto: Irwin.

Blair, L. (1991). Developing student voices with multicultural literature. *English Journal, 80* (8), 24–28.

Bullard, S. (1992). Sorting through the multicultural rhetoric. *Educational Leadership, 49* (4), 4–7.

Carnegie Forum on Education and the Economy: The Task Force on Teaching as a Profession (1986), *A nation prepared: Teaching for the 21st century.* Washington, DC: Author.

Chen, T.L., & Winder, A.E. (1986). *A cross-cultural study of smoking among youth in the United States and the Republic of China.* (ERIC Document Reproduction Service No. ED 28212)

Collins, J., & Harper, J. (1974). Problems of adolescents in Sydney, Australia. *Journal of Genetic Psychology, 125,* 189–194.

Christenbury, L. (Ed.). (1995). *Books for you: A booklist for senior high students.* Urbana, IL: National Council of Teachers of English.

Delpit, L. (1988). The silenced dialogue: Power and pedagogy in educating other people's children. *Harvard Educational Review, 58* (3), 280–298.

Donelson, K., & Nilsen, A. P. (1980). *Literature for today's young adults.* Glenview, IL: Scott, Foresman.

Ehle, M. (1982, February). *The velveteen rabbit, the little prince, and friends: Posacculturation through literature.* Paper presented at the Annual Meeting of the Professional Clinic of Association of Teacher Educators, Phoenix, AZ. (ERIC Document Reproduction Service No. ED 221 881)

Eme, R., Maisiak, R., & Goodale, W. (1979). Seriousness of adolescent problems. *Adolescence, 14,* 93–98.

Erikson, E. (1959). *Identity and the life cycle*. New York: Norton.

Frankson, M. S. (1990). Chicano literature for young adults: An annotated bibliography. *English Journal, 79* (1), 30–35.

Freire, P. (1990). *Pedagogy of the oppressed*. New York: Continuum.

House Select Committee on Children, Youth, and Families. (1991). U.S. Children and Their Families. In *Report on Education Research* (p. 1). Alexandria, VA: The Capitol Publishers.

Johnson, K. (1989, August 27). A new generation of racism is seen. *New York Times*, p. 20.

Mitchell, A.H. (1988). Black adolescent novels in the curriculum. *English Journal, 77* (5), 95–97.

Moir, H. (1989). Current trends and lasting values: A five-year retrospective on children's books. *Ohio Media Spectrum, 41* (4), 5–11.

Nicholson, S. I., & Antill, J. K. (1981). Personal problems of adolescents and their relationships to peer acceptance and sex-role identity. *Journal of Youth and Adolescence, 10*, 309–325.

Ravitch, D. (1990). Multiculturalism yes, particularism no. *Chronicle of Higher Education, 37*, A44.

Rochman, H. (1989). Booktalking: Going global. *Horn Book, 65* (1), 30–35.

Romero, P., & Zancanella, D. (1990). Expanding the circle: Hispanic voices in American literature. *English Journal, 79* (1), 24–29.

Samuels, B. G., & Beers, G. K. (Eds.). (1995/1996). *Your reading: A book-list for junior high and middle school students* (10th ed.) Urbana, IL: National Council of Teachers of English.

Schone, I. (1988). *An Hispanic heritage: A guide to juvenile books about Hispanic peoples and cultures, Series III*. Metuchen, NJ: Scarecrow.

Smith, B. O. (1983). Contingencies of value. *Critical Inquiry, 10*, 1–35.

Steele, S. (1989). On being black and feeling blue. *American Scholar, 58*, 4977–5012.

Stover, L., & Karr, R. (1990). Glasnost in the classroom. *English Journal, 79* (8), 47–53.

Tiedt, P.L., & Tiedt, I.M. (1986). *Multicultural teaching: A handbook of activities, information, and resources* (2nd ed.). Boston: Allyn & Bacon.

Violato, C., & Holden, B. (1988). A confirmatory factor analysis of a four-factor model of adolescent concerns. *Journal of Youth and Adolescence, 17*, 101–113.

Waggoner, D. (1988). Language minorities in the United States in the 1980s: Evidence from the 1980 census. In F.L. McKay & S.C. Wong (Eds.), *Language diversity: Problem or resource?* (pp. 69–108). New York: Newbery.

Wigginton, E. (1992). Culture begins at home. *Educational Leadership, 49* (4), 60–64.

Wilson, R., & Hughes, D. (1981). Appreciating different cultures. In E. Tway (Ed.), *Reading ladders for human relations* (6th ed., pp. 223–313). Urbana, IL: National Council of Teachers of English.

9

Media and Young
Adult Literature

Educators have for many years faced the problem of making the English classroom an exciting, relevant, meaningful place for students to learn. It is no different now that we are moving toward the twenty-first century. Many young people are dissatisfied, characterizing the English classroom as a boring place with no connection to the outside world.

It is quite evident that society is changing. At the turn of the twentieth century, the United States moved from a society fueled by agriculture to one dependent on industry. Education was forced to restructure itself to accommodate the new era. Since the late 1940s, society has begun another era, one that seems to have raced upon us in the last twenty years: the Information Age.

Today students through the Internet Public Library (http://ipl.sils.umich.edu/ – = – ipl@umich.edu) can access the work of many young adult authors and receive a tremendous amount of information. In addition, students can ask specific questions of selected authors and receive responses. As of this writing, authors participating include Lois Lowry, Robert Cormier, Jane Yolen, Avi, Gary Paulsen, Katherine Paterson, Phyllis Reynolds Naylor, and Joan Blos. For example, the following question and response are from the entry for Robert Cormier: Question: "Did you like writing FADE?" Response: "The writing of FADE was virtually a labor of love. Because I wanted the reader to willingly suspend disbelief when the fade arrived, I tried to create a real world (Frenchtown), a real family, a real boy (the most autobiographical writing I've ever done)."

Heinich, Molenda, and Russell (1993) discuss how this most recent change has affected the state of education. They contend that while our overall society in the United States is entirely receptive to new technology, the subculture of education is not. The authors concede that in areas unrelated to instruction, such as attendance and pupil class scheduling, technology has been incorporated effectively. They believe that, unfortunately, "the organization of instruction is basically the same as 100 years ago" (p. 401). When this information is coupled with Nash's (1995) report, "Whiz Kids," in which she contends that U.S. classrooms are lagging behind children's computer interests and abilities, we can begin to see how we are nurturing student apathy. We teach these children of the Information Age as if they are preparing for the Industrial Age (sometimes for the Agricultural Age). In addition, we do not provide them with stimulating content materials that address their social predicaments and personal interests.

Thus, the state of education faces a dilemma, a dilemma we can solve if we only listen to those most affected by education, our young people. They want more interesting materials and a variety of media equal to what they already may have at home to be an integral part of their learning environment. Teachers of varying disciplines can grant this request by learning to incorporate educational technologies into their classroom instruction. Language arts teachers can provide more insurance that future students will be interested and involved in their education by combining the use of technologies with material of social and personal relevance to students—young adult literature.

THEORY AND RESEARCH

Most people think of discussions about instructional technology as discussions about the computer. However, instructional technology includes many types of media and hardware. It is necessary to understand exactly what instructional technology is so that such misconceptions cease to exist. Heinich et al. (1993) define *instructional technology* as "the application of our scientific knowledge about human learning to the practical tasks of teaching and learning" (p. 16). It relies on a variety of media, hardware, and modes of communicating messages for educational purposes. Educators hope to incorporate instructional media technology into the classroom so that students use and manipulate it, taking greater control in their educational settings. Common media used include film, computer disks and CD-ROMs, and audiocassettes.

The roles of media in instruction vary from teacher-directed and –controlled lessons to self-instructing lessons for independent learning purposes. Closely related to self-instruction is cooperative learning, in which students collaborate with teachers and each other in their education. Hypermedia, discussed later, is an example of a newer educational technology that encourages students to rely on their own diverse cognitive strategies of learning as they respond to the information presented.

Heinich et al. (1993) cite a recent survey of patterns of media use in education in Virginia, showing computers to be "the most numerous item of instructional equipment in elementary and secondary schools" (p. 19). Closely following in popularity are audiocassette recorders, filmstrip projectors, overhead projectors, and television receivers/monitors. Adoption of new technologies, such as videodiscs and teleconferencing systems, is slow due to expense and the usability of the "older" instructional aides (p. 19).

As the use of these technologies began increasing in the 1980s, educators feared that technology, specifically the microcomputer, would replace the need for human teachers, according to Higgins (1991). However, teachers came to find that they were still the educational leaders functioning in a facilitator's role and that "students became more involved with their learning as a result" (p. 49). He notes that the computer has become a tool to enhance instruction and student writing skills, with the research indicating that "students now write more than in the pre-word processing days" (p. 50). Higgins emphasizes that current research does not prove that the rate of writing improvement has significantly increased, but it would appear that using the computer takes the drudgery out of composing, rewriting, and editing, motivating students to have greater interest in their work. One could surmise from this that improvement will eventually be manifest, as student use and practice naturally sharpen skills.

Even though educational technology in the 1990s is less threatening to teachers than it was in the 1980s, "only a small number of schools nationwide have gone . . . wholeheartedly into high-technology education" (Lewis, 1991, p. 6). One reason has to do with cost. In addition, Lewis points out that even schools with enough funds have difficulty keeping up with the latest technology because of the constant changes in the industry. For instance, one of the newest items is virtual reality technology, which allows students to travel to distant locations and "sense that they are physically present" (p. 7) through the use of special goggles and gloves.

Mendrinos (1994) provides a unique and insightful argument for incorporating technology into education by focusing on learning styles. The use of instructional technology in schools produces a form of learning Mendrinos refers to as "resource-based," which is learning that promotes several kinds of literacy, as well as critical thinking, skills (p. 2). In this type of learning, information reaches students through many formats, such as the traditional book, periodical, and newspaper, and increasingly from online databases, compact disc—read-only memory (CD-ROM) and laser videodiscs, videotapes, television, satellite transmission, audiovisual materials, and telecommunications. She contends that "these are not supplemental resources but necessary elements integrated within the curriculum to stimulate different literacies (i.e., visual, auditory, textual, information) to increase the learning achievement of the student" (p. 2). Auditory literacy involves students listening to certain material, such as a musical piece, and being able to analyze its underlying meaning. Mendrinos argues that possessing these two forms of literacy enables students to become literate concerning information and to use critical thinking strategies "necessary to seek, gather, evaluate, and apply information in all formats" (p. 3).

Mendrinos (1994) concurs with Heinich et al. (1993) that one of the most attractive aspects of resource-based learning is its adaptability to various learning styles, ranging from individual to group. She asserts that resource-based learning incorporating educational technologies, especially multimedia, "accommodates differences in learning styles and, thus, increases student productivity" (p. 4). She refers to studies that emphasize cultural learning style differences, such as those of African Americans and some Native Americans, who are found to be visual learners, in contrast to, for example, Greek and some western hemisphere cultures, who are shown to have a stronger dependence upon auditory learning. Thus, multimedia, such as the CD-ROM with its combination of visual, tactile, textual, and auditory sensory modalities, becomes an effective form of instruction for diverse populations of students.

Image Projection

Because we live in a technology-laden society, with new items on the market everyday, we sometimes tend to forget the "older" instructional technologies. These technologies still retain their original value when used in the classroom, as for example "projected visuals" (Heinich et al., 1993, p. 134), enlarged still images displayed to or by students in the classroom using overhead, slide, or filmstrip projectors.

In recent decades, the overhead projection system has become "the most widely used audiovisual device in North American classrooms" (Heinich, et al., 1993, p. 134). An overhead projector allows the presenter to manipulate and emphasize materials for the audience. Information can be overlaid to build complexity; eye contact with the audience is more easily maintained; and it is less messy than a chalkboard. Students can make their own transparencies to "act" as teacher for the day during a peer instruction lesson (Heinich et al., 1993). For example, a group of students who have read several works by Chris Crutcher may want to create a visual (chart, diagram, pictogram) on a transparency to illustrate similarities and differences of several of Crutcher's characters. By using various colors and overlays, the rest of the class will better be able to visualize the ideas presented.

Another system used frequently by teachers and students is the slide presentation. Slides offer flexibility unavailable with the more widely used filmstrip because users may easily resequence slides. Heinich et al. (1993) note that making a slide show has become fairly easy for amateurs to do because photographic equipment is now refined and simplified, and automatic projectors are easily available in schools. This type of media use lends "immediacy and specificity" (p. 143) to class lessons that would otherwise be lacking if using commercially produced instructional materials: with only a small amount of guidance, students may work independently or collaboratively to complete multimedia projects that otherwise would be restricted to text only. Teachers and students alike presenting booktalks can make and display slides of the book jacket, cover art, or their own original art while persuading others in the class to read (or not read) the work.

The last projected visual Heinich et al. (1993) present is that of the filmstrip, defined as "a roll of 35 mm transparent film containing a series of related still pictures intended for showing one at a time" (p. 148). Usually, soundtracks recorded on audiocassette accompany filmstrips. Filmstrips are popular because they are less expensive than slides and overhead transparencies, and there is no chance of material becoming unorganized or unsequenced. Most importantly, the pace of viewing a filmstrip may be controlled, in contrast to audio and motion media, making it an attractive vehicle for independent learners who "enjoy using filmstrips on their own" (p. 151) so that they can work at their own speeds.

Audio Instruction

Another form of educational technology that seems to be losing ground in the video/computer age is that of audio instruction. Ironically, Heinich et al. (1993) state that "typical elementary and secondary students spend about 50 percent of their school time just listening" (p. 162). For college students, this percentage jumps to 90 percent. However, educators offer little formal instruction in the development of listening skills. Audio media can help with the acquisition of such skills as following directions or listening for main ideas. The cassette tape recorder and the audio card reader are commonly used for this purpose.

Some advantages to using audio media, besides its support in developing and refining listening skills, include its availability, low cost, and ease of use. Audiotapes can be manipulated on any vocabulary level and employed for individual or group instruction. Audio media's primary strength is with low-level readers or nonreaders, anyone who needs reading improvement. This is due primarily to its ability, as Heinich et al. (1993) state, to "present stimulating verbal messages more dramatically than print can" (p. 164).

The main audio formats used in regular classrooms today are audiocassette tapes and compact discs. Tape recorders and audiocassettes are extremely accessible in schools for students to listen to commercial products or to produce their own materials. Compact discs have replaced phonograph records, but they are more expensive and cannot currently be reused for repeated recording as audiocassettes may. Currently, their use centers around "musical and dramatic reproductions" (Heinich et al., 1993, p. 166) in voice and drama classes.

Video Instruction

Ornstein (1991) details the versatility of using video for educational purposes. He contends that as video increases in its "domination as a mode of communication" (p. 40), students have a great chance for broadening the tools they may use for learning, just as teachers have the chance to incorporate new and different instructional techniques into their classrooms. This domination has created the need "to help children to become critical video consumers" (p. 38). Teachers can do this by incorporating video into their curriculum and ensuring that students are not only passively watching but actively creating their own materials for educational purposes. In doing so, they will have heightened "awareness of how visual images impact upon us as individuals and as a society" (p. 38). Ornstein reviews three options for video use in the classroom appropriate for this discussion: videotapes, videodiscs, and interactive video.

Videotapes allow teachers and learners to record, explain, and replay data. Equipment has become increasingly more portable, sophisticated, and lightweight. Camcorders can record scenes and play them back directly to a television, doubling the equipment's original abilities. Videodiscs are more durable and store greater amounts of information than do videotapes. Digitized information stored on videodiscs is read by beams of laser light, allowing for quality that is unsurpassed in all other video media (Ornstein, 1991, p. 39). However, videodiscs currently are nonrecordable and nonerasable, and are more expensive than videotapes.

Incorporating video production into the classroom allows students more educational independence. Directed by teachers, students experiment and explore in order to discover their own paths. Because students work cooperatively in groups in schools, Brown (1993) asserts that students build life skills involving patience and respect necessary to fulfill requirements of any team project.

INTERACTIVE VIDEO.   Interactive video involves coupling videotapes or discs with a computer to offer learners "realistic situations, simulations, and action-reaction situations" with which to respond and interact (Brown, 1993, p. 39). The computer displays outcomes of learners' responses, providing immediate feedback concerning decision-making skills. Ornstein (1991) suggests that "seeing consequences" (p. 39) through visual images has greater effects on learners than do teachers' written responses.

Brooks and Perl (1991) seem to support Ornstein's position concerning interactive video by adding that such technology inspires greater student interest and longer attention spans. Also, they discuss the use of CD-ROMs as instructional devices that offer students high-quality full-motion and sound instruction as opposed to the "static images" that accompany a "read-only" text (p. 21). One example of the benefits of this technology presently being used for educational purposes is *Compton's Multimedia Encyclopedia*. With a computer that has CD-ROM capability, students can explore "5,000 articles, 63,000 entries, 15,000 photographs and charts, 60 minutes of sound, and 45 animation sequences" (p. 21).

As CD-ROM use becomes more sophisticated, educators are beginning to see other options for its employment in the educational arena. Bennett (1994) reviews how teachers can depend on CD-ROMs for more than just replacing volumes of print dictionaries and encyclopedias. Novels may now appear on computer screens as "living books" (p. 84). Presently, most discs offer "established" materials to learners, such as the *Tale of Peter Rabbit* or *20,000 Leagues Under the Sea*. However, the hope exists that CD-ROM as a genre will gain wide acceptance, and that current authors will begin to produce original material for it. Bennett believes that this genre will evolve quickly because of its employment of graphics, animation, sound effects, narration, and music. Consequently, he warns that having technological capabilities at hand may cause some writers for computer-based children's materials to exploit those capabilities unnecessarily. For instance, in his review of Orange Cherry's *20,000 Leagues Under the Sea,* he criticizes that "animation takes on the role of gimmick rather than as a technique which adds something to the substance of the story" (1994, p. 86).

This genre will likewise be available to amateurs through the use of such CD-ROMs as *Textbook Toolbox,* licensed by Ebook. It involves using a HyperCard®-based tool for Apple Macintosh computers that guides writers as they create electronic books of their own. Students are able to determine how the computer will react to a user's responses (Bennett, 1994).

One title Bennett (1994) finds exciting is "White House Child," written by Greg Bear and published by Ebook, an award-winning science fiction story of a boy's struggle with "his blossoming imagination and with people who would suppress creativity" (p. 92). What makes this title particularly attractive for young adults is its theme of censorship. This CD-ROM includes a video interview with Greg Bear, who discusses why and how he wrote the story, as well as his own feelings concerning censorship of creativity. Bennett believes that this title is a forerunner for a new medium that "cannot be simply dismissed as [a] straightforward [copy] of [a] print book" (p. 94).

Computers

While video is a popular instructional tool in and of itself, computers are recognized as the base component for all discussions concerning the transformation of educational technology in recent history (Lewis, 1991). They can process, store, and transfer information as well as accomodate video displays and various input devices. The physical form of the computer itself continues to evolve, with more laptop and notebook styles becoming available. This creates a multitude of possibilities for the classroom.

For instance, every student and teacher could have their own notebook computer, a "powerful tool which could be carried from class to class" (Lewis, 1991, p. 6). Eliminated would be the messy, overstuffed student notebook from which important assignments vanish into the depths of student lockers. These units (some smaller than the length and width of a sheet of notebook paper) "can store as much as [60 million characters of data]. . . . That's the equivalent of about 30,000 book pages of text information" (p. 6).

Multimedia

Multimedia is an especially attractive and fast-growing area of instructional technology. Galbreath (1994) reviews several definitions of the term *multimedia,* which has been recognized as "the computer-based blending of graphics, sound, and video" or as a bringing together of "video, graphics, animation, text, and sound in a single, computer-controlled presentation" (p. 17). Basically, multimedia involves technologies used in some form of simultaneous combination. Galbreath believes that multimedia is an overall learning system composed of "intelligent integration of two or more communications" (p. 17) under the user's control.

Kalmbach (1994) examines the instructional uses of multimedia and the effect such instruction has on the role of the teacher as instructor. Multimedia application can be as linear as watching a video or sound filmstrip, which students view from start to finish without interaction or interruption. Multimedia also can allow intensive interaction when using a computer to supply options to the user as to selection of study material, and its arrangement and presentation. This versatility of the medium changes the role of the instructor from that of "a dispenser of information to . . . a facilitator of learning" (Kalmbach, 1994, p. 29).

HYPERMEDIA.   Heinich et al. (1993) explain how computer hypermedia systems go a step further than multimedia by permitting students to link related bits of information into a larger framework that they create. "The goal of hypermedia is to immerse users in a richly textured information environment, one in which words, sounds, and still and motion images can be connected in diverse ways" (p. 269), giving students the abilities to construct their own educational outcomes. Thus, students need not be concerned with traditional sequencing in their learning because hypermedia provides the tools to make the connections for them. Students who want to use HyperCard® to create a report with sound, text, and video, can gather their information nonsequencially and use the computer to help form the webbing for their presentations.

Currently, interactive multimedia and hypermedia are available in two major forms: as tools and as educational products. Tools include those materials that grant students the freedom to construct knowledge and explore links, building webs of information between ideas presented in a variety of forms. Most programs fall into the second category, as educational products incorporating fixed subject matter with a selected set of paths to choose for exploration, "representing strands or themes in the topic" (Heinich et al., 1993, p. 28). These often function much like a textbook.

For example, hypertext, a tool, provides a format for writing that encourages both nonlinear and linear organizations of material; nonlinear organization occurs when "active links or 'buttons' . . . take the reader from one section of text to another that the author has decided is related in some fashion and which may or may not be contained in the same document" (Heinich et al., 1993, p. 27). Polin (1991) offers the example of a user of such software who moves from a line of poetry in T. S. Eliot's "The Hollow Men" to a paragraph in Joseph Conrad's *Heart of Darkness*. This student may even wish to incorporate the use of a laser videodisc to provide a link to Francis Ford Coppala's film, *Apocalypse Now.*

Polin (1991) describes a specific example of a hypermedia program called *Media Text,* created by Elliot Soloway. This program is an "illustrated text processor" with multimedia applications that allow learners to use one-step links to connect sections of a text "in a single file and files containing other documents or media formats" (p. 29). Users may complete three tasks: writing a text in paragraph form, creating "buttons" that initiate employment of other media, and linking the media displays by placing them alongside portions of text. The media displays may be accessed by a videodisc player, CD-ROM, original sound or visual images made by the writer, or other documents. Polin feels that one distinct advantage to using *Media Text* is that it is easily learned even without the manual. Polin believes that such programs enhance a teacher's ability to motivate her students, saying, "I have not yet seen a student who is not drawn into a deeper interaction with subject matter by the opportunity to work in a variety of media, literally creating meaning by building connections among ideas and sharing that thinking with peers through a multimedia essay" (p. 28).

Telecommunications and the Internet

A natural progression in this discussion of computers and their multimedia uses is to next view how telecommunications and the Internet are, and soon will be, affecting education. The Internet is a child of telecommunications, one that has 20 million users taking advantage of an "information network of voice, data, images, and full-motion video" (Mendrinos, 1994, p. 42). A user can retrieve information about the poetry of the Dead Sea Scrolls or the complete text of a Shakespearian play (Medrinos, 1994). Its three primary functions include electronic mail (e-mail) for one-to-one or one-to-many communications, "remote login," which allows users to "talk directly to any remote computer," and file exchange, which gives users a way to "capture" and download to a disk files on a variety of topics. The Internet provides educators and students with a new, fast, and relatively easy way to make world contacts without ever leaving home or school.

Of the three mentioned above, e-mail seems to be the fastest-growing area in telecommunications used for educational purposes. Lowry (1994) focuses on the incorporation of e-mail into educational technology, coupled with the exchange and development of ideas through the traditional instructional strategy of class discussion. Lowry asserts that e-mail offers a powerful tool for the enrichment of class discussions on many subjects, and that it is especially effective for including students, who normally are reluctant in traditional settings, in discussions. This seems to happen because more time is allotted for reflection and interaction on the students' part due to the "self-paced," "flexible" character of e-mail (p. 23).

PROJECT BOOKREAD.   Saccardi (1991) offers an exciting example of possible e-mail use in schools. Saccardi is the director of the Fairfield-Westchester Children's Reading Program and a founding member of Project Bookread, a computer-literature program allowing students and authors to interface via technology. Saccardi and her committee formed this group because they wanted to engage their students in reading and discussion, but had been unsuccessful using traditional instructional models. They decided to attempt using e-mail as a way to spark student interest. They selected Gary Paulsen and Sue Ellen Bridgers to be their first guest authors to present information to their students by computer.

Before any interaction between authors and students occured, the committee, representing two schools, began having students in different classes read one of the author's major works. Books for classes of middle schoolers included Paulsen's *Hatchet, The Voyage of the FROG,* and others; classes of high schoolers read from such Bridgers titles as *Home Before Dark* and *Notes From Another Life*. After reading the materials, groups of students from the same grade level, but in different classes, practiced holding online discussions by talking about the plots of the books assigned to them, as well as the similarities and differences between certain titles and styles of their author (Saccardi, 1991). The students then became involved with the authors by posing questions to them and receiving answers they could print and save. Not only did students get a direct perspective from its author about the novel they had read, but they actually witnessed the author's process for writing as he or she "paused to phrase . . . answers in text" (Saccardi, 1991, p. 37).

One teacher concluded that Project Bookread did not make her students "overnight" lovers of reading, but that it did help to increase their participation in class readings and discussion (Saccardi, 1991). Similarly, by having bookshare discussions in this manner, students were more excited about reading books suggested to them by their "on-line" peers (Saccardi, 1991). The computer's importance in this project cannot be ignored: "The computer acted as an equalizer . . . one child [would] not speak throughout the entire [class] exchange, but he sent and received mail on the computer often throughout the demonstration" (Saccardi, 1991, p. 38).

It appears that when technology is incorporated into a content area, students become more highly motivated to learn their material. This is natural, as students today are part of the generation of the Information Age. As a result, they are hungry for interaction with materials that will afford them opportunities to demonstrate their diverse capabilities and learning styles. It is no longer acceptable for teachers to believe that they alone can control the course of students' interests and studies. Educators may be afraid to share some of their power with technological media. If that is the reason schools and teachers "lag behind" on technology incorporation, they are mistaken, and it is today's students who will suffer. Properly applied technology can serve only to enhance teacher instruction, which should motivate teachers as well as students.

CURRICULUM IMPLEMENTATION: YOUNG ADULT LITERATURE AND TECHNOLOGY

We suggest the following four projects as methods for using a variety of technologies and young adult literature.

Project 1: Using Audio and Videocassette to Increase Low-Level Readers' Motivation

> *Required Technology:* **audiotape recorder, videocassette player and monitor, computers with word processing software**

This project focuses on low-level readers in the middle grades. These students usually are placed in "remedial" classes and have skills well below their grade level. As such, they usually maintain attitudes toward learning and school that are not responsive to the traditional literature curriculum. It is simply not enough to tell such students to pick up a book, especially one unrelated to their interests, and read it at home independently. Most of the time they will be unable to read well enough to maintain interest needed to complete a whole novel. In this situation, you may use technology and young adult literature to bring about miraculous results.

It is most important to first establish an environment of trust among you and your students. They must feel safe in the knowledge that no one will be permitted to ridicule or judge them based on their "deficient" skills. After such a climate is set, literature that is of interest and is accessible to them is required. The characters and themes of young adult literature will interest them, and it will be accessible because dialogue often imitates their spoken language. Novels that are suggested with these low-level readers include *The Lottery Rose,* by Irene Hunt; *That Was Then, This Is Now,* by S. E. Hinton, and *A Teacup Full of Roses,* by Sharon Bell Mathis.

For this project, we chose to use *The Outsiders* by S. E. Hinton, for several reasons. First, it is a timeless novel of a young man's battle with society because of his socioeconomic status. The story focuses on loyalty to family and to a gang that inadvertently drags the protagonist, Ponyboy, into dangerous situations. Hence, it is a high-interest story, especially for students who may identify with being on the outside of what is acceptable to mainstream society. Second, this title may be incorporated in an educational technology classroom because both an audio and a video (theatrical film) version of the novel exist. By employing both audio and video, you can provide low-level readers with a better opportunity for success in a literary experience, as well as motivate them to respond through discussion and writing.

To introduce this project, begin with a journal entry in which you ask students to list the rules they believe society expects them to follow in order to become acceptable members of society. After discussing the lists as a class, ask students to choose five rules they can all agree on. Then, ask them to write in their journal the reasons they think some people have a more difficult time abiding by these rules than others do. Most will be able to relate well to this assignment. After further discussion, introduce the novel and ask students to predict the meaning of the title.

As you pass out the novel to students, explain that instead of reading as is normally done, they will be reading along with an unabridged audiocassette. In this process, students will follow along with the novel, which will reinforce correct reading of dialogue and, more importantly, will erase the air of frustration that exists for low-level readers when confronted with literature. In this way, they will be free to enjoy the story and be more motivated to discuss their feelings and ideas.

At least twice a week, have students write in their journals, to an imaginary or real friend, letters explaining what was happening in the life of one of the characters in the book. This activity should be accessible to any level of student, since most enjoy writing notes to their peers. More importantly, it will improve their summary and response skills in a nonthreatening way, since grades will be based on content and participation, not grammar and spelling.

It may take two weeks at the minimum to complete the reading of *The Outsiders* because the audiocassette is five and one-half hours long. Once students have finished reading, ask them to work with a partner to devise a list of events they feel would be most important to include in a movie based on the novel. Collect each pair's list to keep until after the viewing of the movie, *The Outsiders,* directed by Francis Ford Coppala. After viewing the movie, return the lists to them so that they can compare their "director's cuts" with those of the actual movie. This should provide for lively discussion prior to the culminating assignment. This assignment involves students, working in pairs, drafting a letter to you similar to those they have been writing in their journals. In their letters, they explain whether they preferred the movie or the novel based on class discussion and their lists. After they finish their initial draft, the students decide which member has the responsibility for typing the draft and which member has the responsibility for editing it on the computers in the computer lab. In this way, students are allowed to work cooperatively to complete the project while being afforded the aid of the computer program's spell checking and grammar checking applications.

Based on educators' work with remedial readers, both young adults and adults, the single most effective way to encourage their motivation to read is to provide them with a stress-free environment for practice. Using audiocassettes helps reduce stress until readers are confident enough to read independently. In addition, low-level readers lose much of the content of a novel when they read independently, which makes it difficult for them to participate in journal and discussion activities. With audiocassette, students have a better chance to receive all the content and to be prepared for class discussions and assignments. Likewise, by using the computer, their fear of the written work will be significantly reduced.

Project 2: E-mail Discussion Groups Meet the Authors of Young Adult Novels

Required Technology: a telecommunications system—computers with a modem. Also requires the teacher to solicit and arrange for the chosen author's participation.

Many students coming to school today have computer systems at home that outperform those used in the schools. Some young people are already Internet literate and well versed in using e-mail for discussion. Many students logon as soon as they get home from school and logoff when it is time for bed. Obviously, such a tool is a great motivator for young adults growing up in the Information Age.

This project involves students on the same grade levels but from different classes, or even schools, reading two young adult novels by the same author, then discussing them among themselves, followed by actually "meeting" the author online. Each class is assigned the reading of one of the novels and is to complete it on a set date so that e-mail discussions may begin within a week from that date. E-mail discussions among the students will focus on the author's style as well as the different storylines. Students online will ask questions selected with the help of peers in their same class. After receiving basic instruction and demonstration on using e-mail, students share their personal experiences with the book their class read and review the book for their e-mail partners, who in turn do the same with the other novel.

The major goal of this portion of the project is to engage all students at some point in a literary discussion. Too often, five or six students in a class and the teacher discuss the literature while the other twenty members of the class idly sit and listen. By using e-mail, each student may participate with an e-mail discussion partner or group and show you a printout of the discussion. If students have the capability and desire, they could continue their discussions and recommendations at home with their own systems. In this manner, students practice discussion techniques and improve social skills, too.

Part two of this project is for students to converse with and question the books' author on line. You or a colleague must arrange for the chosen author's participation. E-mail partners and class members work together to produce a list of discussion questions to ask the author. After selecting five questions per novel, members in each class would form small groups of four or five students, and each group will ask one of the selected questions, using the telecommunications system at school. Students in both classes at the same time will be viewing the discussion between their peers and the author, and all may receive a printout of the discussion.

Imagine how engaging it would be for students to receive answers quickly and to see authors actually composing the answers. To actually discuss the novel with its author, instead of only being able to hear the teacher act as the spokesperson with all the correct answers, would serve to motivate students to prepare careful, thought-provoking questions.

For example, if you are working with middle school students, you might want to invite Walter Dean Myers to be the class's e-mail guest speaker, using his novels *Scorpions* and *Somewhere in the Darkness*. These novels have different themes but similar character types and settings. Scorpions's plot line centers on the life of Jamal Hicks, a junior high schooler from a "bad" neighborhood who is not doing well in school and is being pressured into replacing his imprisoned brother as the leader of a neighborhood gang. Jamal wants no part of the gang because he wants to have a better life than his brother. As the action develops, Jamal must rely on his friend, Tito, to help him out of this tough situation. In *Somewhere in the Darkness,* the protagonist, Jimmy Little, is confronted with meeting his father for the first time since he was three years old, when his father, Crab, was sent to prison. This story focuses on the father–son relationship with the underlying theme of personal discovery through a journey. Both novels offer a high level of interest and realism for young readers, regardless of socioeconomic or ethnic background, who previously may only have been presented with stereotypical views of urban youth.

If you are working with high school students, especially students in the eleventh or twelfth grades, you may want to ask Chris Crutcher to be the guest author. His novels *Chinese Handcuffs* and *Staying Fat for Sarah Byrnes* provide material rich with mature themes for discussion among youth on the very edge of adulthood. *Chinese Handcuffs* deals with the story of Dillon Hemingway and Jennifer Lawless, both of whom are in the midst of serious situations that affect their everyday lives. Dillon must accept his brother's suicide while Jennifer must find a way to escape a sexually abusive parent. *Staying Fat for Sarah Byrnes* provides another emotionally charged reading, one which produces more questions than answers. In this novel, Eric Calhoune and his friend Sarah Byrnes, while in junior high, are outcasts within their peer group due to their physical appearances. However, as they reach their senior year of high school, Eric has changed his appearance; Sarah has not, as she is severely scarred from a childhood burning, the product of her father's abuse. As in *Chinese Handcuffs,* the theme of escaping an abusive atmosphere with the help of a friend is prevalent. Students who read these novels would surely have many questions for the author and be well motivated to participate in the e-mail discussion groups.

As a followup to this project, you may have students spend a day in the computer lab to write a response paper concerning their experience. In it, they may include how this assignment differed from previous classroom literature experiences they have had, and which ones they preferred. In addition, you may want to know how discussing the novels with the author enriched their understanding of the author's style and his process in writing. Finally, students should relate how this experience has improved their technology skills, as well as what their future uses of e-mail will be.

Project 3: Creating a Multimedia Thematic Presentation

> *Required Technology:* **computers, camcorders, videocassette player and monitor, audio recorders, slide and overhead projectors, and CD player**

This project is more student centered and controlled, than the previous two, allowing for maximum enrichment and critical thinking. It can be adapted for grades 7 through 12, as most teens are quite familiar with using the required equipment. In addition to affording students active participation in designing a lesson to be presented to classmates, this assignment should be motivating because it is collaborative in nature. Thus, it will allow for a great deal of response-based literature discussion among class members.

The project involves self-selected groups of classmates (no more than five to a group) choosing one of five novels with a specific theme for which each group must connect with another form of young adult literature, either short stories or poetry, or with song lyrics, in order to display a multimedia thematic presentation to the class. Before group and novel selection, spend part of one class period discussing the project with the students, explaining that students would be expected to work together in groups and that all members would receive the same grade based on group cooperation, level of content, and use of media.

Next, briefly introduce the novels and their subsequent themes from which groups may choose, establishing that only one group per class may use a particular novel and theme. Then, discuss the expectations of the final products: each group should present the theme of its novel and a selected poem, song, or short story using a combination of media in their presentation. Students will be free to decide among themselves which media they wish to use and how to incorporate the poem, song, or short story; presentations should run no longer than twenty minutes. You might offer suggestions such as turning the novel into a one-act play to be videotaped, or selecting passages to incorporate into a radio play complete with sound effects. Students could use live performances and original artwork as well. Once you have explained these basic guidelines, your role will be that of facilitator in charge of time management and equipment procuring. Other problems, such as differences of opinion or location of stories and poems within the presentation, would be up to each group to resolve.

Examples of materials to provide to student groups include the following titles: *The Brave,* Robert Lipsyte; *Lizard,* Dennis Covington; *If Rock and Roll Were a Machine,* Terry Davis; *Running Loose,* Chris Crutcher; and *Beyond the Chocolate War,* Robert Cormier. These works are appropriate for high school classrooms. The themes to explore would include establishing personal identity in *Lizard,* exploring through a journey in *The Brave,* dealing with abuse in *If Rock and Roll Were a Machine,* dealing with loss and death in *Running Loose,* and navigating peer situations in *Beyond the Chocolate War.* In order for groups to form their thematic connections with another form of young adult literature, keep in the classroom copies of *Crossroads: Classic Themes in Young Adult Literature* (Scott, Foresman, 1995); *Connections: Short Stories by Outstanding Writers for Young Adults,* Don Gallo, editor, (1989); *American Street: A Multicultural Anthology of Stories,* written by Anne Mazer (1993), *Preposterous: Poems of Youth,* Paul Janeczko, editor, (1991); and *My Friend's Got This Problem, Mr. Candler,* written by Mel Glenn (1991). Students would not be limited to these resources and could present others for permission to use.

The hope is that by requiring minimal structure in presentation, only a thematic connection between two works be presented through the use of multimedia. Students will be free to explore their imaginations, examining their feelings about and responses to the theme and novel they select. By working with group members, students will be sharing responses during every segment of their work, receiving guidance and feedback from peers instead of from a teacher. Most empowering to students will be that by presenting their final product to their classmates, they become teachers themselves. To assess the success of the project, you could ask for written personal responses from all students concerning both the cooperative and the technological aspects of the assignment.

Project 4: Electronic Book Report

Required Technology: **computers with CD-ROM or laserdisc player hookup; *Media Text*™, *HyperStudio*™, *Digital Chisel*™, or other appropriate software**

The goal of this project is to provide students with a motivating alternative to the traditional written book report. Instead of summarizing details and pinpointing facts, *Media Text*™, *HyperStudio*™, *Digital Chisel*™ or similar programs allow students to create a written text on the computer, with visual and auditory effects gathered from other sources or crafted by the writer. Before assigning such a project, you must (1) know how to use all the available components of the program, (2) design a simulated model for training students, and (3) guide students through a practice session in the computer lab. Students are then free to produce some really innovative book reports. Students can share their projects by exchanging their "electronic books" with peers. In this way, students can motivate each other to read future titles as well as share processes for creating their books.

For this project, each student independently reads a self-chosen young adult title by a set date. On that date, the class begins work in the computer lab. Students need to develop an abridged form of their novel by using these programs to write the text, create buttons to activate media displays, and locate their buttons strategically in columns running alongside the text. These buttons, once activated by the reader, can bring up graphics or animations, find and run a section of video from a laserdisc player, find and display images or play sounds from a CD-ROM player, play digitized sound the writer has recorded, display images of drawings the writer has scanned in, or open other documents in order to build connections. Each electronic book should be five to ten minutes in length. Such a program presents infinite possibilities for students to explore and use their critical thinking skills as they actually create their own electronic book.

Allow five full days in the computer lab to create the books (perhaps more with inexperienced users), and approximately two for exchanging and sharing. This project is adaptable to any grade level: although younger teens would have more "fun" reading each other's finished products. However, high school students could experiment with creating a professional book and, as an extension of the project, investigate the work's commercial potential. This is an exciting project because hypertext programs and CD-ROM books are still novel ideas. Thus, students will be expressing themselves in an entirely new way, one with immediate relevance to the Information Age.

In addition to these projects, you and your students can also develop a hypertext "home page" for disseminating your reactions, opinions, art, or responses of any kind to the young adult books that you are reading. Too, classes can develop their own database about the literature used in and out of the classroom. This database could include, but not be limited to, reviews of selected works written by the students and other critics, general responses to works read, biographical information about authors, and other information that is relevant to the students' study of young adult literature. This approach connects reading, writing, research, and technology, and provides a forum for exchange.

The projects described in this chapter offer diverse uses of instructional technology and young adult literature. They address a variety of learning styles and offer learning activities that will motivate all students on some level. Young adult literature offers students stimulating reading material that can still fulfill all the requirements of any literature curriculum. Incorporating technology allows teachers to make the material relevant to the skills that will be required of present-day young adults as they enter the job market. Together, the two provide an empowering and motivating air to the English classroom.

Young Adult Technology

Audiocassettes

Angell, Judie. *Ronnie and Rosey*. Level: 7–9. Theme: Family. Time: 81 min.

Avi. *The Fighting Ground*. Level 7–9. Theme: Historical. Time: 68 min.

Avi. *Wolf Rider*. Level: 7–10. Theme: Historical. Time: 5 hrs.

Bennett, James. *I Can Hear the Mourning Dove*. Level: 7–9. Theme: Death. Time: 7.5 hrs.

Blume, Judy. *Are You There God? It's Me, Margaret*. Level: 7–9. Theme: Puberty. Time: 197 min.

Blume, Judy. *Deenie*. Level: 7–9. Theme: Illness. Time: 66 min.

Blume, Judy. *It's Not the End of the World*. Level: 7–9. Theme: Puberty. Time: 197 min.

Bonham, Frank. *Durango Street*. Level: 7–10. Theme: Gangs. Time: 79 min.

Byars, Betsy. *The Pinballs*. Level: 7–9. Theme: Family. Time: 84 min.

Cleary, Beverly. *Fifteen*. Level: 7–10. Theme: Dating. Time: 85 min.

Cleary, Beverly. *Jean and Johnny*. Level: 7–10. Theme: Dating. Time: 75 min.

Cormier, Robert. *The Chocolate War*. Level: 9–11. Theme: Peer pressure. Time: 338 min.

Cooney, Caroline B. *The Face on the Milk Carton*. Level 7–10. Theme: Family/Suspense. Time: 180 min.

Danziger, Paula. *Can You Sue Your Parents for Malpractice?* Level: 7–9. Theme: Humor. Time: 89 min.

Danziger, Paula. *The Cat Ate My Gymsuit*. Level: 7–9. Theme: Self-esteem. Time: 56 min.

Danziger, Paula. *The Divorce Express*. Level: 7–9. Theme: Divorce. Time: 81 min.

Danziger, Paula. *The Pistachio Prescription*. Level: 7–9. Theme: Humor. Time: 80 min.

Danziger, Paula. *There's a Bat in Bunk Five*. Level: 7–9. Theme: Humor. Time: 81 min.

Duncan, Lois. *Down a Dark Hall*. Level: 8–11. Theme: Suspense. Time: 93 min.

Duncan, Lois. *Killing Mr. Griffin*. Level: 9–12. Theme: Suspense/Peer pressure. Time: 88 min.

Duncan, Lois. *Stranger with My Face*. Level: 8–11. Theme: Suspense. Time: 91 min.

Duncan, Lois. *Summer of Fear*. Level: 8–11. Theme: Suspense/Supernatural. Time: 72 min.

Frank, Anne. *Anne Frank: The Diary of a Young Girl*. Level: 7–9. Theme: Holocaust. Time: 64 min.

Gallo, Donald R., ed. *Sixteen: Short Stories by Outstanding Writers for Young Adults*. Level: varies. Theme: varies. Time: 335 min.

Gallo, Donald R., ed. *Visions: Nineteen Short Stories by Outstanding Writers for Young Adults*. Level: varies. Theme: varies. Time: 464 min.

George, Jean Craighead. *Julie of the Wolves*. Level: 6–8. Theme: Survival. Time: 4.5 hrs.

Golding, William. *Lord of the Flies*. Level: 8–11. Theme: Survival. Time: 351 min.

Hamilton, Virginia. *M. C. Higgins, the Great*. Level; 7–9. Time: 8.5 hrs.

Hinton, S. E. *The Outsiders*. Level: 8–11. Theme: Friendship/Belonging. Time: 309 min.

L'Engle, Madeleine. *Camilla*. Level: 7–9. Theme: Family/Romance. Time: 73 min.

L'Engle, Madeleine. *A Wrinkle in Time*. Level: 6–8. Theme: Fantasy. Time: 345 min.

LeGuin, Ursula K. *A Wizard of Earthsea*. Level: 6–8. Theme: Fantasy. Time: 7.25 hrs.

MacLachlan, Patricia. *Journey*. Level: 7–9. Theme: Family. Time: 180 min.

Mazer, Harry. *The Last Mission*. Level: 7–9. Theme: War. Time: 74 min.

Mazer, Harry. *Snow Bound*. Level: 7–9. Theme: Survival. Time: 86 min.

Mazer, Norma Fox. *Taking Terri Mueller*. Level 7–9. Theme: Family. Time: 85 min.

Paulsen, Gary. *Hatchet*. Level: 7–9. Theme: Survival. Time: 210 min.

Paulsen, Gary. *The Monument*. Level: 7–9. Theme: Honor. Time: 180 min.

Paulsen, Gary. *The River*. Level: 7–9. Theme: Survival. Time: 180 min.

Paterson, Katherine. *Lyddie*. Level: 6–8. Theme: Relationships. Time: 6.75 hrs.

Peck, Richard. *Remembering the Good Times*. Level: 8–11. Theme: Suicide. Time: 60 min.

Peck, Robert Newton. *A Day No Pigs Would Die*. Level: 7–9. Theme: Family. Time: 56 min.

Rawls, Wilson. *Where the Red Fern Grows*. Level: 7–9. Theme: Adventure. Time: 80 min.

Sleator, William. *Interstellar Pig*. Level: 8–11. Theme: Fantasy/Humor. Time: 55 min.

Voight, Cynthia. *Homecoming*. Level: 7–9. Theme: Family. Time: 14.25 hrs.

VIDEO TITLES

Across Five Aprils: War and Hope (1990). Author: Hunt, Irene (1964). Level: 7–10. Theme: Civil War. Time: 30 min.

All Summer in a Day (1982). Author: Bradbury, Ray (1958). Level: 7–9. Theme: Peer conflict. Time: 28 min.

Almos' a Man (1977). Author: Wright, Richard. Level: 8–12. Theme: Racial strife. Time: 39 min.

Anne Frank: Diary of a Young Girl (1959). Author: Frank, Anne (1956). Level: 7–9. Theme: Holocaust. Time: 151 min.

Back to the Future (1985). Author: Fleming, Robert. Level: 7–9. Theme: Science fiction. Time: 116 min.

Between Two Loves (1984). Author and original title: Miller, Sandy. *Two Loves for Jenny* (1982). Level: 7–10. Theme: Love. Time: 27 min.

The Black Stallion (1979). Author: Farley, Walter (1941). Level: 7–9. Theme: Adventure. Time: 117 min.

Bridge to Terabithia (1985). Author: Paterson, Katherine (1977). Level: 6–8. Theme: Friendship/Death. Time: 58 min.

Brighton Beach Memoirs (1986). Playwright: Simon, Neil (1984). Level: 10–12. Theme: Jewish family. Time: 110 min.

Can a Guy Say No? (1988). Author and original title: Strasser, Todd. *A Very Touchy Subject* (1985). Level: 9–12. Theme: Sexual relationship. Time: 58 min.

The Cap (1985). Based on short story entitled "A Cap for Steve." Author: Callaghan, Morley. Level: 6–8. Theme: Father/Son relationship. Time: 26 min.

The Chocolate War (1988). Author: Cormier, Robert (1974). Level: 10–12. Theme: Peer pressure. Time: 103 min.

The Chronicles of Narnia (1991). Author: Lewis, C. S. (1955). Level: 6–8. Theme: Fantasy/Adventure. Time: 9 hrs.

City Boy (1992). Author and original title: Stratton-Porter, Gene. *Freckles*. Level: 6–9. Theme: Coming of age. Time: 42 min.

Daddy, I'm Their Mama Now (1984). Author and original title: Byars, Betsy. *The Night Swimmers* (1980). Level: 7–9. Theme: Family. Time: 26 min.

The Day They Came to Arrest the Book (1987). Author: Hentoff, Nat (1982). Level: 9–12. Theme: Censorship. Time 47 min.

Dear Lovey Hart: I Am Desperate (1977). Author: Conford, Ellen (1975). Level: 8–12. Theme: Humor/Love. Time: 32 min.

Dinky Hocker (1979). Author and original title: Kerr, M. E. *Dinky Hocker Shoots Smack!* (1972). Level: 8–11. Theme: Overeating. Time: 30 min.

The Face on the Milk Carton (1995). Author: Cooney, Caroline B. (1993). Level: 7–10. Theme: Suspense/Family/Identity. Time: 2 hrs. (made for t.v. movie)

A Family of Strangers (1978). Author and original title: Bates, Betty. *Bugs in Your Ears* (1977). Level: 7–10. Theme: New family. Time 46 min.

The Fig Tree (1992). Author: Porter, Katherine Anne. Level 6–8. Theme: Death. Time: 59 min.

Freaky Friday (1976). Author: Rodgers, Mary (1972). Level: 6–8. Theme: Humor. Time: 98 min.

A Girl of the Limberlost (1991). Author: Stratton-Porter, Geneva Grace (1986). Level: 7–9. Theme: Adventure. Time: 105 min.

The Glass Menagerie (1987). Playwright: Williams, Tennessee (1975). Level: 10–12. Theme: Identity. Time: 132 min.

A Hero Ain't Nothin' but a Sandwich (1977). Author: Childress, Alice (1973). Level: 6–9. Theme: Urban life/Drugs. Time: 107 min.

The House of Dies Drear (1991). Author: Hamilton, Virginia (1968). Level: 6–8. Theme: Mystery. Time: 107 min.

Island of the Blue Dolphins (1964). Author: O'Dell, Scott (1960). Level: 6–8. Theme: Survival. Time: 99 min.

Jacob Have I Loved (1989). Author: Paterson, Katherine (1980). Level 7–9. Theme: Sibling relationship. Time: 57 min.

The Lilith Summer (1985). Author: Hadley, Irwin (1979). Level: 7–10. Theme: Friendship. Time: 28 min.

Lord of the Flies (1990). Author: Golding, William. Level: 9–12. Theme: Survival. Time: 90 min.

My Mother Was Never a Kid (1981). Author and original title: Pascal, Francine. *Hangin' Out with Cici* (1977). Level: 6–8. Theme: Mother–daughter relationship. Time: 46 min.

Ordinary People (1980). Author Guest, Judith (1979). Level 10–12. Theme: Suicide/Family. Time: 124 min.

The Outsiders (1983). Author: Hinton, S. E. (1967). Level: 8–11. Theme: Friendship/Family. Time: 91 min.

Roll of Thunder, Hear My Cry (1978). Author: Taylor, Mildred D. (1976). Level: 7–10. Theme: Family/Racism. Time: 135 min.

Runaway (1989). Author and original title: Holman, Felice. *Slake's Limbo* (1974). Level: 6–8. Theme: Suspense. Time: 58 min.

The Screaming Woman (1986). Author: Bradbury, Ray. Level: 7–9. Theme: Horror/Suspense. Time: 26 min.

A Single Light (1984). Author: Wojciechowska, Maia (1968). Level: 7–9. Theme: Acceptance. Time: 55 min.

Snow Bound (1978). Author: Mazer, Harry (1973). Level: 7–9. Theme: Survival. Time: 50 min.

Sounder (1972). Author: Armstrong, William H. (1969). Level 7–9. Theme: Coming of age/Family. Time: 105 min.

Tex (1982). Author: Hinton, S. E. (1979). Level: 8–11. Theme: Family. Time: 103 min.

Welcome Home, Jellybean! (1986). Author: Shyer, Marlene Fanta (1980) Level: 7–10. Theme: Family situations. Time: 30 min.

When We First Met (1984). Author: Mazer, Norma Fox (1982). Level 9–11. Theme: Love. Time: 54 min.

Where the Red Fern Grows. Author: Rawls, Wilson. Level: 7–9. Theme: Adventure/Coming of age. Time: 100 min.

Where the Red Fern Grows II (1992). Level: 7–9. Theme: Coming of age. Time: 105 min.

Words by Heart (1991). Author: Sebestyen, Ouida (1979). Level: 7–9. Theme: Racism/Historical. Time: 110 min.

MEET THE AUTHOR VIDEOS

A Talk with Jerry Spinelli. Hosted by Tim Podell. 27 min.

A Talk with Paula Fox. Hosted by Tim Podell. 24 min.

A Talk with Jean Craighead George. Hosted by Tim Podell. 26 min.

A Talk with Phyllis Reynolds Naylor. Hosted by Tim Podell. 26 min.

CD-ROMs—LITERATURE AND WRITING

Media Text. Soloway, Elliot. Links to video clips, QuickTime® movies, and more. Macintosh CD, $99.

Microsoft Publisher. Uses Page Wizards™ to produce professional pieces. Win CD, $138.95.

The Multimedia Workshop. Incorporates text, video clips, and sound effects. Macintosh CD, $129.95.

Storybook Weaver—Deluxe CD Version. Students can create their own storybooks with pictures, words, and sounds. Macintosh CD, $78.95.

CATALOGS CITED FOR MULTIMEDIA LISTS

Film Archives, 1994 (Botsford, CT)

Listening Library, Media Treasures, 1994 (Old Greenwich, CT)

Perma-Bound: Books, Media and Technology, 1995 (Jacksonville, IL)

Software Source, 1995 (Plano, TX)

Sunburst: Multimedia Materials for Education, 1994 (Sunburst Communications, Pleasantville, NY)

TEACHER RESOURCE

For an excellent exploration of how the World Wide Web can be used with Young Adult Literature, see Carter, Betty. (Ed.). (1966). "The Library Connection" in *The ALAN Review, 23* (2), 46–48.

❧ Learning Log Responses ❧

Write a rationale to your administrator for any technology named in this chapter that you could use in your classroom.

Plan a multimedia activity using three works of young adult literature.

Plan a young adult literature activity with students in another school using e-mail.

REFERENCES

Bennett, H. (1994). To instruct and delight: Children's and young adult's literature on CD-ROM. *CD-ROM Professional, 7* (4), 84–94.

Brooks, R., & Perl, B. (1991). Interactive technology for education. *Principal, 71* (2), 20–21.

Brown, K. (1993). Video production in the classroom: Creating successes for students and schools. *Tech Trends, 38* (3), 32–35.

Galbreath, J. (1994). Multimedia in education: Because it's there? *Tech Trends, 39* (6), 17–20.

Heinich, R., Molenda, M., & Russell, J. D. (1993). *Instructional media and the new technologies of instruction.* Englewood Cliffs, NJ: Merrill/Prentice Hall.

Higgins, J. E. (1991). The technological evolution in schools: Reflections and projections. *Contemporary Education, 63* (1), 49–51.

Kalmbach, J. A. (1994). Just in time for the 21st century: Multimedia in the classroom. *Tech Trends, 39* (11), 29–32.

Lewis, P. H. (1991). The technology of tomorrow. *Principal, 71* (2), 5–7.

Lowry, M. (1994). Electronic discussion groups. *Tech Trends, 39* (2), 22–24.

Mendrinos, R. (1994). *Building information literacy using high technology: A guide for schools and libraries.* Loveland, CO: Libraries Unlimited.

Nash, K. (1995). Whiz kids. *Computerworld, Inc., 8* (May), 2–5.

Ornstein, A. C. (1991). The video curriculum. *Contemporary Education, 63* (1), 38–41.

Polin, L. (1991). The multimedia essay, or designing is thinking. *The Writing Notebook* (April/May), 27–29.

Saccardi, M. (1991). The interactive computer: Authors and readers online. *School Library Journal, 37* (10), 36–38.

CHAPTER

10

The Censorship Issues

The whole issue of censorship is concerned with who's on top, who's in charge, who's in power. Can you read this, can you listen to this, can you watch this. . . . I always tell kids in these places where the books have been taken off the school shelves that the most important things are the things your parents don't want you to find out. So when they ban a book I tell them run, don't walk, to the nearest bookstore and get it so you can find out what your elders don't want you to know. Those secrets have power.

Stephen King (1990)

The power to control what one reads, hears, and views is the essential component in the philosophical base of the censor. The censor takes many forms, some that are generally acceptable and others that are not: government (these materials are classified because they may hurt national security); courts (decisions are kept closed because they may infringe on the rights of individuals); public agencies, most notably school boards (books, films, and records/tapes have offensive material of some sort and are not appropriate for young people in general); and parents (this book, film, record/tape has offensive material of some sort and is not appropriate for our children).

The general public has accepted the government's and courts' decisions, although many file suits and base arguments on the Freedom of Information Act, which makes some material open to the public. Those issues do not directly concern those who read or teach young adult literature, although individuals may have concerns in these matters. In addition, most people would agree that parents have every right to decide the reading, listening, and viewing habits of their own children— even if many parents do not exercise that right. What *is* of concern to librarians, teachers, students, and some of the general public is the attempt by special interest individuals and groups to keep specific works of literature, film, and recordings away from groups of students in an educational setting. This chapter discusses these important issues as they relate to the English classroom.

A HISTORICAL VIEW

Censorship is not a twentieth-century American phenomenon. Ideas have been censored since the beginning of time, or so it seems. Some argue that many of the same measures suggested by contemporary censors were first used by Plato. He believed that many of the writers of his time were out of step with his thinking, and he made sure that they were banished from society because they were not working for the well-being of the young. This may have laid the ground work for the censors of the 1990s. Since Plato, numerous incidents over the centuries have added to censorship's long and notorious history.

History records that the works of Confucius were burned in China, Julius Caesar burned the Library of Alexandria, and the Bible was destroyed publicly in England. The Catholic Index of Forbidden Works, the first known "hit list," was published in 1555 in England. The Soviet Union was notorious for altering encyclopedias and journals prior to dissemination throughout the country. For example, *Science,* along with other foreign publications, was routinely censored. Whole articles, usually from the "News and Comment" section, were removed. Many people remember reading about the book burning that took place in Nazi Germany. There are many others, too many to mention here. Suffice it to say that censorship throughout the world has been alive and well for many, many years.

In America, censorship was rooted in the Blue Law controversy. These laws were enacted to close most businesses on Sundays; however, very little was done to enforce the closing. Anthony Comstock, upset that most business and law enforcement people ignored the laws, founded the Society for the Suppression of Vice in New York in 1872. He went on to Washington to lobby for the passage of a federal statute against obscenity, abortion, and other evils as he saw them. With this new law in hand, Comstock began his journey, destroying what he considered bad literature and imprisoning the authors of these works. Comstock's most famous book, *Traps for the Young* (1883), listed the "traps" that young people could fall into: reading light literature, newspaper advertisements, and literature received through the mail. His list of taboos also included gambling, playing pool, using contraceptives, smoking, and drinking alcoholic beverages.

As more literature was written and available to the general public, the censors had more targets. During the early history of American and British literature, the works censored were, of course, from the traditional, classic menu. Attacks on young adult literature did not start until the mid 1990s. In the early days, *Gulliver's Travels* was condemned as being "wicked and obscene," and Shakespeare's *The Merchant of Venice* was removed from New York high schools as anti-Semitic. Voltaire's *Candide* was seized and labeled obscene in 1929; Mark Twain's *Huckleberry Finn* was banned by the Concord (Massachusetts) Public Library the year it was published because of its interracial heresy; the Texas State Board of Education banned the Merriam Webster *New Collegiate Dictionary* because it included seven particular words thought to be obscene; Whitman's *Leaves of Grass* was banned in 1855 by the Boston Society for the Suppression of Vice; and *Ulysses,* considered one of the world's most significant pieces of literature, was seized by the Collector of Customs in 1930 before it could get to the publishers. It also was labeled "obscene." Steinbeck's *Grapes of Wrath* and *Of Mice and Men* are continually censored in one way or another. In fact, between the years of 1982 and 1991, *Of Mice and Men* held the title as the most challenged book (People for the American Way, 1991, p. 123).

As young adult literature began to mature, it too received its share of censorship. Prior to the 1960s, young adult literature was considered "safe"; i.e., the themes were harmless and were certainly not offensive to any segment of society. Most of the novels centered around the "all-American" family, with young people participating in a very sterile environment. The literature was phony; the language was pure and clean; the plots involved prom dates and similar activities; and the characters were WASPs. This unrealistic literature made no mention of pregnancy, drugs, sexual abuse, divorce, alcohol abuse, violence, prejudice, suicide, profanity, or other realistic concerns.

Then two important phenomena changed everything: after World War II, the paperback book became popular, and in the late 1960s, realism invaded the literature. As a result, the censor has been knocking at the schoolroom door ever since. The paperback brought literature to the hands and pockets of almost every student. It was easy to read, certainly easy to carry around, and the price was right. Paperbacks had not been popular in the classroom up to this point. Teachers did not use them primarily because of their lack of quality and appearance.

The second event that changed the relationship between young adults and their reading was the publication of J.D. Salinger's *The Catcher in the Rye* (1951), Ann Head's *Mr. and Mrs. Bo Jo Jones* (1967), S.E. Hinton's *The Outsiders* (1967), and Paul Zindel's *The Pigman* (1968). With the publication of these works and those that followed, young people were off and running with literature that spoke directly to them. Consequently, the censors were also off and running because they now had something more to denounce: the literature used in the schools.

Following on the heels of these first publications were others that also received harsh reviews: Robert Lipsyte's *The Contender* (1967), John Donovan's *I'll Get There, It Better Be Worth the Trip* (1969), and Paul Zindel's *My Darling, My Hamburger* (1969). The field of young adult literature continued to grow and change as it reflected a more sophisticated and complex society. The literature of the 1970s, 1980s, and 1990s became increasingly mature in its treatment of the issues of the day. When this happened, those books that dealt with controversial topics were open to criticism from those who disagreed with the issues or the placement of those issues in classrooms and libraries.

Who Are the Censors?

Censors have various motivations and agendas, and they make their attitudes and criticisms known to the classroom teacher in different ways. Some are individuals that simply do not want a particular piece of literature to be taught in the classroom; others are members of special interest groups that have taken stands against having particular literature taught in schools. A few censors take the form of public agencies. Whatever the form, these censors often place an insurmountable burden on the classroom teacher. On some occasions, teachers are the censors themselves. We rarely think of teachers as censors; normally we think of them as those who feel the brunt of the censor. However, there are times when the teacher, perhaps acting as a parent, will file a challenge to a work.

Some argue that teachers are censors when they select the materials to be used in the classroom; however, we do not consider them censors in this role. Teachers should make the decisions on what materials will be ordered by school districts and what books students will read. Since all published books cannot be ordered for the classroom or the library, some selection must be made. We hope that books will be chosen based on the quality of the literature and how the literature best meets the needs of young people. The major difference between people making decisions on the selection of the materials and those who wish to censor materials is that "selection seeks to promote the right of the reader to read; censorship seeks to protect not the right—but the reader himself from the fancied effects of his reading. The selector has faith in the intelligence of the reader; the censor has faith only in his own" (Asheim, 1953, p. 67).

School administrators, both at the building and district levels, often find themselves acting as censors. Whether as a result of input from another source or simply from their own objections, administrators have a tremendous amount of power in determining what is in the curriculum and what is not. Many administrators are very concerned about public relations and would rather not have to fight a battle about whether a piece of literature should be retained in the curriculum. Therefore, the literature may be stopped before it gets into the classroom.

Administrators may act after the works are in the classroom as well. The well-known incident in Drake, North Dakota, (Massie, 1980) involved the burning of several books, including Vonnegut's *Slaughterhouse Five*. In 1990, a school official in Palm Springs, California, objected to having *Julie of the Wolves* (George) on the required reading list for seventh-grade English classes. The official thought that some sections of the work might be interpreted as describing an incestuous relationship. The book was removed from the core reading list for being too controversial. In Longview, Washington, *Stotan!* (Crutcher) was challenged by a school official for alleged profanity, sadism, violence, sexism, racism, and jokes about sex, and removal from the eighth-grade optional reading list was requested. On appeal, the school board agreed to retain the book (*People*, 1991).

In some states, state education agencies approve lists of books to be used. These agencies may also act as censors. Acquiescing to pressure from national groups, in 1990 the Alabama State Textbook Committee removed 10 books from the state-approved list for fear of "Eastern religious practices" and discussion of homosexuality (People, 1991). While the 10 books were not novels and therefore not really of concern to English teachers, the state agency's influence in determining curriculum is worth noting. State committees do not always follow the wishes of censors: The Texas State Textbook Committee withstood an effort to have some 100 items of literature removed from the list it recommends to school districts (Simmons, 1991).

Perhaps the largest group of censors is comprised of parents. Sometimes parents act in accordance with their own beliefs; other times they are simply pawns for special interest groups. As we have noted, parents who do not want their child to read a certain selection have every right to ask that a different book be read; however, when parents request that books be kept from all students, censorship is rearing its ugly head. A few examples of censorship and attempts to censor that took place in 1990–1991 are worthy of note.

One parent in Alabama brought action against *A Wrinkle in Time* (L'Engle) because "the book deals with New Age religion and describes women dressed as witches" (People, 1991, p. 17). After evaluation by various school officials, the book remains in use. Blume's *Starring Sally J. Friedman as Herself* was objected to in Arkansas for discussing anti-Semitism and homosexuality. School officials decided to remove the book from the required reading list in the fourth grade but kept it in the library. In Harwinton, Connecticut, a parent objected to *The Pigman* (Zindel), *A Day No Pigs Would Die* (Peck), *Summer of My German Soldier* (Greene), *The Chocolate War* (Cormier), and *Bridge to Terabithia* (Paterson) because of profanity and discussion of prejudice, rebellion, and the death of friends. *Bridge to Terabithia* was used in the fifth grade; the rest were used in the eighth grade. The books were retained. In Middleton, Idaho, a parent objected to and asked for the removal of *The Catcher in the Rye* (Salinger), which was being used in a tenth-grade class. The objections were that characters used profanity and questioned religion. As a result, "the teacher, who was in the first quarter of her first year, was stopped on the way to class, told to collect the books immediately, not to give the quiz she had planned for that day, and to begin teaching something new. The book was removed immediately with no formal process, despite the fact that she had received school permission to use the book before assigning it and had offered to provide alternate assignments to those who objected" (People, 1991, p. 46).

A parent in Paola, Kansas, objected to Cormier's *The Chocolate War,* although in his request to have the book reconsidered, he called the novel *Chocolate Wars.* He objected to "negative religious overtones," "sexual implications utilized by the author," and "inappropriate language" (Dilmore, 1990, p. 1A). A review committee was established to hold a formal hearing. The committee, comprised of school and community leaders, voted 6 to 3 to recommend to the Board of Education that the book be retained. In its meeting of October 30, 1990, the Board of Education voted 4 to 3 to retain the use of *The Chocolate War* (Dilmore, 1990). After the meeting, a teacher was overheard saying, "Well, it stays for now, but after the next [Board of Education] election, it could go the other way."

The goals of many special interest groups are to purge school systems of offensive materials. These materials may be young adult novels; reading anthologies; textbooks used in English, biology, or history classes; films; and records and tapes. The definition of *offensive* is, of course, determined by the special interest group. Based on *Attacks on the Freedom to Learn* (People, 1991), the names of some of the major special interest groups that made some objection to school materials follow. Because representatives of these interest groups frequently invite themselves into a censorship problem in a local school, educators need to be aware that local issues often become national issues when these interest groups are present.

- American Family Association Law Center
- Central Council of Parent Teacher Associations
- Citizens for Excellence in Education (CEE)
- Committee to Restore Ethical and Traditional Education (CREATE)
- Concerned Women in America
- Eagle Forum (Phyllis Schlafly)
- Educational Research Analysts (Mel and Norma Gabler)
- Excellence in Children's Educational Literature (EXCELL)
- Focus on the Family
- National Association for the Advancement of Colored People (NAACP)
- Parents Exercising Action for Children and Education (PEACE)

Other groups with similar objectives include People of America Responding to Educational Needs of Today's Society (PARENTS), Citizens United for Responsible Education (CURE), Let's Improve Today's Education (LITE), and American Christians in Education (ACE).

And censorship continues. The 1995 edition of *Attacks on the Freedom to Learn* indicate that censorship in schools is growing. More books and other educational material were removed from schools during 1994–1995 because of parental and community objections than ever before. The book lists 338 confirmed incidents of attempted censorship of books, films, and other educational materials in the 1994–1995 school year, down from a record 375 in the previous year. But 50 percent, or a record 169, of the challenges were successful, up from 157, or 42 percent, the year before.

The most challenged book in the 1994–1995 year was *More Scary Stories to Tell in the Dark* by Alvin Schwartz (People, 1995).

The Basis for Censorship

The major difference between the objectives of the private interest groups and those of public education is the philosophical base from which the groups operate. Public education wants change to occur; that is, educators believe that the truth is found through open but guided inquiry. The censors act from a position of absolute certainty. The conflict occurs between the inquiry process of learning and the absolutist doctrine of "I know what is right!" The former believe books are for finding out what is and making judgments about it; the censor is afraid of what is and thinks it will hurt the book reader.

These philosophical differences are quite broad and need further clarification through detailed objections raised by the censors. Many of these objections have been cited in challenges to specific books earlier in this chapter. The objections seem to fall into four different types: moral, political, religious, or social. Censorship has also been broken into the three S's: Sex, Satanism, and Swearing. Donelson (1974) places the objections into eight specific categories:

Sex

Politics

War and Peace

Religion

Sociology and Race

Language

Drugs

Inappropriate Adolescent Behavior (p. 48)

In "Dirty Dictionaries, Obscene Nursery Rhymes, and Burned Books," Jenkinson (1979b) increases the categories for objections to 14. In addition to those already mentioned, Jenkinson includes literature of homosexuals; ideas, methods, or books that seem to emulate "secular humanism"; role playing; absence of grammar rules; materials that contain negative statements about parents; and phase-elective English programs. In later writings, Jenkinson adds to his list to make a grand total of 67 objections (1979a, 1979c, 1980).

Julian Thompson, well-known young adult author (*Grounding of Group 6, A Band of Angels, Simon Pure,* and *Herb Seasoning*), has clear views on defending books against censorship. His position includes his reasons for why people censor books: "It seems to me three main reasons for burning, banning, and avoiding are that they're alleged to promulgate (or just contain) one or more of the following: 1) vulgar language, 2) sexual activity, and 3) anti-establishment attitudes" (Thompson, 1991, p. 2). In his defense of young adult literature, he argues that it is "normal and appropriate for kids to have a relationship of some sort with vulgarity . . . to be curious about sex—in terms of its mechanics and its context . . . to question and, at times, resist the edicts of those elements of the 'Establishment' they deal with day by day—the authority of parents, or of teachers, or of any other adult in their lives" (p. 4). He cautions readers not to be horrified by his suggestions without first realizing that by "normal and appropriate" he means behavior that most adults used when they were growing up. He continues:

> Don't misunderstand me here. I do believe that there are ways for kids to exercise their new-found and emerging sense of self. I'm not in favor of a world made up of bands of foul-mouthed, promiscuous kids running up to tell me, "I know what I can do." The pharisees and censors paint the issues that we're raising here in blackest blacks and whitest whites, as either-or. My point is: there is a golden mean, a middle ground. What I'm speaking for is moderation, understanding—yes, appreciation of the way that normal people grow into a genuine adulthood. (p. 5)

Now, for the other side of the issue. Is there something to be said in support of some of those who wish to question what is taught in the public schools? Small (1979) takes an interesting position when he points out that most educators are quite knowledgeable about the specific censorship cases (the specific dimension), arguments against censorship and defense of the freedom to read (the freedom dimension), and advice on what to do when the attack occurs (the professional dimension). He suggests that we must go beyond those dimensions. To be fair to all those who have some argument against what is taught in the schools, we must also be knowledgeable about the historical and social dimension, the educational dimension, and the human dimension.

To be knowledgeable in the historical and social dimension, educators must be aware of the basic premises that lead to schooling and the community school. Understanding the relationship between society and schools may help explain the "ownership" some school patrons have about what is taught in the classroom. The educational dimension that Small describes includes the basic questions of why literature is taught and whether there is some consistency between our thinking that "bad" literature will not harm the reader (that's our reaction to the censors) and that "good" literature will benefit young people. Small points out:

> We have led parents—our former students, after all—to believe that great works contain great truths and that masterpieces are such because of their power to influence. Why should it now be so surprising that parents, discovering curse words, scenes of sexual relations, arguments against the current American social order, questions about the existence of God, believe that we are now pushing those ideas as we formerly pushed the ideas in *Silas Marner* and *Julius Caesar*? (p. 59)

Those who argue against censorship very often have few good things to say about the censors. We think of them as "out of touch," ignorant, or even evil. We fail to understand the last dimension—the human dimension. Many parents, for whatever reasons, are often frustrated about their relationship with the schools. "The schools are not responsive," they say. Whether or not this is true, the parents may very well be concerned but they get little help from the establishment. As a result, they strike out at something very specific—what is taught in the classroom, especially if they believe that it is incongruous with what they believe is appropriate. The ever-changing society, and, thus, the ever-changing school, brings about the climate for censorship attacks. From all of this, we learn that we must know the community in which the school is set; we must know its culture and its historical roots and, to some extent, the expectations that the community has for its schools. We would argue that if one or two parents object to a novel being in the library or being used in the classroom and the objections are based on "dirty words" or "sexual situations," for example, then the objection should be treated as an isolated incident by these parents. However, if these parents are supported by the vast majority of the community and the objections are based on differences in cultural heritage and basic philosophy that seem to be in conflict with materials presented in the classroom, then the school has a major concern to be worked out with the community at large.

This seems to be the case in the struggle that occurred in Kanawha County, West Virginia, in 1974. This textbook controversy was by far the most unsettling and far-reaching conflict in the censorship history of America. At the center of the conflict was James Moffett's *Interaction,* a reading/language arts series comprised of two film series, dozens of card and board games, 800 activity cards, hundreds of recorded selections, and other materials besides the 182 paperback books that completed the program. In describing the people of Kanawha County, Moffett (1988) says:

> The majority who opposed the books in Kanawha County were mountaineer fundamentalists who have seldom received any attention but ridicule and who have been as grossly exploited as any group in our society. No region of the United States has been so plundered and taken over by outsiders. Miners die because companies cut corners on the expense of safety measures. But the mountaineer's proud code disdains welfare. . . . In fact, I have taken most seriously what was for them the heart of their outcry—their religious beliefs. (p. xi)

Although the controversy may have been started by the local school patrons because of a conflict between cultural and religious views and the materials selected for students, it quickly mushroomed into the large-scale conflict brought on, primarily, due to the influx of outside support groups: The Hard Core Parental Group (Louisiana), The Heritage Foundation (Washington, DC), Mel and Norma Gabler (Texas), Citizens for Decency Through Law (Los Angeles), and other groups.

Since the 1974 uproar, Jim Moffett has spent a lot of time and energy reflecting on the Kanawha County controversy, and he has published a case study in *Storm in the Mountains: A Case Study of Censorship, Conflict, and Consciousness* (1988). Moffett explains why this book was so long in coming:

I wanted very much to speak out about the issues but felt that my remarks might be taken as the vinegar of sour grapes. Actually, my reactions were very complex and included many other feelings and thoughts besides just hurt and anger. After ruminating them for a good decade, I decided to set forth my views of what happened and explain how this case may illuminate phenomena bigger today than then. (p. x)

WHAT DOES THE TEACHER DO?

Before the Challenge

Teachers of English as well as teachers in other departments in schools must have a strong sense about the community in which they teach. Frequently, schools, perhaps at the district levels, create task forces comprised of school employees and school patrons to investigate, discuss, and explore a variety of social and educational issues. While this procedure may look as if the school district is pampering the positions of the community, it isn't; it is simply exploring, in a partnership arrangement, the issues facing both groups.

The schools and the community seem to be the beneficiaries of such a process. Teachers have an opportunity to learn about the community before they select materials for students. Whether these decisions are made in district wide curriculum committees, school committees, or by individual teachers, information about the materials to be selected and the students who will use these materials will make the selection process more effective.

We are not suggesting that the community or its representatives need to be asked before materials are selected; on the contrary, professional educators ought to make those decisions. But they must make these decisions with as much information as possible. It may just avoid future confrontations. However, if the teacher or teachers believe that some particular material is important and should be a part of the curriculum, then that material should, indeed, be used even if there is a possibility of challenges. If the selection meets the objectives set down by the decision makers and no alternatives are available, the material should be used.

How the selection is to be used also will affect the decision-making process. For example, will the young adult novel be read by every student, or will there be many novels from which each student will choose one novel to read? Another consideration involves the way the novel is used. Will students read the work as an in-class assignment, or will students read the work as an out-of-class assignment, similar to a book report? The more choices students have, the less potential there is for censorship. Chapter 2 discussed the importance of thematic units as an effective curriculum design. We reinforce that here because that design allows for diversity in the selection and treatment of literature.

We have also covered the importance of methodology in teaching young adult literature, in particular the use of reader-response practices in teaching the literature. We want to emphasize one component of that procedure because it may have some impact on the censorship issue. It is important for teachers, students, and parents to know that novels taught in the English classes will do more than just allow students to relate to a work from a humanistic view. Although students may respond to values and the portrayal of life, there is more to the study of the literature. The quality of the work, which includes the author's craft, plays an important part in the consideration of the novel. Study that includes the use of literary strategies and elements as well as other more personal responses to the literature forces students to have a well-rounded understanding of the literature, which may help quiet the would-be censor. Teachers, administrators, boards of education, and the general public should understand how the selection process works—who's involved and the basis on which decisions are made.

Teachers must know why they are teaching a particular piece of literature. Teachers should write and have available rationales for the longer selections. Although it is not necessary to write rationales for each short story or each poem, it is practical to be able to support the use of the anthologies that include these pieces of literature. Our position here, however, suggests written rationales for longer pieces, such as novels and plays. These rationales should be on file and available for anyone to read. Granted, these may take time to prepare, but in the long run, statements that reflect that teachers have given thought to why they are teaching a particular book may stop any challenge.

In *Dealing with Censorship,* Shugert (1979) suggests eight elements that should be in a rationale:

> For what classes is this book especially appropriate?
>
> To what particular objectives, literary or psychological or pedagogical, does this book lend itself?
>
> In what ways will the book be used to meet those objectives?
>
> What problems of style, tone, or theme or possible grounds for censorship exist in the book?
>
> How does the teacher plan to meet those problems?
>
> Assuming that the objectives are met, how would students be different because of their reading of this book?
>
> What are some other appropriate books an individual student might read in place of this book?
>
> What reputable sources have recommended this book? What have critics said of it? (This answer should cite reviews, if any are available.) (p. 188)

Rationales for two young adult novels follow. The rationale for *The Chocolate War* (Cormier) was written by the language arts teachers of Paola High School (Kansas) after a parent tried to have the text removed from the ninth-grade curriculum. The rationale for *Sex Education* (Davis) was written by Paul Clark, University of Kansas, prior to any official challenge.

THE CHOCOLATE WAR: A RATIONALE

The Chocolate War is taught in the ninth-grade curriculum at Paola High School.

Although it is a dark and sometimes disturbing book, *The Chocolate War* does increase students' awareness of the values, attitudes, and goals inherent in the human experience. It also allows them to examine some of the moral and social problems that face human beings in the modern world. The book provides the students with an image of good in the person of the protagonist, Jerry. He is an admirable character who tries in spite of overwhelming odds to do "the right thing." The book raises the issue of peer pressure and teaches that when you give in to peer pressure and do what you know you shouldn't, you feel worse. It focuses on the problem of the individual's responsibility for his own actions and teaches the student to be true to himself. It is only when Jerry tries to oppose his enemies with their own methods that he is ultimately defeated.

That defeat is realistic because it is a result of both his own actions and the world around him. Life doesn't always end happily, and institutions are not perfect. Jerry does not believe that he has any support system within his family, his church, or his school, and he doesn't reach out and try to gain any. This idea is extremely important for students, many of whom are dealing with problems in their own lives.

The language choices are appropriate to the characters. It is the antagonists who demonstrate their lack of morals, values, and ethical standards by the language they use. Jerry resorts to profanity only once and only under the most extreme pressure. The characters do not use profanity or vulgarity in the presence of authority figures or in the classroom, only when in their peer group. Although this is not desirable behavior for students, it is realistic.

This book is on the recommended reading lists of the American Library Association, the National Council of Teachers of English, Reading Circle, and, according to the State Department of Education, it is commonly taught in Kansas high schools and is available in virtually all of the middle and high school and public libraries in Kansas. It is included in college adolescent literature courses as a recommended text for middle and high school students. Area colleges and universities that we know include the text in their adolescent literature courses. These are Kansas State University, Pittsburgh State University, Missouri Western State College, The University of Missouri at Kansas City, and The University of Kansas. It is included in the catalogues of the major educational publishing companies. *The Chocolate War* has been selected as an American Library Association Best Book for Young Adults, a School Library Journal Best Book of the Year, and a *New York Times* Outstanding Book of the Year.

As soon as we received the first objection to *The Chocolate War,* we offered an alternative novel, *The Old Man and the Sea* by Ernest Hemingway, and included assignments that would allow those students an opportunity to earn the same credit as students reading *The Chocolate War.* Perhaps we should have anticipated the controversy generated by *The Chocolate War,* but we feel we have dealt with it in a manner that was fair to everyone concerned. Because this is a newly adopted and somewhat controversial book, those students who have objections to the book have been provided with alternative literature. However, we are absolutely opposed to the removal of this book from the PHS curriculum, and we do not feel that the previously established curriculum would warrant other alternative assignments.

The issue has gone beyond the right of a parent to determine what his own child will read and study. We have seen to it that students whose parents object will not have to read *The Chocolate War.* What is at issue here is the removal of that same right from every other parent.

Sex Education: A Rationale

The young adult novel, *Sex Education,* may not, at first reading, appear to be geared toward the young adult reader. The novel begins as the narrative of a mental patient describing the chain of events that rendered her institutionalized. She explains how a class assignment led to her first-hand experience with a wife abuser, mental torment, and the tragic death of her boyfriend. The assignment was to care for someone. Objections may be raised to *Sex Education* because of its candid approach toward sexual slang, its graphic description of the abused wife, the detailed death scene of David, the unorthodox methods of the teacher, the fact that the main character is institutionalized, and the very title of the book itself.

In my 10th-grade classroom, I would explain the slang issue in much the same way that Mrs. Fulton does in the novel. I might also point out that it is the embarrassed and uneducated person—the person lacking respect for others—who uses such language. I think that the title is great as it would get the students to read the novel. It's a little trick to get them hooked! The tragic events surrounding Livvie's breakdown, David's death, and the abuse of Maggie are vital and essential to the story. I would explain to the students that knowledge sometimes comes through pain and that they can learn a great deal by reading about the suffering of others without having to experience it themselves. I heard a joke once that fits this idea: "Learn from the mistakes of others, you can't possibly live long enough to make them all yourself."

The title of the book is somewhat misleading. Once the initial introduction has been established and the reader has been intrigued by the excellent writing style of the author, the subject of sex is rarely broached. Although there are some references to sexual reproduction in the course of the novel, they are rendered in a scientific manner, one that can be found in any high school biology book.

Slang used within the first 20 pages of the novel can be shocking. However, students (and their parents) should be aware of the intent of these words before a judgment is passed. Mrs. Fulton, the teacher in the story, explains quite eloquently that the slang words have developed through the embarrassment people encounter when discussing an issue such as sex. She explains that the slang words directly reflect the uncomfortable feelings associated with such issues and how education can help alleviate these emotions. It must be understood that, through education, the students will be less likely to engage in illicit sexual union, not more so. Throughout the novel, the main characters learn what it really means to love someone, to truly care. They, and the reader, experience other ways of expressing this love and learn that true love, although it includes sex, is not centered on the sexual act. Rather, sexual intercourse is the fulfillment of a lasting, sincere relationship and should not be engaged in lightly.

The abuse of the wife, Maggie, and the death of David are essential to the theme of the novel: caring. Maggie is involved in a relationship that does not involve caring; it involves selfishness. Maggie's husband cares only about himself, ensuring that only he has a good time. Their relationship is purely a one-sided affair that Maggie should detach herself from if help cannot be obtained. Maggie's marriage provides an extreme example of the kind of relationship to avoid, a kind of anti-caring. David's tragic end at the hand of Maggie's husband hammers this concept home—stay away from a relationship that does not include genuine caring, sharing, and love.

Through Livvie's (the main character) mental breakdown, the reader is again exposed to the idea that a sincere relationship is vital. The fact that David died and Livvie suffered mental collapse also directs the reader to seek help in a situation that is over his or her head. This type of guidance is crucial to the young adult who tries to conquer the world alone. It's all right to reach out to others, to ask for help.

Teaching methods could bring up some legitimate complaints in this work. The teacher is vague in her grading procedures, and the classroom discussions revolve around some highly controversial subjects. The school principal is present during one of these discussions and presents some valid views. It must be remembered that the young adult is faced with many decisions on a daily basis, and many of these decisions can be legally decided without the consultation of a parent or legal guardian. The way in which the author, Jenny Davis, presents the classroom structure is the same way that young adults are faced with difficult issues in real life. A decision must be made, and they won't be graded on it, except perhaps with their very lives. Students should be allowed to discuss such issues with their peers, and no better place exists than a controlled and guided classroom.

In addition to what is stated earlier, I would deal with objections to this novel by explaining the importance of it as I have above. This novel should be read by everyone, young and old alike. I have identified 13 key elements that this novel teaches; I am sure that there may be more. I would like to list these "lessons" here, as I would point them out to anyone objecting to my using the novel in the classroom. *Sex Education* gives excellent advice and instructions on sex, abuse, true love, caring, seeking assistance, rationale for sexual abstinence, seeing people as people—not objects, fears about relationships and death, death, relationships, coping, compassion, and trust. *Sex Education* is one book that no adolescent literature program should be without.

One additional decision should be made in advance of any challenge brought on by the censor. What is the policy that will be in effect when the challenge comes? Will it be given to a committee for consideration? What is the make up of that committee? Will there be a district review committee as well? Who will serve on that committee? All of these questions should be answered before any part of the process has to be initiated.

After the Challenge

The thought of having to face the censors and what they stand for is scary at best. As professional educators, teachers sense that what they do and the decisions they make, either individually or in concert with others, will be accepted by the community. Although this professionalism prevails throughout most communities, pockets of educational unrest surface from time to time, and teachers are faced with, "Why are you teaching that filth to your students?" When that question raises its ugly head and enters the classroom, teachers are at the beginning of what can be a very long journey. There will be times within that journey when teachers will wonder why they ever thought they wanted to get involved with "kids." If the procedures have been thought through and are in place, the journey should be a little easier.

It would seem that the first step that ought to occur when the challenge has been made is for the challenger to meet with the teacher who is responsible for using the challenged material. In doing this there is no attempt to put off the formal, official objection, but to bring the two people together so that some discussion can take place about the concerns of the would-be censor. Often after some clarification about why the novel was chosen, what objectives are being met by using such literature, or how the novel is being used in the classroom, the person making the challenge may understand and accept the decisions. There may be, too, a chance for the suggestion of alternative literature to be assigned instead of the challenged work. If the person or persons are not willing to make any change in their challenge, then the formal policy is implemented, and the censor is given a form to have the work or works formally reconsidered. That form may have been prepared by the local teachers or may be the one recommended by the National Council of Teachers of English (NCTE) or other similar groups. The Citizen's Request for Reconsideration of a Work prepared by NCTE is reprinted in Figure 10.1. This document is available along with other useful information in a booklet titled *The Students' Right to Read*. A single copy of this document is available from NCTE at no cost.

A Teacher's Library on Censorship

The following list of recommended sources does not and cannot include all of the books, articles, and helpful organizations that are available to the classroom teacher concerning censorship; however, it is intended to help the classroom teacher get started about censorship. Teachers will want to add to the list as they continue their reading in literary and professional journals. A well-informed teacher may very well affect in a positive way the results of a literature challenge.

BOOKS

American Library Association (1983). *Censorship litigation and the schools*. Chicago: Author.

American Library Association (1983). *Intellectual freedom manual* (2nd ed.). Chicago: Author.

American Library Association (1989). *Hit list: Frequently challenged young adult titles; References to defend them*. Chicago: Author.

Bosmajian, H. A. (Ed.). (1983). *Censorship: Libraries and the law*. New York: Neal-Schuman.

	Hardcover___

Author _____ Paperback___

Title_____

Publisher (if known)_____

Request initiated by_____

Telephone _____ Address _____

City_____ Zip Code _____

Complaint represents

____ himself/herself

____ organization (please identify) _____

____ other group (please identify) _____

1. To what in the work do you object? Please be specific; cite pages _____

   _____

2. What of value is there in this work?_____

   _____

3. What do you feel might be the result of reading this work? _____

   _____

FIGURE 10.1
Citizen's request for reconsideration of a work

Bosmajian, H. A. (1987). *The first amendment in the classroom* (Vols. 1–5). New York: Neal-Schuman.

Burress, L., & Jenkinson, E. B. (1982). *The students' right to know*. Urbana, IL: National Council of Teachers of English.

Committee on Bias and Censorship in the Elementary School. (1978). *Censorship: Don't let it become an issue in your schools*. Urbana, IL: National Council of Teachers of English.

Cox, B. C. (1977). *Censorship game and how to play it* (Bulletin No. 50). Washington, DC: The National Council for the Social Studies.

4. For what age group would you recommend this work? _____

_____

5. Did you read the entire work?_____ What pages or sections?_____

_____

6. Are you aware of the judgment of this work by critics?_____

_____

7. Are you aware of the teacher's purpose in using this work? _____

_____

8. What do you believe is the theme or purpose of this work?_____

_____

9. What would you prefer the school do about this work?

____Do not assign or recommend it to my child.

____Withdraw it from all students.

____Send it back to the English department for re-evaluation.

10. In its place, what work of equal value would you recommend that would convey as valuable a picture and perspective of a society or a set of values? _____

_____

_____

Signature of Complainant

Davis, J. E. (Ed.). (1979). *Dealing with censorship*. Urbana IL: National Council of Teachers of English.

Haight, A. L. (1978). *Banned books* (4th ed.). New York: R. R. Bowker.

Jenkinson, E. B. (1979). *Censors in the classroom: The mind benders*. Carbondale, IL: Southern Illinois University Press.

Lewis, F. F. (1976). *Literature, obscenity and law*. Carbondale, IL: Southern Illinois University Press.

Lobbying for freedom: A citizen's guide to fighting censorship at the state level. (1975). New York: St. Martin's.

Moffett, J. (1988). *Storm in the mountains: A case study of censorship, conflict, and consciousness*. Carbondale, IL: Southern Illinois University Press.

People for the American Way. (1991). *Attacks on the freedom to learn, 1990–1991 report*. New York: Author. (All yearly reports are interesting.)

Stanek, L. W. (1976). *Censorship: A guide for teachers, librarians, and others*. New York: Dell.

The Students' Right to Read. (1982). Urbana, IL: National Council of Teachers of English.

ARTICLES

Arons, S. (1979). Book burning in the heartland. *Saturday Review, 21,* 24–29.

Burger, R. H. (1982). The Kanawha County textbook controversies: A study of communication and power. *Library Quarterly, 48,* 584–589.

Byorklun, E. C. (1988). Secular humanism: Implications of court decisions. *Educational Forum, 52,* 211–221.

Donelson, K. L. (1981). Shoddy and pernicious books and youthful piety: Literary and moral censorship, then and now. *Library Quarterly 51,* 4–19.

Edwards, J. (1986). The new right, humanism, and "dirty books." *Virginia English Bulletin, 36,* 94–99.

Hentoff, N. (1983). When nice people burn books. *Progressive, 47,* 42–44.

Janeczko, P. (1975). How students can help educate the censors. *Arizona English Bulletin, 17,* 78–80.

Larsen, T. J. (1980). The power of the board of education to censor. *Educational Leadership,* 139–142.

Peck, R. (1986). The genteel unshelving of a book. *School Library Journal, 32,* 37–39.

Rationales for commonly challenged taught books. (1983). *Connecticut English Journal, 15.* (Entire collection of rationales will be helpful.)

Simmons, J. (1991). Censorship in the schools—No end in sight. *The ALAN Review, 18* (2), 6–8.

Small, R. C., Jr. (1976). Censorship and English: Some things we don't seem to think about very often (but should). In J. Davis (Ed.), *Dealing with Censorship* (pp. 54–62). Urbana, IL: National Council of Teachers of English.

ORGANIZATIONS

Only information regarding censorship is included here. See Appendix A for additional information about these and other organizations related to reading and teaching young adult literature.

American Library Association, 50 East Huron Street, Chicago, IL 60611 *(Hit List)*

Office of Intellectual Freedom *(Newsletter on Intellectual Freedom)* Freedom to Read Foundation, 50 East Huron Street, Chicago, IL 60611 *(Freedom to Read Foundation News)*

National Coalition Against Censorship, 2 West 64th Street, New York, NY 10023 (*Censorship News*)

National Council for the Social Studies, 3615 Wisconsin Avenue, NW, Washington, DC 20016

National Council of Teachers of English, 1111 Kenyon Road, Urbana, IL 61801 (*Censorship and Professional Guidelines; Censorship: Don't Let It Become an Issue in Your Schools; The Students' Right to Know; The Students' Right to Read*)

NEA Human and Civil Rights, 1201 16th Street, NW, Washington, DC 20036

People for the American Way, 2000 M Street, NW, Suite 400, Washington, DC 20036 (*Attacks on the Freedom to Learn* [Yearly reports on censorship])

❧   Learning Log Responses   ❧

Choose a young adult novel not discussed in this chapter and write a defense for its use in a middle or high school classroom.

What is your understanding of why censors try to remove books from classrooms and libraries?

What will you do in your classroom to make it less likely that censors will make a challenge?

Become familiar with at least one of the publications listed in this chapter. Write a brief summary of what that publication offers the classroom teacher.

REFERENCES

Asheim, L. (1953). Not censorship but selection. *Wilson Library Bulletin, 28,* 67.

Comstock, A. (1883). *Traps for the Young.* (n.p.).

Dilmore, K. (1990, October 31). *The Chocolate War* Trials. *The Miami County Republican,* pp. 1A, 10A.

Donelson, K. (1974). Censorship in the 1970s: Some ways to handle it when it comes (and it will). *English Journal, 63* (2) 47–51.

Jenkinson, E. (1979a). *Censors in the classroom: The mind benders.* Carbondale, IL: Southern Illinois University Press.

Jenkinson, E. (1979b) Dirty dictionaries, obscene nursery rhymes, and burned books. In J. Davis (Ed.), *Dealing with censorship,* (pp. 2–13). Urbana, IL: National Council of Teachers of English.

Jenkinson, E. (1979c). Protest groups exert strong impact. *Publishers Weekly, 216,* 42–44.

Jenkinson, E. (1980). Sixty-seven targets of the textbook protesters. *Missouri English Bulletin, 38,* 27–32.

King, S. (1990, October 5). Powerful secrets. *Kansas City Times,* p. PE-1.

Massie, D. (1980). Censorship in the schools: Something old and something new. *Today's Education, 59* (4), 30–34.

Moffett, J. (1988). *Storm in the mountains: A case study of censorship, conflict, and consciousness.* Carbondale, IL: Southern Illinois University Press.

People for the American Way. (1991). *Attacks on the freedom to learn,* 1990–1991 report. Washington, DC: Author.

People for the American Way. (1995). Attacks on the freedom to learn, 1994–1995 report. Washington, DC: Author.

Shugert, D. (1979). How to write a rationale in defense of a book. In J. Davis (Ed.), *Dealing with censorship* (pp. 187–191). Urbana, IL: National Council of Teachers of English.

Simmons, J. (1991). Censorship in the schools—No end in sight. *The ALAN Review, 18* (2), 6–8.

Small, R. C., Jr. (1979). Censorship and English: Some things we don't seem to think about very often (but should). In J. Davis (Ed.), *Dealing with censorship* (pp. 54—62). Urbana, IL: National Council of Teachers of English.

The Students' right to read. (1982). Urbana, IL: National Council of Teachers of English.

Thompson, J. (1991). Defending YA literature against the Pharisees and censors: Is it worth the trouble? *The ALAN Review, 18* (2), 2–5.

11

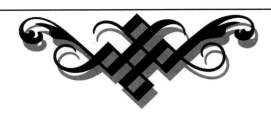

Young Adult Literature: A Brief History

Many think the beginning of literature for young people occurred in the 1950s and 1960s with the publication of Salinger's *The Catcher in the Rye* (1951) or Hinton's *The Outsiders* (1967); however, the literature directed to and for young people began much earlier.

Although it seems impossible, we can trace the emphasis on modeling good behavior for children and young adults through literature back to the fifteenth and sixteenth centuries. This literature was written for adults, not young people. It would be an understatement to say that that literature was different from the literature young adults have today, but it did exist, and adults wanted young people to read it. This chapter traces the changes from the didactic literature of the early periods to the current body of literature.

LITERATURE: RULES TO LIVE BY

The literature that adults wanted children and young adults to read reflected the mores of the time and was used to guide young people in their behavior. Literature closely tied to religion and mythology was set before young people as models. Wintle and Fisher (1974) discuss the characteristics of education in the Middle Ages:

> Education in the Middle Ages was grounded in Latin. Ideally, children were taught to read and write in a foreign language. . . . At a precociously early age, they could tackle the works of the masters. An understanding of literature in the vernacular was not regarded as the proper object of learning, even though popular romances had as much appeal to the young as to the old. (p. 11)

The books found in this time took stands, which adolescents were to emulate. *A Book of Courtesy* (1477) is said to be the first book published specifically for young readers in England. At approximately the same time, *Aesop's Fables* appeared primarily as a book for adults, but its audience shifted to children and young adults. Malory's *Le Morte d'Arthur* enjoyed a considerable circulation among older children.

During this period adults felt strongly that young people should read the classics and not the more popular romances that were available (which sounds much like the 1990s). The philosophy appears ever so strongly in Hugh Rhodes's *Book of Nurture* (c. 1545), which "fulminated against reading for pleasure and this reflected common opinion among the literate" (Wintle & Fisher, 1974 p. 12). The prevailing attitude was that children (especially the well-born) were to read to learn how to act like adults and take on adult responsibilities if the need arose. Wintle and Fisher characterize this attitude toward children well: "Throughout the Tudor century childhood was merely an inconvenient period when one was not an adult" (p. 12).

The seventeenth century, while holding on to the traditions of the past, did see some changes, however slight. A somewhat different attitude toward children was found in a picture book, *The Visible World in Pictures* by John Amos Comenius (1659). This was the first book to convey information to children through pictures of real children. It should be said, however, that the primary emphasis in the seventeenth century was on religious publication and faith in the Christian word. *The King James Bible* (1611) was standard reading for young and old; John Milton's *Paradise*

Lost (1667), the twelve-book epic based on the creation, the fall of Satan, and Adam and Eve, was written to put man right with God; and John Bunyan's *The Pilgrim's Progress from This World to That Which Is to Come* (1678) taught God's way through religious allegory with people and places representing vices and virtues.

As the eighteenth century dawned, children were still seen as deficient adults who needed all the help they could get. Books of the time reflected this didactic attitude: for example, Benjamin Keach's *War with the Devil, or The Young Man's Conflict with the Powers of Darkness, in a Dialogue Discovering the Corruption and Vanity of Youth, the Horrible Nature of Sin, and the Deplorable Condition of Fallen Man* (1707) and James Janeway's *A Token for Children: Being an Exact Account of the Conversion, Holy and Exemplary Lives & Joyful Deaths of Several Young Children to Which is Added: A Token for the Children of New England* (1700). Smith (1967) quotes Janeway's purpose for writing the book:

> You may now hear (my dear Lambs) what other good Children have done, and remember how they wept and prayed by themselves; how earnestly they cried out for an interest in the Lord Jesus Christ. . . . Would you be in the same condition as naughty Children? O Hell is a terrible place, that is a thousand times worse than Whipping. God's Anger is worse than your Father's Anger. (p. 42)

In addition to this religious and didactic literature of the sixteenth and seventeenth centuries, two very important works were published that made a tremendous impact on children's literature. In 1719 Daniel Defoe published *The Life and Strange Surprising Adventures of Robinson Crusoe,* and shortly thereafter Jonathan Swift published *Gulliver's Travels.* These two works were quickly adapted for younger readers and became early children's classics.

In the mid 1700s, John Newbery began publishing children's books as a business. Newbery wrote and published attractive, small books for children. His attitude, contrary to the prevalent philosophy, was that children could read just for fun. However, Newbery's attitude was not the prevailing one. Most of the literature was still moralistic and didactic. Hannah More was the prolific writer of *Repository Tracts,* in which she preached moralistic lessons. These became standard reading for young people, as did the writing of Mary Sherwood (1778–1851). Sherwood's morally didactic fiction was widely read throughout the end of the eighteenth century and into the nineteenth century.

The nineteenth century was "the first age of great children's books" (Wintle & Fisher, 1974, p. 14). Literature for young women emphasized home and family values conforming to societal expectations. Literature for boys largely emphasized that hard work would be rewarded by success, and traditional values were upheld even by their literary heroes. Wintle and Fisher comment on the literature of this period:

> It was the first age of great children's books: . . . *The Adventures of Tom Sawyer* (1876) and *The Adventures of Huckleberry Finn* (1885) by Mark Twain; *Black Beauty* (1877) by Anna Sewell; *The Wind in the Willows* (1908) by Kenneth Grahame, and so on and so on. There is no single explanation for such an assemblage. The accidents of genius, the dynamics of the market, cheaper printing methods, the swelling of the middle class, the increased sophistication of editors, the post-romantic senti-

> mentalizing of the child, an abundance of literacy, the loosening of church morality,
> the awareness of class, the growth of advertising, and so on and so on again. (p. 14)

Also in the 1800s, Mason Locke Weems (also known as The Parson) wrote his adventurous, and reportedly inaccurate, books about Washington's exploits (*A History of the Life and Death, Virtues and Exploits, of General George Washington; The Life of George Washington;* and *The Life of Washington the Great*), which were widely read by young readers in search of adventure. In 1825, the first of 170 Peter Parley books on moralistic standards appeared.

In the mid 1800s, a new genre appeared: the domestic novel. This new literature made a tremendous impact on the American book-reading public. Leading the list of domestic novels was *The Wide, Wide World* by Susan Warner. Domestic novels, including Warner's, successfully taught and preached traditional values and moral lessons—no tobacco, alcohol, adultery, or divorce were allowed in domestic novels. Warner wrote approximately twenty novels of this kind. *The Wide, Wide World* was one of the four most widely read books during the 1890s; the other three were the Bible, *Pilgrim's Progress,* and *Uncle Tom's Cabin* (Stowe). Donelson and Nilson (1989) describe the domestic novel:

> Born out of a belief that humanity was redeemable, the domestic novel preached morality; woman's submission to man; the value of cultural, social, and political conservatism; a religion of the heart and the Bible; and the glories of suffering. . . . Heroines differed more in name than in characteristics. Uniformly submissive to—yet distrustful of—their betters and men, they were self-sacrificing and self-denying beyond belief, interested in the primacy of the family unit and a happy marriage as the goal of all decent women. They abhorred sin generally, but particularly tobacco, alcohol, divorce, and adultery. (p. 468)

One other domestic novel that must be mentioned is *St. Elmo,* by Augusta Jane Wilson. It is said to be the most popular domestic novel written—only *Uncle Tom's Cabin* exceeded it in sales. Its popularity came from its strong domestic novel components, especially the dominance of a good woman who triumphs over an evil man. Donelson and Nilson (1989) comment on the popularity of Wilson's novel: "No other novel so literally touched the American landscape—thirteen towns were named or renamed St. Elmo, as were hotels, railway coaches, steamboats, one kind of punch, and a brand of cigars" (p. 469).

About the same time of the domestic novels, the dime novel made its entrance with the publication of Ann Stephens' *Malaeska: The Indian Wife of the White Hunter*—a 128-page book that sold some 65,000 copies. These short, 10-cent novels were first written for adults, but when publishers realized that young boys were reading them, they changed the audience and the price. (They sold for 5 cents and the books were shorter, but people still called them dime novels.) Some of the most popular characters included Revolutionary War scout Seth Jones, detectives "Old Sleuth" and Nick Carter, and Western hero Deadwood Dick. The novels were quick, formulaic reading. They included standard characters, contrived plots, and values that reinforced family life.

The series books began with the publication of *The Boat Club* by Oliver Optic. *The Boat Club* was the first of six volumes and 60 editions. Optic was a prolific writer—over 123 novels are credited to him. Since this book was the first, it set the pattern that was to follow for later series. Harry Castlemon wrote *Frank, the Young Naturalist,* the first of five adventurous Frank books. Martha Farquharson Finley wrote primarily for women. Her Elsie Dinsmore series (which included *Elsie Dinsmore* [1867], *Christmas with Grandma Elsie* [1888], *Elsie in the South* [1899]) is said to be the most popular series of its time for young women. The virtuous and Christian Elsie can be followed from childhood to grandmotherhood in 28 popular and profitable volumes.

These various novels—domestic, dime, and series—gave rise to a great deal of literature that was read by young people. It also gave rise to competition between publishing houses. As a result of the popularity of Optic's books, a competing publisher urged Louisa May Alcott to write a book especially for young girls. The novel *Little Women* was born. The story appeared in two volumes, *Little Women: Meg, Jo, Beth, and Amy. The Story of Their Lives: A Girls Book* and *Little Women: Meg, Jo, Beth, and Amy, Part Second.* Alcott and Horatio Alger, Jr., were the first writers for young people to gain national attention. Alger published the first of his estimated 119 novels in 1867. Alger's most successful books (they have sold some 16 million copies) were the Ragged Dick books, such as *Ragged Dick and Mark, the Watch Boy,* and the Richard Hunter books. Ragged Dick is a young and poor hero who is honest above everything else—he drinks, smokes, and gambles, but refrains from lying or stealing, even in the worst of times and situations.

Literature went though a number of changes from the Middle Ages to the mid 1800s. There was one constant, however. Practically all the literature still held values and morals high and came down on the side of what was considered "right." One difference between *A Book of Courtesy* in 1477 and Alcott's *Little Women* in 1868 was the intended audience. The major shift during this time was that the earlier literature was written by adults, but read by children to model behavior. In *Little Women,* Alcott wrote specifically for young female readers.

A shift in the treatment of characters occurred in 1870 with the publication of Thomas Bailey Aldrich's *The Story of a Bad Boy.* With Aldrich's work—partly autobiographical—there soon appeared literature about "bad boys," literature that told about boys as they were, not as parents wished them to be. Other authors followed his lead, and bad boy stories flourished. The realism about boys in literature mirrored the realism of Alcott's *Little Women.* Other "bad boy" literature included Mark Twain's *The Adventures of Tom Sawyer,* soon to become the most loved, mischievous bad boy of the nineteenth century. *Peck's Bad Boy and His Pa* by George Wilbur Peck followed in 1883. Two years later, Twain's *The Adventures of Huckleberry Finn* became an immediate hit with young readers, despite being immediately banned as trashy, vicious, and unfit by libraries in Concord, Massachusetts, and Brooklyn, New York. Both Tom Sawyer and Huck Finn would be frequently banned ever after, yet remain reading favorites.

Other literature read by young people continued to flourish. *Twenty Thousand Leagues Under the Sea* was written by Jules Verne in 1872 and provided young readers with one of the first examples of science fiction. A second novel by Verne, *Around the World in Eighty Days,* appeared in 1873. In 1877, Anna Sewell wrote the extremely popular *Black Beauty* as a protest against cruelty to horses.

Two adventure stories published in 1883 made an immediate impact on the reading of young people and have continued to be popular reading to this day. Robert Louis Stevenson's *Treasure Island* and Howard Pyle's *The Merry Adventures of Robin Hood* are two of literature's all-time great adventure tales. In 1892 Arthur Conan Doyle contributed to the mystery and suspense genre with his *Adventures of Sherlock Holmes.*

Formula fiction dominated literature for young adults in the late 1800s and into the twentieth century. Variations of stock plots and themes made the stories predictable, but young readers loved them. Edward Stratemeyer is credited with developing formula fiction to its fullest. Writing under numerous pen names, Stratemeyer first created the Old Glory series, centered around two young boys and war themes. This series was followed by numerous other series of books—many of which are still read today. Among Stratemeyer's successes are contemporary battle books, Soldiers of Fortune; school-like and sports books, the Lakeport series; the adventurous Rover Boys books of which 30 adventures were published; and mystery books centered around the Hardy Boys and Nancy Drew. Remarkable young inventor Tom Swift also proved to be exciting and popular reading for young adults.

Although Stratemeyer is credited with producing over 1,000 titles, it is well known that many of the novels were written by a writing syndicate headed by Stratemeyer. He provided other writers with chapter-by-chapter plots, and they completed the stories. Stratemeyer ensured the accuracy of events by comparing new books to others in the series, making changes as he wished, and then sending them off to be published.

The Stratemeyer books were widely popular. In a major survey of reading interests conducted by the American Library Association (1926), 98 percent of the young people surveyed listed a Stratemeyer title as a favorite. These stories displayed the elements that young readers most admired: mystery, excitement and suspense, and a protagonist who would always triumph against terrible odds. Although far from good literature—stereotyped characters, poorly constructed plots, no relationship to reality—these books did keep young people reading and paved the way for the better young adult literature to follow. An interesting phenomenon surfaced again with the Stratemeyer books: Popularity and quality did not necessarily go hand in hand. This is true even today, and not only in young adult literature.

An early young adult novel that broke away from the surreal characteristics of the earlier literature was *Seventeen* by Booth Tarkington. Written in 1902, this novel is one of the first "reality" novels about the joys and problems of young people, with no sugar coating. The literature of this period was a mixed bag. Tarkington's novel offered some sense of reality, but other literature seemed to stay with the tried and true. Laura Lee Hope's *The Bobbsey Twins* (1904) series was a great success. It offered pure entertainment for young readers. Also in 1904, Kate Douglas Wiggin's *Rebecca of Sunnybrook Farm* becomes one of the first of many popular novels in which young children significantly brighten the lives of people around them. Between 1906 and the 1920s, Zane Grey romanticized the Old West in more than 60 novels. Among the most successful were *The Spirit of the Border, The Wanderers of the Wasteland,* and *Riders of the Purple Sage.*

In 1934, publishers started a direct attempt to publish literature for young adults. The publishing company of Longmans, Green marketed Rose Wilder Lane's novel *Let the Hurricane Roar* (published earlier as an adult novel) as the first of their novels in a new marketing division termed "Junior Books." Other publishers would soon follow Longmans' lead and establish their own junior book divisions. The "official" junior or young adult novel was off and running. Although many of the young adult books were steeped in the popular romances or in the series books, a few, such as Lane's novel, broke out of that tradition.

Let the Hurricane Roar was historical because it told about the pioneering days of Dakota and the struggle of a young couple fighting for survival in the hostile environment of the northern plains. *Shuttered Windows,* written by Florence Crannel Means in 1938, is considered the first novel for adolescents to portray blacks realistically. The novel tells of the trials of a 16-year-old girl who leaves Minnesota and lives with her grandmother in South Carolina. The quality of writing leaves much to be desired, but the work does portray blacks as worthwhile and dignified people. One other book of historical fiction published about this time was Esther Forbes' *Johnny Tremain* (1944). The story tells of a 14-year-old silversmith's apprentice and his life during the American Revolution.

Sports stories dominated the reading of young adult males. John Tunis was said to be the most widely read sports author with such titles as *The Iron Duke* (1938), a novel about the football hero Jim Wellington, and *All-American* (1942), the story of black athlete Ronald Perry and the injustices he suffered because of racial prejudice. Many critics believe that Tunis's greatest story is *His Enemy, His Friend* (1967), which combines the aftermath of war memories with Tunis's favorite topic, sports.

A phenomenon that flourished in the 1930s and 1940s and peaked in the 1950s was the career novel. For every vocation (except the least desirable) a publisher was eager to provide young readers with a book about their favorite field. Unquestionably, books about nursing led the group in numbers and popularity. A representative writer in the genre was Helen Boylston whose Sue Barton series (1936–1952) ran to seven volumes. Another widely read book was *Peggy Covers the News* (1936) by Emma Bugbee (Hauck, 1984).

LITERATURE: INACCURATE REPRESENTATION

Generally, young adult novels of the 1940s and 1950s focused on traditional social behavior: family, jobs, sports, dating, etc. The themes of most of these novels were moralistic and superficial. However, realism began to creep into the writing of a few popular young adult writers and this became a significant milestone in the direction of young adult literature. Hauck (1984) comments:

> Throughout the '40's and '50's lesser novelists also focused on genuine adolescent concerns, although the range of adolescent experience examined was still fairly narrow. Families, jobs, dating, and athletics were common themes, but such controversial

subjects as drugs, alcohol, illegitimate pregnancy and the like were seldom introduced except to be decried. . . . All the protagonists in the novels are good, clean-hearted, clean-limbed, middle class Americans. In the antiseptic settings, sexual dilemmas are never allowed to intrude and difficulties rather readily overcome. (p. 90)

Seventeenth Summer (1942) by Maureen Daly is frequently credited with being the first contemporary young adult novel to meet these new criteria. It was the first classic love story for teenagers. The realistic portrayal of teenagers as they really were set this story apart from others of its time. Daly recognizes drinking, smoking, homosexuality, and other "taboo" topics as realistic aspects of life. As one might expect, Daly's book was not well received by the adult population, but it did not go unnoticed by young adult readers.

Henry Gregor Felsen joined Daly in writing about young adults in an honest and serious fashion. He, too, ruffled the feathers of adults by writing about such taboo topics as adolescent failure and teenage pregnancy. One of his most popular books was *Two and the Town,* about a young girl who becomes pregnant, which forces her boyfriend and her to marry. In the 1950s, Felsen's books about cars were immensely popular among young adult males. *Hot Rod, Street Rod,* and *Crash Club* were the hot titles.

In 1951, the novel that began the shift to what is called the "new realism" was J. D. Salinger's *The Catcher in the Rye.* The literature that followed this novel is cynical and reflects economical, political, and social problems of the era. *Catcher* remains noteworthy in part due to its frankness in both language and the negative light in which it portrays adults. Ironically, the novel was written for the adult market, but it captured the young adult reader's attention like no other book has done.

Two other novels, although they did not have the impact of *Catcher,* did make contributions to the literary field. *Miracles on Maple Hill* (1957) by Virginia Sorenson received the Newbery Medal, but it was heavily criticized for dealing with subject matter inappropriate for young adult readers: dissension in the home and the possibility of divorce. During this time, restrictions on subject matter were declining, but many adults still attempted to maintain unrealistic values of the past in current literature. The second book was *To Kill a Mockingbird* (1960) by Harper Lee. This novel depicts racial problems in the South and, to the horror of many adults of the time, it does not portray the white population favorably.

In this period of young adult literature, but for a few exceptions, "much of the literature written for young adults from 1940 through 1966 goes largely and legitimately ignored today" (Donelson & Nilson, 1989, p. 555).

LITERATURE: SELF-DISCOVERY

Meanwhile, the influence of the media, especially television, and the more permissive climate of the sixties were also having their effect. . . . The middle sixties ushered in this "new realism" as it came to be called. These novels depicted young people in ordinary situations without censoring their language or glossing over their conduct. Premarital sex, unwed motherhood, abortion, illicit drugs, all these issues and many more found their way into the stories. . . . With few exceptions, these new problem novels, as they were also called, have several characteristics in common. They are told from the point of view of a rather precocious adolescent . . . parents are unsympathetic or incompetent . . . they generally end with the protagonist taking a small step forward in maturity or self-understanding. The language is conversational, with a few descriptive passages or niceties of style and the setting is a mere backdrop for the action. (Hauck, 1984, p. 91)

The early books in this new age of realism emphasized this "unsympathetic or incompetent" parent characteristic. Leading the pack is Paul Zindel. In his 1968 novel *The Pigman,* John and Lorraine are the two narrators who have little positive to say about their parents. John always refers to his father as "Bore," and Lorraine realizes that her mother has an obsession about the dangers that men may bring. In Zindel's next book *My Darling, My Hamburger* (1969), the parents don't fare much better. Liz's father is extremely abusive, and her decision to have an abortion is due to her boyfriend's father, who believes it is better to spend a little to remove the embarrassment.

Although this attitude toward parents may be the negative side of young adult literature at this time, Zindel and other authors offered a great deal more on the positive side for adolescents. *The Pigman* has been widely praised by critics and the young adults who read it. It offers young readers an understanding of and compassion for human nature. In addition, it lifts up the quality of the writer's craft. Alternating points of view between John and Lorraine is one example of writing skill that is not common in previous literature.

In *The Outsiders* (Hinton, 1967), parents are not effective or not present, but this is not the emphasis that Hinton brings to this novel. Her motive for writing *The Outsiders* was the realism that is found in street gangs, rigid social class structure, and violence in the community and the schools. She tells of the Greasers and the Socs from the point of view of Ponyboy, a Greaser. This new age of realism also was found with stories of the poor and minority groups. *Where the Lilies Bloom* (Cleaver & Cleaver, 1969) is set in the Appalachian mountains where 14-year-old Mary Call Luther struggles to keep her family together after the death of her father. The reader experiences the struggles of a poverty-stricken family. Readers also experience a well-written novel.

Also in 1969, William Armstrong wrote about a poverty-stricken black family of tenant farmers in *Sounder.* In *The Contender* (1967), Robert Lipsyte writes about a black young adult boxer who hopes his athletic ability will get him out of the slums. Hunter's *The Soul Brothers and Sister Lou* (1968) has a similar theme. It portrays the life of blacks in a northern ghetto and shows the conditions that give rise to racial strife. The bleak and stark realities of racial prejudice are also presented most effectively in Mildred Taylor's writings. Her novels follow the lives of the Logan family as they experience the struggle to hold their land and the persecution of white neighbors.

Books by Judy Blume also contributed to this new realism in young adult literature. *Are You There God? It's Me, Margaret* (1970) focuses on a pre-adolescent girl's fears and concerns about menstruation and other problems of growing up. In *Blubber* (1974), Blume writes to the issue of obesity as well as to a lesser issue (perhaps) of teacher weakness and ineffectiveness. In the same year, Paula Danziger also wrote about school and the unhappy life of an overweight girl in *The Cat Ate My Gymsuit*. In this novel, however, the teacher has a more positive role and is portrayed as courageous and compassionate. In *Deenie* (1973), Blume writes of a pretty girl whose mother wants her to become a model, but this dream seems unachievable since Deenie develops scoliosis and must wear a back brace. A realistic view comes with Deenie's concern that the back problem may be because she masturbates. Perhaps the most controversial of Blume's novels is *Forever* (1976), which addresses teenage romance with graphic details of sexual intercourse.

Readers experience another type of realism in the works of Jean Craighead George. In *Julie of the Wolves* (1972), a young Eskimo woman struggles with two cultures: the past and the modern way of life. The agonizing conflicts that this woman faces to choose the "right" direction for her are described vividly.

As the continuum evolves, the literature reflects more conditions of society, and these conditions are told in straightforward stories that young people want to read. As we look at the evolution of young adult literature, we find that the literature from the mid 1970s to the present not only reflects the mountains and valleys of society, but it does it with high-quality writing. Yes, some of the earlier novels were written well, but quality was not generally the most important characteristic of young adult literature. There is more of a push in that direction as literature for young adults continues.

Most, if not all, of Robert Cormier's novels reflect this quality of writing. *The Chocolate War* (1974), *I am the Cheese* (1977), *After the First Death* (1979), *Fade* (1988), and *We All Fall Down* (1991) offer complicated, sophisticated plot structure, fully developed characters, settings that complement the plot and characters, a variety of literary devices, and complex, universal themes. Although some criticize Cormier for his pessimistic view of life in his early novels, it is important to note that many of life's problems are difficult to overcome and, for a few, cannot be overcome.

Chris Crutcher, a writer and child abuse therapist, believes that if stories are to be told, they must be told in an honest, forthright way. His literature—*Running Loose* (1983), *Stotan!* (1986), *The Crazy Horse Electric Game* (1987), *Chinese Handcuffs* (1989), and *Athletic Shorts* (1991)—reflect this attitude. Crutcher believes that there are stories to be told about love, death, racism, bigotry, and sexual abuse, and these stories need to be told to young adults with honesty, for if they are not, young people will see through them in a flash. Crutcher writes with an honest, straightforward style. He includes just the right amount of humor and other literary techniques to make his writing the quality that young people read.

LITERATURE: THE PRESENT AND BEYOND

Other young adult writers who could be mentioned in this history of young adult literature have been included in other parts of this book, usually in discussions of their quality of writing and their positive contributions to the field of young adult literature. Certainly, the quality writers in the immediate past and present who will continue to write and contribute to the reading of young adults in the future include Norma Fox Mazer, Harry Mazer, Sue Ellen Bridgers, Richard Peck, Cynthia Voigt,

Julian Thompson, Gary Paulsen, Mildred Taylor, Sandy Asher, Paul Zindel, S. E. Hinton, Judy Blume, Lois Duncan, Walter Dean Myers, Katherine Paterson, Robert Lipsyte, M. E. Kerr, Robert Cormier, Chris Crutcher, and others discussed in this text. Many others who are just publishing their first young adult novels will also be important young adult authors.

What will the literature of the future be like? Certainly, like the literature of the past, it will reflect the concerns of an ever-changing society. Donelson and Nilson (1989) suggest the following differences between young adult literature of the 1970s and future literature:

Less reliance for interest on shock and titillation.

More excitement, romance, and optimism.

More variety and less stereotyping of characters, plots, and settings.

A more balanced and convincing view of parents.

More sophisticated and varied approaches to problems connected with racism and ethnic identification. (p. 95)

To this list, we would add that the young adult literature of the present and the future will include stories about abuses that young people face: child and sexual abuse; the family and its inability to stay together; political abuses in the United States and abroad; the stress of economic instability; sexually transmitted diseases and their effects on young people; and the general conflicts that go with growing up in a society that is sometimes unkind to its youth.

In addition, there will be an increase in the series books. M. E. Kerr will continue her Fell series: *Fell* (1987); *Fell Back* (1989); and *Fell Down* (1991). Other series will probably continue as well: the Tillerman series by Cynthia Voigt, the alphabet—*A, My Name Is Amy; B, My Name Is Bunny,* etc.—series by Norma Fox Mazer, and Alvin Schwartz's *Scary Stories.* Perhaps one of the most widely known series is by Mildred Taylor. Books such as *Roll of Thunder, Hear My Cry* and *Let the Circle Be Unbroken* trace the lives of the Logan family, in particular the life of Cassie Logan. Gary Paulsen adds his name to the list with the Culpepper series, which combines mystery, adventure, and humor. Walter Dean Myers also has added a series to his accomplishments. *18 Pine St.* includes realistic stories about family, friendship, and romance with a multicultural cast.

Sequels will continue to be available to the young adult reader. Well-known sequels in the past may give rise to additional companion novels. Robert Cormier continues the lives of the characters at Trinity High School from *The Chocolate War* in *Beyond The Chocolate War;* Betty Greene wrote *Summer of My German Soldier,* which preceded *Morning Is a Long Time Coming.* Robert Lipsyte wrote *The Contender* in 1967 and then continued the story in *The Brave* in 1991.

We also suggest that the nonfiction genre will continue to grow and will meet the needs of the young adult. A renewed interest will be apparent in the books on preparing for college and careers. There will be more how-to books and self-help books. Young adults will continue to read the books of Milton Meltzer, Brent Ashabranner, David Macaulay, and others who write nonfiction.

❧   Learning Log Responses   ❧

What realizations did you uncover during the reading of this chapter? Does a continuum evolve?

How do the recent series novels compare with the earlier series novels?

REFERENCES

American Library Association. (1926). *Children's reading interests*. Chicago: Author.

Donelson, K., & Nilson, A. (1989). *Literature for today's young adults*. Glenview, IL: Scott, Foresman.

Hauck, P. (1984). "Literature for Adolescents: Gold or Dross?" *Journal of Educational Research, 18* (2), 88–102.

Smith, J. (1967). *A critical approach to children's literature*. New York: McGraw-Hill.

Wintle, J., & Fisher, E. (1974). *The pied pipers*. New York: Paddington.

Support for Teaching Young Adult Literature

Teachers are a very busy group of professionals. Since both authors taught (and one is still teaching) in the public schools, we know what it is like to teach 100 to 140 students each day. Simply trying to keep up with lesson plans, grading, and all of the administrative/clerical work that is asked of teachers is a full-time job. Little time is left for library research to find appropriate sources of support of teaching young adult literature. This appendix attempts to provide an easy reference to these sources.

ADDRESSES OF YOUNG ADULT LITERATURE PUBLISHERS

Archway,
Pocket Books
1230 Avenue of the Americas
New York, NY 10020

Atheneum, McElderry, Scribner's
866 Third Avenue
New York, NY 10022

Avon Books
105 Madison Avenue
New York, NY 10016

Ballantine, Del Ray, Fawcett Books
201 East 50th Street
New York, NY 10022

Bantam, Doubleday, Dell
666 Fifth Avenue
New York, NY 10103

Bradbury Press
866 Third Avenue
New York, NY 10022

Delacorte Press
1 Dag Hammarskjold Plaza
245 E. 47th
New York, NY 10017

Dial Press
2 Park Avenue
New York, NY 10016

Doubleday
245 Park Avenue
New York, NY 10167

E. P. Dutton
2 Park Avenue
New York, NY 10016

Farrar, Straus & Giroux
19 Union Square West
New York, NY 10003

Fawcett Juniper
201 E. 50th Street
New York, NY 10022

Greenwillow Books
105 Madison Avenue
New York, NY 10016

Grosset & Dunlap
51 Madison Avenue
New York, NY 10010

Harcourt Brace Jovanovich
HBJ Building
Orlando, FL 32887

HarperCollins
10 E. 53rd Street
New York, NY 10022

Henry Holt and Company
115 West 18th Street
New York, NY 10011

Houghton Mifflin, Clarion Books
2 Park Street
Boston, MA 02108

Alfred A. Knopf, Random House
201 East 50th Street
New York, NY 10022

Lippincott Junior Books
10 East 53rd Street
New York, NY 10022

Little, Brown & Company
34 Beacon Street
Boston, MA 02106

Methuen, Inc.
733 Third Avenue
New York, NY 10017

William Morrow
105 Madison Avenue
New York, NY 10016

New American Library
1633 Broadway
New York, NY 10019

Orchard Books
387 Park Avenue South
New York, NY 10016

Pantheon Books
201 E. 50th Street
New York, NY 10022

Penguin Books
625 Madison Avenue
New York, NY 10022

Scholastic Books
730 Broadway
New York, NY 10003

Simon & Schuster
1230 Avenue of the Americas
New York, NY 10020

Viking Penguin
40 West 23rd Street
New York, NY 10010

Warner Books
666 Fifth Avenue
New York, NY 10103

Franklin Watts
387 Park Avenue
New York, NY 10016

SOURCES THAT INCLUDE REVIEWS OF YOUNG ADULT BOOKS

The ALAN Review
Assembly on Literature for Adolescents, NCTE
1111 Kenyon Road
Urbana, IL 61801

Booklinks
50 E. Huron Street
Chicago, IL 60611

Booklist
American Library Association
50 E. Huron Street
Chicago, IL 60611

Books for the Teen Ager
Office of Young Adult Ser.
New York Public Library
Fifth Avenue & 42nd Street
New York, NY 10018

Bulletin for the Center for Children's Books
P.O. Box 37005
Chicago, IL 60637

Children's Literature in Education: An International Quarterly
Agathon Press
111 8th Avenue
New York, NY 10011

English Journal
NCTE
1111 Kenyon Road
Urbana, IL 61801

Horn Book
14 Beacon Street
Boston, MA 02108

Horn Book Guide
14 Beacon Street
Boston, MA 02108

Interracial Books for Children Bulletin
1841 Broadway
New York, NY 10023

The Journal of Reading
International Reading Association
P.O. Box 8139
Newark, DE 19714

Journal of Youth Services in Libraries
American Library Association
50 East Huron Street
Chicago, IL 60611

Kirkus Reviews
200 Park Avenue, South
Suite 1118
New York, NY 10003

Kliatt Young Adult Paperback Book Guide
425 Watertown Street
Newton, MA 02158

Language Arts
NCTE
1111 Kenyon Road
Urbana, IL 61801

McNaughton Young Adult Reviews
McNaughton Book Service
P.O. Box 926
Williamsport, PA 17705

The New Advocate
480 Washington Street
Norwood, MA 02062

The New York Times Book Review
New York Times Company
229 W. 43rd Street
New York, NY 10036

Publishers Weekly
P.O. Box 1979
Marion, OH 43302

The School Library Journal
P.O. Box 1978
Marion, OH 43305

SIGNAL Newsletter
IRA
P.O. Box 8139
Newark, DE 19714

Voice of Youth Advocate
52 Liberty Street
Metuchen, NJ 08840

Wilson Library Review
950 University Avenue
Bronx, NY 10452

INDEXES OF REVIEWS OF YOUNG ADULT LITERATURE

Book Review Digest
1905 to date
H. W. Wilson Company

Book Review Index
1965 to date
Gale Research Company

Children's Book Review
1975 to date
Gale Research Company
A. Block and C. Riley (Ed.)

Children's Literature Review
1976 to date
Gale Research Company

High-Interest Books for Teens: A Guide to Book Review and Biographical Sources
Joyce Nakamura, Ed.
Gale Research Company
1988

Masterplots II, Juvenile and Young Adult Literature
Frank N. Magill, Ed.
Salem Press
1991

Olderr's Young Adult Fiction Index
Stevn Olderr, Ed.
St. James Press
1988

Young Adult Book Review Index
Barbara Beach, Ed.
Gale Research Company
1988

AWARDS PRESENTED TO YOUNG ADULT BOOKS

Best Books for Young Adults—The annual list of books is chosen by a committee of the American Library Association. The list is published in the March issue of *School Library Journal* or is available from the American Library Association.

Booklist Editors' Choices—The list of best books is published each January in *Booklist*.

Books for the Teenager—The best books list is published yearly by the New York Public Library.

Books for Young Adults—The list is generated from the evaluations sent in by young adult readers. It is published by the University of Iowa.

Boston Globe-Horn Book Award—Awards are given annually for best of fiction and nonfiction. Acceptance speeches of those receiving the awards are pub-

lished in the January/February issue of *Horn Book Magazine*.

Horn Book Fanfare Books—This list of best books is selected by the editors of *Horn Book Magazine* and is published in the December issue of *Horn Book Magazine*.

Newberry Award—The annual award winner and the honor books are chosen by a committee of the American Library Association. The award is announced in January. The winning author's acceptance speech appears in the July/August issue of *Horn Book Magazine*.

Recommended Books for the Reluctant Young Adult Reader—The annual list of books is chosen by a committee of the American Library Association.

School Library Journal Best Books of the Year—The annual list of books is published in the December issue of *School Library Journal*.

OTHER SOURCES IMPORTANT TO THE CLASSROOM TEACHER

PERIODICALS

The ALAN Review—In addition to the reviews of young adult literature, the journal includes articles written by professional writers of young adult literature as well as by professional educators who offer criticisms and practical applications of young adult literature.

Bulletin of the Center for Children's Books—In addition to the reviews, this source also includes articles about the way young adult literature may be used in the curriculum.

Children's Literature in Education: An International Quarterly—The interna-

tional journal offers readers a more detailed analysis and scholarly criticism than many others.

English Journal—Although the journal tries to meet the needs and interests of the junior high/middle and high school English teacher with articles covering all aspects of teaching English, it does often have a focus, frequently on young adult literature.

Horn Book Magazine—Primary emphasis is given to scholarly reviews of children's and young adult literature; however, there are feature articles of interest to the classroom teacher.

Interracial Books for Children Bulletin—In addition to the reviews, this bulletin does include articles. The main emphasis is on social issues and their treatment in literature.

Journal of Reading—Aimed at the high school reading teacher, the journal emphasizes the teaching of reading; however, it does include articles on reading interests and literature.

Voice of Youth Advocates (VOYA)—Although primarily aimed at the librarian, this periodical offers interesting articles that would also be of interest to classroom teachers.

Wilson Library Bulletin—In addition to the reviews of books, the *Bulletin* includes interesting and relevant articles of interest to the young adult literature teacher.

BOOKS

Bodart, J. (1992). *Booktalker.* Englewood, CO: Libraries Unlimited.
   Explores booktalks and booktalking.

Carlsen, G. R. (1980). *Books and the teen-age reader* (2nd ed.). New York: Harper & Row.
   The first edition was one of the early books on young adult literature that connected with teachers. This book continues to connect.

Carter, B., & Abrahamson, R., (1990). *Nonfiction for young adults: From delight to wisdom.* Phoenix, AZ: Oryx.
   A thorough presentation of the nonfiction field, the book also includes interviews with prominent nonfiction writers.

Christenbury, L. (Ed.). (1995). *Books for you: A booklist for senior high students.* Urbana, IL: National Council of Teachers of English.
   Books are described by subject or theme. This publication is revised every 5 years.

Criscoe, B. L. (Ed.). (1990). *Award-winning books for children and young adults: An annual guide, 1989.* New York: Scarecrow.

This directory of awards includes information on award sponsors, award background, and biographies of the winners.

Donelson, K., & Nilsen, A. (1989). *Literature for today's young adults* (3rd ed.). Glenview, IL: Scott, Foresman.
   This book is often described as the complete text on young adult literature.

Feehan, P., & Barron, P. (Eds.). (1991). *Writers on writing for young adults: Exploring the authors, the genre, the readers, the issues, and the critics of young-adult literature.* New York: Omnigraphs.
   Essays in this work discuss the various aspects of young adult literature.

Gallo, D. (Ed.). (1990). *Speaking for ourselves: Autobiographical sketches by notable authors of books for young adults.* Urbana, IL: National Council of Teachers of English.
   This useful book contains sketches of well-known young adult authors, with information about each author's life and works.

Lynn, R. N. (1989). *Fantasy literature for children and young adults.* New York: R. R. Bowker.
   The book contains annotated bibliographies of fantasy novels and short story collections.

Matthews, D. (Ed.). (1988). *High interest—easy reading: For junior and senior high school students* (5th ed.). Urbana, IL: National Council of Teachers of English.
   The emphasis is on books that meet the interests of reluctant adolescent readers.

Nathan, R. (Ed.). (1991). *Writers in the classroom.* Norwood, MA: Christopher Gordon.
   In this book, writers share their writing, and writers and teachers share how they would teach writing. Chapters were written by young adult writers as well as professional educators.

Probst, R. (1988). *Response and analysis: Teaching literature in junior and senior high school.* Portsmouth, NH: Boynton/Cook.

This book teaches about the teaching of literature in general and response-based teaching in particular.

Samuels, B. G., & Beers, G. K. (Eds.), (1995/1996). *Your Reading: A Booklist for Junior High and Middle School Students.* (10th ed.). Urbana IL: National Council of Teachers of English.

A companion to *Books for you,* this publication presents summaries of literature that are appropriate for junior high and middle school students.

Twayne's United States Author Series: Young Adult Authors Books. Boston: G. K. Hall.

This series presents the life and work of various young adult authors, including Judy Blume, Sue Ellen Bridgers, Robert Cormier, Rosa Guy, S. E. Hinton, M. E. Kerr, Norma Klein, Norma Fox Mazer, Richard Peck, Walter Dean Myers, and Paul Zindel. A list of specific titles in the Twayne series appears in Chapter 2; bibliographic information is included in Appendix B.

Walder, E. (Ed.). (1988). *Book bait: Detailed notes on adult books, popular with young people* (4th ed.). Chicago, IL: American Library Association.

This bibliography provides detailed information about books that are of interest to young adults. It attempts to bridge the gap between young adult books and adult books.

Ward, M., & Marquardt, D. (1990). *Authors of books for young people* (3rd ed.). New York: Scarecrow.

This book provides a snapshot reference of information about children's and young adult authors.

Weiss, J. (Ed.). (1979). *From writers to students: The pleasures and pains of writing.* Newark, DE: International Reading Association.

The book contains interviews with selected young adult authors including Judy Blume, M. E. Kerr, and Norma and Harry Mazer.

We recommend the thorough collection of sources presented in the Fall 1991 issue of *The ALAN Review.* "The Library Connection" column, by Donald J. Kenney, was titled "Familiarity with Reference." The column is very extensive and demands the attention of any teacher of young adult literature.

CONFERENCES

Reading journals and books is just one of many ways to stay abreast of what is happening in the field of young adult literature. An effective way to come into contact with the literature, its writers, and its critics is to attend a conference that includes a young adult literature component. Most state English and reading organizations, perhaps affiliated with their national organizations, have annual conferences in which authors are invited to speak, and sessions on the writer's craft or the work itself are available for discussion. Teachers can learn a great deal from these conferences.

National conferences attract a wider audience and, thus, attract more and varied authors and sessions. In the national arena, prominent young adult authors participate in large group presentations as well as small group sessions. It is an excellent way for teachers of young adult literature to interact with the authors of the literature they are teaching in the classroom. Many groups across the nation meet and discuss young adult literature to some extent. Two in particular are the International Reading Association (IRA) and the Assembly on Literature for Adolescents—NCTE (ALAN). Both groups have extended workshops that include general presentations by authors, critics, and teachers of young adult literature as well as small-group sessions on related issues relevant to the classroom teacher.

LITERATURE FESTIVALS

Literature festivals also provide contact with popular young adult authors. These are particularly beneficial because they connect these authors with teachers, children, and young adults. These festivals usually last two to three days and involve hundreds of young people interacting with authors and specialists in young adult literature. Usually sessions are offered for the classroom teacher as well.

The field of young adult literature is growing rapidly. The quality of literature that is now available for young people demands that classroom teachers and librarians pay close attention to this genre. Resources are available so that teachers can keep up with this rapidly growing field. When teachers become knowledgeable about young adult literature, they and their students can only benefit.

❧   Learning Log Responses   ❧

Read the latest issue of *The ALAN Review*. Make an entry in your log about its content and its usefulness to you as a teacher of literature.

Peruse two other publications that may be helpful to the teacher of young adult literature. Make an entry showing how you might use these publications.

Works of Literature Cited

Books that are appropriate for middle school students are marked with an asterisk (*). Also, because many older titles are either no longer in print or are in the public domain and available from several sources, we do not list publishers for these works.

Achebe, C. (1960). *No Longer at Ease*. Greenwhich, CT: Fawcett.

Achebe, C. (1988). *Things Fall Apart*. Portsmouth, NH: Heinemann.

*Adoff, A. (1986). *Sports Pages*. New York: Lippincott.

Aesop. (c. 6th cent. B.C.E.). *Fables*.

Aiken, J. (1969), *Night Fall*. New York: Dell.

Aiken, J. (1978). *Street*. New York: Viking.

Aiken, J. (1984). *A Whisper in the Night*. New York: Delacorte.

Albery, N. (1978). *Balloon Top*. New York: Pantheon.

Alcott, L. M. (1868). *Little Women: Meg, Jo, Beth, and Amy. The Story of Their Lives: A Girl's Book*.

Alcott, L. M. (1869). *Little Women: Meg, Jo, Beth, and Amy, Part Second*.

Aldrich, T. (1870). *The Story of A Bad Boy*.

*Aleskin, A. (1975). *My Brother Plays the Clarinet*. New York: Henry Walck.

Alger, H. (1962). *Ragged Dick and Mark, The Watch Boy*. New York: Collier.

*Almazov, B. (n.d.). *The Most Beautiful Horse*. Chicago: Imported Publications.

*Ames, L. (1977, 1978, 1981, 1986). *Draw 50* Books (series). Garden City, NY: Doubleday.

Anaya, R. (1972). *Bless Me, Ultima*. Berkely, CA: Tonatiuh, Quinto Sol International.

Anderson, M. (1954). *The Bad Seed*. New York: Dramatists.

Angelou, M. (1970). *I Know Why the Caged Bird Sings*. New York: Random House.

Angelou, M. (1971). *Just Give Me a Cool Drink of Water 'fore I Die*. New York: Random House.

Angelou, M. (1975). *Oh, Pray My Wings Are Gonna Fit Me Well*. New York: Random House.

Angelou, M. (1978). *And Still I Rise*. New York: Random House.

Angelou, M. (1987). *Now Sheba Sings the Song*. New York: Dial.

Anonymous. (1971). *Go Ask Alice*. New York: Prentice Hall.

Anthony, M. (1985). *The Games Were Coming*. Portsmouth, NH: Heinemann.

*Anthony, M. (1985). *The Year in San Fernando*. Portsmouth, NH: Heinemann.

Anthony, M. (1987). *Green Days by the River*. Portsmouth, NH: Heinemann.

Appleman-Jurman, A. (1988). *Alicia: My Story*. New York: Dell.

Argheta, M. (1990). *A Day in the Life*. New York: Random House.

— *Armstrong, W. (1969). *Sounder*. New York: Harper & Row.

*Arrick, F. (1981). *Chernowitz*. New York: New American Library.

Arrick, F. (1992). *What You Don't Know Can Kill You*. New York: Bantam.

Arundel, H. (1972). *Emma In Love*. New York: Elsevier-Nelson.

*Ashabranner, B. (1982). *Morning Star, Black Sun*. New York: G. P. Putnam's Sons.

*Ashabranner, B. (1983). *The New Americans*. New York: G. P. Putnam's Sons.

*Ashabranner, B. (1984). *To Live in Two Worlds: American Indian Youth Today*. New York: Dodd, Mead.

*Ashabranner, B. (1985). *Dark Harvest*. New York: G. P. Putnam's Sons.

*Ashabranner, B. (1989). *People Who Make a Difference*. New York: Cobblehill.

*Ashabranner, B. (1989). *Born to the Land: An American Portrait*. New York: G. P. Putnam's Sons.

*Ashabranner, B., & Ashabranner, M. (1987). *Into a Strange Land: Unaccompanied Refugee Youth in America*. New York: G. P. Putnam's Sons.

* Asher, S. (1980). *Summer Begins*. New York: E. P. Dutton.

*Asher, S. (1987). *Everything Is Not Enough*. New York: Dell.

Asher, S. (1987). "Great Moves." In *Visions*, ed. Don Gallo. New York: Dell.

*Asher, S. (1989). *A Woman Called Truth*. Woodstock, IL: Dramatic Publishing.

Asher, S. (1989). *Little Old Ladies in Tennis Shoes*. New York: Dramatic Publishing.

*Asher, S. (1992). *The Wise Men of Chelm*. New York: Dramatic Publishing.

Asher, S. (1993). *Out of Here*. New York: Lodestar.

Asher, S. (1994). *Sunday Sunday*. New York: Dramatic Publishing.

Asher, S. (1994). *Dancing with Strangers*. New York: Dramatic Publishing.

Asimov, I., ed. (1985). *Young Monsters*. New York: Harper & Row.

Austin, J. (1813). *Pride and Prejudice*.

*Avi. (1988). *Wolf Rider: A Tale of Terror*. New York: Macmillan.

Avi. (1989). *The Man Who Was Poe*. New York: Avon.

Avi. (1990). *The True Confession of Charlotte Doyle*. New York: Orchard.

*Avi. (1991). *Nothing But the Truth*. New York: Orchard.

*Avi. (1992). *The Blue Heron*. New York: Avon.

*Babbitt, N. (1975). *Tuck Everlasting*. New York: Farrar, Straus & Giroux.

*Bachrach, S. (1994). *Tell Them We Remember*. Boston: Little, Brown.

Baldwin, J. (1985). *Go Tell It on the Mountain*. New York: Dell.

Bambara, T. (1981). *Gorilla, My Love*. New York: Random House.

Barrett, P. (1986). *To Break the Silence: Thirteen Short Stories for Young Readers*. New York: Dell.

*Bauer, J. (1992). *Squashed*. New York: Dell.

Bauer, M. D., ed. (1994). *Am I Blue: Coming Out from the Silence*. New York: HarperCollins.

Beirhorst, J. (1987). *In the Trail of the Wind: American Indian Poems and Ritual Orations*. New York: Farrar, Straus & Giroux.

Bell, W. (1990). *Forbidden City*. New York: Bantam.

Benard, R., ed. (1988). *All Problems Are Simple*. New York: Dell.

Benard, R., ed. (1989). *Do You Like It Here? And Other Stories—Twenty-one Views of the High School Years*. New York: Dell.

Benjamin, C. (1991). *Nobody's Baby Now*. New York: Bantam.

*Bennett, J. (1980). *The Pigeon*. New York: Avon.

Bennett, J. (1982). *The Executioner*. New York: Avon.

*Bennett, J. (1990). *Sing Me a Death Song*. New York: Fawcett.

*Bennett, J. (1994). *Dakota Dream*. New York: Scholastic.

Bennett, J. (1995). *The Squared Circle*. New York: Scholastic.

Bishop, R. (1990). *Presenting Walter Dean Myers*. New York: Twayne.

Bloom, S., & Mercier, C. (1991). *Presenting Zibby Oneal*. New York: Twayne.

Blos, J. (1979). *A Gathering of Days: A New England Girl's Journal*, 1830–32. New York: Aladdin.

*Blume, J. (1970). *Are You There God? It's Me, Margaret*. New York: Bradbury.

*Blume, J. (1974). *Blubber*. New York: Bradbury.

*Blume, J. (1973). *Deenie*. New York: Bradbury.

Blume, J. (1976). *Forever*. New York: Bradbury.

*Blume, J. (1981). *Tiger Eyes*. New York: Dell.

*Blume, J. (1990). *Fudge-A-Mania*. New York: Dell.

*Bode, J. (1986). *New Kids in Town: Oral Histories of Immigrant Teens*. New York: Franklin Watts.

Bode, J. (1990). *The Voices of Rape*. New York: Franklin Watts.

Bode, J. (1992). *Kids (Still) Having Kids*. New York: Franklin Watts.

*Bode, J., & Mack, S. (1994). *Heartbreak and Roses: Real Life Stories of Troubled Love*. New York: Delacorte.

Bograd, L. (1981). *The Kolokol Papers*. New York: Bantam.

Bograd, L. (1983). *Los Alamos Light*. New York: Farrar, Straus & Giroux.

Boissard, J. (1977). *A Matter of Feeling*. Trans. Mary Feeley. Toronto: Little, Brown.

*Bonham, F. (1965). *Durango Street*. New York: Dell.

A Book of Courtesy. (1477).

Borland, H. (1963). *When the Legends Die*. New York: Lippincott.

Boylston, H. (1936–1952). *Sue Barton* (series). Boston: Little, Brown.

Bradbury, R. (1973). *When Elephants Last in the Dooryard Bloomed*. New York: Alfred A. Knopf.

Brancato, R. (1977). *Winning*. New York: Dell.

Brancato, R. (1978). *Blinded By the Light*. New York: Alfred A. Knopf.

*Brancato, R. (1982). *Sweet Bells Jangled Out of Tune*. New York: Alfred A. Knopf.

*Brancato, R. (1984). *Facing Up*. New York: Scholastic.

*Brancato, R. (1986). *Uneasy Money*. New York: Alfred A. Knopf.

Breznitz, S. (1992). *Memory Fields*. New York: Alfred A. Knopf.

Bridgers, S. E. (1976). *Home Before Dark*. New York: Bantam.

*Bridgers, S. E. (1979). *All Together Now*. New York: Bantam.

Bridgers, S. E. (1981). *Notes for Another Life*. New York: Bantam.

Bridgers, S. E. (1987). *Permanent Connections*. New York: Harper & Row.

Bridgers, S. E. (1993). *Keeping Christina*. New York: HarperCollins.

Brontë, E. (1847). *Wuthering Heights*.

Brooks, B. (1984). *The Moves Make the Man*. New York: Harper & Row.

Brooks, B. (1986). *Midnight Hour Encores.* New York: Harper & Row.

Brooks, B. (1989). *No Kidding.* New York: Harper & Row.

Brooks, G. (1982). *Selected Poems.* New York: HarperCollins.

Brophy, B. (1983). *The Prince & the Wild Geese.* London: Harnish Hamilton.

Bugbee, E. (1936). *Peggy Covers the News.* New York: Dodd, Mead.

Bunting, E. (1982). *The Great White Shark.* New York: Julian Messner.

Bunyan, J. (1678, 1684). *The Pilgrim's Progress from This World to That Which Is to Come.*

Burns, O. (1984). *Cold Sassy Tree.* New York: Dell.

*Butler, O. (1981). *Kindred.* New York: Pocket Books.

*Byars, B. (1985). *Cracker Jackson.* New York: Viking Penguin.

*Byars, B. (1991). *The Moon and I.* New York: Simon & Schuster.

Bykov, V. (1981). *Pack of Wolves.* Trans. Lynn Solataroff. New York: Crowell.

*Cadnum, M. (1992). *Breaking the Fall.* New York: Viking.

Caine, C. (1985). *How to Get Into College: A Step-by-Step Manual.* New York: Greene.

Cameron, P. (1986). *One Way or Another.* New York: Harper & Row.

Campbell, P. (1989). *Presenting Robert Cormier.* New York: Twayne.

Camus, A. (1954). *The Stranger.* New York: Random House.

Castlemon, H. (1864). *Frank, the Young Naturalist.*

— Carter, A. (1985). *Wart, Son of Toad.* New York: Berkley.

Carter, A. (1987). *Sheila's Dying.* New York: Scholastic.

Carter, A. (1988). *Birth of the Republic.* New York: Franklin Watts.

Carter, A. (1988). *Colonies in Revolt.* New York: Franklin Watts.

Carter, A. (1988). *Darkest Hours.* New York: Franklin Watts.

Carter, A. (1988). *At the Forge of Liberty.* New York: Franklin Watts.

Carter, A. (1989). *The Shoshoni.* New York: Franklin Watts.

Carter, A. (1989). *Up Country.* New York: Scholastic.

Carter, A. (1990). *The Battle of Gettysburg.* New York: Franklin Watts.

Carter, A. (1990). *Dancing on Dark Water.* New York: Scholastic.

Carter, A. (1990). *Last Stand at the Alamo.* New York: Franklin Watts.

*Carter, A. (1990). *RoboDad.* New York: G.P. Putnam's Sons.

Carter, A. (1992). *The American Revolution: War for Independence.* New York: Franklin Watts.

Carter, A. (1992). *The Civil War: American Tragedy.* New York: Franklin Watts.

Carter, A. (1992). *The Colonial Wars: Clashes in the Wilderness.* New York: Franklin Watts.

Carter, A. (1992). *The Mexican War: Manifest Destiny.* New York: Franklin Watts.

Carter, A. (1992). *The Spanish-American War: Imperial Ambitions.* New York: Franklin Watts.

Carter, A. (1992). *The War of 1812: Second Fight for Independence.* New York: Franklin Watts.

Carter, A. (1993). *Battle of the Ironclads: The Monitor and Merrimack.* New York: Franklin Watts.

Carter, A. (1994). *China Past—China Future.* New York: Franklin Watts.

Carter, A. (1994). *Dogwolf.* New York: Scholastic.

Carter, A. (1995). *Between a Rock and a Hard Place.* New York: Scholastic.

Chambers, A. (1985). *Out of Time.* New York: Harper & Row.

Chambers, A. (1986). *Shades of Dark.* New York: Harper & Row.

— *Childress, A. (1973). *A Hero Ain't Nothin But a Sandwich.* New York: Avon.

*Childress, A. (1981). *Rainbow Jordan.* New York: G. P. Putnam's Sons.

*Childress, A. (1989). *Those Other People.* New York: G. P. Putnam's Sons.

*Chukovsky, K. (1976). *The Silver Crest: My Russian Boyhood.* Trans. Beatrice Stillman. New York: Holt, Rinehart & Winston.

Cisneros, S. (1988). *The House on Mango Street.* Houston, TX: Arte.

Clark, M. H., ed. (1995). *Bad Behavior.* Orlando, FL: Harcourt Brace.

*Cleaver, V., & Cleaver, B. (1969). *Where the Lilies Bloom.* New York: Lippincott.

Cline, R. (1990). *Focus on Families: A Reference Handbook.* Santa Barbara, CA: ABC-CLIO.

*Cohen, B. (1982). *King of the Seventh Grade.* New York: Lothrup.

*Cohen, B. (1989). *Tell Us Your Secret.* New York: Bantam.

*Cole, B. (1987). *The Goats.* New York: Farrar, Straus & Giroux.

Cole, B. (1989). *Celine.* New York: HarperCollins.

Coleman, H. (1978). *Rachael's Legacy.* New York: Morrow.

*Collier, J., & Collier, C. (1974). *My Brother Sam Is Dead.* New York: Macmillan.

*Collier, J., & Collier, C. (1976). *The Bloody Country.* New York: Macmillan.

Comenious, J. (1659). *The Visible World in Pictures.*

Comer, J. (1988). *Maggie's American Dream.* New York: NAL-Dutton.

— *Conford, E. (1983). *If This is Love, I'll Take Spaghetti.* New York: Scholastic.

*Conford, E. (1994). *I Love You, I Hate You, Get Lost.* New York: Scholastic.

*Conley, J. (1993). *Crazy Lady.* New York: HarperCollins.

Conley, P. (1983). *The Code Breaker.* New York: Anchorage.

— Conrad, J. (1921). *Heart of Darkness.*

Conton, W. (1982). *The African.* Portsmouth, NH: Heinemann.

*Cooney, C. (1987). *Among Friends.* New York: Bantam.

*Cooney, C. (1990). *The Face on the Milk Carton.* New York: Bantam.

*Cooney, C. (1991). *The Party's Over.* New York: Scholastic.

*Cooney, C. (1992). *Flight #116 Is Down.* New York: Scholastic.

*Cooney, C. (1992). *Operation Homefront.* New York: Bantam.

*Cooney, C. (1993). *Whatever Happened to Janie?* New York: Delacorte.

*Cooney, C. (1994). *Driver's Ed.* New York: Delacorte.

*Cooney, C. (1995). *Flash Fire.* New York: Scholastic.

*Cooper, S. (1973). *The Dark Is Rising.* New York: Atheneum.

*Cooper, S. (1975). *The Grey King.* New York: Collier.

— Cormier, R. (1974). *The Chocolate War.* New York: Dell.

— Cormier, R. (1977). *I Am the Cheese.* New York: Dell.

Cormier, R. (1979). *After the First Death,* New York: Dell.

Cormier, R. (1980). *8 Plus 1.* New York: Pantheon.

Cormier, R. (1980). "The Moustache." In *8 Plus 1.* New York: Pantheon.

Cormier, R. (1983). *The Bumblebee Flies Anyway.* New York: Dell.

— Cormier, R. (1985). *Beyond the Chocolate War.* New York: Dell.

Cormier, R. (1988). *Fade.* New York: Dell.

*Cormier, R. (1990). *Other Bells for Us To Ring.* New York: Delacorte.

Cormier, R. (1991). *We All Fall Down.* New York: Delacorte.

Cormier, R. (1992). *Tunes for Bears to Dance To.* New York: Delacorte.

*Cormier, R. (1995). *In the Middle of the Night.* New York: Delacorte.

Covington, D. (1991). *Lizard*. New York: Delacorte.

Covington, D. (1995). *Lasso the Moon*. New York: Delacorte.

— Crane, S. (1894). *The Red Badge of Courage*.

Creech, S. (1994). *Walk Two Moons*. New York: HarperCollins.

Crew, L. (1989). *Children of the River*. New York: Delacorte.

Cross, G. (1983). *Born of the Sun*. New York: Dell.

Crossroads. (1995). Glenview, IL: Scott, Foresman.

Crutcher, C. (1983). *Running Loose*. New York: Dell.

Crutcher, C. (1986). *Stotan!* New York: Dell.

— Crutcher, C. (1987). *The Crazy Horse Electric Game*. New York: Dell.

Crutcher, C. (1989). *Chinese Handcuffs*. New York: Greenwillow.

Crutcher, C. (1991). *Althletic Shorts*. New York: Greenwillow.

Crutcher, C. (1993). *Staying Fat for Sarah Byrnes*. New York: Greenwillow.

Crutcher, C. (1995). *Ironman*. New York: Greenwillow.

*Cushman, K. (1994). *Catherine, Called Birdy*. New York: Clarion.

*Daly, J. (1989). *Presenting S. E. Hinton*. New York: Twayne.

*Daly, M. (1942). *Seventeenth Summer*. New York: Dodd, Mead.

*Daly, M. (1986). *Acts of Love*. New York: Scholastic.

*Daly, M. (1990). *First a Dream*. New York: Scholastic.

— *Danziger, P. (1974). *The Cat Ate My Gymsuit*. New York: Dell.

— *Danziger, P. (1983). *The Divorce Express*. New York: Dell.

— *Danziger, P. (1985). *It's an Aardvark-Eat-Turtle World*. New York: Delacorte.

—✳ *Danziger, P. (1986). *This Place Has No Atmosphere*. New York: Dell.

Davis, J. (1988). *Sex Education*. New York: Dell.

*Davis, J., & Davis, H. (1991). *Presenting William Sleator*. New York: Twayne.

Davis, O. (1981). *Mass Appeal*. New York: Avon.

Davis, O. (1982). *Langston*. New York: Delacorte.

Davis, O. (1992). *Just Like Martin*. New York: Simon & Shuster.

Davis, T. (1991). *Vision Quest*. New York: Dell.

Davis, T. (1993). *If Rock and Roll Were a Machine*. New York: Delacorte.

Deem, J. (1994). *3 NB's of Julian Drew*. Boston: Houghton Mifflin.

Defoe, D. (1719). *The Life and Strange Surprising Adventures of Robinson Crusoe*.

*Dhondy, F. (1976). *East End at Your Feet*. London: Macmillan/Topliner.

*Dhondy, F. (1978). *Come to Mecca*. London: Collins/Armada.

*Dhondy, F. (1993). *Black Swan*. Boston: Houghton Mifflin.

— Dickens, C. (1859). *A Tale of Two Cities*.

— Dickens, C. (1860–1861). *Great Expectations*.

Dickinson, P. (1988). *Eva*. New York: Dell.

Dickinson, P. (1992). *AK*. New York: Delacorte.

Dillon, E. (1992). *Children of Bach*. New York: Charles Scribner's Sons.

Donovan, J. (1969). *I'll Get There. It Better Be Worth the Trip*. New York: HarperCollins.

Doyle, A. C. (1892). *The Adventures of Sherlock Holmes* (and others).

· Drimmer, F. (1985). *The Elephant Man*. New York: G. P. Putnam's Sons.

— *Duncan, L. (1976). *Summer of Fear*. New York: Dell.

— *Duncan, L. (1978). *Killing Mr. Griffin*. New York: Dell.

— Duncan, L. (1979). *Daughters of Eve*. New York: Dell.

*Duncan, L. (1982). *Chapters: My Growth as a Writer*. Boston: Little, Brown.

*Duncan, L. (1985). *Locked in Time*. Boston: Little, Brown.

*Duncan, L. (1987). *The Twisted Window*. New York: Dell.

— *Duncan, L. (1989). *Don't Look Behind You*. New York: Dell.

Duncan, L. (1992). *Who Killed My Daughter?* New York: Dell.

Dunning, S., Lueders, E., & Smith, H., eds. (1966). *Reflections on a Gift of Watermelon Pickle and Other Modern Verse*. New York: Scott, Foresman.

Dunning, S., Lueders, E., & Smith, H., eds. (1969). *Some Haystacks Don't Even Have Any Needles: and Other Complete Modern Poems*. New York: Lothrop, Lee & Shepard.

Dunning, S., Lueders, E., & Smith, H., eds. (1995). *Reflections on a Gift of Watermelon Pickle, Second Ed.* Glenview, IL: Scott, Foresman.

*Dygrad, T. (1992). *Backfield Package*. New York: William Morrow.

Edelman, B., ed. (1985). *Dear America: Letters Home from Vietnam*. New York: W. W. Norton.

*Edgell, Z. (1987). *Beka Lamb*. Portsmouth, NH: Heinemann.

Eliot, G. (1861). *Silas Marner*.

Emecheta, B. (1976). *The Bride Price*. New York: Braziller.

Emmens, C. (1991). *The Abortion Controversy*. New York: Julian Messner.

Eyerly, J. (1987). *Someone To Love Me*. New York: Lippincott.

Farmer, N. (1994). *The Ear, the Eye, and the Arm*. New York: Orchard.

*Fast, H. (1961). *April Morning*. New York: Crown.

*Felsen, H. G. (1950). *Hot Rod*. New York: E. P. Dutton.

*Felsen, H. G. (1952). *Two And the Town*. New York: Scribner's.

*Felsen, H. G. (1953). *Street Rod*. New York: Random House.

*Felsen, H. G. (1958). *Crash Club*. New York: Random House.

*Filipovac, Z. (1994). *Zlata's Diary: A Child's Life in Sarajevo*. New York: Viking.

Finley, M. F. (1867). *Elsie Dinsmore* (series).

Fitzgerald, F. S. (1925). *The Great Gatsby*.

*Forbes, E. (1944). *Johnny Tremain*. Boston: Houghton Mifflin.

Ford, M. T. (1993). *100 Questions and Answers About AIDS: What You Need to Know Now*. New York: Beech Tree.

*Forman, J. (1988). *Presenting Paul Zindel*. New York: Twayne.

Forshay-Lunsford, C. (1990). "Riding Out the Storm." In *Center Stage: One Act Plays for Teenage Readers and Actors,* ed. Don Gallo. New York: Harper & Row.

*Fox, P. (1973). *The Slave Dancer*. New York: Dell.

*Fox, P. (1984). *The One-Eyed Cat*. New York: Bradbury.

*Frank, A. (1956). *The Diary of a Young Girl*. New York: Random House.

Freedman, R. (1983). *Children of the Wild West*. New York: Clarion.

*Freedman, R. (1989). *Lincoln: A Photobiography*. New York: Clarion.

*Freedman, R. (1994). *Kids at Work*. New York: Clarion.

*Freierman, R. (1940). *The Dingo: A Story of First Love*. Chicago: Imported Publications.

Friedman, C. (1991). *Nightfather*. New York: Persea.

— *Fritz, J. (1982). *Homesick: My Own Story*. New York: Dell.

Fritz, J. (1985). *China Homecoming*. New York: G. P. Putnam's Sons.

Fritz, J. (1988). *China's Long March*. New York: G. P. Putnam's Sons.

Gaines, E. (1983). *A Gathering of Old Men*. New York: Alfred A Knopf.

Gale, D., ed. (1992). *Funny You Should Ask*. New York: Delacorte.

*Gallo, D. (1989). *Presenting Richard Peck.* New York: Twayne.

*Gallo, D., ed (1984). *Sixteen.* New York: Dell.

*Gallo, D., ed. (1987). *Visions.* New York: Dell.

*Gallo, D., ed. (1989). *Connections.* New York: Dell.

*Gallo, D., ed. (1990). *Center Stage: One-Act Plays for Teenage Readers and Actors.* New York: Harper & Row.

*Gallo, D., ed. (1993). *Join In: Multiethnic Short Stories by Outstanding Writers for Young Adults.* New York: Delacorte.

*Gallo, D., ed. (1993). *Within Reach: Ten Stories.* New York: HarperCollins.

Garfield, L. (1974). *The Sound of Coaches.* New York: Viking.

Garland, S. (1992). *Song of the Buffalo Boy.* Orlando, FL: Harcourt Brace.

Garland, S. (1993). *Shadow of the Dragon.* Orlando, FL: Harcourt Brace.

*George, J. (1972). *Julie of the Wolves.* New York: Harper & Row.

*George, J. (1991). *Shark Beneath the Reef.* New York: Harper.

*George, J. (1994). *Julie.* New York: HarperCollins.

Gerber, M. (1990). *Handsome as Anything.* New York: Scholastic.

Gibson, W. (1959). *The Miracle Worker.* New York: French.

Gilsenan, N. (n.d.). *A Separate Peace* (play). Woodstock, IL: Dramatic Publishing.

*Ginsburg, M., ed. (1976). *The Air of Mars and Other Stories.* New York: Macmillan.

Girion, B. (1984). *A Very Brief Season.* New York: Macmillan.

*Gleitzman, M. (1990). *Three Weeks with the Queen.* London: Pan.

*Glenn, M. (1982). *Class Dismissed! High School Poems.* New York: Clarion.

*Glenn, M. (1986). *Class Dismissed II: More High School Poems.* New York: Clarion.

*Glenn, M. (1987). *Back to Class.* New York: Clarion.

*Glenn, M. (1991). *My Friend's Got This Problem, Mr. Candler.* New York: Clarion.

Gold, R., ed. (1981). *Point of Departure: 19 Stories of Youth and Discovery.* New York: Dell.

Gold, R., ed. (1981). *Stepping Stones: 17 Powerful Stories of Growing Up.* New York: Dell.

Golding, W. (1955). *Lord of the Flies.* New York: Coward, McCann.

Gordon, R. (1987). *Under All Silences: Shades of Love.* New York: Harper & Row.

Gordon, S. (1987). *Waiting for the Rain.* New York: Dell.

Goldreich, G. (1979). *Lori.* New York: Holt.

Graham, R. (1972). *Dove.* New York: Harper & Row.

*Grahame, K. (1908). *The Wind in the Willows.*

Gravelle, K., & Peterson, L. (1992). *Teenage Fathers.* New York: Julian Messner.

Green, H. (1964). *I Never Promised You a Rose Garden.* New York: Holt, Rinehart & Winston.

*Greenburg, J. (1983). *No Dragons to Slay.* New York: Farrah, Straus & Giroux.

Greene, B. (1973). *Summer of My German Soldier.* New York: Dial.

Greene, B. (1978). *Morning Is a Long Time Coming.* New York: Dial.

Greene, B. (1989). *Homecoming: When the Soldiers Returned from Vietnam.* New York: G. P. Putnam's Sons.

Greene, B. (1991). *The Drowning of Stephan Jones.* New York: Bantam.

Grey, Z. (1906). *The Spirit of the Border.*

Grey, Z. (1912). *Riders of the Purple Sage.*

Grey, Z. (1923). *The Wanders of the Wasteland.*

Grollman, E. (1993). *Straight Talk About Death for Teenagers: How to Cope with Losing Someone You Love.* Boston: Beacon.

*Grover, W. (1993). *Ali and the Golden Eagle.* New York: Greenwillow.

Guest, J. (1977). *Ordinary People.* New York: Ballantine.

*The Guinness Book of Amazing Achievements. (1990). New York: Bantam.

*The Guinness Book of World Records. (1989). New York: Bantam.

Gunther, J. (1953). *Death Be Not Proud: A Memoir.* New York: Modern Library.

Guy, R. (1979). *The Disappearance.* New York: Delacorte.

Guy, R. (1983). *The Friends.* New York: Bantam.

*Guy, R. (1989). *The Ups and Downs of Carl Davis III.* New York: Delecorte.

Guy, R. (1992). *The Music of Summer.* New York: Delacorte.

Haley, B. (1990). *Focus on School.* Santa Barbara, CA: ABC-CLIO.

Hall, B. (1990). *Dixie Storms.* New York: Harcourt.

*Hamilton, V. (1974). *M. C. Higgins, The Great.* New York: Macmillan.

*Hamilton, V. (1982). *Sweet Whispers, Brother Rush.* New York: Philomel.

Hamilton, V. (1984). *A Little Love.* New York: Berkley.

*Hamilton, V. (1985). *Junius Over Far.* New York: Harper & Row.

Hamilton, V. (1987). *The People Could Fly: American Black Folktales.* New York: Alfred A. Knopf.

Hamilton, V. (1987). *A White Romance.* New York: Philomel.

Hamilton, V. (1990). *Cousins.* New York: Philomel.

Hansen, J. (1994). *The Captive.* New York: Scholastic.

Hartnett, Sonya. (1995). *Sleeping Dogs.* New York: Viking.

Haskins, J. (1990). *Black Dance in America.* New York: HarperCollins.

Haskins, J. (1992). *One More River to Cross.* New York: Scholastic.

Hawthorne, N. (1850). *The Scarlet Letter.*

Hayden, R. (1985). *Collected Poems.* New York: Liveright.

Hayes, J. (n.d.). *Seven Ages of Anne.* Charlottesville, VA: New Plays, Inc.

Hayslip, L. L. (1989). *When Heaven & Earth Changed Places.* New York: Doubleday.

Hazelgrove, W. E. (1992). *Ripples.* New York: Pantonne.

Head, A. (1967). *Mr. and Mrs. Bo Jo Jones.* New York: New American Library.

Hemingway, E. (1952). *The Old Man and the Sea.* New York: Scribner's.

Hentoff, N. (1981). *Does This School Have Capital Punishment?* New York: Dell.

Hentoff, N. (1982). *The Day They Came to Arrest the Book.* New York: Dell.

*Herriot, J. (1972). *All Creatures Great and Small.* New York: St. Martin's.

*Hesse, K. (1994). *Phoenix Rising.* New York: Holt.

Hettinga, D. R. (1993). *Presenting Madeleine L'Engle.* New York: Twayne.

Heyerdahl, T. (1984). *Kon-Tiki.* New York: Random House.

Highwater, J. (1985). *Ceremony of Innocence.* New York: Harper & Row/Zolotow.

*Highwater, J. (1984). *Legend Days.* New York: Harper & Row.

Hinojosa, M. (1995). *Crews.* Orlando, FL: Harcourt Brace.

*Hinton, S. E. (1967). *The Outsiders.* New York: Dell.

*Hinton, S. E. (1975). *Rumblefish.* New York: Dell.

*Hinton, S. E. (1979). *Tex.* New York: Dell.

*Hinton, S. E. (1988). *Taming the Star Runner.* new York: Dell.

*Hinton, S. E. (1989). *That Was Then, This Is Now.* New York: Dell.

Hipple, T. (1990). *Presenting Sue Ellen Bridgers.* New York: Twayne.

*Hobbs, W. (1989). *Bearstone.* New York: Avon.

*Hobbs, W. (1991). *Downriver.* New York: Atheneum.

*Hobbs, W. (1993). *Beardance.* New York: Atheneum.

*Hobbs, W. (1995). *Kokopelli's Flute.* New York: Atheneum.

*Hohler, R. (1986). *I Touch the Future: The Story of Christa McAuliffe*. New York: Random House.

*Holbrook, S. (1990). *The Dog Ate My Homework*. Bay Village, OH: KID POEMS.

*Holbrook, S. (1990). *Feelings Make Me Real*. Bay Village, OH: KID POEMS.

*Holbrook, S. (1990). *Some Families*. Bay Village, OH: KID PEOMS.

*Holbrook, S. (1992). *I Never Said I Wasn't Difficult*. Bay Village, OH: KID POEMS.

*Holbrook, S. (1995). *Nothing's the End of the World*. Honesdale, PA: Boyds Mills.

*Holbrook, S. (1995). *Walking on the Boundaries of Change*. Bay Village, OH: KID POEMS.

Holland, I. (1994). *Behind the Lines*. New York: Scholastic.

Holman, F. (1983). *The Wild Children*. New York: Scribner's.

*Holtze, S. (1989). *Presenting Norma Fox Mazer*. New York: Twayne.

The Holy Bible, Authorized King James Version. (1611).

Homer. (c. 850 B.C.E.). *The Odyssey*.

*Hope, L. L. (1904). *The Bobbsey Twins* (series).

Hopkins, L., ed. (1983). *Love and Kisses*. Boston: Houghton Mifflin.

Howker, J., ed. (1985). *Badger on the Barge and Other Stories*. New York: Greenwillow.

Hughes, L. (1989). "A Dream Deferred." In *Prentice Hall Literature—Gold*. Englewood Cliffs, NJ: Prentice Hall.

Hughes, L. (1990). *Selected Poems*. New York: Random House.

*Hunt, I. (1964). *Across Five Aprils*. New York: Grosset & Dunlap.

*Hunt, I. (1966). *Up A Road Slowly*. New York: Berkley.

Hunt, I. (1987). *The Lottery Rose*. New York: Berkley.

*Hunter, K. (1968). *The Soul Brothers and Sister Lou*. New York: Szebineh's Sons.

Hurst, J. (1960). "The Scarlet Ibis." In *Prentice Hall Literature—Gold*. Englewood Cliffs, NJ: Prentice Hall.

*Irwin, H. (1984). *I Be Somebody*. New York: NAL-Penguin.

*Irwin, H. (1988). *So Long at the Fair*. New York: McElderry.

*Irwin, H. (1992). *The Original Freddie Ackerman*. New York: McElderry.

Jackson, S. (1949). "The Lottery."

Janeczko, P. (1986). *Bridges To Cross*. New York: Macmillan.

*Janeczko, P. (1993). *Stardust Hotel*. New York: Orchard.

*Janeczko, P. (1994). *Poetry from A to Z*. New York: Bradbury.

Janeczko, P., ed. (1979). *Postcard Poems: A Collection of Poetry for Sharing*. New York: Bradbury.

Janeczko, P., ed. (1981). *Don't Forget to Fly*. New York: Bradbury.

Janeczko, P., ed. (1983). *Poetspeak: In Their Work, About Their Work*. New York: Bradbury.

Janeczko, P., ed. (1984). *Strings: A Gathering of Family Poems*. New York: Bradbury.

Janeczko, P., ed. (1985). *Pocket Poems: Selected for a Journey*. New York: Bradbury.

Janeczko, P., ed. (1987). *Going Over to Your Place: Poems for Each Other*. New York: Bradbury.

Janeczko, P., ed. (1990). *The Place My Words Are Looking For*. New York: Bradbury.

Janeczko, P., ed. (1991). *Preposterous: Poems of Youth*. New York: Orchard.

Janeway, J. (1700). *A Token for Children: Being an Exact Account of the Conversion, Holy and Exemplary Lives & Joyful Deaths of Several Young Children to Which Is Added: A Token for the Children of New England*.

Jennings, C., & Berghammer, G. (n.d.). *Theatre for Youth: Twelve Plays with Mature Themes*. New Orleans: Anchorage.

*Johnson, A. (1993). *Toning the Sweep*. New York: Orchard.

*Jones, D. (1985). *Witchweek.* London: Methuen.

Jones, D., ed. (1985). *Warlock at the Wheel & Other Stories.* New York: Greenwillow.

Jones, R. (1993). *The Beginning of Unbelief.* New York: Atheneum.

Justice, D. (1989). "Incident in a Rose Garden." In *Prentice Hall Literature—Gold.* Englewood Cliffs, NJ: Prentice Hall.

Kafu, N. (1965). "The River Sumida." In *Kafu the Scribbler: The Life and Writings of Nagai Kafu,* by Edward Seidensticker. Stanford, CA: Stanford University Press.

*Karl, H. (1992). *The Toom County Mud Race.* New York: Delacorte.

Karolides, N. (1991). *Focus on Physical Impairments.* Santa Barbara, CA: ABC-CLIO.

*Karr, K. (1994). *The Cave.* New York: Farrar.

*Kassem, L. (1990). *A Haunting in Williamsburg.* New York: Avon.

*Kaye, M. (1993). *Real Heroes.* Orlando, FL: Harcourt Brace.

Keach, B. (1707). *War with the Devil, or The Young Man's Conflict with the Powers of Darkness, in a Dialogue Discovering the Corruption and Vanity of Youth, the Horrible Nature of Sin, and the Deplorable Condition of Fallen Man.*

Kennemore, T. (1984). *Changing Times.* New York: Faber & Faber.

Kerr, M. E. (1972). *Dinky Hocker Shoots Smack.* New York: Dell.

*Kerr, M. E. (1975). *Is That You, Miss Blue?* New York: Harper & Row.

*Kerr, M. E. (1981). *Gentlehands.* New York: Bantam.

*Kerr, M. E. (1982). *What I Really Think of You.* New York: Harper & Row.

*Kerr, M. E. (1983). *Me, Me, Me, Me, Me, Not a Novel.* New York: Harper & Row.

*Kerr, M. E. (1984). *Him She Loves.* New York: Harper & Row.

Kerr, M. E. (1986). *Night Kites.* New York: Harper & Row.

*Kerr, M. E. (1987). *Fell.* New York: Harper & Row.

Kerr, M. E. (1987). "The Sweet Perfume of Good-bye." In *Visions,* ed. Don Gallo. New York: Dell.

*Kerr, M. E. (1989). *Fell Back.* New York: HarperCollins.

*Kerr, M. E. (1991). *Fell Down.* New York: HarperCollins.

Kerr, M. E. (1993). *Linger.* New York: HarperCollins.

Kerr, M. E. (1994). *Deliver Us from Evie.* New York: HarperCollins.

Kincaid, J. (1985). *Annie John.* New York: Farrar, Straus & Giroux.

Kingston, M. (1976). *Women Warriors.* New York: Alfred A. Knopf.

Kittredge, M. (1991). *Teens with AIDS Speak Out.* New York: Julian Messner.

Klaus, A. (1990). *The Silver Kiss.* New York: Dell.

Klein, N. (1974). *Sunshine.* New York: Avon.

Knowles, J. (1960). *A Separate Peace.* New York: Macmillan.

Koch, K. (1974). *Where Did You Get That Red?* New York: Random House.

Koch, K. (1980). *Wishes, Lies, and Dreams.* New York: Chelsea House.

Korman, G. (1985). *Don't Care High.* New York: Scholastic.

*Korman, G. (1987). *A Semester in the Life of a Garbage Bag.* New York: Scholastic.

Korschunow, I. (1978). *Who Killed Christopher?* New York: Collins.

Kuklin, S. (1989). *Fighting Back: What Some People Are Doing About AIDS.* New York: G.P. Putnam's Sons.

Kuklin, S. (1993). *Speaking Out: Teenagers Talk on Sex, Race, and Identity.* New York: G.P. Putnam's Sons.

Kunitz, S. (1983). "The Portrait." In *Poetspeak: In Their Words, About Their Work,* ed. P. Janeczko. New York: Bradbury.

*Kuroyanagi, T. (1981). *Totto Chan: The Little Girl in the Window.* Trans. Dorothy Britton. New York: Kodansha International.

Lamb, W. (1979). *Always Begin Where You Are: Themes in Poetry and Song.* New York: McGraw-Hill.

Lamb, W., ed. (1986). *Meeting the Winter Bike Rider and Other Prize Winning Plays.* New York: Dell.

Lane, R. W. (1934). *Let the Hurricane Roar.* New York: Longmans, Green.

*Lasky, K. (1983). *Beyond the Divide.* New York: Macmillan.

*Lasky, K. (1994). *Beyond the Burning Time.* New York: Scholastic.

Laurents, A. (1956). *West Side Story in Romeo and Juliet/West Side Story.* New York: Dell.

Lawrence, J., & Lee, R. (1955). *Inherit the Wind.* New York: Dramatists.

Lawrence, J., & Lee, R. (1972). *The Night Thoreau Spent in Jail.* New York: Bantam.

Lederer, R. (1987). *Anguished English.* Charleston, SC: Wyrick.

Lee, H. (1960). *To Kill a Mockingbird.* New York: Fawcett.

*LeGuin, U.K. (1976). *Very Far Away From Anywhere Else.* New York: Atheneum.

*L'Engle, M. (1968). *A Wrinkle in Time.* New York: Dell.

*LeShan, E. (1992). *What Makes You Special?* New York: Dial.

Lester, J. (1984). *Do Lord, Remember Me.* New York: Holt, Rinehart & Winston.

Lester, J. (1986). *To Be a Slave.* New York: Scholastic.

Leuders, E., & St. John, P., eds. (1976). *Zero Makes Me Hungry: A Collection of Poems for Today.* New York: Scott, Foresman.

*Levine, E. (1993). *Freedom's Children.* New York: Avon.

Lightfoot, S. (1988). *Balm in Gilead.* New York: Addison-Wesley.

*Likhanov, A. (1983). *Shadows across the Sun.* New York: Harper & Row.

Lillington, K. (1989). *An Ash-Blond Witch.* London: Penguin.

*Lipsyte, R. (1967). *The Contender.* New York: Bantam.

*Lipsyte, R. (1977). *One Fat Summer.* New York: Harper & Row.

*Lipsyte, R. (1991). *The Brave.* New York: HarperCollins.

*Lipsyte, R. (1992). *The Chemo Kid.* New York: HarperCollins.

*Lipsyte, R. (1993). *The Chief.* New York: HarperCollins.

Loughery, J., ed. (1995). *Into the Widening World: International Coming-of-Age Stories.* New York: Persea.

Lowry, L. (1977). *A Summer to Die.* Boston: Houghton Mifflin.

*Lowry, L. (1978). *Find a Stranger, Say Goodbye.* New York: Pocket Books.

*Lowry, L. (1989). *Number the Stars.* New York: Dell.

*Lowry, L. (1993). *The Giver.* Boston: Houghton Mifflin.

Lund, D. (1974). *Eric.* New York: Harper & Row.

Lynch, C. (1994). *Iceman.* New York: HarperCollins.

*Lyon, G. (1988). *Borrowed Children.* New York: Bantam.

*Macaulay, D. (1980). *Unbuilding.* Boston: Houghton Mifflin.

*Macaulay, D. (1988). *The Way Things Work.* Boston: Houghton Mifflin.

MacLachlan, P. (1991). *Journey.* New York: Delacorte.

Mahy, M. (1987). *Memory.* New York: Dell.

Major, K. (1978). *Hold Fast.* New York: Delacorte.

Malmgren, D. (1989). *The Ninth Issue.* New York: Dell.

Malmgren, D. (1990). "Large Fears, Little Dreams." In *Center Stage: One Act Plays for Teenage Readers and Actors,* ed. Don Gallo. New York: Harper & Row.

Malory, T. (1485). *Le Morte d'Arthur.*

Mamlin, G. (n.d.). *Hey There—Hello!* Charlottesville, VA: New Plays, Inc.

*Mark, J. (1985). *Handles.* New York: Atheneum.

Markandaya, K. (1954). *Nectar in a Sieve.* New York: Signet.

Marshall, C. (1967). *Christy.* New York: Avon.

Martinez, M. (1988). *Schoolland: A Novel.* Houston, TX: Arte.

*Maruki, T. (1982). *Hiroshima No Pika.* New York: Lothrop.

Mason, S. (1986). *Johnny's Song: Poetry of a Vietnam Veteran.* New York: Bantam.

*Matas, C. (1993). *Daniel's Story.* New York: Dell.

*Matas, C. (1993). *Sworn Enemies.* New York: Dell.

*Mathis, S. (1972). *Teacup Full of Roses.* New York: Avon.

Mazer, A., ed. (1993). *America Street: A Multicultural Anthology of Stories.* New York: Persea.

Mazer, A., ed. (1995). *Going Where I'm Coming From.* New York: Persea.

*Mazer, H. (1979). *The Last Mission.* New York: Delacorte.

*Mazer, H. (1981). *The Island Keeper.* New York: Delacorte.

*Mazer, H. (1985). *When the Phone Rang.* New York: Scholastic.

*Mazer, H. (1993). *Who is Harry Leonard?* New York: Delacorte.

*Mazer, N. F. (1976). *Dear Bill, Remember Me? & Other Stories.* New York: Delacorte.

*Mazer, N. F. (1981). *Taking Terri Mueller.* New York: Avon.

*Mazer, N. F. (1982). *Summer Girls, Love Boys.* New York: Delacorte.

*Mazer, N. F. (1982). *When We First Met.* New York: Scholastic.

Mazer, N. F. (1987). *After the Rain.* New York: Avon.

*Mazer, N. F. (1987). *B, My Name is Bunny.* New York: Scholastic.

*Mazer, N. F. (1990). *C, My Name is Cal.* New York: Scholastic.

*Mazer, N. F. (1991). *A, My Name is Amy.* New York: Scholastic.

*Mazer, N. F. (1991). *D, My Name is Danita.* New York: Scholastic.

*Mazer, N. F. (1991). *E, My Name is Emily.* New York: Scholastic.

Mazer, N. F. (1993). *Out of Control.* New York: Morrow.

*Mazer, N. F., & Mazer, H. (1989). *The Solid Gold Kid.* New York: Bantam.

*Mazer, N. F., & Mazer, H. (1990). *Heartbeat.* New York: Bantam.

McDaniel, W. (1985). "Who Said We All Have To Talk Alike," In *The Things That Divide Us,* ed. F. Conlon, R. da Silva, & B. Wilson. Seattle: Seal.

Means, F. C. (1938). *Shuttered Windows.* Boston: Houghton Mifflin.

Medoff, M. (1980). *Children of a Lesser God.* New York: Dramatists.

Meltzer, M. (1976). *Never to Forget: The Jews of the Holocaust.* New York: Harper & Row.

Meltzer, M. (1982). *The Truth about the Ku Klux Klan.* New York: Franklin Watts.

Meltzer, M. (1985). *Ain't Gonna Study War No More: The Story of America's Peace Seekers.* New York: Harper & Row.

Meltzer, M. (1987). *The American Revolutionaries: A History in Their Own Words.* New York: HarperCollins.

Meltzer, M. (1988). *Rescue: The Story of How Gentiles Saved Jews in the Holocaust.* New York: HarperCollins.

Meltzer, M. (1989). *Voices From the Civil War.* New York: Crowell.

*Meltzer, M. (1990). *Columbus and the World Around Him.* sNew York: Franklin Watts.

Meltzer, M. (1994). *Cheap Raw Material.* New York: Viking.

Melville, H. (1851). *Moby-Dick, or, the Whale.*

Melville, H. (1924). *Billy Budd, Foretopman*.

Merriam, E. (1976). *Rainbow Writing*. New York: Atheneum.

Merriam, E. (1983). *If Only I Could Tell You: Poems for Young Lovers and Dreamers*. New York: Alfred A. Knopf.

Meyer, C. (1994). *Rio Grande Stories*. Orlando, FL: Harcourt Brace.

*Miklowitz, G. (1985). *The War Between the Classes*. New York: Dell.

Miklowitz, G. (1987). "The Fuller Brush Man." In *Visions*, ed. Don Gallo. New York: Dell.

*Miklowitz, G. (1987). *Good-Bye Tomorrow*. New York: Dell.

*Miklowitz, G. (1990). *Anything to Win*. New York: Dell.

—— Miller, A. (1949). *Death of a Salesman*. New York: Viking.

✳ Miller, A. (1952). *The Crucible*. New York: Dramatists.

*Miller, R. (1986). *Robyn's Book*. New York: Scholastic.

Milton, J. (1667). *Paradise Lost*.

Mohr, N. (1973). *Nilda*. New York: Harper & Row.

*Mohr, N. (1986). *Going Home*. New York: Dial.

Momaday, N. S. (1969). *House Made of Dawn*. New York: Signet.

*Momaday, N. S. (1976). *The Way to Rainy Mountain*. Albuquerque, NM: University of New Mexico Press.

Monseau, V. (1994). *Presenting Ouida Sebestyn*. New York: Twayne.

Moore, L. (1994). *Lifelines*. New York: E. P. Dutton's Children's Books.

More, H. (1795–1798). *Repository Tracts*.

—— Mowat, F. (1979). *Never Cry Wolf*. New York: Bantam.

Murphy, J. (1982). *Death Run*. New York: Clarion.

*Myers, W. D. (1975). *Fast Sam, Cool Clyde, and Stuff*. New York: Penguin.

*Myers, W. D. (1981). *Hoops*. New York: Dell.

*Myers, W. D. (1987). *Crystal*. New York: Viking Kestrel.

Myers, W. D. (1987). "Jeremiah's Song." In *Visions*, ed. Don Gallo. New York: Dell.

*Myers, W. D. (1987). *Motown and Didi*. New York: NAL-Dutton.

*Myers, W. D. (1987). *The Outside Shot*. New York: Dell.

Myers, W. D. (1988). *Fallen Angels*. New York: Scholastic.

*Myers, W. D. (1988). *Scorpions*. New York: Harper.

*Myers, W. D. (1988). *Won't Know Till I Get There*. New York: Puffin.

Myers, W. D. (1991). *Now Is Your Time*. New York: HarperCollins.

*Myers, W. D. (1992). *Somewhere in the Darkness*. New York: Scholastic.

*Myers, W. D. (1993). *Malcolm X: By Any Means Necessary*. New York: Scholastic.

Myers, W. D. (1994). *The Glory Field*. New York: Scholastic.

Myers, W. D. (1995). *Shadow of the Red Moon*. New York: Scholastic.

*Naidoo, B. (1989). *Chain of Fire*. New York: J. B. Lippincott.

Namioka, L. (1994). *April and the Dragon Lady*. Orlando, FL: Harcourt Brace.

Naughton, J. (1989). *My Brother Stealing Second*. New York: Harper & Row.

Naylor, P. (1986). *The Keeper*. New York: Bantam.

Naylor, P. (1989). *Alice in Rapture, Sort Of*. New York: Macmillan.

*Naylor, P. (1990). *Send No Blessings*. New York: Atheneum.

*Needle, J. (1978). *My Mate Shofiq*. London: Deutsch/Armada.

Newman, S. (1991). *Don't Be S.A.D.: A Teenage Guide to Handling Stress, Anxiety, and Depression*. New York: Julian Messner.

Neufeld, J. (1969). *Edgar Allan*. New York: Signet.

—— Neufeld, J. (1969). *Lisa, Bright and Dark*. New York: Phillips.

Neufeld, J. (1982). *A Small Civil War.* New York: Ballentine.

Neufeld, J. (1983). *Sharelle.* New York: New American Library.

*Nilsen, A. (1986). *Presenting M. E. Kerr.* New York: Twayne.

*Nixon, J. L. (1986). *The Other Side of Dark.* New York: Bantam.

*Nixon, J. L. (1987). *A Family Apart.* New York: Bantam.

*Nixon, J. L. (1988). *Secret Silent Screams.* New York: Dell.

*Nixon, J. L. (1990). *Whispers from the Dead.* New York: Dell.

*Nixon, J. L. (1991). *A Candidate for Murder.* New York: Dell.

*Nixon, J. L. (1992). *The Weekend Was Murder.* New York: Delacorte.

*Nixon, J. L. (1994). *A Dangerous Promise.* New York: Delacorte.

Norman, R. (1992). *Albion's Dream.* New York: Delacorte.

*Norris, G. (1967). *A Feast of Light.* New York: Alfred A. Knopf.

Norris, J. (1988). *Presenting Rosa Guy.* New York: Twayne.

O'Brien, R. (1974). *Z for Zacharia.* New York: Macmillan.

O'Dell, S. (1986). *Streams to the River: River to the Sea.* New York: Ballentine.

O'Dell, S. (1990). *My Name Is Not Angelica.* New York: Dell.

Optic, O. (1855). *The Boat Club.*

Orwell, G. (1950). *1984.* New York: E. P. Dutton.

Orwell, G. (1954). *Animal Farm.* New York: Harcourt Brace Jovanovich.

Oswald, D. (n.d.). *Dags.* Woodstock, IL: Dramatic Publishing.

Parker, D. (1989). "Solace." In *Prentice Hall Literature—Gold.* Englewood Cliffs, NJ: Prentice Hall.

Parks, G. (1989). "The Funeral." In *Prentice Hall Literature—Gold.* Englewood Cliffs, NJ: Prentice Hall.

*Paterson, K. (1977). *Bridge To Terabithia.* New York: Avon.

*Paterson, K. (1979). *The Great Gilly Hopkins.* New York: Avon.

Paterson, K. (1980). *Jacob Have I Loved.* New York: Avon.

*Paterson, K. (1988). *Park's Quest.* New York: Penguin.

*Paulsen, G. (1978). *The Night the White Deer Died.* New York: Dell.

*Paulsen, G. (1985). *Dogsong.* New York: Bradbury.

*Paulsen, G. (1986). *Sentries.* New York: Scholastic.

*Paulsen, G. (1987). *Hatchet.* New York: Puffin.

*Paulsen, G. (1988). *The Island.* New York: Dell.

*Paulsen, G. (1989). *The Voyage of the FROG.* New York: Dell.

*Paulsen, G. (1990). *Woodsong.* New York: Bradbury.

*Paulsen, G. (1991). *The Cookcamp.* New York: Orchard.

*Paulsen, G. (1991). *The Monument.* New York: Delacorte.

*Paulsen, G. (1991). *The River.* New York: Delacorte.

*Paulsen, G. (1992). *The Haymeadow.* New York: Delacorte.

*Paulsen, G. (1993). *Harris and Me.* New York: Harcourt Brace.

*Paulsen, G. (1993). *Nightjohn.* New York: Bantam Doubleday Dell.

Paulsen, G. (1993). *Sisters.* Orlando, FL: Harcourt Brace.

Paulsen, G. (1994). *The Car.* Orlando, FL: Harcourt Brace.

*Paulsen, G. (1994). *Mr. Tucket.* New York: Delacorte.

*Paulsen, G. (1995). *The Rifle.* Orlando, FL: Harcourt Brace.

Peck, G. W. (1883). *Peck's Bad Boy & His Pa.*

Peck, R. (1973). *Dreamland Lake.* New York: Dell.

— Peck, R. (1976). *Are You In The House Alone?* New York: Dell.

Peck, R. (1978). *Father Figure.* New York: Dell.

*Peck, R. (1985). *Remembering the Good Times.* New York: Dell.

*Peck, R. (1987). *Princess Ashley.* New York: Dell.

*Peck, R. (1988). *Those Summer Girls I Never Met.* New York: Delacorte.

*Peck, R. (1989). *Voices After Midnight.* New York: Dell.

Peck, R. (1991). *Unfinished Portrait of Jessica.* New York: Delacorte.

*Peck, R. (1993). *Bel-Air Bambi and the Mall Rats.* New York: Bantam Doubleday Dell.

*Peck, R. (1995). *The Last Safe Place on Earth.* New York: Delacorte.

*Peck, R., ed. (1990). *Mindscapes: Poems for the Real World.* New York: Dell.

*Peck, R., ed. (1990). *Sounds and Silences: Poetry for Now.* New York: Bantam.

— Peck, R. N. (1972). *A Day No Pigs Would Die.* New York: Dell.

*Peck, R. N. (1989). *Arly.* New York: Walker & Co.

*Peck, R. N. (1994). *A Part of the Sky.* New York: Alfred A. Knopf.

*Petersen, P. J. (1984). *Nobody Else Can Walk It for You.* New York: Dell.

Petry, A. (1971). *Harriet Tubman, Guide to Freedom.* New York: Fawcett.

Pettepiece, T., & Aleksin, A. (1990). *Face to Face.* New York: Philomel.

Peyton, J., ed. (1989). *The Stone Canoe and Other Stories.* New York: McDonald.

Peyton, K. M. (1972). *Pennington's Seventeeth Summer.* New York: Crowell.

Pfeffer, S. (1980). *About David.* New York: Dell.

Pfeffer, S. (1987). "A Hundred Bucks of Happy." In *Visions,* ed. Don Gallo. New York: Dell.

— Pfeffer, S. (1987). *The Year Without Michael.* New York: Dell.

*Philbrick, R. (1993). *Freak the Mighty.* New York: Scholastic.

Phy, A. (1988). *Presenting Norma Klein.* New York: Twayne.

Pines, T., ed. (1991). *Thirteen Tales of Horror.* New York: Scholastic.

Pirsig, R. (1974). *Zen and the Art of Motorcycle Maintenance: An Inquiry into Values.* New York: Morrow.

Poe, E. (1990). *Focus on Sexuality.* Santa Barbara, CA: ABC-CLIO.

*Pogodin, R. (1980). *Of Jolly People and Fine Weather.* Chicago: Imported Publications/ Progress Publishers.

Porte, B. (1987). *I Only Made up the Roses.* New York: Greenwillow.

Potok, C. (1972). *My Name Is Asher Lev.* New York: Alfred A. Knopf.

Potok, C. (1985). *The Chosen.* New York: Fawcett.

Pyle, H. (1883). *The Merry Adventures of Robin Hood.*

Rapp, A. (1994). *Missing the Piano.* New York: Viking.

Reaver, C. (1990). *Mote.* New York: Delacorte.

Reaver, C. (1994). *Bill.* New York: Delacorte.

Reed, D. (1989). *The Dolphins and Me.* Boston: Sierra Club/Little, Brown.

Reid, S. (1995). *Presenting Cynthia Voigt.* New York: Twayne.

Reiss, J. (1984). *The Upstairs Room.* New York: Bantam.

Rhodes, H. (c. 1545). *Book of Nurture.*

Rinaldi, A. (1990). *The Last Silk Dress.* New York: Bantam.

Rinaldi, A. (1991). *Wolf by the Ears.* New York: Scholastic.

Rinaldi, A. (1992). *A Break with Charity.* Orlando, FL: Harcourt Brace.

Rinaldi, A. (1993). *In My Father's House.* New York: Scholastic.

Rinaldi, A. (1994). *Finishing Becca.* Orlando, FL: Harcourt Brace.

Rinaldi, A. (1994). *A Stitch in Time.* New York: Scholastic.

Rinaldi, A. (1995). *Broken Days.* New York: Scholastic.

Ripslinger, J. (1994). *Triangle.* Orlando, FL: Harcourt Brace.

Robinson, M. (1990). *A Woman of Her Tribe.* New York: Fawcett Juniper.

Rodriguez, R. (1982). *Hunger of Memory: The Education of Richard Rodrigues.* New York: Bantam.

*Rodowsky, C. (1994). *Hannah In Between.* New York: Farrar.

*Rodowsky, C. (1995). *Sydney, Invincible.* New York: Farrar.

*Rofes, E., ed. (1985). *The Kid's Book About Death and Dying: By and For Kids.* Boston: Little, Brown.

Rose, R. (1969). *Twelve Angry Men.* In *Great Television Plays,* ed. William Kaufman. New York: Dell.

Rossetti, C. (1989). "Uphill." In *Prentice Hall Literature—Gold.* Englewood Cliffs, NJ: Prentice Hall.

Roth, A. (1974). *The Iceberg Hermit.* New York: Scholastic.

Ruby, L. (1993). *Miriam's Well.* New York: Scholastic.

Ruby, L. (1994). *Skin Deep.* New York: Scholastic.

*Ruby, L. (1994). *Steal Away Home.* New York: Macmillan.

Rylant, C. (1990). *A Couple of Kooks and Other Stories about Love.* New York: Franklin Watts.

Salinger, J. D. (1951). *The Catcher in the Rye.* Boston: Little, Brown.

Salisbury, G. (1992). *Blue Skin of the Sea.* New York: Delacorte.

Salisbury, G. (1994). *Under the Blood-Red Sun.* New York: Lodestar.

Sander, D. (1991). *Focus on Teens in Trouble.* Santa Barbara, CA: ABC-CLIO.

Santiago, D. (1983). *Famous All Over Town.* New York: Simon & Schuster.

Schami, R. (1990). *A Handful of Stars.* Trans. Rika Lesser. New York: E. P. Dutton.

Schwartz, A., ed. (1981). *Scary Stories to Tell in the Dark.* New York: Harper & Row.

Schwartz, A., ed. (1984). *More Scary Stories to Tell in the Dark.* New York: Harper & Row.

Sebestyn, O. (1981). *Words by Heart.* New York: Bantam.

Sebestyn, O. (1982). *IOU's.* New York: Dell.

Sebestyn, O. (1983). *Far From Home.* New York: Bantam.

Sebestyn, O. (1987). *Girl in the Box.* New York: Dell.

Sebestyn, O. (1987). "Playing God." In *Visions,* ed. Don Gallo. New York: Dell.

Sebestyn, O. (1994). *Out of Nowhere.* New York: Orchard.

Sefton, C. (1989). *Frankie's Story.* London: Methuen.

Segel, E., ed. (1986). *Short Takes: A Collection of Short Stories.* New York: Lothrop, Lee & Shephard.

*Sergel, C. (n.d.). *The Outsiders* (play). Woodstock, IL: Dramatic Publishing.

Service, P. (1989). *Vision Quest.* New York: Fawcett Juniper.

Sewell, A. (1877). *Black Beauty.*

Shakespeare, W. (1595). *Romeo and Juliet.*

Shakespeare, W. (1599). *Julius Caesar.*

Shakespeare, W. (1606). *Macbeth.*

Shaw, G. B. (1913). *Pygmalion.*

Shiras, F. (n.d.). *Go Ask Alice* (play). Woodstock, IL: Dramatic Publishing.

*Sleator, W. (1974). *House of Stairs.* New York: E. P. Dutton.

*Sleator, W. (1983). *Fingers.* New York: Bantam.

*Sleator, W. (1984). *Interstellar Pig.* New York: E. P. Dutton.

*Sleator, W. (1985). *Singularity.* New York: E. P. Dutton.

*Sleator, W. (1989). *The Duplicate.* New York: Dell.

*Sleator, W. (1989). *Strange Attractors.* New York: E. P. Dutton.

Smith, R. (1982). *Sumitra's Story.* New York: Coward-McCann.

Sorenson, V. (1957, 1990). *Miracles on Maple Hill*. New York: Harcourt Brace.

*Soto, G. (1990). *Baseball in April and Other Stories*. New York: Harcourt.

*Soto, G. (1990). *A Fire in My Hands*. New York: Scholastic.

*Soto, G. (1992). *Pacific Crossing*. Orlando, FL: Harcourt Brace.

*Soto, G. (1993). *Local News*. Orlando, FL: Harcourt Brace.

Soto, G. (1994). *Jesse*. Orlando, FL: Harcourt Brace.

*Soto, G. (1995). *Summer on Wheels*. New York: Scholastic.

*Speare, E. (1958). *The Witch of Blackbird Pond*. Boston: Houghton Mifflin.

*Speare, E. (1983). *The Sign of the Beaver*. New York: Dell.

*Spinelli, J. (1982). *Space Station Seventh Grade*. New York: Dell.

*Spinelli, J. (1990). *Maniac Magee*. Boston: Little, Brown.

*Staples, S. (1989). *Shabanu, Daughter of the Wind*. New York: Alfred A. Knopf.

Steinbeck, J. (1937). *Of Mice and Men*. New York: Viking

Steinbeck, J. (1937). *The Red Pony*. New York: Covici-Friede.

Steinbeck, J. (1939). *The Grapes of Wrath*. New York: Viking.

Steinbeck, J. (1947). *The Pearl*. New York: Viking.

Stephens, A. (1860). *Malaeska: The Indian Wife of the White Hunter*.

Stevenson, R. L. (1883). *Treasure Island*.

Stevenson, R. L. (1886). *Kidnapped*.

*Stone, B. (1990). *Been Clever Forever*. New York: Harper & Row.

Stowe, H. B. (1852). *Uncle Tom's Cabin*.

Strasser, T. (1979). *Angel Dust Blues*. New York: Dell.

*Strasser, T. (1981). *Friends 'til the End*. New York: Dell.

*Strasser, T. (1982). *Rock N' Roll Nights*. New York: Delacorte.

Strasser, T. (1985). *A Very Touchy Subject*. New York: Dell.

Strasser, T. (1987). "On the Bridge." In *Visions*, ed. Don Gallo. New York: Dell.

*Strasser, T. (1988). *The Accident*. New York: Dell.

*Strasser, T. (1991). *Beyond the Reef*. New York: Dell.

*Stratemeyer, E. (1899–1926). *The Rover Boys* (series).

*Stratemeyer, E. (1900–1906). *Soldiers of Fortune* (series).

*Stratemeyer, E. (1904–1912). *Lakeport* (series).

*Stratemeyer, E. (1927–   ). *Nancy Drew* (series).

*Stratemeyer, E. (1927–   ). *The Hardy Boys* (series).

Strelkova, I. (1983). *Playing the Game*. Trans. J. C. Butler. Chicago: Imported Publications.

Swanson, J. (1978). *142 Ways to Make a Poem*. St. Paul, MN: EMC Corporation.

Swartout, G. (1984). *Bless the Beasts and the Children*. New York: Pocket Books.

Swift, J. (1726). *Gulliver's Travels*.

*Talbert, M. (1992). *The Purple Heart*. New York: HarperCollins.

Tamar, E. (1993). *Fair Game*. Orlando, FL: Harcourt Brace.

Tarkington, B. (1902). *Seventeen*.

*Tate, E. (1987). *The Secret of Gumbo Grove*. New York: Bantam.

Tate, E. (1992). *Front Porch Stories at the One-Room School*. New York: Bantam.

Tatum, C., ed. (1990). *Mexican American Literature*. Chicago: Harcourt Brace Jovanovich.

Taylor, M. (1975). *Song of the Trees*. New York: Bantam.

Taylor, M. (1976). *Roll of Thunder, Hear My Cry*. New York: Bantam.

Taylor, M. (1981). *Let the Circle Be Unbroken*. New York: Bantam.

Taylor, M. (1990). *Mississippi Bridge*. New York: Dial.

Taylor, M. (1990). *The Road to Memphis.* New York: Dial.

*Taylor, T. (1976). *The Cay.* New York: Avon.

Taylor, T. (1989). *Sniper.* New York: Avon.

*Taylor, T. (1993). *Timothy of the Cay.* Orlando, FL: Harcourt Brace.

Teal, E. (1989). "The Death of a Tree." In *Prentice Hall Literature—Gold.* Englewood Cliffs, NJ: Prentice Hall.

Teasdale, S. (1989). "There Will Come Soft Rains." In *Prentice Hall Literature—Gold.* Englewood Cliffs, NJ: Prentice Hall.

Terkel, S. (1980). *American Dreams Lost and Found.* New York: Pantheon.

Terkel, S. (1992). *Ethics.* New York: Lodestar.

Terris, S. (1987). *Nell's Quilt.* New York: Scholastic.

Terris, S. (1990). *Author! Author!* New York: Farrar.

Thackeray, W. (1847). *Vanity Fair.*

Thomas, J. (1982). *Marked by Fire.* New York: Avon.

*Thomas, J. (1986). *Water Girl.* New York: Avon.

Thomas, J., ed. (1990). *A Gathering of Flowers: Stories about Being Young in America.* New York: Harper & Row.

Thompson, J. (1986). *A Band of Angels.* New York: Scholastic.

Thompson, J. (1987). *Simon Pure.* New York: Scholastic.

Thompson, J. (1990). *Herb Seasoning.* New York: Scholastic.

Thompson, J. (1993). *Shepherd.* New York: Henry Holt.

Thoreau, H. D. (1854). *Walden.*

Toffler, A. (1970). *Future Shock.* New York: Bantam.

Townsend, S. (1982). *The Secret Diary of Adrian Mole, Aged 13¾.* New York: Avon.

Trelease, J. (1989). *The New Read-Aloud Handbook.* New York: Penguin.

*Tunis, J. (1938). *The Iron Duke.* New York: Harcourt Brace.

*Tunis, J. (1942). *All-American.* New York: Harcourt Brace.

*Tunis, J. (1967). *His Enemy, His Friend.* New York: William Morrow.

Twain, M. (1876). *The Adventures of Tom Sawyer.*

Twain, M. (1885). *The Adventures of Huckleberry Finn.*

*Uchida, Y. (1972). *The Samurai of Gold Hill.* New York: Scribner's.

*Uchida, Y. (1982). *A Jar of Dreams.* New York: McElderry.

*Uchida, Y. (1984). *The Best Bad Thing.* New York: Atheneum.

Verne, J. (1872). *Twenty Thousand Leagues Under the Sea.*

Verne, J. (1873). *Around the World in Eighty Days.*

*Voigt, C. (1981). *Homecoming.* New York: Atheneum.

*Voigt, C. (1982). *Dicey's Song.* New York: Ballentine.

*Voigt, C. (1983). *A Solitary Blue.* New York: Atheneum.

*Voigt, C. (1985). *The Runner.* New York: Atheneum.

*Voigt, C. (1986). *Izzy, Willy-Nilly.* New York: Atheneum.

*Voigt, C. (1986). *Jackaroo.* New York: Fawcett.

Voigt, C. (1992). *Orfe.* New York: Scholastic.

Voigt, C. (1983). *Wings of a Falcon.* New York: Scholastic.

Voigt, C. (1994). *When She Hollers.* New York: Scholastic.

Vonnegut, K. (1969). *Slaughterhouse-Five, or, The Children's Crusade.* New York: Dell.

Wadds, G. (n.d.). *Who Cares?* Woodstock, IL: Dramatic Publishing.

Walker, A. (1979). *Good Night Willie Lee, I'll See You in the Morning.* New York: Dial.

Walker, A. (1982). *The Color Purple.* New York: Harcourt Brace Jovanovich.

Warner, S. (1850). *The Wide, Wide World.*

Wartski, M. C. (1980). *A Long Way from Home.* New York: Signet Vista.

*Wartski, M. C. (1981). *A Boat to Nowhere*. New York: New American Library.

Weems, M. L. (1800). *A History of the Life and Death, Virtues and Exploits, of General George Washington*.

Weems, M. L. (1806). *The Life of Washington the Great*.

Weems, M. L. (1808). *The Life of George Washington*.

*Weidt, M. (1989). *Presenting Judy Blume*. New York: Twayne.

*Westall, R. (1976). *The Machine Gunners*. New York: Greenwillow.

*Westall, R. (1988). *Urn Burial*. New York: Greenwillow.

*Westall, R. (1989). *Blitzcat*. New York: Scholastic.

*Westall, R. (1990). *The Promise*. New York: Scholastic.

*Westall, R. (1992). *Yaxley's Cat*. New York: Scholastic.

*Westall, R. (1994). *A Place to Hide*. New York: Scholastic.

*White, E. (1983). *Friends for Life*. New York: Avon.

*White, E. (1987). *Life Without Friends*. New York: Scholastic.

*White, E. (1989). *Long Live the Queen*. New York: Scholastic.

White, R. (1972). *Deathwatch*. New York: Dell.

Wieler, D. (1992). *Bad Boy*. New York: Delacorte.

Wiesel, E. (1960). *Night*. New York: Bantam.

Wiggin, K. D. (1904). *Rebecca of Sunnybrook Farm*.

Wigginton, E., ed. (1972–   ). *The Foxfire Books* (series). New York: Doubleday.

Wilder, T. (1938). *Our Town*. New York: Samuel French.

Wilson, A. J. (1867). *St. Elmo*.

Windsor, P. (1991). *The Christmas Killer*. New York: Scholastic.

Wolff, V. E. (1993). *Make Lemonade*. New York: Henry Holt.

*Woodson, J. (1994). *I Hadn't Meant to Tell You This*. New York: Delacorte.

Wrinkler, A. (1994). *Cassie's War*. Unionville, NY: Royal Fireworks.

*Yee, P. (1990). *Tales from the Golden Mountain: Stories of the Chinese in the New World*. New York: Macmillan.

*Yep, L. (1975). *Dragonwings*. New York: Harper & Row.

*Yep, L. (1977). *Child of the Owl*. New York: Harper Junior.

*Yep, L. (1982). *Dragon of the Lost Sea*. New York: Harper & Row.

*Yep, L. (1992). *Dragon War*. New York: HarperCollins.

Yep, L., ed. (1993). *American Dragons: Twenty-Five Asian American Voices*. New York: HarperCollins.

*Yolen, J. (1987). *The Sending of Dragons*. New York: Delacorte.

*Yolen, J. (1990). *The Devil's Arithmetic*. New York: Puffin.

Yolen, J., ed. (1991). *2041*. New York: Delacorte.

Yolen, J., & Greenburg, M., eds. (1989). *Things That Go Bump in the Night: A Collection of Original Stories*. New York: Harper & Row.

*Young, A. (1978). *Land of the Iron Dragon*. New York: Doubleday.

*Zindel, P. (1968). *The Pigman*. New York: Bantam.

*Zindel, P. (1969). *My Darling, My Hamburger*. New York: Harper & Row.

Zindel, P. (1970). *The Effect of Gamma Rays on Man-in-the-Moon Marigolds*. New York: Dramatists.

*Zindel, P. (1974). *Let Me Hear You Whisper*. New York: Harper & Row.

*Zindel, P. (1985). *Harry and Hortense at Hormone High*. New York: Bantam.

*Zindel, P. (1987). *The Amazing and Death-Defying Diary of Eugene Dingman*. New York: Harper & Row.

*Zindel, P. (1989). *A Begonia for Miss Applebaum*. New York: Bantam.

Zindel, P. (1993). *David and Della*. New York: HarperCollins.

*Zindel, P. (1994). *Loch*. Orlando, FL: Harcourt Brace.

*Zindel, P., & Zindel, B. (1980). *A Star for the Latecomer*. New York: Harper & Row.

Zolotow, C. (1986). *Early Sorrow: Ten Stories of Youth*. New York: Harper & Row.

Book Lists

ONE, BOOK, ONE CLASS

The following books are particularly appropriate for teachers to use when considering a book selection for all students in a class to read.

After the First Death, Robert Cormier

After the Rain, Norma Fox Mazer

All Together Now, Sue Ellen Bridgers

— *Are You in the House Alone?*, Richard Peck

A Band of Angels, Julian Thompson

Beardance, Will Hobbs

Bearstone, Will Hobbs

Been Clever Forever, Bruce Stone

A Begonia for Miss Applebaum, Paul Zindel

— *Beyond the Chocolate War*, Robert Cormier

Bless Me, Ultima, Rudolfo Anaya

✦ *Bridge to Terabithia*, Katherine Paterson

The Bumblebee Flies Anyway, Robert Cormier

— *The Catcher in the Rye*, J. D. Salinger

Chapters: My Growth As a Writer, Lois Duncan

Chernowitz, Fran Arrick

Children of the River, Linda Crew

Chinese Handcuffs, Chris Crutcher

— *The Chocolate War*, Robert Cormier

Cold Sassy Tree, Olive Burns

The Contender, Robert Lipsyte

— *The Crazy Horse Electric Game*, Chris Crutcher

Crazy Lady, Jane Conley

Daniel's Story, Carol Matas

A Day No Pigs Would Die, Robert Newton Peck

The Day They Came To Arrest the Book, Nat Hentoff

Deathwatch, Robb White

— *Dicey's Song*, Cynthia Voigt

Dogwolf, Alden Carter

— *Don't Look Behind You*, Lois Duncan

Dove, Robin Graham

Downriver, Will Hobbs

Dragonwings, Lawrence Yep

Driver's Ed, Caroline Cooney

Eva, Peter Dickinson

The Face on the Milk Carton, Caroline Cooney

Fallen Angels, Walter Dean Myers

Far from Home, Ouida Sebestyn

Father Figure, Richard Peck

Flash Fire, Caroline Cooney

Forbidden City, William Bell

Freak the Mighty, Rodnum Philbrick

Freedom's Children, Ellen Levine

Gentlehands, M. E. Kerr

— *The Giver,* Lois Lowry

The Glory Field, Walter Dean Myers

Home Before Dark, Sue Ellen Bridgers

— *I Am the Cheese,* Robert Cormier

I Touch the Future: The Story of Christa McAuliffe, Robert Hohler

In the Middle of the Night, Robert Cormier

Interstellar Pig, William Sleator

Into a Strange Land, Brent Ashabranner

The Island, Gary Paulsen

— *Jacob Have I Loved,* Katherine Paterson

The Keeper, Phyllis Naylor

— *Killing Mr. Griffin,* Lois Duncan

The Kolokol Papers, Larry Bograd

The Last Safe Place on Earth, Richard Peck

— *Let the Circle Be Unbroken,* Mildred Taylor

Loch, Paul Zindel

Make Lemonade, Virginia Euwer Wolff

Memory, Margaret Mahy

Miriam's Well, Lois Ruby

Mississippi Bridge, Mildred Taylor

Mote, Chap Reaver

The Moves Make the Man, Bruce Brooks

New Kids in Town: Oral Histories of Immigrant Teens, Janet Bode

Night Kites, M. E. Kerr

The Ninth Issue, Dallin Malgrem

No Dragons To Slay, Jan Greenburg

No Kidding, Bruce Brooks

Notes for Another Life, Sue Ellen Bridgers

Nothing But the Truth, Avi

Number the Stars, Lois Lowry

One Fat Summer, Robert Lipsyte

Ordinary People, J. Guest

The Other Side of Dark, Joan Lowry Nixon

Out of Control, Norma Fox Mazer

Out of Here, Sandy Asher

The Outsiders, S. E. Hinton

Park's Quest, Katherine Paterson

Permanent Connections, Sue Ellen Bridgers

Phoenix Rising, Karen Hesse

— *The Pigman,* Paul Zindel

Remembering the Good Times, Richard Peck

Rescue: The Story of How Gentiles Saved Jews in the Holocaust, Milton Meltzer

The Road to Memphis, Mildred Taylor

— *Roll of Thunder, Hear My Cry,* Mildred Taylor

Running Loose, Chris Crutcher

— *A Separate Peace,* John Knowles

Skin Deep, Lois Ruby

Steal Away Home, Lois Ruby

Stotan!, Chris Crutcher

Streams to the River, River to the Sea, Scott O'Dell

— *Summer of My German Soldier,* Bette Greene

Sworn Enemies, Carol Matas

Taming the Star Runner, S. E. Hinton

Tunes for Bears to Dance To, Robert Cormier

Voices from the Civil War, Milton Meltzer

Waiting for the Rain, Shiela Gordon

The War Between the Classes, Gloria Miklowitz

— *Wart, Son of Toad,* Alden Carter

We All Fall Down, Robert Cormier

— *Whatever Happened to Janie?,* Caroline Cooney

The Whole Nine Yards, Dallin Malgren

Winning, Robin Brancato

Words by Heart, Ouida Sebestyn

┼ *A Wrinkle in Time,* Madeleine L'Engle

Z for Zacharia, Robert O'Brien

ONE BOOK, ONE STUDENT

Teachers may use the following books on an individual reading list, as well as using any of the books from the previous list. Again, as in any literature program, it is so important to realize that a book appropriate for one student may not be so for another.

About David, Susan Pfeffer

The Accident, Todd Strasser

Acts of Love, Maureen Daly

AK, Peter Dickinson

Ali and the Golden Eagle, Wayne Grover

Alicia: My Story, Alicia Appleman-Jurman

Among Friends, Caroline Cooney

Angel Dust Blues, Todd Strasser

Anything to Win, Gloria Miklowitz

April and the Dragon Lady, Lensey Namioka

Bel-Air Bambi and the Mall Rats, Richard Peck

Bill, Chap Reaver

Blinded by the Light, Robin Brancato

Blitzcat, Robert Westall

Blue Skin of the Sea, Graham Salisbury

Born of the Sun, Gillian Cross

The Boy Who Could Reverse Himself, William Sleator

The Brave, Robert Lipsyte

A Break with Charity, Ann Rinaldi

Broken Days, Ann Rinaldi

A Candidate for Murder, Joan Lowery Nixon

The Captive, Joyce Hansen

The Car, Gary Paulsen

Catherine, Called Birdy, Karen Cushman

The Cave, Kathleen Karr

The Cay, Theodore Taylor

Celine, Brock Cole

The Chemo Kid, Robert Lipsyte

The Chief, Robert Lipsyte

The Christmas Killer, Patricia Windsor

Christy, Catherine Marshall

Crews, Maria Hinojosa

Dakota Dream, James Bennett

Dancing in the Dark, Alden Carter

A Dangerous Promise, Joan Lowery Nixon

The Dark is Rising, Susan Cooper

Daughters of Eve, Lois Duncan

David and Della, Paul Zindel

Deliver Us from Evie, M. E. Kerr

The Devil's Arithmetic, Jane Yolen

— *Does This School Have Capital Punishment?,* Nat Hentoff

Dogsong, Gary Paulsen

Don't Care High, Gordan Korman

Dragon of the Lost Sea, Laurence Yep

Dragon War, Laurence Yep

The Drowning of Stephan Jones, Bette Greene

The Duplicate, William Sleator

The Ear, the Eye, and the Arm, Nancy Farmer

Edgar Allan, John Neufeld

The Executioner, Jay Bennett

Facing Up, Robin Brancato

A Family Apart, Joan Lowery Nixon

Famous All Over Town, Danny Santiago

Fell, M. E. Kerr

Fell Back, M. E. Kerr

Fell Down, M. E. Kerr

Fingers, William Sleator

Finishing Becca, Ann Rinaldi

First a Dream, Maureen Daly

Flight #116 Is Down, Caroline Cooney

The Friends, Rosa Guy

Friends for Life, Ellen White

Friends 'till the End, Todd Strasser

— *Fudge-A-Mania*, Judy Blume

Girl in the Box, Ouida Sebestyn

Go Ask Alice, Anonymous

The Goats, Brock Cole

Good-Bye Tomorrow, Gloria Miklowitz

The Grey King, Susan Cooper

Hannah In Between, Colby Rodowsky

Harris and Me, Gary Paulsen

— *Harris and Hortense at Hormone High*, Paul Zindel

Hatchet, Gary Paulsen

The Haymeadow, Gary Paulsen

Heartbeat, Norma Fox Mazer and Harry Mazer

Herb Seasoning, Julian Thompson

— *Him She Loves*, M. E. Kerr

I Hadn't Meant to Tell You This, Jacqueline Woodson

— *I Never Promised You a Rose Garden*, Hannah Green

Iceman, Chris Lynch

If Rock and Roll Were a Machine, Terry Davis

In My Father's House, Ann Rinaldi

IOU's, Ouida Sebestyn

Ironman, Chris Crutcher

— *Is That You, Miss Blue?*, M. E. Kerr

— *Izzy, Willy-Nilly*, Cynthia Voight

Jackaroo, Cynthia Voight

Jesse, Gary Soto

Journey, Patricia MacLachlan

Keeping Christina, Sue Ellen Bridgers

Lasso the Moon, Dennis Covington

The Last Mission, Harry Mazer

The Last Silk Dress, Ann Rinaldi

Life Without Friends, Ellen White

Linger, M. E. Kerr

— *Lisa, Bright and Dark*, John Neufeld

Lizard, Dennis Covington

Locked in Time, Lois Duncan

Long Live the Queen, Ellen White

Lord of the Flies, William Golding

Los Alamos Light, Larry Bograd

Malcolm X: By Any Means Necessary, Walter Dean Myers

The Man Who Was Poe, Avi

Maniac McGee, Jerry Spinelli

Marked by Fire, Julian Thomas

Midnight Hour Encores, Bruce Brooks

Missing the Piano, Adam Rapp

The Monument, Gary Paulsen

Motown and Didi, Walter Dean Myers

Mr. Tucket, Gary Paulsen

The Music of Summer, Rosa Guy

My Name Is Asher Lev, Chaim Potok

My Name Is Not Angelica, Scott O'Dell

Nell's Quilt, Susan Terris

The Night the White Deer Died, Gary Paulsen

Nightjohn, Gary Paulsen

Nobody Else Can Walk It For You, P. J. Petersen

Nobody's Baby Now, C. Benjamin

Orfe, Cynthia Voigt

Other Bells for Us To Ring, Robert Cormier

Out of Nowhere, Ouida Sebestyen

A Part of the Sky, Robert Newton Peck

The Party's Over, Caroline Cooney

The Pigeon, Jay Bennett

A Place to Hide, Robert Westhall

Princess Ashley, Richard Peck

The Promise, Robert Westall

Real Heroes, Marilyn Kaye

The River, Gary Paulsen

Robyn's Book: A True Diary, Robyn Miller

Rock N' Roll Nights, Todd Strasser

The Runner, Cynthia Voight

Scorpions, Walter Dean Myers

The Secret of Gumbo Grove, Eleanora Tate

Secret Silent Screams, Joan Lowery Nixon

Send No Blessings, Phyllis Naylor

A Sending of Dragons, Jane Yolen

Sentries, Gary Paulsen

Sex Education, Jenny Davis

Shadow of the Dragon, Sherry Garland

Shark Beneath the Reef, Jean Craighead George

Shiela's Dying, Alden Carter

The Silver Kiss, Annette Klaus

Simon Pure, Julian Thompson

Sing Me a Death Song, Jay Bennett

Sisters, Gary Paulsen

The Slave Dancer, Paula Fox

The Solid Gold Kid, Norma Fox Mazer and Harry Mazer

A Solitary Blue, Cynthia Voight

Somewhere in the Darkness, Walter Dean Myers

Squashed, Joan Bauer

Staying Fat for Sarah Byrnes, Chris Crutcher

A Stitch in Time, Ann Rinaldi

Summer of Fear, Lois Duncan

Summer on Wheels, Gary Soto

A Summer To Die, Lois Lowry

Sunshine, Norma Klein

Sweet Bells Jangled Out of Tune, Robin Brancato

Sydney, Invincible, Colby Rodowsky

Taking Terri Mueller, Norma Fox Mazer

A Teacup Full of Roses, Sharon Bell Mathis

Tex, S. E. Hinton

Those Summer Girls I Never Met, Richard Peck

3 NB's of Julian Drew, James M. Deem

Timothy of the Cay, Theodore Taylor

Toning the Sweep, Angela Johnson

The True Confession of Charlotte Doyle, Avi

Tuck Everlasting, Natalie Babbitt

The Twisted Window, Lois Duncan

Uneasy Money, Robin Brancato

Unfinished Portrait of Jessica, Richard Peck

A Very Touchy Subject, Todd Strasser

Vision Quest, Terry Davis

Vision Quest, Pamela Service

The Voyage of the FROG, Gary Paulsen

Walk Two Moons, Sharon Creech

The Weekend Was Murder, Joan Lowery Nixon

What I Really Think of You, M. E. Kerr

What You Don't Know Can Kill You, Fran Arrick

When She Hollers, Cynthia Voigt

When the Phone Rang, Harry Mazer

When We First Met, Norma Fox Mazer

Who Is Harry Leonard?, Harry Mazer

Who Killed My Daughter?, Lois Duncan

Wings of the Falcon, Cynthia Voigt

Wolf by the Ears, Ann Rinaldi

Wolf Rider, Avi

A Woman of Her Tribe, Margaret Robinson

Yaxley's Cat, Robert Westall

The Year Without Michael, Susan Beth Pfeffer

Index